BERNARD SHAW

The Drama Observed

The Pennsylvania State University Press
University Park, Pennsylvania

BERNARD SHAW

The Drama Observed

Volume I: 1880–1895

Edited and with an Introduction by
Bernard F. Dukore

Library of Congress Cataloging-in-Publication Data

Shaw, Bernard, 1856–1950.
    The drama observed / Bernard Shaw ; edited and with an
introduction by Bernard F. Dukore.

        p.   cm.
    Includes bibliographical references and index.
    Contents: v. 1. 1880–1895 — v. 2. 1895–1897 — v. 3. 1897–1911 —
v. 4. 1911–1950.
    ISBN 0-271-00872-5 (alk. paper)
    1. Theater—England—London—Reviews.   2. Drama—History and
criticism.   I. Dukore, Bernard Frank, 1931–   . II. Title.
PN2596.L6S48   1993
792.9′5′09421—dc20   92-4566
                                                                                      CIP

Published by the Pennsylvania State University Press,
Barbara Building, Suite C, University Park, PA 16802-1003

It is the policy of The Pennsylvania State University Press to use acid-free paper
for the first printing of all clothbound books. Publications on uncoated stock
satisfy the minimum requirements of American National Standard for Information Sciences—Permanence of Paper for Printed Library Materials, ANSI Z39.
48–1984.

CONTENTS

VOLUME II

VOLUME III

VOLUME IV

INTRODUCTION

Shaw observed the drama professionally for seven decades—seventy-one years and a month, to be exact, from 7 April 1880, when he wrote a review, unpublished until now, of Henry Irving's production of *The Merchant of Venice*, to 6 May 1950, when he debated Terence Rattigan on ideas in the drama. To Shaw, drama involved presentation before an audience, which made it inseparable, except for purposes of analysis, from performance, regardless of whether the performance was on a stage with live actors. He regarded theater, as he did drama, in the widest sense of the term. Drama may be verbal or nonverbal, may include pantomime plays and silent movies, radio and talking films and television—all of which tell stories about characters. Shaw observed—saw, perceived, took notice of, regarded, contemplated, studied, examined, reviewed—all these forms of drama, believing that to restrict theater to live performances by human beings is as narrow a view as to restrict drama to the printed page.

Shaw's best-known criticisms of the drama are *The Quintessence of Ibsenism*, the first book on Ibsen in English, published in 1891 but derived from a lecture given to the Fabian Society the previous year, and his weekly theater reviews that appeared in the *Saturday Review* for three and a half years from 1895 to 1898. Ibsen himself expressed satisfaction with a newspaper report of Shaw's lecture on him.[1] G. K. Chesterton, who disagreed with Shaw at least as often as he agreed with him, admiringly declared of the book, "every paragraph is provocative."[2] Shaw's "vigorous" theater reviews, said Maurice Valency, exhibit "his eminently sound taste and good judgment. They afford us also an unparalleled perspective of the theatrical world in London during a most significant period in the

1. Letter to Hans Lien Braekstad, 18 August 1890, in *Ibsen: Letters and Speeches*, ed. Evert Sprinchorn (New York: Hill & Wang, 1964), 292.
2. *George Bernard Shaw* (New York: Hill & Wang, 1956), 82.

development of the English stage."³ According to St. John Ervine, himself a critic and dramatist, they contain "witty and virile prose" and reveal that "a new and powerful mind had come to the criticism of the English stage." Other theater critics, continued Ervine, had written with distinction and authority, but none had or would have such authority as Shaw. "His critical faculty had been sharpened more keenly and in a greater variety of ways than any other critic then in practice or, indeed, any critic since."⁴ On 1 June 1898, eleven days after the appearance of his "Valedictory" notice in the *Saturday Review*, the Irish Shaw married Charlotte Frances Payne-Townshend, whom he had described to Ellen Terry as "my Irish lady with the light green eyes and the millions of money."⁵ Without the need to earn his living by writing regular criticism, since his wife provided him with a marriage settlement that guaranteed an annual income, he stopped, putting most of his dramatic energies into his playwriting, which flourished, although from time to time, when occasion demanded or only suggested, he returned to criticism of the drama—on page, stage, film screen, radio, and television screen. However, Shavian biography or the relationship between his life and his critical writings— his composition of a study of Ibsen, his turn to weekly reviewing, or its cessation when he married—which has been and continues to be written by others, is not the subject of this introduction. Rather, its subject is what follows the introduction, Shaw's criticism itself, his seventy-one-year observation of the drama.

"The childhood shows the man," said Milton, "As morning shows the day."⁶ When Shaw began to criticize the drama, he was twenty-three; hardly a child, but young. During the next seven decades, his fundamental views changed little. His early ideas influenced the way he viewed new developments in dramatic media: cinema, radio, and television. What changed were the increasing skill with which he expressed himself, the occasions that informed his utterances, and the greater opportunities he had to present his views.

Unsurprisingly present at the very outset is his wit. Reviewing Henry Irving's production of *The Merchant of Venice*, he advises those who wish to become acquainted with the play's beauties "to procure the book and read for themselves."⁷ Playing with words, he calls Oscar Wilde "our only

3. *The Cart and the Trumpet* (New York: Oxford University Press, 1973), 23.

4. *Bernard Shaw: His Life, Work and Friends* (New York: William Morrow, 1956), 275.

5. 12 October 1896, in Shaw, *Collected Letters 1874–1897*, ed. Dan H. Laurence (London: Max Reinhardt, 1965), 676.

6. John Milton, *Paradise Regained* (1671), book 4, lines 220–21.

7. "The Merchant of Venice at the Lyceum," 7 April 1880. In this Introduction, citations to works in this collection, which are arranged chronologically, are to dates of the original (published, spoken, unpublished).

thorough playwright. He plays with everything: with wit, with philosophy, with drama, with actors and audience, with the whole theatre."[8] Turning his wit toward his own profession, he praises an actor in *The Sign of the Cross*, which his readers knew he had panned, for having published "a long letter in defence of that play against the adverse opinion of an eminent colleague of mine," since "[n]ot only ought actors to write occasionally, so as to shew the critics their ideas of dramatic criticism; but the critics ought to act from time to time, so as to shew the actors their notion of acting."[9]

Among the characteristics of Shaw's criticisms, before and after he became a dramatist in 1892 and a regular theater reviewer in 1895, is an astonishingly wide range of literary, social, and popular allusions, whose sources he does not usually announce. Shakespeare, Dickens, and the Bible appear most frequently, but there are references to poets, novelists, dramatists, painters, composers, musicians, philosophers, critics, politicians, socialists, feminists, theologians, financiers, military men, cartoonists, music-hall performers, well- or little-known statements, politically significant events, popular culture, shops, slang, law cases, theater practices and terminology (not always mentioned in theater history texts), now-forgotten characters and plays and performers, as well as simply the news of the day, week, year, or decade. As early as 29 February 1884, for instance, in a speech on Shakespeare's *Troilus and Cressida*, he refers to Dekker, Chettle, and Homer's *Iliads* (as it was called in Shakespeare's time), and he also compares Homer's description of the battle between Achilles and Asteropaios to an account of a boxing match in an 1859 magazine. As a dramatic critic in the mid-nineties, he parodies Shakespeare, calling a female character "more kissed against than kissing"; adverting to Lyly, he proclaims an actress "ever fair and fortunate."[10] More than thirty-five years later, he refers to Shakespeare, calling Lillah McCarthy "of imagination all compact."[11] As a theater critic he remarks, alluding to an axiom of corrupt American politics, that "the free list comes early and comes often" and, referring to an aspect of mundane London life, that an actress seems partly costumed as a waitress in an Aerated Bread shop.[12] A single paragraph in one review refers to over a dozen artists, a Gilbert and Sullivan operetta, a play by Scribe, several English dramatists, and two English poets; a paragraph in another, to the American debate about the gold and silver standards, a Dickensian character, a

---

8. "Two New Plays," 12 January 1895.
9. "Dear Harp of My Country," 1 February 1896.
10. "The Return of Mrs Pat," 8 March 1896; "Mr Pinero on Turning Forty," 3 April 1897.
11. "An Aside," [May] 1933.
12. "Poor Shakespear!" 2 February 1895.

Scottish-American grammarian, a theologian, a Christian socialist, an art critic, and a fraudulent financier.[13] He uses then-common theatrical phrases: no fee houses, star traps, and the crutch and toothpick brigade.[14]

After he wrote plays, his criticism became self-referential. He mentions *Arms and the Man*, produced the year before he became a regular reviewer, or quotes a passage from an unnamed "recent play" (the same one).[15] He compares William Archer's criticisms with his own and opines that in some respects George Henry Lewes anticipated himself.[16] Making a case for the dramatist as critic, he names himself as "a particularly flagrant example"; in arguing that dramatic criticism and musical criticism are not different callings, he identifies Lewes and Archer as critics who wrote both, yet "[m]odesty forbids me to cite another obvious case."[17]

His critical observations reflect themes in his plays. An 1897 review of Meredith's *Essay on Comedy* mentions Englishmen's "invincible determination to tell and be told lies about everything, and their power of dealing acquisitively and successfully with facts whilst keeping them [. . .] rigidly in their proper place; that is, outside their moral consciousness"[18]— an echo of Napoleon's remarks in *The Man of Destiny*, completed two years earlier. In 1905 he expresses a preference, "under existing circumstances," for the Theatrical Trust, a syndicate, to independent managers. While he believed municipal theaters "with no object except the good of the town" would be better than both, these did not yet exist. Of the different types of private venture that did, he knew as a businesslike playwright that the syndicate was more responsible, for which reason he "provisionally" favored it.[19] He made these remarks nine months after the first performance of *John Bull's Other Island*, which argued similarly in favor of land syndicates over individual owners. Frequently, Shaw advocated the establishment of an endowed theater as an alternative to private, commercial ventures. Because high art is minority art, he said in 1918, the fact that it pays does not mean it can attract commercial capital. If it pays ten percent while commercial plays pay twenty-five to two hundred, theatrical speculators will go for the latter. Despite the facts that its losses are less common and small profits more probable, speculators

13. "King Arthur," 19 January 1895; "Daly Undaunted," 18 July 1896.

14. "The Chili Widow," 12 October 1895; "The Theatre in England," 28 March 1896; "More Masterpieces," 26 October 1895.

15. "Mr Daly Fossilizes," 29 June 1895; "Mr Pinero's New Play," 16 March 1895.

16. "Mr William Archer's Criticisms," 13 April 1895; "Some Other Critics," 20 June 1896.

17. "The Case for the Critic-Dramatist," 16 November 1895; "Quickwit on Blockhead," 5 June 1897.

18. "Meredith on Comedy," 27 March 1897. For [. . .], spelling, and similar matters, see "A Note on the Text."

19. "G.B.S. and the Trust," 28 July 1905; "Is a Theatre Trust Desirable?" 2 August 1905.

aim for a commercial windfall. "Without endowment private enterprise can do nothing with high art in such a market. The habit of gambling at huge risks for monstrous profits is too firmly established."[20] He held that the same was true for the cinema. If the capitalists who control the movie industry "let themselves be seduced from their pursuit of profits to the enchantments of art, they would be bankrupt before they knew where they were. You cannot combine the pursuit of money with the pursuit of art."[21] All of these remarks echo *The Dark Lady of the Sonnets* (1910), in which he has Shakespeare plead with Queen Elizabeth I to create an endowed theater, since "this writing of plays is a great matter, forming as it does the minds and affections of men," but "[o]nly when there is a matter of a murder, or a plot, or a pretty youth in petticoats, or some naughty tale of wantonness, will your subjects pay the great cost of good players and their finery."[22]

From the start, Shaw was an original thinker, not one who parrots received opinions. Before and after he put Shakespeare in a play, he made unconventional remarks on Shakespeare's plays, among other subjects. *Troilus and Cressida* "washes the paint off many persons whose natural complexions are so bad that we can hardly help wishing that Shakespear had left them as they were; but the process sets us laughing and thinking, and it may be doubted whether Homer achieved any result comparably beneficial to this." He called Cressida "one of Shakespear's most captivating women. She has been blamed for inconstancy; but as we may forgive Romeo for jilting Rosaline, we may forgive Cressida for jilting Troilus."[23] A dozen years later, he called this work Shakespeare's only attempt to hold the mirror to nature.[24] Not too many critics were making such statements in the 1880s or 1890s—or are making them in the 1990s. His championship of Ibsen in the eighties and nineties placed him in the vanguard of drama. In the early days of talking films, he flatly declared that dramatically the arts of stage and screen were the same. Both try "to tell a story and make its characters live and seize and hold and guide the attention [. . .]."[25] In telling that story, a drama may use "the stage, the camera, the microphone, the actor," and other means, but cinema "is a new art form" only to the extent that it is like a new instru-

20. "Repertory Theatre Finance," 10 January 1914.

21. "The Drama, The Theatre, and The Films," 1 September 1924.

22. Shaw, *Collected Plays with Their Prefaces* [CPP], ed. Dan H. Laurence (London: Bodley Head, 1970–74), 4:322–23.

23. "Troilus and Cressida," 29 February 1884.

24. "Ibsen Ahead!" 7 November 1896. For Shavian spelling and related matters, see "A Note on the Texts."

25. "Films, Plays, and G. B. Shaw," 1937.

ment in an orchestra or a new verse form.[26] In 1930, few people in the theatrical profession predicted, as Shaw did, "The theatre may survive as a place where people are taught to act, but apart from that there will be nothing but 'talkies' soon."[27] Nor did many predict, two years later, that once actors and other artists master its technique, "ninetynine percent of the present occupation of the theatre will be gone" and that the theater will "cater for small and select audiences [. . .] by doing a class of work not yet popular enough to bear the huge capital expenditures of the film studios."[28]

In the 1880s, to return to Shaw's utterances on Shakespeare, his independent ideas produced a statement unorthodox even today, that Shakespeare's "manysidedness included a remarkable power of writing badly."[29] Above the pseudonym of a woman, he called *The Taming of the Shrew* "one vile insult to womanhood and manhood from the first word to the last" and urged all men and women who respect each other to boycott it.[30] In the 1890s he called *Cymbeline* "for the most part stagey trash of the lowest melodramatic order, in parts abominably written, throughout intellectually vulgar, and, judged in point of thought by modern intellectual standards, vulgar, foolish, offensive, indecent, and exasperating beyond all tolerance." Condemning Shakespeare's fustian, intellectual sterility, and platitudinousness, he professed, in a now-famous passage, to "despise" him when measuring their minds against each other. Less famous is what follows: Shakespeare "has outlasted thousands of abler thinkers, and will outlast a thousand more." His gift of storytelling, his linguistic power, his sense of character, and his vital energy constitute "the true differentiating property behind the faculties, good, bad, or indifferent, of the man of genius [. . .]."[31] His magic derives not from his "commonplace meaning" but from "the sound of it," which Shaw called "word-music" that vivified the speaker's "mood and temperament." Like Ben Jonson, Shaw did "honor his memory on this side idolatry as much as any."[32] He coined a word for uncritical idolatry of the Bard, "Bardolatry," and he pointedly stated that too much surprise at his criticisms "betrays an acquaintance with Shakespear criticism so limited as not to include even the prefaces of Dr Johnson and the utterances of Napoleon."[33]

---

26. "The Cinema as an Art Form," 1 January 1930.
27. "Shaw Asserts Theatre Is Lost, Signs for Films," 8 August 1930.
28. "Relation of the Cinema to the Theatre," 9 May 1932.
29. "Troilus and Cressida," 29 February 1884.
30. "The Taming of the Shrew," 8 June 1888.
31. "Blaming the Bard," 26 September 1896.
32. Ben Jonson, *Timber, or Discoveries Made Upon Men and Matter* (1620–25).
33. Preface (1900) to *Three Plays for Puritans*, in *CPP*, 2:40–41.

Though not an uncritical admirer of Shakespeare, Shaw was a *devotée*. His first dramatic criticism condemns Irving's mutilation of *The Merchant of Venice* as capricious, inconsistent, and destructive of the play. "Mr Irving calls his arrangement of the Merchant an 'acting version,' " says Shaw, adding, "What does he call the original?"[34] The "usual principles" of managers were "altering, transposing, omiting, improving, correcting, and transfering speeches from one character to another." In *Two Gentleman of Verona,* "Shakespear shews lucidly how Proteus lives with his father (Antonio) in Verona, and loves a lady of that city named Julia." In the work "founded by Augustin Daly" on this play, "Daly, by taking the scene in Julia's house between Julia and her maid, and the scene in Antonio's house between Antonio and Proteus, and making them into one scene, convinces the unlettered audience that Proteus and Julia live in the same house with their father Antonio." Whereas Shakespeare shows the other gentleman of Verona traveling from there to Milan, Daly "just represents the two scenes as occuring in the same place; and immediately the puzzle as to who is who is complicated by a puzzle as to where is where."[35] Despite admonitions to Ellen Terry on how to cut *Cymbeline,* Shaw savaged Irving's excisions: "In a true republic of art Sir Henry Irving would ere this have expiated his acting versions on the scaffold. He does not merely cut plays; he disembowels them."[36]

By contrast, the chief merit of Beerbohm Tree's production of *Henry IV,* Part I is its fidelity to Shakespeare's text.[37] Shaw extols Forbes-Robertson's *Hamlet*: "He does not superstitiously worship William: he enjoys him and understands his methods of expression. Instead of cutting every line that can possibly be spared, he retains every gem, in his own part or anyone else's [. . .]."[38] To Shaw, cutting Shakespeare means trying to improve him. Once you do this, "you are launched on a slope on which there is no stopping until you reach the abyss where Irving's Lear lies forgotten." Your cuts, symptoms of the differences between you and Shakespeare, will result in the lowering or raising of Shakespeare to your level. Besides, the effect of a cut version of a play "is not the same as that of the whole play."[39] Citing the Bible as authority that if you try to root up the tares you will also root up the wheat, he maintains that Shakespearean mutilators seem to have been fonder of the tares than of the wheat, but even if the reverse were the case, "A play is not a string of pearls

34. "The Merchant of Venice at the Lyceum," 7 April 1880.
35. "Poor Shakespear!" 6 July 1895.
36. Letter to Ellen Terry, 6 September 1896; "Blaming the Bard," 26 September 1896.
37. "Henry IV," 16 May 1896.
38. "Hamlet," 2 October 1897.
39. "On Cutting Shakespear," August 1919.

which you can shorten by taking out some of the pearls when you are casting it before swine."[40]

One reason for the mutilation of Shakespeare's plays was to force them into a form "dictated by the notions that the mechanical illusions attempted by the scene painters of the XVIII and XIX centuries were indispensable in a modern theatre, and that Elizabethan plays must therefore be tortured into five acts with long waits between each for the 'striking' and setting of elaborate stage pictures."[41] Thus, *All's Well That Ends Well* was "pulled to pieces in order that some bad scenery, totally unconnected with Florence or Rousillon, might destroy all the illusion [. . .]. Briefly, the whole play was vivisected, and the fragments mutilated, for the sake of accessories which were in every particular silly or ridiculous." Far from heightening the illusion, "they rendered illusion almost impossible. If they were intended as illustrations of place and period, they were ignorant impostures."[42] Every scenic accessory in Daly's *Midsummer Night's Dream* destroyed the spell created by the words. "His 'panoramic illusion of the passage of Theseus's barge to Athens' is more absurd than anything that occurs in the tragedy of Pyramus and Thisbe in the last act."[43]

Shaw was an early admirer of William Poel, who directed readings and sceneryless stagings of Elizabethan plays. He welcomed the Elizabethan Stage Society, founded by Poel to present Shakespeare's plays on the type of stage for which he wrote them. Shaw too believed that the pictorial stage was less favorable to Elizabethan acting and stage illusion than the platform stage, which brought the actor so close to the spectators that the need to overact subtle moments "to overcome the remoteness of the 'living picture' stage, all but vanishes."[44] He also perceived that spectators "are less conscious of the artificiality of the stage when a few well-understood conventions, adroitly handled, are substituted for attempts at impossible scenic verisimilitude."[45] But he was not dogmatic. "The poetry in The Tempest is so magical that it would make the scenery of a modern theatre ridiculous." Poel frankly asks the audience to pretend that a gallery is a ship, which the audience does, but which it would not do if faced with a stagey imitation of one. The reason is not that one can always imagine something more vividly than art can simulate it, "but that it takes an extraordinary degree of art to compete with pictures which the imagination makes when it is stimulated by [. . .] the poetry of Shakespear." It requires discretion to determine how much

40. "Cutting Shakespear," November 1920.
41. "Cutting Shakespear," November 1920.
42. "Poor Shakespear!" 2 February 1895.
43. "Toujours Daly," 13 July 1895.
44. "Criticism on the Hustings," 20 July 1895.
45. "The Spacious Times," 11 July 1896.

help the imagination needs. "There is no general rule, not even for any particular author. You can do best without scenery in The Tempest and A Midsummer Night's Dream, because the best scenery you can get will only destroy the illusion created by the poetry; but it does not follow that scenery will not improve a representation of Othello." Symbolist plays would be spoiled by Elizabethan methods. Melodramas so heavily depend on realistic scenery that "a representation would suffer far less by the omission of the scenery than of the dialogue. That is why the manager who stages every play in the same way is a bad manager, even when he is an adept in his own way."[46]

Among Shaw's concerns was why post-Shakespearean literary drama failed. Early on, he articulated a key distinction between dramatic and undramatic: the latter is "descriptive." The nondramatic poet "has a theory of the motives and feelings of his characters, and he describes his theory," whereas the dramatic poet "puts the character before you acting and speaking as it would in actual life." In "Caliban upon Setebos," Browning has Caliban "minutely describe his own feelings and analyze his own thoughts." Since so brutish a creature "would not be able to do anything of the sort," the result is essentially undramatic. In The Tempest, Shakespeare's Caliban "does not reason about God; but he is terrified by a thunderstorm." A man gives a bottle of strong spirits to Caliban, who worships him like a god. Upon discovering this man to be a fool, he is angry with himself for having worshiped him. Whereas Shakespeare dramatizes Caliban's character and theology naturally, Browning gives Caliban, undramatically and unnaturally, "the introspective powers of a Hamlet."[47] Also early on, Shaw discerned a key reason for the failure of post-Shakespearean tragedy. In The Cenci, Shelley "got hold of the wrong vehicle when he chose the five-act tragedy in blank verse which had sufficed for Otway and Nicholas Rowe." This form's encumbrances and traditions required him "to write constantly as Shakespear only wrote at the extreme emotional crises in his plays [. . .]."[48]

Such failures notwithstanding, Shaw stumped for literary drama. Seven years before he completed his first play, he noted that Colombe's Birthday, which the Browning Society produced, had key weaknesses from the commercial viewpoint: long speeches and an appeal to "the higher faculties of an educated and thoughtful audience. Both of these features materially contributed [. . .] to its success, which was complete and unequivocal."[49] He found these features in Ibsen's plays. Unlike the

46. "Shakespear and Mr Barrie," 13 November 1897.
47. "[Shakespear's and Browning's Caliban]," 25 April 1884.
48. "[The Cenci]," June 1886.
49. "[Colombe's Birthday]," 21 November 1885.

hypocritical, twaddling works that held the stage, in which opposition to unconventional conduct was considered morality, in which "serious problems of life and conduct were either glozed or shirked," and in which mechanical stagecraft devitalized the action, *A Doll's House* eschewed "conventional lies of the stage," providing instead "a vital truth searched out and held up in a light intense enough to dispel all the mists and shadows that obscure it in actual life."[50] If the literary world, he argued in defense of Henry James's *Guy Domville*, were as "dominated by the admirers of Mr Rider Haggard as the dramatic world is by their first cousins, we should be told that Mr James cannot write a novel." The life depicted in James's play, which is graceful and dignified, lacks the vulgarity and hokum to which theatergoers are accustomed, but it is nonetheless theatrical, with beautiful speech and "a story of fine sentiments and delicate manners."[51] Shaw derided pseudoliterature: "Great works in fiction are the arduous victories of great minds over great imaginations: Miss [Marie] Corelli's works are the cheap victories of a profuse imagination over an apparently commonplace and carelessly cultivated mind."[52] As he declared in a tribute to William Morris, "we have no theatre for quite ordinary cultivated people." The only people who go there are those "who also go to Madame Tussaud's." Theater "has no share in the leadership of thought: it does not even reflect its current. It does not create beauty: it apes fashion."[53] After he retired as a reviewer, he complained not that theater offered commercial works, but that "there is no theatre in the country at which we can enjoy ourselves by the recreation of our higher appreciative faculties."[54]

To Shaw, drama, like all vital art, is drawn from life, not from playland. Minor dramatists live in a world of imagination, not "the world of politics, business, law, and the platform agitations by which social questions are ventilated." They may be clever and imaginative, but the real world infrequently enters their plays.[55] Because Incas had to marry their siblings, "an average Inca was worth about as much as an average fashionable drama bred carefully from the last pair of fashionable dramas, themselves bred in the same way, with perhaps a cross of novel." To cross art and life is always possible. Although a dramatist may be incapable of bringing his art in contact with the religion, philosophy, science, and statesmanship of his time, "he can at least bring it into contact with the obvious life and common passions of the streets. [. . .] When art becomes effete, it is

50. "Is Mr Buchanan a Critic with a Wooden Head?" 13 June 1889.
51. "Two New Plays," 12 January 1895.
52. "Satan Saved at Last," 16 January 1897.
53. "William Morris as Actor and Dramatist," 10 October 1896.
54. "On the University Dramatic Society," January 1900.
55. "The Problem Play," May 1895.

realism that comes to the rescue."[56] This belief was lifelong. In the 1930s, he called Osaka, Japan, "a huge industrial hell, all slum and factory," whose Kabuki plays in a magnificent theater "had nothing to do with the slums and factories: they dealt with the old feudal life that the factories have swept away forever."[57]

Life was among the qualities missing from the fashionable well-made play, which he derided in 1885, with an antithesis he would often employ: story (a set of circumstances that reveal character) and plot (a "dramatic cancer"). In *Othello*, "Desdemona does not in the last act turn out to be Bianca's half-sister, and heiress to a large fortune left by Brabantio. Emilia does not interrupt her death-speech to inform Iago that Roderigo was their child, stolen in infancy by gypsies under circumstances known only to Cassio under seal of an oath of secrecy." By contrast, Henry Arthur Jones's *Hoodman Blind* contains such "childish make-believe" as "suppressed wills, long lost relatives, [and] documents hidden in safes." To make room for them, Jones distorts the action and introduces irrelevant incidents.[58] A decade later, Shaw expressed surprise that Pinero's *The Second Mrs Tanqueray* was praised for its stagecraft, as its first act exposition contains "naïve machinery" with two actors "wasted on sham parts, and the hero, at his own dinner party, is compelled to get up and go ignominiously into the next room 'to write some letters' when something has to be said behind his back"; as it has a confidant to whom both husband and wife "explain themselves for the benefit of the audience"; and as it requires an array of doors and French windows to get its characters on- and offstage. Stagecraft, he concluded, means "the substitution of dead machinery and lay figures for vital action and real characters."[59] Sardou's method of playwriting is to invent the action, carefully keep it offstage, and then have it announced by letters and telegrams. He coined the term "Sardoodledom" for the well-made play.[60] After he stopped reviewing plays regularly, he summarized its formula: "the manufacture of a misunderstanding," whose culmination is at the end of the penultimate act. The first act consists of introducing the characters to the audience through "elaborate explanations, mostly conducted by servants, solicitors, and other low life personages (the principals must all be dukes and colonels and millionaires), of how the misunderstanding is going to come about." The last act consists "of clearing up the misunderstanding, and generally geting the audience out of the theatre as best you can."[61]

56. "Chin Chon Chino," 6 November 1897.
57. "[Traditional Japanese Theatre and Contemporary Japanese Society]," 30 April 1934.
58. "[Hoodman Blind and Olivia]," October 1885.
59. "An Old New Play and a New Old One," 23 February 1895.
60. "Two Bad Plays," 20 April 1895; "Sardoodledom," 1 June 1895.
61. Preface to *Three Plays by Brieux*, 1909.

Marking the watershed of drama, Ibsen's plays dramatize problems of real life and discuss these problems. As Shaw pointed out after Ibsen's death, Ibsenites had "strength of character to stand up to his terrible searchlight without blinking" and rejected the sentimental, snobbish, and conventional desire to view the world "through rose colored romantic spectacles."[62] Although he claimed, perhaps surprisingly in view of his reputation, that "people's ideas, however useful they may be for embroidery, especially in passages of comedy, are not the true stuff of drama, which is always the naïve feeling underlying the ideas"[63] and that since social questions are too topical and temporal to form the basis of great poetry, "A Doll's House will be as flat as ditchwater when A Midsummer Night's Dream will still be as fresh as paint," he recognized that Ibsen's plays had feeling beneath their ideas and the same essay with his statements on great poetry and the freshness of Shakespeare's comedy gives Peer Gynt as an example of such poetry, adding that Ibsen's seminal work "will have done more work in the world" than any by Shakespeare, "and that is sufficient for the highest genius, which is always intensely utilitarian." More than half a century later, Shaw insisted that ideas must underlie dramatic dialogue, for "without a stock of ideas, mind cannot operate and plays cannot exist."[64]

In Ibsen's plays, drama derives not from attachments and misunderstandings that raise no moral questions but from unsettled ideals. Rather than a conflict between simple right and wrong, they raise issues of what is right and wrong. Not only is the villain as conscientious as the hero, but questions arise as to who, if anyone, is the villain or hero.[65] Partly, this means that a character must act on the basis of his own beliefs, not that of preordained conventional morality. Whether his views are right or wrong is irrelevant: "he must follow his star, right or wrong [. . .]."[66] As he says in his 1903 Preface to Man and Superman, all his characters "are right from their several points of view; and their points of view are, for the dramatic moment, mine also."[67]

Less than a week after the first London production of a faithful translation of A Doll's House, he placed Ibsen's impact on the level of Wagner's, Whistler's, and Monet's. Even people who found no merit in Wagner could not thereafter tolerate Donizetti; even those who derided Whistler and Monet found "to their dismay" that when they returned "to their pet pictures" there was "no art in the landscapes and no light—except studio

62. "Ibsen," The Clarion, 1 June 1906.
63. "Daly Undaunted," 18 July 1896.
64. "The Problem Play: A Symposium," May 1895; "The Play of Ideas," 6 May 1950.
65. "The Technical Novelty in Ibsen's Plays," The Quintessence of Ibsenism, 1913.
66. "Michael and His Lost Angel," 18 January 1896.
67. Shaw, CPP, 2:517.

light—on the figures." London playgoers may not like Ibsen, but after *A Doll's House* they will not regard oldfashioned plays in the same way,[68] for, he said two years later, they "suddenly become conscious of absurdities and artificialities" that "never troubled them before." He predicted that "nobody will write for the stage after him as most playwrights wrote before him."[69] In practical business terms, the issue was "not how people liked Ibsen, but how they liked Byron, Sardou, and Tom Taylor after Ibsen." The theater manager must "measure as exactly as possible the effect on public taste produced by the series of experiments, by the Independent Theatre Society and others," between the production of *A Doll's House* in 1889 and that of *Arms and the Man* the previous year. "Never mind whether these experiments were pecuniary successes or not: the question is how far they altered the fashion in pecuniarily successful pieces."[70] At the time of Ibsen's death, Shaw saw no evidence that Ibsen had changed English drama. Only a new generation would show signs of Ibsen's influence—the contemporaries of Granville-Barker, not of Pinero.[71] Fifteen years later he noted Ibsen's influence in the development of modern tragicomedy, a type of drama other than tragedy and comedy, which began "as tragedy with scraps of mirth in it" and ended "as comedy without mirth in it, the place of mirth being taken by a more or less bitter and critical irony. [. . .] Ibsen was the dramatic poet who firmly established tragicomedy as a much deeper and grimmer entertainment than tragedy."[72]

A mark of Shaw's greatness as a critic is that one can disagree with his appraisal yet be illuminated by it. He unfavorably reviewed *The Importance of Being Earnest*, which many rank among the best comedies in the English language. "It amused me, of course; but unless comedy touches me as well as amuses me, it leaves me with a sense of having wasted my evening. I go to the theatre to be moved to laughter, not to be tickled or bustled into it [. . .]." Such tickling and bustling as lies, deceptions, cross-purposes, and the christening of two grown men, he argued, could only be raised from the level of farce by making them occur to characters who convince us they are real and thereby make us sympathize with them as human beings.[73] Similarly, he disparaged the farces of Georges Feydeau. "To produce high art in the theatre, the author must create persons whose fortunes we follow as those of a friend or enemy: to produce base laughter, it is only necessary to turn human beings on to the

68. "Is Mr Buchanan a Critic with a Wooden Head?" 13 June 1889.
69. Appendix to *The Quintessence of Ibsenism*, 1891.
70. "Mr Daly Fossilizes," 29 June 1895.
71. "Ibsen," 1 June 1906.
72. "Tolstoy: Tragedian or Comedian?" May 1921.
73. "An Old New Play and a New Old One," 23 February 1895.

stage as rats are turned into a pit, that they may be worried for the entertainment of the spectators."[74] The basis of both these criticisms is a different kind of comedy, in which he had begun to make his mark. Without ceasing to admire George Meredith's analysis of high comedy, which includes wit and satire, one can appreciate Shaw's disagreement, since he argues for a more radical type of satire. Against Meredith's view that the English public has as the basis of the comic, "an esteem for commonsense," Shaw asserts that it has a "common nonsense," which "is not only not 'the basis of the comic,' but actually makes comedy impossible" because it is "self-satisfiedly unconscious of its moral and intellectual bluntness, whereas the function of comedy is to dispel such unconsciousness by turning the searchlight of the keenest moral and intellectual analysis right on to it." To Shaw, comedy's function "is nothing less than the destruction of old-established morals."[75]

Such a view brought him in conflict with a major institution of English theater, the censorship. When the Lord Chamberlain's Office, which administered censorship, forbade the Shelley Society from giving the first production of *The Cenci*, about seventy years old, since it would cause public depravity, the Society employed the subterfuge of a performance for members, who paid dues rather than bought tickets. As Shaw reported, "the anticipated depravation of the public seems not to have come off; for the conduct of the nation has not perceptibly altered for the worst"; instead, the performance "accentuated the anomaly, folly, and hypocrisy of the censorship [. . .]."[76] As a regular dramatic critic he called censorship "as effective a safeguard as a deathbed repentance." The Lord Chamberlain's formula for what will pass "does not prevent the exhibition [. . .] of sensational sexuality, brutality, drunkenness, and murder; but it takes care that all these things shall end happily, charmingly, respectably, prettily, lady-and-gentlemanlikely for all parties concerned."[77] When the House of Lords and House of Commons established a Joint Select Committee to examine the censorship of drama, Shaw prepared drafts of humorous models to guide cooperative witnesses. In his own testimony, he stated unequivocally that "the censorship ought to be abolished." He objected to any control of theaters that "excludes rights which are accorded to all other citizens in the conduct of their business and the pursuit of their livelihood." Furthermore, "the danger of crippling thought, the danger of obstructing the formation of the public mind" by suppressing drama "is far greater than any real danger that there is from

74. "The Farcical Comedy Outbreak," 9 May 1896.
75. "Meredith on Comedy," 27 March 1897.
76. "[The Cenci]," June 1886.
77. "The Drama Purified," 23 April 1898.

such representations."[78] With the advent of films, he reiterated these views. The true issue is whether films, like plays, "are detrimental to public morals." Censorship gives the job of making this decision "to some frail and erring mortal man, and making him omnipotent on the assumption that his official status will make him infallible and omniscient," which is "silly." If a public inquiry is again established, "people who consider sex as sinful in itself must be excluded from it like other lunatics, and its business [should] be to ascertain whether, on the whole, going to the films makes worse or better citizens of us."[79] All censorships are pretexts "to suppress works which the authorities dislike." An example was the ban on Eisenstein's *Potemkin*, which Shaw like many considered "[o]ne of the best films ever produced as a work of pictorial art [. . .]." Authorities objected to it because it did not show naval officers as popular and gallant. Its proscription had nothing to do with morality and everything to do with class warfare. "The screen may wallow in every extremity of vulgarity and villainy provided it whitewashes authority. [. . .] That is what censorship means."[80]

When he began to criticize the drama, Great Britain had no acting schools. Like orators, actors learned their profession at the expense of the public, but whereas "a public speaker practises his entire art each time he speaks," a novice actor "applies only a small portion of his art to such minor parts as he is likely to obtain at first." Repeating his minor roles nightly for six months or six years would not make him a skilled actor.[81] After ten years, he said ten years later, most professional actors acquire only "a habit of brazening out their own incompetence." Ninety percent of actors and actresses have spent much of their career touring London successes in roles "thoughtlessly copied from the performances of their London 'creators,' with long intervals spent between each tour in the ranks of the unemployed." The old stock-company system was no better. Its actors were "the least versatile of beings," each helplessly stuck to his "line of heavy or light, young or old," playing every role exactly the same. His ability to learn the words of a role quickly and disgorge them, usually inaccurately, "was incompatible with his ever knowing his part in any serious sense at all." His few thrusts and parries were not fencing nor his few steps dancing, and his obnoxious elocution was a far cry from natural or artistic speech. Traveling companies superseded the stock actor, who vanished "unwept, unhonored, and unsung, because the only sentiment he had inspired in the public was an intense desire for some means of

78. "[Testimony on the Censorship of Plays]," 30 June 1909.
79. "Mr G.B. Shaw on Film Censorship," 20 January 1935.
80. "Views on the Censorship," April–May 1928.
81. "Qualifications of the Complete Actor," 19 September 1885.

doing without him."[82] With the actor-manager system, authors abetted the limited capacities of star actors. Once they learned that these actors had one or at most half a dozen notes, they wrote roles confined to those notes.[83] Perhaps the worst aspect of the long-run system is that it drives the actor "to limit himself to such effects as he can repeat to infinity without commiting suicide." Yet at its worst it is superior to the stock company system. In giving the actor a chance to vary his performance, he may "exhaust the possibilities of his part before it exhausts him, whereas the stock actor, having barely time to apply his bag of tricks to his daily task, never varies his treatment by a hair's breadth from one half century to another."[84] This system did not help the neophyte. With such prominent actors and actresses as Herbert Beerbohm Tree, who under Shaw's direction played Higgins in *Pygmalion*, Shaw worked to establish a school of acting. The result was the Royal Academy of Dramatic Art. In 1941 he wrote a long, unsigned introduction for a booklet, obtained comments from theatrical notables, and underwrote its printing costs. The booklet, *The R.A.D.A. Graduates' Keepsake & Counsellor*, was for two decades presented to graduates of the Academy; Shaw's introduction is reprinted here, the first time, in a collection of his writings.

Very early, he perceived, in terms that still have a contemporary ring, that the conditions under which the public saw plays made "most reasonable people regard a visit to the theatre rather as a troublesome and costly luxury to be indulged in three or four times a year under family pressure, than as the ordinary way of passing an unoccupied evening." To go there, a family had to leave home after dinner, travel by trains, cabs, or buses, and pay high prices for comfortable seats, since the cheaper seats were "below the standard of comfort now expected by third-class travelers on our northern railway lines." People therefore seldom went to the theater, and then only to see star actors of a play that was the current rage.[85] As a critic he attended the theater for his livelihood, but he would not do so for "an average London play with an average London cast [. . .]."[86] He advocated the spread of theater to the suburbs, so that there would be no part of London where one could not go to a neighborhood theater and enjoy oneself for a reasonable price in a comfortable chair.[87] Almost thirty years later, with the advent of radio and the imminence of television, the Victorian Shaw, far from resisting the media, found that they confirmed his views: "if I could see and hear

82. "The Old Acting and the New," 14 December 1895.
83. "Henry IV," 16 May 1896.
84. "Hamlet Revisited," 18 December 1897.
85. Preface to *The Theatrical "World" of 1894*, 1895.
86. "Two Plays," 22 February 1896.
87. "Municipal Theatres," 21 March 1896.

a play from my fireside I would never enter a theatre again." Broadcasting was cheaper and more comfortable than live theater; it was accessible in the country as well as the city; and "it has made the theatre and the trouble of getting there as intolerable as the motor car has made the railway train." Since theaters were expensive, inconvenient, and stuffy, he predicted that unless theater managers "overcome these disadvantages by the overpowering fascination of good plays, good acting, and theatres that are like enchanted palaces instead of hotel smoking rooms, broadcasting will knock them out."[88] When movie houses became picture palaces, he declared that their comparative comfort and wider cultural and intellectual range would supersede the old theatres.[89]

In harmony with his views of the drama are his views of presenting it, which were formed before he completed his first play. He believed the director, whom he usually called by the nineteenth-century term *stage-manager*, to be "as important a functionary as the conductor of an orchestra" and an adequate arrangement of all production elements to be "necessary to the complete effect of a theatrical representation [. . .]."[90] Seeking the illusion of reality, he mocked such shoddy direction as allowing an actress to trail "a robe of white China silk about an African hut,"[91] having a Shakespearean actor, after a thunderstorm, sit down "on a bank of moss, as an outlaw in tights naturally would after a terrific shower," and Roman soldiers after a battle carry their javelins as neatly packed in their rug straps as they were before the battle.[92] Direction includes ensemble acting rather than star turns by actor-managers. Shaw praised Charles Wyndham not only for having his supporting cast react to him but also for reacting to them, the result being better acting at his theater than at those run by most actor-managers; he honored Wilson Barrett for "good and unselfish" direction that sacrificed no role to his own and for having "honestly sunk the actor in the author," thereby doing "his best for the play, instead of for himself personally."[93] Since supernumeraries are part of the ensemble, in *Hamlet* "[t]he courtiers should be taught how flatteringly courtiers listen when a king shews off his wisdom in wise speeches to his nephew."[94] To guide directors, he published "The Art of Rehearsal" in 1922 and "Rules for Directors" in 1949.

The art of acting, Shaw maintained, was prostituted "into the art of

88. "The Drama and the Microphone," March 1925.

89. "Relation of the Cinema to the Theatre," 9 May 1932.

90. "Ten Minutes with Mr Bernard Shaw," 28 April 1894.

91. "The Gold Craze," 2 December 1889.

92. "Poor Shakespear!" 6 July 1895; "Tappertit on Cæsar," 29 January 1898.

93. "Trilby and L'Ami des Femmes," 9 November 1895; "Plays of the Week," 11 January 1896.

94. "Hamlet," 2 October 1897.

pleasing. The actor wants 'sympathy': the actress wants affection. They make the theatre a place where the public comes to look at its pets and distribute lumps of sugar to them."[95] As he recommended dramatists depicting characters from their viewpoints, so he advocated acting from the viewpoint of the character rather than substituting the actor's charms or peculiarities for it, or inviting admiration for a performance rather than conveying a character's qualities. Irving's Hamlet and Lear, said Shaw, were not Shakespeare's. He could not adapt himself to "an author's conception: his creations were all his own; and they were all Irvings."[96] Shaw praised Martin Harvey for playing Osric "from Osric's own point of view, which is, that Osric is a gallant and distinguished courtier, and not, as usual, from Hamlet's, which is that Osric is a 'waterfly.' "[97] He censured actresses for calling attention to their technique rather than their character. "Sarah Bernhardt has nothing but her own charm, for the exhibition of which Sardou contrives love scenes," whereas Eleonora Duse's "own private charm has not yet been given to the public. She gives you [. . .] the charm [. . .] belonging to the character she impersonates."[98] When they appeared in London at the same time, playing the same roles, Marguerite in Dumas *fils*'s *La Dame aux Camélias* and Magda in Sudermann's *Heimat*, he vividly etched the numerous external details with which Bernhardt achieved her effects and coaxed admiration for herself—her "bag of tricks"—and he contrasted them with an equally vivid, detailed analysis of how Duse's internal methods of performing revealed, without calling attention to these methods or to herself as an actress, the complexities of the human beings she portrayed. He concluded that Duse's "stock of ideas and sense of character [. . .] distinguish the master actor from the mere handyman." By common consent, his review "Duse and Bernhardt" is the best criticism of acting in the English language.[99]

In comedy perhaps especially, Shaw believed it important that actors play from the viewpoint of their characters. What they should not do, he urged, was to ensure as broadly as possible that the audience knows it is supposed to laugh. He deduced that actors in *Love's Labor's Lost*, having gathered that they should be amusing and highly spirited, tried to produce that effect by obstreperous action and arch speech.[100] Performances marked by "tomfoolery," "larking," or flagrant consciousness of one's fun-

95. "Mr Bancroft's Pilgrimage," 19 December 1896.
96. "Sir Henry Irving," 25 October 1905.
97. "Hamlet," 2 October 1897.
98. "Two Plays," 8 June 1895.
99. "Duse and Bernhardt," 15 June 1895.
100. "[Love's Labor's Lost]," August 1886.

niness differ from artistic comedy.[101] This did not mean he wanted comic performers "to be 'funny without being vulgar.' " Although they should be capable of vulgarity, "vulgarity in the wrong place, or slovenliness of speech in any place as a matter of personal habit instead of artistic assumption, is not to be tolerated from any actor or in any entertainment." Horseplay or silliness must be performed artistically.[102]

A practical difficulty in performing Ibsen's realistic characters, Shaw perceived, was that experienced actors did not understand them and those without experience were unskilled. The complexity of Ibsen's characters puzzled conventional actors, who assumed that if a character were selfish he must be villainous; if self-sacrificing or scrupulous, comic. They therefore tried to bring his characters onto familiar ground by reducing them to theatrical stereotypes with which they were familiar. Since laughter meant derision to them, they did not want to be laughed at when playing serious roles and Ibsen required them to make themselves ridiculous, sometimes during their most emotional passages, his point often being to expose the conventions from which stereotyped characters derived. Not only did he make "lost" women sympathetic, he made this quality the basis on which he awarded them the sympathy usually granted to traditionally righteous figures. "Hence Ibsen cannot be played from the conventional point of view [...]." Whereas the new school regarded the old as ignoramuses who for this reason could not perform Ibsen properly, the old school regarded the new as amateurs who for that reason could not perform him properly. But because the old technique is useless in Ibsen's theater, then, "taking amateur in its sense of unpractised executant, both schools are amateur as far as Ibsen's plays are concerned." Shaw anticipated an improvement in Ibsen performances by the young players, after experience matured them as artists.[103] He did not reckon on the tendency of actors to treat solemnly a writer with serious ideas, marking important speeches with "pathetic sentimentality and an intense consciousness of Ibsen's greatness." This method, which falsifies Ibsen, "is gradually establishing a funereally unreal tradition which is likely to end in making Ibsen the most portentous of stage bores." To act his plays as tragedies lends itself, ruinously for Ibsen, to rhetorical acting in which people talk "at each other from opposite sides of the stage, taking long sweeping walks up to their 'points' " and striking deliberately artificial attitudes. Failing the services of such "geniuses" as Irving and Mansfield, masters of "homely-imaginative, the realistic-fateful" style, Shaw begs the director "to treat Ibsen as comedy. That will not get the business

101. "The Chili Widow," 12 October 1895.
102. "At the Pantomime," 23 January 1897.
103. Appendix to *The Quintessence of Ibsenism*, 1891.

right; but it will be better than the tragedy plan." Particularly important, the actor should recognize that his job "is not to supply an idea with a sounding board, but with a credible, simple, and natural human being to utter it when its time comes and not before."[104]

Shaw was vitally concerned with scenery as well as acting. Even contemporary authors were undone by nineteenth-century scene changes. When Réjane brought *Madame Sans-Gêne* to London, she exhibited "elaborate Empire interiors requiring half an hour between the acts to set, and not worth looking at when they are set."[105] As with acting, Shaw wanted scenery to convey the illusion of the play's reality and atmosphere. He deplored the scenery of *John Gabriel Borkman* as so makeshift as to destroy what the imagination might create. Between actors reading a play while seated on chairs and adequate scenery, "there is no middle course." The pioneers of the drama may be poor, "but in art, what poverty can do unhandsomely and stingily it should not do at all."[106] In itself, realism is insufficient. "It is one thing to banish vulgarity and monstrosity from the stage and replace them by conventional refinement and scrupulous verisimilitude. It is quite another to surround a real drama with its appropriate atmosphere, and provide a poetic background or an ironically prosaic setting for a tragic scene."[107]

Perceiving that the appeal of Ibsen and the new drama, including his own, was to younger generations, Shaw held high hopes for them. At one point he went so far as to declare, "I have never, I hope, underrated the importance of the amateur; but I am now beginning to cling to him as the savior of theatrical art."[108] Looking to the universities for appreciation of dramatic art, he offered criticism and encouragement. "It is characteristic of the authorities at Oxford that they should consider a month too little for the preparation of a boat race, and grudge three weeks to the rehearsal of one of Shakespear's plays." Consequently, student accomplishments on the Thames outpaced those of the Oxford University Dramatic Society. Amateurs have one advantage over professionals which, if exhaustively used, makes their best performances instructive: "the possibility of unlimited rehearsal." If they spent two nights a week all year reading Elizabethan plays, they would establish a tradition of skill and practice "and the O.U.D.S. will in course of time become popular as a club of artistic athletes instead of being ridiculed [. . .] as a set of unrepresentative esthetes." Only on these lines might a drama club become a vital part of an

104. "John Gabriel Borkman," 8 May 1897.
105. "Toujours Daly," 13 July 1895.
106. "John Gabriel Borkman," 8 May 1897.
107. "Mr John Hare," 21 December 1895.
108. "The Old Acting and the New," 14 December 1895.

English university and force the authorities to build a theater as an indispensable part of a university's educational equipment.[109] When university actors produced old-fashioned commercial drama, he was astonished. "The professional actress accepts what she calls 'a rotten part' instead of a part by Ibsen or Shakespear because she is paid to do it. But why do University students do it when all the dramatic poetry of the ages lies at their command?" He does not believe that despite their education they know no better than uneducated people, but that not having thought seriously about the matter, they do what other amateurs do, which is to imitate the professionals.[110]

In the nineteenth century and some years thereafter, amateurs meant ladies and gentlemen of "stagestruck stupidity" who amused themselves by giving performances of a fashionable play, which they insultingly called "theatricals," and to ensure that no one mistook them for members of a dishonorable profession, gave the profits, if any, to charity.[111] The author's fee was five guineas for a full-length play, two or three for a shorter piece. In the early twentieth century, a new type of amateur emerged, who pioneered the new drama, including Ibsen's and Shaw's, in little theaters throughout the United Kingdom and the United States. Since the usual amateur fee, Shaw was early to recognize, would bankrupt this type and prevent drama from reaching audiences, he charged them what he charged professionals: a sliding scale from five to fifteen percent of the gross receipts. His distinction was not between unpaid and paid actors, full-time or part-time actors, the quality of acting, or the place of performance. A few dramatic enthusiasts trying to create a theater in a remote country town, spending their savings and charging low admission prices, might one day establish a permanent theater there. Instead of demanding an exorbitant five guineas from "these heroic pioneers," Shaw charged a percentage, even if it came to sixpence, for they were "planting theatrical art where it never grew before, whilst the West End syndicates spend a good deal of their money in dealing deathblows to it." His distinction between amateur and professional was simple. To the traditional lady and gentleman amateur he charged the traditional five guineas, but to those trying "to establish a permanent theatrical organization and [. . .] keeping all profits in the concern except what they need for their bread and butter," he gave "business terms." He gave school actors professional terms if all profits went to "a fund to be used exclusively for giving their annual theatrical performances. If there were continuity, and the profits

109. "Elizabethan Athletics at Oxford," 5 March 1898.
110. "On the University Dramatic Society," January 1900.
111. " 'The Starving Art': Mr Bernard Shaw and the Amateur Actors," 15 February 1906.

spent on performances," he accepted the enterprise as a legitimate theatre enterprise.[112]

His views of dramatic critics and criticism did not change. "Dramatic
criticism," he said in 1889, "is the quintessence of art criticism, which is
itself the essence of human folly and ignorance [. . .]."[113] "Unhappily,"
he stated six years later, "most of our theatre criticism is born stale [. . .]
and its republication would almost justify the immediate abolition of the
freedom of the press."[114] As late as 1929, he reiterated this theme, comparing the late 1920s with the late 1890s, when he practised that trade:
"dramatic criticism today is not worse than the criticism of that time. It
could not be. After all, there are limits to what can be done by incompetence, by ignorance, by carelessness, and by the irresponsible, and in
those days, several times a week, those limits were reached cheerfully.
[. . .] Criticism is, has been, and eternally will be as bad as it possibly can
be." One reason may be that nobody asks a dramatic critic for his qualifications. "Whether we are qualified or not is pure accident."[115]

At one time, the "average newspaper dramatic critic" was not necessarily a regular playgoer but a newsman assigned to the theater beat. In the
1890s, he was still little more than a reporter who wrote on what happened at the theater the way he would write about what happened in a
court. The bulk of such articles "is only called dramatic criticism by courtesy."[116] In small towns, "the critic is so abysmally beneath contempt that
nobody would dream of taking him seriously enough to call him an imposter."[117] Even in large cities, papers need theatrical advertisements, and
since some editors and owners ask managers for complimentary tickets, a
critic is not always reliable "even as a newsman where the plain truth
would give offence to any individual."[118] Criticism is "simply an advertisement," and the manager who advertises will "threaten and dictate freely if
the notices are not of the most abjectly complimentary character." Matters
were only somewhat better in London, where newspaper editors or owners made critics understand that if their notices offended anyone influential, they would "probably be superseded by writers who may be depended
on to give no trouble." Shaw resigned one critical position because he was
told that his duties included puffing the editor's friends (ironically, the
name of the paper was *Truth*).[119] Compounding the problem, he main-

---

112. "Amateur and Professional Fees for Performing Licenses," July 1928.
113. "Acting, by One Who Does Not Believe in It," 3 February 1889.
114. "Mr William Archer's Criticisms," 13 April 1895.
115. "[On Drama Critics and Drama Criticism]," 11 October 1929.
116. Appendix to *The Quintessence of Ibsenism*, 1891.
117. "Not Worth Reading," 24 April 1897.
118. "Appendix" to *The Quintessence of Ibsenism*, 1891.
119. "Mr William Archer's Criticisms," 13 April 1895.

tained, critics could not boycott producers because, as most critics were paid by the column or line, they would fine themselves whenever they did so, and because the work of some dramatists and actors is part of the news a paper is obliged to cover. While this does not mean the entire press is corrupt, it means the odds are weighted against independent journalistic criticism.[120]

When Ibsen died, Shaw berated most critics for having judged the "greatest dramatic genius of the XIX century" as criminal, imbecilic, and ephemeral. But what else could anyone expect? "Contemporary journalism, like democracy, is always a better judge of second-rate than of first-rate."[121] As he declared a few years later, the average critic is "always wrong"—which a few lines later he modified to "nine times out of ten"— "when a new genius and his school give the critic the chance of his lifetime."[122] This is consistent with his earlier statement: "Criticism may be pardoned for every mistake except that of not knowing a man of rank in literature when it meets one."[123] "We have great dramatists," he announced, "but the critics are not educated up to them and cannot appreciate their efforts." As examples, he cited Ibsen and Frank Wedekind, whom "the ignorant critics" did not admire, and he lamented the "little connection between the appearance of genius and its recognition." He also cited himself: "Every time one of my new plays is produced the critics declare it is rotten," though they always call "the next to the last play [. . .] the greatest thing Ive done."[124]

One reason for poor criticism, Shaw believed, is that formulas replace ideas.[125] Since most dramatists write according to a formula, it takes a great deal of talent to acquire a good reputation, and "the talent, being all expended on the formula, [. . .] consecrates the formula in the eyes of the critics." They not only do not understand that the talent transcends the formula, they think the formula makes the work good. Perniciously, they become so used to the formula, they cannot enjoy or understand a play that does not use it, although "No writer of the first order needs the formula any more than a sound man needs a crutch."[126] By contrast, Shaw in *The Quintessence of Ibsenism* reminds "those who may think that I have forgotten to reduce Ibsenism to a formula for them, that its quintessence is that there is no formula."[127]

120. "Appendix" to *The Quintessence of Ibsenism*, 1891.
121. "Ibsen," 1 June 1906.
122. "[On Our Stage and Its Critics]," 1910–11.
123. "The New Ibsen Play," 30 January 1897.
124. "Shaw Answers James Bryce," 5 May 1907.
125. "The Author to the Dramatic Critics," 1893.
126. Preface to *Three Plays by Brieux* (1909).
127. Preface to *The Quintessence of Ibsenism*, 1913.

Another reason is that some critics are "too illiterate and incompetent in the sphere of dramatic poetry to conceive or relish anything more substantial than the theatrical fare to which they are accustomed."[128] They "are not traitors to literature because they do not belong to it"; rather, they are at one with mass audiences who prefer fluff. As for critics who appear to be cultured in literature and art, "they are bad critics," perhaps "not critics at all," but "simply petulant pleasure hunters." Possibly, "their disapproval may be entirely justified: the play may be verbose, dull, untheatrical, repugnant, or whatnot; but this does not justify a critic in writing uncritical nonsense about it" based on an assortment of ignorant commonplaces.[129]

To Shaw, criticism was a difficult art and critics not merely failed authors. He called authorship "child's play compared to criticism [. . .]. Ask any novelist whether he can write a better novel or play than I; and he will blithely say Yes. Ask him to take my place as critic for one week; and he will blench from the test. The truth is that the critic stands between popular authorship, for which he is not silly enough, and great authorship, for which he has not genius enough."[130] The purpose of a skilled critic is "to educate [. . .] dunces, not to echo them." He "must act as the watchdog of art, and [. . .] bark very vigorously." What he cannot be is a gentleman, since his duties "consist largely in making painful remarks in public about the most sensitive" people; rather, "he is the policeman of dramatic art; and it is his express business to denounce its delinquencies."[131] Politeness is not his business. "Good manners in him consist in sincerity, not in smooth speech."[132] Teacher, watchdog, policeman— Shaw more often compared the critic to a dentist. If a critic, like a dentist, drills "the rot out of a tooth he can't always help hurting the patient."[133] Critics, like dentists, hurt sensitive people, and as they do it entertainingly, they may seem to enjoy it;[134] but when he must inflict pain, he uses "all the anesthesia I can produce."[135] Still, he advised the critic, "Never insult an author or artist by sparing his feelings. [. . .] If you are going to hit him, hit him straight in the face—exuberantly, as if you enjoyed it—

---

128. Appendix to *The Quintessence of Ibsenism*, 1891.

129. "[On Our Stage and Its Critics]," 1910–11.

130. "The Author to the Dramatic Critics," 1893.

131. "Two New Plays," 12 January 1895; "The Chili Widow," 12 October 1895; "On the Living and the Dead," 25 December 1897.

132. "As You Dont Like It," 15 July 1899.

133. Quoted in St John Adock, "G.B.S. at Home" (revised and corrected by Shaw), *Bookman*, December 1924, reprinted in A. M. Gibbs, ed., *Shaw: Interviews and Recollections* (Iowa City: University of Iowa Press, 1990), 414.

134. Preface to *Ellen Terry and Bernard Shaw: A Correspondence*, 26 June 1929.

135. Letter to H. A. Silverman, 6 January 1930, *Collected Letters 1926–1950* (New York: Viking, 1988), ed. Dan H. Laurence, 4:168–69.

and give him credit for being able to stand up to it."[136] He tried "to hit out at remediable abuses rather than at accidental shortcomings, and at strong and responsible people rather than weak and helpless ones."[137] His utterances may be irritating, but "if you do not say a thing in an irritating way, you may just as well not say it at all, since nobody will trouble themselves about anything that does not trouble them."[138]

Impartiality, he stated, was an abjuration of criticism.[139] "Never in my life have I penned an impartial criticism; and I hope I never may."[140] However, he provided what we now call truth in packaging, warning readers to discount his opinion of *The Notorious Mrs Ebbsmith* since he writes plays in reaction to Pinero's. Disarmingly, he added, "my criticism has not, I hope, any other fault than the inevitable one of extreme unfairness."[141] Reviewing a book by William Archer, to which he contributed a preface, he frankly admitted, "We are intimate personal friends; and we roll each other's logs with a will. [. . .] If my judgment were not so exquisitely balanced that the slightest touch of personal bias upsets it, I should be a very poor critic: consequently my opinion as to Mr Archer's merits is flagrantly unjudicial.[142] Furthermore, "I have never claimed for myself the divine attribute of justice." In his reviews, "I set up my own standard of what the drama should be and how it should be presented; and I used all my art to make every deviation in aiming at this standard, every recalcitrance in approaching it, every refusal to accept it seem ridiculous and oldfashioned." In doing so, he was no more impartial than critics with different views.[143]

Welcoming diversity of informed opinion, he contrasted Archer's criticisms with his own: "For him there is illusion in the theatre: for me there is none." To Archer, "acting, like scenepainting, is merely a means to an end, that end being to enable him to make believe. To me the play is only the means, the end being the expression of feeling by the arts of the actor, the poet, the musician. Anything that makes the expression more vivid, whether it be versification, or an orchestra, or a deliberately artificial delivery of the lines is so much to the good to me, even though it may destroy all the verisimilitude of the scene." This does not mean he regards his critical stance as right and Archer's wrong. He mentions his belief to

136. "[On Criticism]," June 1894.
137. "The Case for the Critic-Dramatist," 16 November 1895.
138. "Mary Anderson," 4 April 1896.
139. " 'Spectator's' Book," 9 January 1892.
140. "The Effects of Electioneering," *The World*, 6 July 1892, reprinted in *Shaw's Music* (London: Bodley Head, 1981), ed. Dan H. Laurence, 2:666.
141. "Mr Pinero's New Play," 16 March 1895.
142. "Mr William Archer's Criticisms," 13 April 1895.
143. "The Author's Apology [for *Saturday Review* Criticisms]," October 1906.

clarify Archer's by contrast.[144] At one time, he called Arthur Bingham Walkley "the best dramatic critic in London" because he excels in impressionistic criticism, inviting the actor and dramatist: "Impress me; and I will describe my impressions. [. . .] I have no prepossessions except those of artistic temperament." Since he does this so well, "he beats us all as a critic. Whilst we are laboriously measuring the difference between what the performance is and what it ought to be, and complaining because it is not the latter: whilst we are [. . .] moralizing, or immoralizing, or backing our side in every political or religious issue raised by the dramatist," Walkley simply draws a picture of what has happened on stage, "with charming ingenuity, humor, and grace."[145] Surprisingly, Shaw praised the anti-Ibsenite Clement Scott. His criticisms express "the warmest personal feeling and nothing else. They are alive: their admiration is sincere and moving: their resentment is angry and genuine." His shortcoming is a susceptibility "to the direct expression of human feeling, and to that alone. Interpose any medium between him and the moving, uttering, visible human creature, and he is insulated at once." Whether the medium is music, painting, "reflective thought inspired by passion instead of the direct instinctive cry of the passion itself," the moment it is interposed, he "writes like any Philistine citizen of ordinary artistic tastes [. . .]." His inability to recognize a feeling when it is presented to him as a thought has brought him in conflict with Ibsen's drama. Scott "is not a thinker: whatever question you raise with him you must raise it as a question of conduct, which is a matter of feeling, and not of creed, which is a matter of intellectual order." The view that "when conduct conflicts with creed, the question as to which of the two is in the wrong is an open one" is central to modern drama. Because he finds this view repugnant, he cannot tolerate its dramatization.[146] Unsurprisingly, Scott was not among those who admired Shavian drama. Indeed, Archer and Walkley too, both publicly and privately, often lambasted Shaw's plays.

Among the qualities of good criticism, Shaw consistently maintained, is its relationship to real life. Thanking critics of *Widowers' Houses* for being "not merely fair, but generous," he adds that "the fairness of criticism is one thing, its adequacy quite another." Many critics did not understand the play because they are "ignorant of society," that is, "they do not know life well enough to recognize it in the glare of the footlights."[147] As for critics who view the public life dramatized by Ibsen as "petty parochial squabblings" that are irrelevant to the complex greatness of public affairs

144. "Mr William Archer's Criticisms," 13 April 1895.
145. " 'Spectator's' Book," 9 January 1892.
146. "G.B.S. on Clement Scott," 30 May 1896.
147. "Bernard Shaw Replies to the Critics of Widowers' Houses," 19 December 1892.

in England, such people "know as much of political life as I know of navigation."[148] He aimed "to widen the horizon of the critic, especially of the dramatic critic, whose habit at present is to bring a large experience of stage life," which replaces reality with conventions, "to bear on a scanty experience of real life, although it is certain that all really fruitful criticism of the drama must bring a wide and practical knowledge of real life to bear on the stage."[149]

He contrasted the critic with the actor. "It is true that dramatists do not write their plays with a view to shewing me off to the best advantage by writing only what fits my style of criticism," as they write plays showing off actors by writing roles that fit only their style of performing, "and that I must know my business all through and take it as the public demand it: Shakespear and Ibsen one week, musical farce the next, light and heavy, 'character' and classical, instead of picking out what is 'in my line.'" However, "my brain gets exercised [. . .]."[150] He denounced "high and mighty criticism, which consists merely of complaints that melodramas are not classical, tragedies not high comedies, Mr Pinero not Aristophanes, and Mr Henry Arthur Jones not Sophocles" as "foolish" and "barren," for "[a] critic who cannot criticize Punch and Judy on its own plane is no critic, but only a partisan of his favorite plane. Nay, a critic who cannot enjoy a good performance of Punch and Judy is not likely to be a very safe judge of Aristophanes."[151] To write dramatic criticism for a daily London newspaper was "tragic," not because the critic who must appraise Euripides, Shakespeare, or Ibsen one day a week must judge melodramas and chorus girls the other five. If the proportions were reversed, such diversity would "be good for the critic and what he criticized, provided he were really capable of the Euripidean end of his job [. . .]." The problem is that too many critics agree with those who, as it were, want no Beethoven and "a continual Yip-i-addy i-ay." They should recognize there are different audiences for both, be able to criticize both, and "make an end of ignorant complaints that Beethoven is not Yipiaddy and uppish complaints that Yipiaddy is not Beethoven"; unfortunately, "the press is practically unanimous in its approval" of "purely commercial plays."[152]

Recognition of varieties of drama includes awareness of differences among dramas of different periods. In time, manners, customs, and morals change "with revolutionary completeness, whilst man remains almost the same." Yet people change, "not only in what they think and what they

148. "L'Œuvre," 30 March 1895.
149. "Criticism on the Hustings," 20 July 1895.
150. "Not Worth Reading," 24 April 1897.
151. "On the University Dramatic Society," January 1900.
152. "[On Our Stage and Its Critics]," 1910–11.

do, but in what they are." While the differences between seventeenth-century and twentieth-century institutions may be as complete as those between a horse and a bicycle, the difference between people of these periods is relatively trivial, smaller than that between Shakespeare and the average Elizabethan. Thus, his plays, while "obsolete as representations of fashion and manners, are still far ahead of the public as dramatic studies of humanity." However, Shaw's point is subtler than the perception that people change more slowly than fashions. "Everything has its own rate of change. Fashions change more quickly than manners, manners more quickly than morals, morals more quickly than passions, and, in general, the conscious, reasonable, intellectual life more quickly than the instinctive, wilful, affectionate one. The dramatist who deals with the irony and humor of the relatively durable sides of life, or with their pity and terror, is the one whose comedies and tragedies will last longer [. . .]." Whereas fashionable plays date in a few years, Shakespeare's "must have 'dated' far more when they were twenty to a hundred years old than they have done since the world gave up expecting them to mirror the passing hour." As a consequence of different rates of change, plays run a familiar course. First, their manners and fashions date. If their matter is substantial enough to overcome this, their reputations will be renewed. After more time, perhaps centuries, their ethical conceptions will make them date again, but if they deal "so powerfully with the instincts and passions of humanity as to survive this also," they will regain their position, this time as antique classics.[153]

Shaw argued that the best critic was a dramatist—if, however, the dramatist were also a good critic. "The advantage of having a play criticized by a critic who is also a playwright is as obvious as the advantage of having a ship criticized by a critic who is also a master shipwright." When one has faced practical questions of casting one's own play, he may realize that there are fewer talented actors than he had thought, and that some he may have felt good enough for other people's plays are not good enough for his. Once a play's author has dealt with this problem in regard to his own play, he deals with it in regard to other people's plays, thereby combining "the first moral with the first technical qualification of the critic: the determination to have every play as well done as possible, and the knowledge of what is standing in the way of that consummation."[154]

In addition, the able critic takes the drama seriously, which "few journalistic critics do." In a frequently repeated theme, Shaw quoted Matthew, 18:20: "A theatre to me is a place 'where two or three are gathered together.' The apostolic succession from Eschylus to myself is a serious

---

153. "The Second Dating of Sheridan," 27 June 1896.
154. "The Case for the Critic-Dramatist," 16 November 1895.

and as continuously inspired as that younger institution, the apostolic succession of the Christian Church." Instead of "alternately petting and snubbing" the theater as entertainment, critics should treat it seriously "as a factory of thought, a prompter of conscience, an elucidator of social conduct, an armory against despair and dullness, and a temple of the Ascent of Man."[155] Since movies are a dramatic medium, he recognized even in the silent-film era the importance of the morality they inculcated. "The cinema is going to form the mind of England. The national conscience, the national ideals and tests of conduct, will be those of the film."[156] Films and records, which he foresaw would be synchronized, will very likely become more revolutionary than writing or printing, "for the number of people who can read is small, the number of those who can read to any purpose much smaller, and the number of those who are too tired after a day's work to read without falling asleep enormous."[157] With the advent of talkies, this belief intensified. He called Hollywood "one of the most immoral places in the world." The reason was not sex but anarchy. Hollywood heroes, anarchists, had "one answer to anything annoying or to any breach of the law": to sock the offender on the jaw, which is a criminal offence. "When will we see a film issuing from Hollywood," he wondered, "in which the hero, instead of socking the gentleman in the jaw, does the civilized thing and calls the policeman?" On the basis of his own experience, "it is not the heroes or the virtuous people who are good at socking jaws," but "exactly the contrary sort of people," for which reason "they are regarded as evil people."[158]

Shaw was under no illusion as to the effectiveness of dramatic criticism: "My labors [. . .] are the labors of Sysiphus: every week I roll my heavy stone to the top of the hill; and every week I find it at the bottom again." The public likes to see the stone tumbling down in a cloud of dust, "blackening the eyes of a beautiful actress here and catching an eminent actor-manager in the wind there, flattening out dramatists, demolishing theatres," but afterward, "The actresses are as beautiful and popular as ever; the actor-managers wallow in the profits of the plays I have denounced; the dramatists receive redoubled commissions; the theatres reopen with programs foolisher than before; and nothing remains of my toy avalanche but the stone at my feet to be rolled up again before the fatigue of the last heave is out of my bones."[159] Rarely did he state that his criticism had impact. In the second edition of *The Quintessence of Ibsen-*

---

155. "The Author's Apology [for *Saturday Review* Criticisms]," October 1906.
156. "The Cinema as a Moral Leveler," *New Statesman*, 27 June 1914.
157. "What the Films May Do to the Drama," May 1915.
158. "[Hollywood's Immoral Influence]," 11 April 1933.
159. "Some Other Critics," 20 June 1896.

ism, he wondered if it would "change people's minds to the extent to which the first did," and added parenthetically, "to my great astonishment."[160] This statement echoed his preface to *Major Barbara*: "I, who have preached and pamphleteered like any Encyclopedist, have to confess that my methods are no use [. . .]."[161] But had he not believed his criticism had value, he would not have continued to criticize theater or society. As he says in the preface to *Plays Unpleasant*, every despot needs a disloyal subject. "Even Louis XI had to tolerate his confessor, standing for the eternal against the temporal throne." Democracy has given the despot's scepter to the people, whose confessor "they call Critic." Criticism "has positive popular attractions in its cruelty, its gladiatorship, and the gratification given to envy by its attacks on the great, and to enthusiasm by its praises. [. . .] Its iconoclasms, seditions, and blasphemies, if well turned, tickle those whom they shock, so that the critic adds the privileges of the court jester to those of the confessor."[162] He recommended a volume of reprints of theater criticism by George Henry Lewes and John Forster partly on the basis of eternal against temporal: "the actor who desires enduring fame must seek it at the hands of the critic, and not of the casual playgoer." The latter may give him money and applause, "but posterity can see him through the spectacles of the elect [. . .]. The world believes Edmund Kean to have been a much greater actor than Junius Brutus Booth solely because Hazlitt thought so." If posterity concerns itself about either contemporary actors or himself, it will see them as he sees them.[163]

To those who considered Shaw the critic a mere banterer or joker, he replied, accurately, "I am only a leg-puller insofar as I pull crooked legs straight."[164] What he said in 1884 about Thersites, a critic of humanity in Shakespeare's *Troilus and Cressida*, may also hold for himself as dramatic critic. "Hypocrisy has no existence for him [. . .]." Like Jonathan Swift, Thersites is an "analyst of human motives and pretences" whom the public considers a "witty railer. [. . .] Like a prophet, he utters the truth that is in him without regard to consequences."[165] As St John Ervine noted, Shaw "could be terrifyingly frank, and some people, whose vanity he disturbed, thought him cruel; but he was not cruel [. . .]. His frankness was almost scarifying; but he was frank because he thought it better to tell people the truth than to involve them in long, obscure dodg-

160. Preface to *The Quintessence of Ibsenism*, 1913.
161. *CPP*, 3:38–39.
162. *CPP*, 1:13–14.
163. "Some Other Critics," 20 June 1896.
164. "Bernard Shaw Piqued," *Daily Express*, 22 February 1924, reprinted in *CPP*, 5:707.
165. "Troilus and Cressida," 29 February 1884.

ings of it." And he "firmly defended his faith."[166] In this introduction to Shaw's seven decades of dramatic criticism, perhaps the last word should be that of Frank Harris, editor of the *Saturday Review*, for which Shaw regularly criticized the drama from 1895 to 1898. In Shaw's observations, said Harris, "the drama of the day"—which we may extend to the days before and after these years—"had never been so pungently criticized; I began to compare Shaw's articles with the [*Hamburg*] *Dramaturgie* of Lessing; and it was Shaw who gained by the comparison."[167]

166. "Bernard Shaw," *The Spectator*, November 1950, reprinted in Gibbs, 505, 507.
167. *Contemporary Portraits*, reprinted in Gibbs, 92.

A NOTE ON THE TEXTS

Shaw observed the drama both publicly and privately, expressing himself differently for each mode. For example, about 7 February 1897, he wrote a letter, not intended for publication, to Robert Blatchford, editor of *The Clarion*, about *John Gabriel Borkman*. To his surprise, Blatchford published the letter on 13 February. Since the letter "would have been more considerately worded" had Shaw wanted it published, he said in another letter, he wrote again "to clear up a point or two which had better not be misunderstood." The first, private letter is published in Shaw's *Collected Letters*; an extract from the second, public letter, printed on 20 February, is published here. With two exceptions, both extracts from private letters, these volumes consist of his public utterances. The first is to Ellen Terry, 6 September 1896, advising her on cutting *Cymbeline* for performance: in conjunction with Shaw's review of Henry Irving's production of *Cymbeline* twenty days later, each casts light on the other. The second is to Gilbert Murray, 14 March 1911, on *Oedipus the King* as a well-made play: it illuminates both the Sophoclean tragedy and the well-made play, and it is Shaw's only examination of a Greek tragedy in this collection. Important public observations of the drama not included in this collection are in his prefaces to his plays, in *Collected Plays with Their Prefaces*, and in his music criticisms, *Shaw's Music*, which are easily available to the reader. Since he recycled many of his views, he made similar utterances in the pieces included in this collection. Other public observations are excluded from this collection because they significantly duplicate material included.

The Drama Observed contains 318 separate items, arranged chronologically, of which 100, almost a third, are new to today's readers: twelve are published for the first time, three published in full for the first time, and eighty-five unpublished since their first, sometimes anonymous, printing. Many pieces, such as dramatic criticisms for the *Saturday Review*, reprinted in *Our Theatres in the Nineties*, and essays republished in *Pen*

Portraits and Reviews—more than 150 in all—have been unavailable for so long that these too may be new to many readers. Shaw wrote the first item in this collection when he was twenty-five years old; the last, two months before his ninety-fourth birthday. Unless otherwise indicated, all were first published in London; "otherwise" includes America, Australia, and India. The pieces collected here range from brief statements to a book—or rather two editions of a book, *The Quintessence of Ibsenism*, which are placed chronologically. The 1891 text has footnotes indicating substantive later revisions; a preface and chapters added in 1913 are placed in that year. To have collated them would have meant either putting in 1891 Shaw's analysis of plays Ibsen wrote later, which is illogical, or placing the entire, revised edition in 1913, which would lack the immediacy and topicality of 1891. Where possible, I have gone to the original publications, which I have checked against reprints (for instance, the *Saturday Review* pieces and *Our Theatres in the Nineties*).

In Shaw's texts, editorial interpolations and ellipses are enclosed by brackets. For easy reference, annotations are footnoted on the same page as the text. With few exceptions, characters in plays by Shakespeare and Ibsen are unannotated, since readers of works about these dramatists should be familiar with them or be able to find them without difficulty. Because these volumes will be read or consulted by scholars, teachers, students, directors, actors, and I hope some nonspecialists interested in a good read, I have otherwise erred in the matter of annotations—if erring it be—on the side of fullness. Having met graduate students and nonspecialists who had not learned or had forgotten the meanings of, for example, *raisonneur* and the Gordian knot, I decided to risk irritating teachers and specialists by annotating both. For the most part, however, my rule of thumb has been not to annotate anything that one could find in a dictionary.

Shaw's idiosyncratic spelling and punctuation have been followed to the best of my ability. Edipus and Eschylus are spelled that way. Dont and Ive lack apostrophes; but since I'll and she'd could be confused with ill and shed, apostrophes are retained. On the other hand, the verb cant is Shavianly unapostrophed, despite possible confusion with the noun cant. Arnt is spelled and punctuated this way, Shakespear and Tchekov that way. Shaw often drops one of two consecutive letters, such as the second p in worshipper, but where a single letter might confusingly create a misreading or a different pronunciation, such as rivalled, he retains both. Yet spelled becomes spelt. I have followed Shavian precedent in hyphenating such words as actor-manager and word-music, not hyphenating such words as music hall and well known, and making one word of terms sometimes written as two or hyphenated, such as commonsense, greenroom, halfhearted, oneanother, postwar, and stagemanager. When Shaw refers to the middle class, the term is spelled as two words, as he also spells "lower class"; when he mentions middleclass morality, he uses one word, as he does for middleaged. I have also followed Shaw's practice in dropping commas before and after interrupting phrases that break a quotation into two parts if no comma is in the original, dropping commas before quotations (He said "Hello"), and retaining commas in series (Tom, Dick, and Harry). Similarly, Shavian precedent requires italics for some words (*genre, mise-en-scène*), but not others (matinée, naïve). Color and labor receive a Shavianly American spelling and quotation marks are Americanly double, not Britishly single; numbers are run together as one word (ninetynine) and fractions lack hyphens; a century is XIX, not nineteenth; periods do not follow some words (Mr, Mrs) but follow others (M., Rev.). Titles of books, plays, and songs have Roman letters, not italics or quotation marks. As some of these examples demonstrate, Shaw believed, Emersonially, that a foolish consistency is the hobgoblin of little minds and that great souls have nothing to do with it.[1] Accordingly, I have not tried to impose consistency where such an imposition would change Shaw's words. For example, while Shaw usually gives singular verbs to nouns like "public," in the American manner ("the public is"), on more than a few occasions he conforms to British usage ("the public are"). These inconsistencies stand, I hope, as evidence of Shaw's greatness of soul.

When people with unhyphenated names later hyphenated them, such as Granville-Barker and Forbes-Robertson, I have followed their wishes and used hyphens. However, the Index cross-references each under what was previously the surname. In letters, salutations and signatures are omitted unless the latter are needed to complete a sentence.

1. Ralph Waldo Emerson (1803–82), "Self-Reliance" (1841).

ABBREVIATIONS

AG   *Agitations* (1985), ed. Dan H. Laurence and James Rambeau

BL   British Library (at the British Museum)

C   Published in a collection of Shaw's writings for the first time

CL   *Collected Letters* (1965–88), 4 vols., ed. Dan H. Laurence.

CPP   *Collected Plays with Their Prefaces* (1970–74), 7 vols.

F   Published in full for the first time

H   Holograph manuscript

HR   Harry Ransom Humanities Research Center, University of Texas at Austin

P   Published for the first time

PP   *Platform and Pulpit* (1961), ed. Dan H. Laurence

PPR   *Pen Portraits and Reviews* (1949)

Ps   Pseudonymously signed (pseudonym given in brackets)

QI   Written interview based on questions submitted

SDI   Self-drafted interview

SI   *Shaw and Ibsen* (1979), ed. J. L. Wisenthal

ST   *Shaw on Theatre* (1958), ed. E. J. West

TS   Typescript

TH   Typescript with holograph corrections

U   Following F, indicates what is previously unpublished by [U:] and [:U]

Un   Unsigned or generically signed (e.g. From Our Correspondent)

VR   Verbatim report

X   Extract

ACKNOWLEDGMENTS

With one exception, this section is the most pleasant to write, as it enables me to express my deep gratitude to those people who and institutions which, by helping me, have made these volumes possible. That exception is my concern that I may have overlooked someone or some institution. If I have, I am extremely sorry.

I am particularly thankful to Dan H. Laurence, whose assistance has been such that when I describe it I can only resort to such clichés as "immense," "unflagging," and "far beyond the call of duty," which serve as reminders that clichés may be based in reality; to Virginia Tech, the popular and affectionate term for Virginia Polytechnic Institute and State University, whose enlightened assistance to scholars and scholarship, chiefly through released time to do research and to write but also through the ambience it has created by its University Distinguished Professorships, should be a model for universities in this country; to the National Endowment for the Humanities, whose Fellowship for Independent Study and Research made it possible for me to gather the material printed here and whose Travel to Collections grant helped me to find annotations; and to the University of Hawaii Research Foundation, whose grant helped me to collect items printed here.

For reading and criticizing my Introduction, I thank Barbara Dukore and David Johnson. For their assistance in obtaining or annotating various items I am indebted to numerous people in several countries. For convenience's sake I list them alphabetically: Sidney P. Albert, Steven Baehr, Rosemarie Bank, Jacques Barzun, John Beaufort, Michael Booth, James Brandon, Oscar G. Brockett, Annette Burr, Marvin Carlson, Charles A. Carpenter, Gay Gibson Cima, L. W. Conolly, Gilbert Cross, Tracy C. Davis, P. Antonie Distler, Ian Donaldson, Joseph Donohue, Barbara Dukore, Martin Esslin, Joanne Eustis, Robert G. Everding, Christopher Faraone, Craig Fields, Rhiannon Finamore, Rolf Fjelde, Helen Foster, Rachel France,

Richard France, Joanne E. Gates, Helen Graeff, Robert Graeff, Marjorie Grene, Nicholas Grene, Mary Louise Hallauer, Joy Harvey, Gordon Hogg, Elizabeth J. Holford, Kent Holliday, Michael Holroyd, Norma Jenckes, Katherine J. Johnson, Gregory Justice, Joel Kaplan, Charles A. Kennedy, Bettina Knapp, Shoshona Knapp, Terence Knapp, Rosette Lamont, Gerald MacDonald, David Male, Anita Malebranch, Dorothy McCombs, Brooks McNamara, Walter B. Meserve, Douglas Muecke, Jeanne T. Newlin, Christopher Newton, Marion O'Connor, Ken Olson, A. A. Orgill, Linda Plaut, Roy Porter, Thomas Postlewait, Felice Proctor, Jennie Rathbun, Leonard C. Pronko, Terence Rees, José M. Reguiero, Vera M. Roberts, Anthony Rota, Michael Saffle, Ruth Salvaggio, Horst Schroeder, Guangren Shen, Anthony W. Shipps, Robert Silvester, George Speaight, Harriet Talan, Michèle Thomas, Joel Trapido, William Tydeman, Bailey Van Hook, Ruth Vasey, André Veinstein, Diane Parr Walker, Michael P. Walters, Randolph W. Ward, Irving Wardle, Betty S. Waterhouse, Stanley Weintraub, Samuel A. Weiss, Elizabeth Wichmann, James Wightman, Don B. Wilmeth, Frederic Woodbridge Wilson, J. L. Wisenthal, Roma Woodnutt, and Katharine Worth.

I am also grateful to the Bibliothèque Nationale, the Billy Rose Collection of the New York Public Library at Lincoln Center, the British Film Institute, the British Library, the Burgunder Collection of Cornell University Library, the Canning House Library (London), the Central Library of the Royal Military Academy at Sandhurst, the editors of *Notes and Queries*, the editors of the "Notes and Queries" section of *Theatre Notebook*, the Fales Library of New York University, the Greater London Council Library, the Harry Ransom Humanities Research Center of the University of Texas at Austin, the Harvard Theatre Collection, the Henry E. Huntington Library, the Library of Congress, the Manchester Central Library, the Marx Memorial Library (London), the Mitchell Library (Sydney, Australia), the National Library of Scotland, the Newman Library of Virginia Polytechnic Institute and State University, the Newspaper Library of the British Library at Colindale, the Newspaper Library of the New York Public Library, the Royal Academy of Dramatic Art, the Royal Naval College at Greenwich, the Society of Authors (London), the Spanish Institute (London), the State Library of New South Wales, the Theatre Museum Library (London), the University College Library of the University of London, the University of Hawaii Library, the University of Virginia Law Library, the University of Virginia Library, the Victoria and Albert Museum Library, the Voltaire Foundation at the Taylor Institute (London), and the Westminster Central Reference Library.

BERNARD
SHAW

The Drama Observed

THE MERCHANT OF VENICE
AT THE LYCEUM
P/H/BL (7 April 1880)

During a phase of taste to suit which all intelligible fictions are obscured by farfetched interpretations, a theory representing Shakespear as a morbid creator of sombre and preposterous figures has been offered to the public by Mr Henry Irving,[1] a man of singular appearance, and full of that love of mysterious and grotesque with which students of the picturesque arts become seized before they have advanced to a conception of the indifferent familiarity with the external machinery of effect which the adept master feels. The theory became popular, and last year when Mr Irving determined to play Shylock beside a Portia whom the public had resolved to admire, his sole difficulty lay in the task of adapting the Jew to himself, whom he had already adapted to the demand of the mob for what it thought profound. He therefore removed Shylock into the shadow, by ignoring the comments of Houndsditch and Bevis Marks[2] upon the poet's text. Perhaps—jumping to the conclusion that their soil was too vulgar to be leavened by the genius of Shakespear—he did not think of looking to them for instruction. Babylon appeared a grander scene, Ezra[3] a sublimer figure, exile a more pathetic condition to study than the barren region and the sordid men whom his audience could see every day between Tower Hill and Bishopsgate. So, in despite of the testimony of every line of his part, he presented Shylock as a noble and mournful man perverted by a sensational dramatist, and publicly taught the lesson that the fruits of persecution were admirable even in their unhappiness.

Having so far outstripped Cibber and Garrick,[4] it was inconsistent, though not strange, that he should have made a scruple which never occurred to either of them. These men altered the letter of the parts they

1. Henry Irving (real name John Henry Brodbribb, 1838–1905), the preeminent English actor of his day, was manager of London's Lyceum Theater. In 1895 he was knighted—the first actor to receive this honor.

2. Streets in the slums of London's East End, as are Tower Hill and Bishopsgate (below), all near Whitechapel, where Jack the Ripper committed his murders eight years later.

3. Old Testament priest and scribe, devout and influential, apparently born in Babylon, he reputedly collected and revised previous writings of the Old Testament. The Book of Ezra relates his return to Jerusalem.

4. Actors, theater managers, and playwrights, Colley Cibber (1671–1757) and David Garrick (1717–79) were infamous for their adaptations of Shakespeare's plays, which included cuts, changes, and additional dialogue.

tinkered [with], in order (as they believed) to reinforce their spirit. When Cibber, because he would have Richard [III] every inch a hero—because the very word "coward" did not, to his taste, become the lips of the gamest of the Plantagenets—made him exclaim "Oh T y r a n t conscience, how thou dost afflict me!" his intention was to improve Shakespear's delineation of the qualities indicated in the text; and his error lay solely in his vanity, which blinded him to the comparatively abysmal depth of his own artistic ignorance. Yet Mr Irving, without hesitating to comport himself with less respect to Shakespear's play than he might have preserved had he rewritten the whole of it, has shrunk from violating the text.

Neither his furtive omissions nor his deliveries which inflect the meaning of the verse, suffice to make consistent his version, the incongruity of which could only have been avoided by two bold alterations. These are, first, the omission of the aside "How like a fawning publican he looks," a licence which would be pardoned by every judicious person, even to an actor who merely sought to play Shakespear's Shylock, because this stagey aside is remarkable as the sole blemish in an unusually perfect play. It is an example of how even Shakespear could not always conceal the coarseness of the method which the dulness of the public forced him to employ, although commonly his successes in explaining and labeling everything for the childlike spectators of his day without seeming to go out of his direct course to do so are amongst the technical triumphs of his genius.

The second alteration would require the services of a poet. It would consist of a speech to be substituted for the words "I am content," expressive of the indomitable resolve of Shylock to die a thousand deaths rather than betray the tears of the captivity and sell his faith like Rachel's turquoise.[5] And, since in view of another act he could not very suitably die or be condemned, Portia might beg his life for Jessica's sake, and he could retire a beggar but invincible. Such is the only possible end to Mr Irving's Shylock, and to it he irrevocably commits himself when he ventures to shew the Jew as only checked in the act of generously lending the money without usury to the man who has unjustly despised him by the shrinking of the latter from his touch. That the conclusion is not adopted can hardly, after such a display of temerity, be due either to veneration for the integrity of the original play, or want of audacity. Possibly Mr Irving did not comprehend as a whole the image he based on Shylock until he had offered it to the public. Possibly he does not comprehend it yet. It is not

---

5. Shylock's daughter Jessica sold (or bartered) a turquoise ring she stole from him, which his late wife Leah had given him while he was still a bachelor. Since the biblical Leah and Rachel were sisters, both of whom Jacob married (Genesis 29), Shaw may have confused the names.

unlikely that the fact of his having, most unfortunately for his progress as an actor, become an object of popular superstition as a Shakespearean scholar, may have influenced him to spare the text that violence which he has offered to the character.

Obviously, the Shylock intended by Shakespear is a moneylender of the common Jewish type, grasping, repellent of Christian friendship, only civil on purpose, fond of his family, and a shrewd arguer in defence of his practice. The proof negative of this is the absence from the play of one single line or word either incongruous with it, or congruous with the higher nature which Mr Irving labors to suggest. The proof positive is the reception by Shylock of Portia's justifiably disingenuous evasion of the bond. Confounded by the decree, he at first exclaims "Is that the law?"— not, be it observed, "Is this justice?" Justice, the denial of which strikes Mr Irving into a statue of dumb protest, does not even occur to Shylock. Angry as he is at being outwitted, he quickly reverts to his habitual greed.

> I take this offer then. Pay the bond thrice
> And let the Christian go.

He is baffled in this too, but he still clings to the money.

> Give me my principal and let me go.

And when even this demand is refused, he retorts, like a true cur, "The devil give him good of it!" and turns to fly. So long as Mr Irving retains these lines in his version, and deports himself in direct defiance of their evident spirit, so long will he be forced to plead against disappointment and ridicule by an effective but perfectly meaningless exit.

Shylock may be dismissed from further consideration with the remark that he and the two Gobbos suffer less than any other characters in the comedy from that depreciation of interest which is wrought by foreknowledge of the plot by the public. The chief losers from this cause are Portia, whose most surprising entry is received as matter of course, and Shakespear, whose comedy, a masterpiece of construction, rapid in action and quite free from superfluities, is mutilated to spare the audience as much of the tedium of listening to it as possible. For instance, the spectators do not take the least interest in the mystery of the caskets. They seek to enliven their appreciation of the Prince of Morocco by regarding him as a compound of Bombastes Furioso and the Shah of Persia, and only tolerate the business of Bassanio's choice from a sense of duty to Shakespear and of chivalry to Portia. As to the Prince of Aragon, he dares not intrude in a modern acting version. Yet his dramatic function of shewing that the lead casket must be the desired one by displaying the contents of the silver as his fellow suitor had already displayed that of the gold, was absolutely necessary in order to enable Shakespear's contemporaries to share Portia's emotions whilst Bassanio doubtfully conned the three enigmas. Again, in the scene where Portia anticipates her appearance in male attire, how many persons nowadays wonder, as Elizabethan audiences wondered, why she is going to play such a prank the moment her husband's back is turned? No intimation of her purpose escapes her; and the first suspicion of it should be suggested by the entry of Nerissa to the court as a lawyer's clerk. Expectation is whetted by delay as the clerk reads Bellario's still further suggestive letter, and the effect is completed by the appearance of Portia in her robes. This must have been the best effect in the play at a time when Shakespear's plots were as little anticipated as Sardou's are at present.[6]

There is another difference between Elizabethan and Victorian audiences which tends to make Shakespear appear dull to the latter. In his time, books and readers were scarce. There was a demand for poetry, and the people expected to find it at the playhouse. The demand still exists; but the supply comes from the library and the magazine. Poetry loses as much as epigram gains by stage delivery; and scenes of pure poetry are no longer produced in the theatre. There are two such scenes in The Merchant of Venice: that of Bassanio's choice, and the return to Belmont in the last act. Both are not merely poetically conceived dramatic episodes, but pieces of poetry intentionally offered as such to the public, and consequently more respected than relished by them; although the first as a lovers' scene, and the second as a picture, are unsurpassed in fiction.

Since the causes which nowadays militate against the interest of Shakespear's plays are so easily discoverable, it is a pity that the process of mutilation by which they are converted into acting versions is not more rationally conducted. In proof of Molière's[7] superiority to Shakespear as a stage craftsman, the fact that the plays of the former alone are still presented in their integrity has recently been adduced. Had Molière been an Englishman, and Shakespear the founder of the Comédie Française,[8] there is no doubt that the reverse might be proved by the same argument. In The Merchant of Venice, the construction is so close that there is not a dispensable speech in the scenes which conduct the action. But, the play

6. Victorien Sardou (1831–1908), one of the most prolific and successful French dramatists of his day, succeeded (Augustin) Eugène Scribe (1791–1861) as the foremost practitioner of the well-made play. To characterize Sardou's practice in this formulaic drama, Shaw coined the term "Sardoodledom" (see below).

7. Molière (real name Jean-Baptiste Poquelin, 1622–73), France's greatest comic dramatist and actor.

8. French national theater, officially founded in 1680, also called le Théâtre Français and known as the House of Molière.

being foreknown, gaps made by excision are not perceived. Yet these are so capriciously made: the timidity evidenced by the respect paid to some of the heaviest scenes so contradicts the recklessness with which others, comparatively amusing, are discarded, that the pruning appears to be the result of a number of traditions dating from different periods and owing their existence to diverse considerations, rather than the work of an intelligence bent on threshing out obsolete forms of entertainment and evaporated plot interest. The Merchant, like the rest of its author's works, was curtailed for the sake of brevity at a time when three substantial pieces were in every playbill. "Star" Shylocks omited the last act, and "star" Portias restored it. The secondary parts were pared away for the sake of a public who cared little for literary propriety or dramatic coherence, provided Edmund Kean[9] declaimed "Hath not a Jew eyes?" with a vehemence which, did he live now, would elicit a monitory repetition of Hamlet's instructions to the player from every newspaper in London.

When Miss Ellen Terry[10] reassumed the part of Portia last year, the public, instead of waiting to judge her performance, waited only to express their admiration: a sentiment which she never fails to justify. Criticism either slept, or, ashamed of its vigilance, remained silent. Yet if ever a treasure of art needed to be jealously watched and grudgingly praised, so does Miss Terry's gift of acting. Like all possessors of genius who have achieved popularity, she probably looks upon encouragement as a thing that would have been worth having once. At present she has happily nothing to fear but that adulation which often tempts notable workers to earn conventional superlatives by doing their second best only. For months past she has been extravagantly praised for a performance which is rather the result of her previous experience than an outcome of any special sensibility to the part of Portia. All her archnesses, like some of her attitudes, have done duty before. Nothing new either in the part or in the actress is revealed, and it may be fairly said, though not in that stale sense which makes the phrase a clumsy cover for a censure which the censor is too lazy to define, that her impersonation of Portia will not add to her reputation. It will not detract from it, because her acquired resources are fully equal to the requirements of her audience, in whose eyes, indeed, she could not fail save by an inconceivable misdirection of ingenuity. But a little consideration will suggest that a complete success as Portia is still less possible for her than a failure.

Portia, in the play, is an incorrigible jester. If her generous dismissal of Bassanio to the side of his unfortunate friend, and her worthily conceived

9. (1737–1833), prominent English tragedian of the Romantic era.

10. Ellen Alice Terry (1847–1928), major English actress. In 1878 she became and remained Irving's leading lady at the Lyceum.

appeals to Shylock in the trial scene were omited, nothing would remain for her to do except to make a little love and a great deal of fun. The last generation would have described her as a tomboy. She mocks her servant by calling him "my lord"; she baffles all Nerissa's attempts to discuss her position seriously; and she brings about the catastrophe by an incredible escapade, which she has hardly achieved when she prepares a discomfiture for her husband by begging the betrothal ring of him. The very nature of the evasion practised on Shylock, a sell, must have commended it to the invention of such a woman. This design of her character, enriched though it has been by Shakespear, must yet be unmistakably shewn on the stage, if the interest of the comedy and the probability of the plot are to be made the most of. This duty is not congenial to Miss Terry's talents. She is skilful in the impersonation of a tender and emotional nature thinly covered by a petulance which savors too pleasantly of youthful spirit to be called flippancy.

But Portia is a more robust character. Her love of fun is part of her nature: not a mere ebullition which misfortune or the sight of sorrow can reduce to sadness. Her jests need expurgation, and her sensibilities are numb in comparison with those of modern nervous organizations. Further, she is not adapted to prevailing ideals. An actress, realizing her, would not be thanked for doing so, because the current taste shrinks from breadth of style, and demands conceptions which it can dub "subtle." Shakespear was too imaginative to deal in subtleties. The character of Portia is neither thick nor hard; there is abundant suppleness in her mind, and variety in the play of her emotions; and she knows her own disposition no more than clever young ladies usually do: but she cannot suitably be made a vehicle of pre-Raphaelite languor. It is because of her presence that a series of scenes in which anxiety and disappointment are so often prominent, will not harbor the least strain of melancholy.

Here, then, was Miss Terry in a dilemma. To attempt a strict rendering of Shakespeare's Portia would have ensured the disappointment of the public, and her own discomfort in straining at that large style of which she has the least command. To pander in the opposite extreme, to the morbid aspect of esthetic culture by manufacturing a Portia of poses and dolours, would have inspired some worthless raptures at the cost of artistic self-respect and the gratitude of the healthier masses. Thus—although she might laugh very heartily at the reasoning here ascribed to her—she was, unconsciously, driven to the safe course of adapting the part to her own personality, with the charming, if not impressive result of Miss Terry, in her most genial vein, partly impersonating Portia, and Portia meeting her halfway by partly merging her substantial beauty in the more evasive fascinations of her representative. The public, having no preconception of the part, and a strong preconception of the actress, find all their expectations gratified,

and, insensible to the extraordinary merit of the dialogue, readily accept the conventionalities of Miss Terry's manner as a sufficient treatment of it, and abandon themselves to admiration of her grace, her costume, her byplay whilst Bassanio considers his choice, her bearing in legal robes, and her fine delivery of the appeal "Shylock, there's thrice thy money offered thee."

Nerissa, whose vivacity is merely the reflection of Portia's, should be a foil to her, in voice and face if possible, but in demeanor and a disposition to be serious, certainly. At the Lyceum, much of Portia's part lacks lustre from the neglect of this condition. There is, besides, a quality in the manner of Miss Florence Terry[11] which is peculiarly destructive to the local illusion of a scene laid in Italy.

The remaining female character, Jessica, demands both personal beauty and what is called "stage presence" from its exponent. Shylock's daughter, thanks to Shylock's training of her, is an odious person. Shakespear evidently calculated the effect of her antecedents. He shews what she is by her flippant elopement, where she throws the casket down and bids her lover wait until she gilds herself with more ducats; yet in the last act, where her susceptibility to the influence of music is shewn, he indicates that she might have been something better. He has given her actress the very difficult task of dumbly filling the stage. Few readers of The Merchant of Venice notice how small this very prominent part appears, when estimated by the number of lines assigned to it. Yet it calls for so little histrionic acquirement, that the injury done to the Lyceum revival by its utter insignificance is the misfortune of Miss Murray,[12] and the fault of the manager who cast her for it.

The parts of Jessica and Nerissa are not the only instances of injudicious selection in the bill. Mr Barnes's[13] performance as Bassanio is in no way discreditable to him; but the allotment to him of the task of impersonating the modest, quickwitted, and generous young Venetian nobleman was apparently dictated by professional etiquet rather than artistic fitness. Mr F. Cooper,[14] as Gratiano, mars every scene in which he appears. His elocutionary defects are so grave that he would probably spoil any sonorous or rhythmic language given him to deliver, but, this consideration apart, his misconception of the character is as complete and no less important in its effect on the trial scene, as Mr Irving's misconception of

11. Florence Floss Terry (1854–96), Ellen's sister.
12. Alma Murray (1854–95) would gain a reputation in London for undertaking challenging roles in works by noncommercial playwrights, such as Robert Browning (1812–89), Percy Bysshe Shelley (1792–1822), and Shaw himself. In 1894 she would create Raina in the first production of Shaw's Arms and the Man.
13. John H. Barnes (1850/52–1925).
14. Frank Kemble Cooper (1857–1918), English actor.

Shylock. Gratiano is not an impertinent youth with a love of practical joking, but a coarsely jovial fellow, who might with advantage to the illusion be made to appear a little older, a little stouter, a little more florid in complexion, and a good deal more of a blackguard, than his boon companions. A man, in short, whom Bassanio might naturally hesitate to introduce to his future wife, and who, when introduced, might as naturally begin at once to court the lady's maid. There should be no trace of sarcasm in his colloquy with Shylock before the judgment. He is then engaged, not in an encounter of wit with the Jew, but in blurting out his choler with a ludicrous sense of discomfiture. When his enemy is at his mercy, instead of suggesting a stinging gadfly, and annoying the audience more than he is supposed to annoy Shylock, as Mr F. Cooper does, he enjoys a boisterous triumph, chuckling at his own boorish sallies. Mr Barnes would have done far more justice to this part than to his own.

Shakespear and his contemporaries were fond of introducing Orientals or Spaniards in their plays, in order to indulge their taste for hyperbole, the stage convention of the time being that these foreigners were outrageous in their habit. If Othello's rants be compared with the most violent utterances of Macbeth or Richard, it will appear that the Moor's nationality was held by the author to justify an excess of bombast which jars in the taste of those critics who pronounce him weakest where he strove most to be sublime. He secured a special licence in The Merchant of Venice by making the first adventurer for Portia's hand a Moor also.

The representative of Tubal has little to do except to simulate the appearance of an elderly Jew, and to shew that in relating Jessica's extravagance and Antonio's ruin alternately, he purposely returns to the latter in order to appease the outbursts elicited by the former. Otherwise the contrast aimed at by the dramatist will not appear to spring naturally out of the situation, and the blemish of imperfectly concealed art will attach to the workmanship of the scene. To appreciate a literary condition such as this is hardly an actor's business; and in the absence of tradition or written direction, Mr Carter[15] cannot be blamed for failing to fulfil it.

The remaining characters may be played very diversely without injury to the balance of the comedy. Antonio, a grave, conscientious blockhead, is not likely to become the subject of histrionic innovation. His sober demeanor, his prejudice against the Jew, and his complacency in the matter of the bond as contrasted with Bassanio's quick suspicion are less important to the romantic impression of the drama than either his friendship or his wealth; and it is well that they should receive, as they do, less emphasis. Salanio and Salarino are shewn in the early acts as a common-

15. John Carter (d. 1907).

place man and a poetic wit respectively; but in the third act the distinction lapses, as though it were not worth sustaining. Lorenzo need not exercise the insight of any young and handsome actor who can deliver a speech fairly. Low comedians who can master the peculiar flavor of the Shakespearean clown are rare, but Mr S. Johnson[16] plays the part of Launcelot Gobbo quite as well as it need be played. After what has been said of Mr Irving's view of Shylock, it would be of little use to criticize his manner of conveying that view to his audience. The subject belongs properly to the consideration of Mr Irving as an actor, and not to the merits of the Lyceum revival. Nor is it expedient to treat of the play itself further than has been done incidentally already. To use the phrase of guide books and manuals: those who are desirous of becoming acquainted with the beauties of this delightful comedy are recommended to procure the book and read for themselves. An analysis of it would be a foolish business at best, though it could be so handled as to prove interesting. A technical study of its construction might, on the other hand, inform future adapters of Shakespear to the modern stage, and countenance some better principle of excision than the leaving in of all popular quotations, and the leaving out of all the passages which serve to prepare the audience for the sequent features of the plot. Even without adaptation, the works of our famous dramatist are not without interest, for he was not ignorant of the mystery of stage effect. Mr Irving calls his arrangement of the Merchant an "acting version." What does he call the original?

TROILUS AND CRESSIDA
C (Speech, read in Shaw's absence,
New Shakespear Society, 29 February 1884)[1]

Troilus and Cressida is a play which appeared at the beginning of the XVII century. It has been attributed to Shakespear, and is included in all editions of his collected works; but certain points concerning it are still disputed, namely, its date, its class, its moral, its authorship, and the

---

16. Sam Johnson (1831–1900), English actor.

1. From *Shaw Review* (May 1971), checked against MS in BL. The New Shakespeare Society, founded 1873 by Shakespearean scholar and editor Frederick James Furnivall (1825–1910), published reprints of First Folio and Quarto texts, plays by Shakespeare's contemporaries, and some of the more important scholarly research of the period.

sources from which the author drew his story. This story, as the play tells it, is as follows.

Helen, the wife of Menelaus, a Greek prince, has eloped to the City of Troy with Paris, a Trojan prince. In revenge, the Greeks leave their country and besiege Troy, demanding that Helen shall be given up to Menelaus. The Trojans are too proud to yield to the Greeks; and a war ensues, and is waged for seven years without a decisive result, except that Helen is seven years nearer to forty, and presumably seven years less worth fighting for. This Trojan war was not a war in the sense given to the term in modern treatises on tactics. The Trojans were walled into their city, and the Greeks were entrenched in their camp by the seashore. In the morning, the Trojan princes sallied into the plain between the camp and the city, and the Greek chieftains came out to meet them. They engaged in single combat, throwing stones and javelins at oneanother; and the victor ransomed his prisoners for his own private profit when he was poor or in a good humor, and slaughtered them when he could afford to indulge his fury at the cost of the ransom. Meanwhile, the rank and file slung stones, shot arrows, and kept their unprotected skins out of the way of the ironclad princes. Hector, one of the many sons of Priam, King of Troy, was the chief Trojan warrior. Among the Greeks, championship honors were divided between Ajax and Achilles. This is the state of things in which the play of Troilus and Cressida begins.

There is in Troy at this time a pretty girl named Cressida, clever, winning in her ways, very sympathetic, fond of men, and kind to them. Prince Troilus, a younger brother of Hector, falls in love with her. As he is handsome and interesting, her affectionate nature goes out to meet his love halfway: or even further. But he is adolescent, full of doubts and diffidence, and so ridiculously shy that he is with difficulty brought to the point of declaring his passion by the encouragement he receives from Cressida's uncle Pandarus, an old gentleman who likes the society of young people, and buys their tolerance by indulging their follies, and, on occasion, acting as go-between in their love affairs. When Troilus at last breaks silence, he is flattered to find that he has inspired love in Cressida, attributes to her all the excellence his poetic imagination can conceive, and has no suspicion that her soft heart holds a wealth of affection sufficient not only for him, but for half a dozen other men besides.

Now it happens that Cressida's father is a renegade serving with the Greeks; and, just at this time, his allies having captured Antenor, a famous Trojan commander, he demands the exchange of the prisoner for his daughter. The Greeks consent, and Cressida is conducted to the camp, leaving Troilus disconsolate, and oppressed with fears that she will be lonely among the hostile warriors of the besiegers.

Hector now challenges the Greeks to select their best man to fight him, and the question arises whether Achilles or Ajax shall respond. These are two men of widely different character. Ajax, a trustworthy soldier, and as honest as he knows how to be, is rough and stupid. Achilles, who despises Ajax as a mere brute, is clever, elegant, sensual, entirely unscrupulous, intolerant of contradiction, and able, through his renowned strength and skill in combat, and his power as a chief, to indulge his selfishness without restraint. As he has been deprived of a favorite slave by Agamemnon, the Greek commander, he has retired sulkily to his tents, forbidden his followers to take part in the war, and left the Greeks to carry on the war as best they can without his assistance. In order to humiliate him, the Greeks select Ajax to fight Hector. This piece of policy is the device of Ulysses, a worldlywise chief, whose shrewdness makes him a man of considerable mark in the camp, where muscle is at a discount, and brain at an extravagant premium. Achilles, quite as clever as he, sees through the plot to make him jealous; holds aloof as before; and, on the combat ending in a harmless exhibition of swordsmanship, invites Hector and the other Trojan chiefs to a banquet at his tent. This invitation gives Troilus an opportunity to see his beloved Cressida again. He begs Ulysses to bring him to her father's tents. Ulysses does so, and Troilus sees his love, but under disappointing circumstances. Since her departure from the city, she has made the acquaintance of her escort from thence to the camp, a fine young man named Diomed, who has enchantingly rough ways with women, speaks his mind freely in dispraise of Helen, yields a little to the charms of Cressida, but will stand no nonsense from her. Cressida is led by him into the presence of the Greek heroes of whom she has heard so much, and when they all kiss her, she recovers from the melancholy induced by her separation from Troilus, and makes an assignation with Diomed. Accordingly, at nightfall, Diomed comes to her tent by appointment, and Troilus and Ulysses come there too—not by appointment—just in time to witness the meeting. Her affectionate remembrance of her former lover in the very act of giving one of his presents to Diomed as a pledge of her faith proves touchingly that she has a heart; but it does not appease Troilus, whose wounded vanity so exasperates him that Ulysses with difficulty keeps him silent and gets him away from the camp in safety.

On the following day the war is resumed. Troilus, seeking through the field for Diomed, and reckless of his own life, ravages the ranks of the Grecians. Hector kills Patroclus, a parasite of Achilles. Achilles, feeling the loss acutely, resumes his arms, and attacks Hector, but, being out of training in consequence of his recent inaction, gets worsted in the encounter by the Trojan hero, who magnanimously spares his life. Finding his courage and skill of no avail, Achilles resorts without the least scruple to foul means. He obtains the assistance of his soldiers, surprises Hector in a defenceless condition, and murders him. Meanwhile Troilus, having at last found Diomed, and received a sound thrashing from him, illogically vents his wrath on Pandarus, who is by no means to blame in the matter. His rage and grief at the death of Hector end the play.

This unfinished story will not strike anyone as a congenial theme for a poet or a reader of refined tastes. What attraction had it for Shakespear, and how comes Troilus and Cressida to be one of the most interesting of his works? The answer is that Shakespear did not invent the story, but found it readymade; and that its attraction for him was that which an idol has for an iconoclast, or a plausible fraud for an ingenious detective. Before it was thrust upon his attention, he had some private reasons for believing himself to be as capable a poet and dramatist as the human race could produce. But he had been arbitrarily taught that certain mysterious writers of remote antiquity had possessed powers beyond the reach of XVI century man. Of these the unapproachable father and master was Homer,[2] a wonderful blind bard supposed to have been born in six different cities, and, later on, not to have been born at all. The works of this famous man were extant and written in very choice Greek; but Shakespear, not understanding Greek, could not read them. His contemporary, George Chapman,[3] was better instructed, and made no secret of his contempt for literary pretenders who only knew their own language. Chapman was Shakespear's rival in the favor of Mr W. H., the "onlie begetter" of the sonnets. He wrote magnificently nonsensical tragedies, and was tremendous where Shakespear, restrained by commonsense and a strong susceptibility to the ridiculous aspects of stage rant, was only ironical, or, at best, tragic. Chapman was an intolerable boaster, paraded his knowledge of dead languages, scorned the writers of his day, and asserted that his dramas were dictated to him by a spirit. This spirit, judged by his fruits, was not at all so clever a playwright as Shakespear; and the description of him in the 86th sonnet as "that affable familiar ghost" is, like the whole of the 85th, a sarcasm. Shakespear had his own opinion of Chapman, and probably his own suspicions of Homer; but these he had no means of verifying, as he could not read his poetry until Chapman himself came to the rescue by translating it. The Iliads, as they were then called, thus came into Shakespear's hands at last; and they found him in no mood to appreciate descriptions of ships and shields which were not at all superior to the descriptions in Romeo and Juliet or Lucrece, and accounts of brutal fights with the combatants Homerized and Chapmanized into heroes and demigods. All the human nature in it seemed spelt backwards. Shake-

2. Greek poet (fl. c. tenth century B.C.).
3. (c. 1560–1634), poet and playwright as well as translator.

spear spelt it forwards, and resolved to make a c o r r e c t version of it for the edification of Chapman.

No agreement upon the merit of this project of Shakespear's is possible between self-satisfied people and cynics, optimists and pessimists. Those whose imaginations are filled and satiated by the beauty of Helen, the devotion of Troy, the valor of Achilles, and the glamor thrown upon the Greek mythology by the art which sprung from it, will be disgusted beyond measure by Troilus and Cressida, in which the kernel of the whole affair is proclaimed to be a frivolous quarrel, savagely prosecuted by a horde of licentious bullies managed and played off against oneanother by a few shrewd worldlings, who are themselves mocked by the overruling gods. The optimists who admire Shakespear will not admit that he took any such view: it being the practice of Shakespear enthusiasts to dwell fondly on such of his ideas as happen to reflect their own, and to deny the existence of the rest unconditionally. Optimists who are not Shakespear enthusiasts (and I, for one, can hardly conceive of an optimist caring for the grimmest and greatest of pessimists) will admit his design readily enough, but they will denounce it as a deliberate attempt to debase a great poem: to write a comic Homer in the spirit of a modern burlesque writer. It certainly involves the presentment of a disagreeable truth emphasized by contrast with a pleasant falsehood. It is Shakespear's protest against Homer's attempt to impose on the world, and against Chapman's exaggeration of Homer's authority. Doubtless it washes the paint off many persons whose natural complexions are so bad that we can hardly help wishing that Shakespear had left them as they were; but the process sets us laughing and thinking; and it may be doubted whether Homer achieved any result comparably beneficial to this. In my opinion The Iliad should never be read without its pungent Shakespearean commentary. As to the general issue between the optimists and the pessimists, it is useless to discuss it. Shakespear adopted the pessimistic view; and it is better, without prejudice to the question whether he was right or wrong, to proceed to consider how he approached it, and when he arrived at it.

Taking the latter point first: Troilus and Cressida is the earliest pessimistic play; and its date is about 1600, or perhaps a year earlier or later. Its cynicism, confined to the Trojan war, and somewhat fitful and superficial, is antecedent to the deeply pessimistic view of the nature and destiny of mankind in general of which Hamlet is the exponent. 1602 is the date of Hamlet. Chapman's translation of The Iliad appeared in 1598, and the 85th and 86th sonnets, referring as Professor Minto[4] has successfully

4. William Minto (1845–93), author of *Characteristics of English Poets from Chaucer to Shirley* (1874).

established, to Chapman, have been traced by Mr Tyler to the same period.[5] Again, 1599 is the date of Henry V, which no sane critic places, or is likely to place, later than Troilus and Cressida. Hence the latter must have been written in 1600, or closely thereabout. In the Stationers' Register of 1602 or 3,[6] February 7th, appears "The booke of Troilus and Cressida as yt is acted by my Lo. Chamberlens men." We may take the date of the play in round numbers as 1600. In that year, Shakespear seemed to have exhausted the possibilities of his art. He had written tragedies, or plays in which the chief characters died; comedies, in which they got married; a fairy extravaganza; and a number of histories. In all of these he had surpassed every known author, and had nothing left to do except to surpass himself. To Shakespear this must have seemed impossible: he probably thought his career at an end. In his novitiate, he had written such romances as The Two Gentlemen and Romeo and Juliet. His early manhood, with its energy and materialistic common sense, had produced The Comedy of Errors and The Taming of the Shrew. A blending of these veins, first perceptible in Love's Labor's Lost, had resulted in The Merchant of Venice, the Midsummer Night's Dream, and Twelfth Night. Then his youth began to stale, and disillusion overtook him. He no longer believed in Romeo and Juliet. The windy energy of such exuberant bullies as Petruchio, Richard III, and Falconbridge [in *King John*] could no longer impose on the imagination of a man approaching forty, and on the verge of creating Hamlet. Falling back on the partly mechanical attraction of interesting stories, he borrowed a couple from Italian novels, and produced the gloomy and unsympathetic All's Well, and Much Ado About Nothing, revolting in plot, but lightened by an afterglow from some of the fancies of Love's Labor's Lost, and by his irrepressible humor, which, like the humor of Swift and Beethoven,[7] remained pessimism proof to the last. In these plays, he seems to have come to the conclusion that the more selfish the hero was, the more natural he was. But there can have been just as little satisfaction to himself as to his audiences in a progress from Romeo and Bassanio to Bertram and Claudio. Thus his prospects in comedy were not encouraging, and he had ceased to write tragedy.

Nor had his histories, into which he had put much serious thought, led him into a fruitful dramatic field. He had developed stage histories as far as their artistic form seemed to admit. He had begun by furbishing up the

5. Thomas Tyler (1826–1902) was a biblical and Shakespearean scholar. In his introduction to a facsimile edition of Shakespeare's *Sonnets*, reviewed by Shaw in 1886, he was the first to suggest Mary Fitton as the Dark Lady, a view that Shaw used in *The Dark Lady of the Sonnets* (1910).

6. 1602 Old Style or 1603 New Style.

7. Jonathan Swift (1667–1745), Irish satirist, and Ludwig van Beethoven (1770–1827), German composer.

works of Marlowe[8] and others, presenting traditional anecdotes dramatically, and supplying plenty of kings, lords, commons, battles, alarums, excursions, and single combats. Further, he had individualized some of the chief characters, and differentiated some of the minor ones in a cheap but effective way, making the 1st Murderer ferocious, the 2nd Murderer remorseful, and so on. He had dwelt on the contrasts between the royal state of kings and the humiliations which they were compelled to endure, and on the leveling influence of misfortune and death. He had even ventured on a history without a single battle in it, relying on the moralizing of King Richard II over his downfall, and on his sensational murder in the last act, to sustain the interest of the spectators. But neither then nor at any time since did the public take kindly to that play, and Shakespear, in Henry IV, shrank back to his battles, single combats, and appeals to Elizabethan jingoism, introducing a most successful innovation in the shape of a set of comic cowards, of whom the chief was Falstaff. It is probable that the elaborate portrait of Prince Henry was intended as a protest against the imputation of dissoluteness of which Shakespear complains in Sonnets 112 and 121; for the stress laid upon the fact that a man may possess great qualities without being ascetic in his habits or exclusive in his society is much greater than the interest which the reader feels in it. Falstaff is introduced simply as a thief and debauchee with whom the Prince associates. But Falstaff unexpectedly grew upon Shakespear. The leading idea of shewing him as a thief was forgotten; and he overran two plays so that they became comedies rather than histories. Nevertheless, neither Falstaff nor the delight of the public in Falstaff were calculated to raise Shakespear's sinking estimate of human nature. He refused to pander to the popular taste by introducing his lamentable old buffoon into Henry V, which he set himself to write as a really great historical play. He did his best, triumphed at the theatre, and then, we may suppose, went home and asked himself what his best came to after all. What, for instance, was the hero in whose image he had attempted to justify his own taste for low company, and whom he had put forward as a King worthy to be the idol of all Englishmen? Only a young man as selfish as Claudio or Bertram, and more odious; for he had broken his father's heart by his wildness when it had suited him to be wild, and broken his old comrade's heart by his righteousness when it had suited him to be righteous. And his attack upon the French, whether regarded as the effect of ambition, or the atrocious policy, enjoined by his dying father, of busying giddy minds with foreign quarrels, may have seemed heroic to the gallery, but not to the reflective author. Shakespear had not created a hero: he

8. Christopher Marlowe (1564–93), playwright and poet, the most outstanding contemporary dramatist when Shakespeare started to write plays.

had only whitewashed a commonplace man very thickly. This was all that the greatest genius in the world could do after ten years practice, during which he had produced nearly twenty plays, and had declared that "not marble, nor the gilded monuments of princes" should outlive the work of his pen.[9] Then came Chapman with his boasted Homeric Iliads, which turned out to be a prehistoric Jingo epic, with force masquerading as greatness, a famous war waged under a claptrap pretext for nothing but pride, ambition, and love of fighting, and a Greek popular hero selfish to the core. In short, Henry V over again, with different dresses and scenery. Two great poets, unknown to oneanother, and separated by vast epochs, driven by the common cure of humanity to the same climax: the glorification of two mean brigands! The book of Ecclesiastes must have seemed cheerfully optimistic in comparison with the reflections of Shakespear when he made this discovery. He bore no malice towards Homer. But towards the ass who had made a demigod of Henry V he had no mercy. It was to expose and revenge that fraud that he set to work with a bitter will on Troilus and Cressida.

It must not be supposed, however, that pessimism was new to Shakespear at this time. We have glimpses of it at times from the very beginning of his career, but only as a disorder brought upon men by unhappiness. For example, Richard II is, in a measure, a pessimist; and Shakespear entered into his feelings without being himself consciously a pessimist, just as he entered into Shylock's feelings without being himself a Jewish usurer. It is one thing to portray a pessimist, and quite another to write a pessimistic play, such as Hamlet. Still, some points in the early plays are worth noting. In the first, The Two Gentlemen of Verona, an ordinary friend is described as one "that's without faith or love." In Love's Labor's Lost, attempts at self-improvement by men are dismissed with ridicule, and their authors recommended to go and learn a little of the reality of life in a hospital. In The Comedy of Errors, Antipholus of Syracuse speaks of his

> earthly gross conceit
> Smothered in errors, feeble, shallow, weak.

Romeo anticipates the fatalism of Cleopatra[10] by exclaiming "I am Fortune's fool." Petruchio, in The Taming of the Shrew, remarks at his wedding, that it would be well for him if he could renew himelf as easily as he can renew his garments. Richard II gives a strong indication of the direction in which Shakespear's mind was traveling. He says:

9. Sonnet 55.
10. "Antony and Cleopatra, V.ii.3." [G.B.S.]

> What e'er I be,
> Nor I, nor any man, that but man is,
> With nothing shall be pleased, til he be eased
> By being nothing.

King Henry IV, speaking of the future, exclaims

> Oh, if this were seen,
> The happiest youth, viewing his progress through,
> What perils past, what crosses to ensue,
> Would shut the book, and sit him down and die.

When it came to this, Troilus and Cressida was evidently not far off; and the attempt to be patriotic and optimistic in Henry V only made the reaction more acid.

In writing a play to demonstrate the vanity and folly of his best previous work, it would have been absurd to cast it in the same mould as that work. Shakespear deliberately threw aside the serious historical style which he had so thoughtfully built up, and went back to the oldfashioned chronicle play, with its combats, its bragging speeches, and its bustling stage business. The gravity of King John and Richard II was discarded, and the comparatively infantile plan of Henry VI recurred to as the most appropriate to the childish passions of warriors and the complacent logic chopping of worldly statecraft. In doing this, Shakespear was not throwing away his experience; he was, on the contrary, profiting by it. He threw away nothing of value. He retained his two recent discoveries of the effect of a comic coward, and of combining comedy with history. He greatly developed the latter expedient by taking a love story from Chaucer[11] and engrafting a romantic comedy based on it upon the Homeric chronicle. He even gave the names of the hero and heroine of this episode as the title of the play. Nevertheless Troilus and Cressida is not a comedy. Its theme is the Trojan war; and Hector's death, though it has nothing to do with the lovers, and leaves their affairs unsettled, ends the play. The proper place for Troilus and Cressida in an edition of Shakespear's works is among the histories, immediately following Henry V. Obvious as this is—or perhaps because it is so obvious—it has not appeared so to Shakespear editors. Heminges and Condell,[12] not being experts in pessimism, could make nothing of the play, and at last ingeniously sandwiched it between the histories and

---

11. *Troilus and Criseyde* (c. 1385) by Geoffrey Chaucer (c. 1343–1400).

12. John Heminges (d. 1630) and Henry Condell (d. 1627) coedited the First Folio of Shakespeare's plays (1623). The "first exant folio" of 1609, to which Shaw refers below, is that of the individual play.

tragedies. Lest the pagination should commit them to a classification, they paged the first leaves wrongly, and the rest not at all. Subsequent editors have judged it safest to imitate the folio, although Malone put the play among the comedies, and Knight put it among the tragedies.[13] Had they followed the first extant folio, that of 1609, which correctly describes the drama as a Historie, they would have had both fact and precedent on their side.

Having selected this oldfashioned form, Shakespear subjected the stories he had taken from Chaucer and Chapman to a severely realistic treatment. Coleridge says justly that he "opposed the inferior civilization, but purer morals, of the Trojans to the refinement, deep policy, but duplicity and sensual corruption of the Greeks."[14] He assumed, in short, that the more men know, the worse they become. But, though he represented the Greeks as being more cunning than the Trojans, he did not rate them absolutely as men of a high intellectual order. He took them scrupulously at Homer's word as being rather athletes than soldiers, and as fighting from mingled ferocity and cupidity. The human type he studied from nature. It has always existed in England. Its representatives, the professional fighting men, were swordsmen in the age of Elizabeth, and their services as instructors must have been in constant requisition among the actors who performed the histories and tragedies of the time, and whose swordplay had to bear the criticism of audiences many of whom were themselves experts. Shakespear must have been struck by the curious inversion of the normal morality which took place in the minds of those professional fighters as a result of the anti-social nature of their social function. To him they were living paradoxes, and had dramatic material in them which his contemporaries did not suspect. Formerly, like Jonson, Beaumont and Fletcher, and others, he had held them up to ridicule by caricatures of such of them as were drunken tavern brawlers, decayed bullies, or imposters. Bobadil, the swordsmen hired by Bessus in A King and No King, Pistol and Nym, are caricatures of this class.[15] But Shakespear must have known fighting men who were sober and skilful; heroes in their own circle; brave, brutal, and honest, like Ajax; brave, crafty, and treacherous, like Achilles; simple and ignorant enough sometimes to be led like children by shrewd and unscrupulous gamesters, as Ajax was led by Ulysses; and sometimes, like Achilles, too clever to be the dupe of

13. Edmund Malone (1741–1812) and Charles Knight (1791–1873).

14. Minor misquotation from manuscript notes and marginalia on *Troilus and Cressida* by Samuel Taylor Coleridge (1772–1834).

15. Bobadil is a character in *Every Man in His Humour* (1598) by Ben Jonson (1572–1637); *A King and No King* (1611) is by Francis Beaumont (1584–1616) and John Fletcher (1579–1625); Pistol appears in Shakespeare's *2 Henry IV* and *Henry V*, Nym in Shakespeare's *The Merry Wives of Windsor*.

aught except their own passions. There must have been many public displays of swordsmanship in the XVI century which furnished parallels to the numerous combats described by Homer. Descriptive reports of these encounters have not come down to us, as sporting papers did not then exist; but as the fighting man remains the same now as he was in Shakespear's day, except that he is now a pugilist instead of a fencer, it is quite easy to match Homer's descriptions from records of our own times. I will give a brief example of such a parallel. The following extract is from Mr Ernest Myer's translation into English prose of the 21st book of The Iliad.

"Goodly Achilles lifted the Pelian ash; but the warrior Asteropaios hurled with both spears together, for he could use both hands alike, and with the one spear smote the shield, but pierced it not right through, for the gold stayed it, the gift of a god; and with the other he grazed the elbow of Achilles' right arm, and there leapt forth dark blood, but the point beyond him fixed itself in the earth, eager to batten on flesh. Then in his turn Achilles hurled on Asteropaios his straight-flying ash, fain to have slain him, but missed the man and struck the high bank, and quivering half its length in the bank he left the ashen spear."

Compare with this the following extract from Bell's Life in London[16] for the week ending the 25th September 1859.

"Number 6. Bob came up looking very serious, and several times led off left and right, but quite out of distance. Tom then stepped in and tried his left, which Bob cleverly avoided, and then returned on the chest. They quickly got to close quarters, and after a sharp exchange on the neck, Brettle fell forward on his hands in Tom's corner, Tom missing a terrific upper cut with his right as he fell."

I should be unjust to the memory of the lamented Messrs Sayers and Brettle if I left it to be inferred that their contest was as shocking in its details or fatal in its results as that between Achilles and Asteropaios, or the duels and tournaments which we read of in the novels of Walter Scott[17] and other XIX century works of fiction; but it is probable that the prizefights of Shakespear's time, being conducted with swords and quarter staves, often led to the infliction of dangerous wounds. Taking the prizefighter, then, for his Greek model, Shakespear took the soldier for his Trojan: a type higher by just so much as patriotism is a higher motive than love of gain. Hector, the chief Trojan, is represented as admirably just, sensible, and magnanimous. He is ill-advised enough to apply these qualities practically; and the result which pessimists consider the usual one follows. His justice is scouted as want of patriotism; his good sense as cowardice; and his magna-

16. A sporting journal.
17. Sir Walter Scott (1771–1832).

nimity costs him his life. Troilus is a young man in the adolescent stage, believing his impulses to be the promptings of abstract virtue. Shakespear had been in that stage himself not many years before, and had actually expressed an opinion that his taste for music was indispensable to a noble nature. Troilus overrules the scruples of Hector by urging a revengeful and vainglorious policy upon him with the air of a moralist reproving a worldling. And, because Cressida has realized his ideal, he is convinced that she must be an angel. Troilus is specially interesting as being the last young man drawn by Shakespear from a young man's point of view, or at least from fresh remembrance of it. With the exception of Orlando, who is mature enough to have resolved to chide no breather in the world but himself, against whom he knows the most faults,[18] Shakespear drew no more young hero lovers until that St Martin's summer of romance which set in Cymbeline, and presently ended with his life. When he created Troilus, he was just young enough to enter into his feelings; just old enough to despise them; and not old enough to have reached that indulgent but imperfect memory of them which he had when he drew Ferdinand in The Tempest. A glance at the other characters in Troilus and Cressida will detect the shadow of pessimism upon them all. Ulysses is grave, worldly wise, and judicious. His gravity gives an air of profundity to his utterances; and his disapproval of Cressida's forwardness stamps him at once as a ruthlessly respectable man: one who, in our time, might be safely invited to take the chair at public meetings. But he is a mere politician, with a few prejudices in favor of conventional propriety in place of a conscience, and no hold on the affections of his comrades, nor any good influence upon their morals. He is superior to Ajax only in the sense in which a fox is superior to a bear, and he imposes on him much as he has since imposed on a few commentators who have taken him to be Shakespear's portrait by himself.

The most important character in the play is Thersites, "a deformed and scurrilous Grecian," who, knowing himself to be detestable, loves to find in the actions of the handsome heroes around him that it is not his humped back or his malicious humor that is detestable in him, but the humanity which he has in common with the handsomest and most heroic of them all. His cynicism is mistaken for envy by those whose follies he exposes; but it is nonetheless true cynicism, simply disbelieving in virtue. Hypocrisy has no existence for him: he knows that the men about him believe in their own worth, and he scorns them for being so preposterously duped by their own vanity. As his genius is purely reflective, and he has no practical turn whatever, either for fighting or politics, he is only tolerated as a buffoon by the Greeks, each of whom thinks him a sharp critic of all the rest. Like

18. "III.ii.263." [G.B.S.] The play is As You Like It.

Jonathan Swift, he is an unhappy pessimistic analyst of human motives and pretences, known to the public as an obscene but witty railer. He does not spare h i m s e l f. He echoes the popular accusation of envy, and says "Ajax beats me, and I rail at him. Oh, worthy satisfaction! would it were otherwise: that I could beat him whilst he railed at me!" This gibe against himself is the bitterest he utters. He actually calls Ajax a camel: a sublime taunt from a hunchback to a first rate athlete. His function in the play, theatrically, is to supply the comic element, which had succeeded so well in Henry IV. Thus he is the Falstaff of Troilus and Cressida, and he would be equally popular if his words had not such a sting in them for all of us. Apart from his theatrical function, he has the philosophical one of interpreting Shakespear's pessimism. "The common curse of humanity, ignorance and folly, be thine in great revenue," he says to Patroclus. He also points out each particular illustration of this pessimism. At his exit in the 2nd scene of Act II he sums up the cause of the Trojan war, and the motives of the heroes with terseness and precision. Like a prophet, he utters the truth that is in him without regard to consequences. When in the grasp of the angry Ajax, he exclaims "Thou scurvy-valiant ass, thou art here but to thrash Trojans; and thou art bought and sold among those of any wit, like a barbarian slave." And accordingly, Ajax, infuriated by the truth of the observation, beats him soundly. When Achilles, after rescuing him, twits him with the drubbing he has suffered, Thersites vents his impotent rage on him by saying "A great deal of y o u r wit, too, lies in your sinews, or else there be liars. Hector shall have a great catch if he knock out either of your brains: 'a were as good crack a fusty nut with no kernel." Achilles, knowing that his brains are as sound as his biceps, laughs at this empty taunt; but Thersites instantly hits him effectually by adding "Theres Ulysses and old Nestor, whose wit was mouldy 'ere your grandsires had nails on their toes, yoke you like draught oxen, and make you plough up the wars." Achilles is quite shrewd enough to see that there is some truth in this. Ajax, though a blockhead, is goodnatured enough to say a few manly things, and to be shocked at Thersites, whom, of course, he cannot understand. Achilles, as selfish, witty, and wicked as a typical French marquis of the XVIII century, enjoys Thersites and calls him his cheese: his digestion.

Cressida is one of Shakespear's most captivating women. She has been blamed for inconstancy; but as we may forgive Romeo for jilting Rosaline, we may forgive Cressida for jilting Troilus. She is certainly not noble, like the heroine of Measure for Measure; but very few men would find Isabella's company agreeable, or be disposed to share Ulysses' objection to Cressida. Shakespear was indulgent to women. In his earliest plays, The Two Gentlemen and Love's Labor's Lost, they are all angels; and though, marrying early, he soon found that this view was erroneous, the discovery did not embitter him against the sex. The women in The Comedy of

Errors are truer to nature than to the romantic instincts of a young poet. In The Taming of the Shrew occurs an allusion to "a woman's gift to rain a shower of commanded tears"; and Bianca, the pet and beauty of the play, is odious. The ladies in the Midsummer Night's Dream are brave lovers, but they are jealous and spiteful. Shakespear gave women credit for being very nice. He created Portia, Viola, and Olivia, although he put Jessica beside them to shew that the rule admitted exceptions. In All's Well, they are treated with deepening seriousness; but it may be said that Cressida is Shakespear's first scientific description of a real woman, all the previous ones being either generous fancies or clever sketches. There is nothing fanciful or superficial about his presentment of Cressida. There is no longer any question of pleasing the sentimental playgoer: an interesting subject is prepared and offered to the humanity student for vivisection; and those who have no taste for such study are at liberty to amuse themselves with the early plays, or, if they must have novelty, to patronize some other author. The same remark applies to Shakespear's entire method of dealing with his characters from 1600 forward.

The part of Pandarus, the last which calls for comment, was either written to suit some actor who excelled as a singer, and as a representative of jocose old libertines such as Merrythought in The Knight of the Burning Pestle;[19] or else some previous drama on the subject of Troilus and Cressida had established comic songs and a certain vein of ribaldry as "traditions" of the character. The first scene of the 3rd act is merely a pretext for exhibiting Helen, and for introducing a song by Pandarus. If we adopt the view that the part was written for some particular actor, we must conclude that the play was written with a view to immediate representation, if not to order for Shakespear's theatre. Now the earliest copies of Troilus and Cressida which we possess were published in 1609, when two quartos appeared. Both were printed from the same type, but one contained a preface implying that the play had never been acted. It has been assumed that this was the first edition, and that the preface was omited in the second because the play had been acted for the first time in the interim. In that case, though written with a view to immediate representation, it must have lain unacted for eight years after its completion. But there is no evidence to shew that the quarto with the preface was the first, nor is the preface itself a document of convincing authority. Little importance has been ascribed to it except by writers who hold that the drama was not completed until 1607 or later.

However, it is possible that it may have been shelved as too shockingly cynical for an audience newly indoctrinated by Chapman with the sublimity of Homer's heroes. It is true that Hamlet, a more pessimistic play than

19. (1607) by Francis Beaumont; sometimes attributed to Beaumont and John Fletcher.

Troilus and Cressida, was produced in or before 1602 with success. But the pessimism of Troilus and Cressida is very obvious and acrid, and it cannot be explained away by any soothing theory of the insanity of the leading character, or covered by the terrors of a ghost, seven murders, and a suicide. Again, it contains no serious part good enough from a professional point of view to tempt a leading actor to study it or encourage its production. Every tragedian wants to play Hamlet, and the result is that Hamlet is frequently played; but no tragedian wants or has ever wanted to play Hector, and hence Troilus and Cressida is unknown upon the stage, and is likely to remain so. On these grounds it might be argued with plausibility that Troilus and Cressida, though written about 1600, was excluded from the stage by a more popular drama on the same subject until 1609, by which date it may have begun to dawn on the managers that Shakespear's pessimism was something more than wanton paradox-mongering.

It is generally believed that such an earlier drama did exist; that portions of it survive in the prologue, 5th act, and a few other passages of Troilus and Cressida; and that it is the work referred to in Henslowe's diary as being in preparation by Dekker and Chettle in 1599.[20] This last supposition requires further support. Henslowe's allusion may refer to Shakespear's play. In 1599, theatrical gossip was probably full of rumors of plays founded on Chapman's then recent publication of "Homer's Iliads"; and it is more likely that Henslowe was misled as to the name of the dramatist who was at work on the subject than that Shakespear was shabby enough to attempt to oust Dekker and Chettle. As to the theory that Shakespear rewrote their work, Dekker and Chettle were not so incompetent nor so unsuccessful as to submit to have their plays rewritten, even by the author of Henry V, before they had been a year on the stage. Besides, Troilus and Cressida is not, like Henry VI, an old play revised by Shakespear. It is an original Shakespearean drama, and the plan is even more Shakespearean than the execution, which is exactly the reverse of what we should expect of a work which he had merely revised. But what then was the play which fixed the traditions of the part of Pandarus, and supplied Achilles with a few lines in the 5th act? Putting Dekker and Chettle out of the question, as they probably never wrote a Troilus and Cressida at all, it was, as I conjecture, some stock piece founded on Chaucer, Caxton, and Lydgate,[21] which had become old-

20. Philip Henslowe (d. 1616), theater owner and manager; Thomas Dekker (c. 1572–1632), dramatist; Henry Chettle (c. 1560–1607), printer and dramatist.

21. William Caxton (1421–91) set up his own press and published *The Recuyell of the Histories of Troy* (1475), the first book printed in English, his translation of Raoul Le Fèvre's *Recuil des histoires de Troye*, a redaction of Guido delle Colonne's *Historia Troiana*. The best-known work of the poet John Lydgate (c. 1370–1451) is *The Troy Book* (1412–20).

fashioned when Chapman's translation appeared in 1598, and which Shakespear could replace by a new play without infringing any patent which could fairly be claimed as unexpired. He composed an entirely new play; but he preserved some features of the old one which the public liked and looked forward to. One of the features so preserved was the part of Pandarus; and the actor who had made it his own in the old play succeeded to it in the new. But in the old one, he had spoken the epilogue, and had the last word and jest with the audience. Shakespear of course did not spoil the artistic form of his last act by retaining this claptrap, and he ended the play with Troilus's speech at the line "Hope of revenge shall hide our inward woe." But the representative of Pandarus, after the manner of actors, protested against being deprived of his "bit of fat,"[22] and, to satisfy him, Shakespear transferred the three lines which follow from Scene 3, where they originally stood, and where, in the Folio, by an oversight, they still bear witness to the incident. They served to introduce the epilogue and to leave Pandarus alone on the stage to speak it.

Although Shakespear adopted the treatment of the character of Pandarus which had proved successful in the old play, there is no reason to suppose that he literally transcribed the dialogue invented by the author of it. But it is not equally certain that he did not do so in other instances; and on this point the internal evidence is somewhat distracting. The style of the play is singularly unsettled, and some of the scenes, though consistent on the whole with Shakespear's manner of writing in 1600, yet contain anticipations of the later dictum of Henry VIII, and reversions to the prettier fashion of The Merchant of Venice, all in one piece. It is curious to observe, too, how Shakespear, when he goes back to the old battlefields and single combats, also goes back involuntarily to the language and style of Henry VI, in which he had first dealt with them. In the 5th scene of the 5th act, where the fighting becomes fast and furious, he relapses into a peculiar vein of blank verse for which he seems to have had a hankering, but which his taste prevented him from indulging at large. It is hyperbolically descriptive, has a swinging rhythm, is crammed with sounding proper names, and strikes modern ears as especially oldfashioned. Chapman did it rather better than Shakespear; but it is Chapman's normal style, whereas it may be regarded as one of Shakespear's aberrations. It occurs also in the prologue; and samples of it are to be found in the recitation of the player in Hamlet, the narrative of the bleeding sergeant in Macbeth, and in many portions of Othello, where a tendency towards it is prevalent throughout. Though one of Shakespear's weak points, it is highly characteristic of him; but its occurrence almost invariably leads commentators to suspect what they call "another hand." For instance, they have made Dekker and Chettle a present of the pro-

22. Good acting opportunity.

logue and 5th act of Troilus and Cressida. In my opinion they might as
well have thrown in the rest of the play when they were in the giving
vein.[23] But there are about sixteen rhymed lines spoken by Achilles in
Scenes 7 and 8 of the 5th act, which Shakespear, finding them good
enough for his purpose, may have retained from the old play, in which
case they may be said to be his by adoption. Such a couplet as

> Follow me, sirs, and my proceedings eye.
> It is decreed Hector the great must die.

ought not to be ascribed to Dekker and Chettle, as they really did nothing
to expose them to such an imputation. Shakespear can hardly have been
prompted to spare these lines by sentiments similar to those which induced Michael Angelo to spare the frescoes of Masaccio when he re-
painted the Sistine Chapel;[24] but it seems that he d i d spare them,
pessimistically thinking that they were good enough for Achilles, for the
public, and for himself too. It was the pessimist Swift who afterwards
described the difference between the art of a popular Italian musician and
that of the composer of the Messiah as a difference between Tweedledum
and Tweedledee. Here again it is possible that some actor, accustomed to
play Achilles in the old version, and thinking the rhymed piece of rant
effective, insisted on retaining it, and that Shakespear did not think it
worth while to put him out of humor with his part by baulking him.
However it came about, a few of the lines in Scenes 7, 8, and 9 might
have been written by the call boy, although they also might have been
written by Shakespear, whose manysidedness included a remarkable
power of writing badly. The part of Hector, though woven into these very
scenes, is written earnestly and well, and, like all the rest of the play, is by
Shakespear's own hand. Troilus and Cressida is the unsettled work of a
transition period, and is unequal, like all works which are too long to be
completed at one sitting, and which are by an author who does not choose
or cannot afford to wait for the recurrence of the state of mind in which
they were first conceived. The pessimistic state of mind is a particularly
uncertain one. A creditor's knock at the door, a cool greeting from a
valued friend, a chance encounter with some fresh evidence of human
selfishness and suffering, or an attack of dyspepsia may produce it at any
moment. On the other hand, a good dinner or a bottle of wine may
extinguish it completely. Shakespear's digestion must have been perfect
when he wrote the 3rd act of Troilus and Cressida. It is comfortably
philosophical and dignified. Thersites only appears once, and the scene

23. An allusion to *Richard III*, IV.ii: "I am not in the giving vein today."
24. Michael Angelo (Michaelangelo Buonarroti, 1475–1564), Masaccio (Tomasso di Giovanni di Simone Guidi, 1401–28?).

he then enacts is a piece of pure buffoonery. But this act is not a reconcilia-
tion with the world. It is only a truce, as may be seen by the words which
close it. Achilles says broodingly

> My mind is troubled like a fountain stirred,
> And I myself see not the bottom of it.

"Would the fountain of your mind were clear again, that I might water an
ass at it" says Thersites. "I had rather be a tick in a sheep than such a
valiant ignorance."

Except in this act, the bitterness of the play is tolerably consistent; but
Shakespear, not yet so ingrained a pessimist as he subsequently shewed
himself by such masterly pessimistic plays as Timon of Athens, occasionally allowed himself to be interested by the easy logic chopping of Ulysses, touched by the passion of Troilus, or excited by the martial ardor of
the warriors. This variability of mood, with the other causes, produced an
unevenness in the play which led Mr Fleay[25] to assume that it is an
ingenious dovetailing of three different dramas, written respectively in
Shakespear's early, middle, and late periods. In one place, a break made
by Shakespear's putting down his pen after writing a scene in the strong
style which afterwards became his normal one, and resuming with relaxed energy on a later and less favorable day, is so perceptible that it has
led Mr Furnivall to deliver a rash judgment on the 5th act, in which it
occurs. It will be found at the entry of Troilus in the 3rd scene.

"How now, young man! mean'st thou to fight today?" says Hector; and
Mr Furnivall declares that this, and all that follows, is spurious. But if
Shakespear did not finish the play, who did? for some of it is first rate
work, inseparable from the best scenes in the admittedly Shakespearean
parts which precede it. The sudden ferocity of Troilus is not mere
thrasonical stage rant: it is the spleen of a disilluded youth, and the direct
effect of Cressida's jilting him. If the scene between Troilus and Pandarus
be spurious, then I see no reason why any of the rest of the play should be
considered genuine. The same remark applies to the 4th scene, in which
Thersites appears on the field of battle, and draws the moral of the
Ulyssean part of the play by exclaiming "O' the t'other side, the policy of
those crafty swearing rascals, that stale old mouse-eaten dry cheese,
Nestor, and that same dog fox, Ulysses, is not proved worth a blackberry.
They set me up in policy that mongrel cur, Ajax, against that dog of as
bad a kind, Achilles: and now is the cur Ajax prouder than the cur
Achilles, and will not arm today; whereupon the Grecians begin to pro-

25. Frederick Gard Fleay (1831–1909), Shakespearean scholar who used verse tests to
determine authorship and date of composition.

claim barbarism, and policy grows into an ill opinion." The impish glee with which Thersites dances round Troilus and Diomed, hounding them on to thrash each other for his amusement; and his sudden terror when he is checked by the thundering voice of Hector close behind him, demanding whether he is of blood and honor, are both highly humorous, and, from the stagemanager's point of view, very effective. Thersites' abject reply, "No, no: I am a rascal; a scurvy railing knave; a very filthy rogue," and Hector's immense answer "I do believe thee. Live," reminding us of Nestor's impression of him as "Jupiter yonder, dealing life," were certainly written by the same hand, whether Shakespear's or not, that wrote the rest of the parts of these two characters. The 5th scene I have already mentioned as an example of a style in which Shakespear sometimes indulged. It is in this instance vividly descriptive, and here, as in the earlier acts, Nestor's mind is full of Hector, Ulysses' of Achilles and Ajax, whilst the more general description is supplied by Agamemnon, who has no particular individuality in the play. In Scene 6 the meeting of Achilles and Hector, and that between Thersites and Margarelon in Scene 7 are above suspicion. In Scene 8 there is an unmistakable foretaste of Hamlet's morbid tendency to dwell on the corruption of the body in Hector's apostrophe to the man in sumptuous armor whom he has just slain: "Most putrefied core, so fair without!" Thersites, at the beginning of the play, introduces this repulsive strain of thought farcically by his reflection on what the Greeks would think of their general Agamemnon, the king of men, if he were covered with boils. Now, at the end, we find Shakespear, with the tragic scope of his pessimism dawning on him, transfering the ideas of the deformed and scurrilous Grecian to a prince and hero in the shadow of death. He had, in fact, come to see in the working out of the play that his cynical view of the Trojan war was only an imperfect apprehension and limited application of the follies, futilities, base necessities, infatuated beliefs in free will, and self-deceptions too subtle and manifold for the most acute and patient judgment to unravel, which are common to all humanity, which impart an aspect of mingled farce and tragedy to even the noblest lives, and which the conventional decorations of romance only obscure or tacitly deny. In finding out the vanity of the Trojan war, he found out, like the writer of Ecclesiastes, the vanity of all things, and with this discovery he must have felt that instead of being at the end of his career he was only at the beginning of it. The access of power which ensued can only be imagined by considering carefully the great gap between Henry V and Hamlet. But Shakespear's growth did not progress by leaps and bounds. There must be a bridge across that great gap. And the only bridge which fits it is Troilus and Cressida, with its cynical history at one end and pessimistic tragedy at the other.

I have no time to deal with the text of the play at present. Perhaps this deficiency will be supplied in the course of discussion. I began by mentioning that opinions differed as to the date of the play, its class, its moral, its authorship, and the sources of the story. I will end by recapitulating my conclusions that the date is within a year either way of 1600; that it should be classed as a history; that its moral is pessimistic; that it was written, with the possible exception of less than twenty lines, by Shakespear; and that it was inspired by Chapman's Iliads, and founded partly on them and partly on the Troylus and Cryseyde of Chaucer.

[SHAKESPEAR'S AND BROWNING'S CALIBAN]
C (VR: Remarks at Meeting of The Browning Society, 25 April 1884)

I have a very few words to say on this subject, and they shall not be connected with Agnosticism or natural theology in any way. I wish to speak of the different treatments of the character of Caliban by Shakespear and Browning.[1] Shakespear, being a dramatic poet, has never labeled any work of his dramatic; Browning, being essentially undramatic, has called this Caliban poem a dramatic monologue. Now, there is a difference between the faculty of the dramatic poet and that of the epic or descriptive poet, and they are often strangely divided. The epic poet has a theory of the motives and feelings of his characters, and he describes his theory. The dramatic poet, whether he has a theory or not, instinctively puts the character before you acting and speaking as it would do in actual life. The merely epic and descriptive poet cannot do this. Milton[2] had not the dramatic faculty very strongly; Shakespear had. In music Beethoven was destitute of it; Mozart[3] possessed it in the highest degree. If you compare Browning and Shakespear, you will find the difference coming out strongly. Browning makes Caliban minutely describe his own feelings and analyze his own thoughts. A creature in the brutish condition of Caliban would not be able to do anything of the sort; and here you have an

1. In Browning's "Caliban upon Setebos" (1864).
2. John Milton (1608–74).
3. Wolfgang Amadeus Mozart (1756–91), Austrian composer.

initial absurdity: an essentially undramatic condition, which shews you at once that what you are reading is no dramatic monologue at all. Shakespear's method is very simple. His Caliban does not reason about God; but he is terrified by a thunderstorm. A man comes in with a bottle of whisky—at least with a liquor which has the effect usually produced by whisky—and gives some to Caliban, who immediately falls down and worships him as a god. Subsequently, finding that the man is a fool, he is disgusted with himself for worshiping him; there you have Caliban's character and his theology put before you in a very natural way. Mr Furnivall bases a high estimate of Caliban's nature upon his musical tastes, and says that if he were now living he would go to the concerts of The Philharmonic Society. I do not know whether he is aware that Negroes possess the musical faculty in a higher degree than Englishmen. Ordinarily, one Negro has more music in him than four average Englishmen. Yet I am not prepared to infer that the Negro race is superior to the English. If all the characters who sing songs in Shakespear's plays were living, and Mr Furnivall's belief that they would attend the Philharmonic concerts be well grounded, you would have an audience in St James's Hall of which I certainly should not care to form one. Browning's Caliban is a savage, with the introspective powers of a Hamlet, and the theology of an evangelical Churchman. I must confess that I cannot conceive an evangelical Churchman possessing the introspective powers of a Hamlet. (*Great laughter.*) Although this character of Caliban is very interesting, and is, in fact, one of my Browning favorites, I am compelled to say that it is unnatural, impossible, and radically undramatic. (*Applause.*)

[A BLOT IN THE 'SCUTCHEON AND THE COMEDY OF ERRORS]
C/Un (*The Dramatic Review*, 2 May 1885)

On Thursday evening at St George's Hall, an amateur company under the direction of Mr Charles Fry, ventured on a performance of Robert Browning's Blot in the 'Scutcheon[1] and Shakespear's Comedy of Errors. Considering that we have few professional actors who would not be heavily

1. (1843).

overweighted by the leading parts in the Blot, the amateurs deserve great credit for the degree of success they achieved. The play was produced more than forty years ago at Covent Garden under Macready's management, with Phelps in the part of Tresham, which he played subsequently at Sadler's Wells.[2] It will furnish to many critics only an additional illustration of their view that Browning's genius is not dramatic. But the tragedy is powerful enough to raise the whole question of what a dramatic play is; for some of the scenes that are least dramatic in the accepted sense of the word impress and interest the spectator very forcibly and deeply. It will be repeated tonight under the auspices of The Browning and New Shakespear Societies.

Mr Charles Fry's[3] acting in the part of Mertoun, though of considerable merit, provoked a little laughter at times, notably in the duel scene. Of the reason [for] this Mr Fry had evidently no suspicion. Perhaps the following quotation from the famous Indian traveller, George Catlin, may enlighten him.[4] The passage is apropos of a duel which was to have come off between an Indian and a Fur Company man on the banks of the Missouri. "When alone with the Indian," says Catlin, "I asked him if he had not felt fears of his antagonist, who appeared much his superior in size and strength; to which he very promptly replied 'No, not in the least: I never fear harm from a man who cannot shut his mouth, no matter how large or strong he may be.' " That Indian would have backed himself at heavy odds against Mr Charles Fry, who fights duels with his mouth wide open, as if he contemplated astonishing his adversary with an exhibition of sword swallowing.

Dr. F. J. Furnivall, alluding to this performance at a recent meeting of The Browning Society, begged the members to wait for The Comedy of Errors, and not to leave the hall immediately after the Blot in the 'Scutcheon. It is to be hoped that he did not omit to ask the members of The New Shakespear Society to arrive in time for the Blot, and not to wait until the Shakespear part of the program began. The Comedy was the worse acted of the two plays. Stickishness, embarrassment, and lapses of memory are never quite absent from amateur performances; and they were more conspicuous in Shakespear's play, which requires all the crispness and impetus of a Criterion comedy, than in Browning's tragedy, which had, besides, been much more thoroughly rehearsed.

2. William Charles Macready (1793–1873), one of the major tragedians of his time, and Samuel Phelps (1804–78), important Shakespearean actor.

3. (d. 1928).

4. Catlin (1796–1872) wrote several books about American Indians, including *Letters and Notes on the Manners, Customs, and Condition of the North American Indians* (1841) and *Life Amongst the Indians* (1861).

AMERICAN STAGE-RIGHT
C/Ps (To the Editor, *The Dramatic Review*, 27 June 1885, signed George Bunnerd)

You have lately given prominence in The Dramatic Review to Mr William Archer's[1] scheme for enabling English dramatists to publish their plays without forfeiting their American stage-right. The plan, if feasible, is an admirable one; but as Mr Archer seems to regard it as a provisional measure pending the final solution of the difficulty by the establishment of full international copyright and stage-right, I venture to ask you to give publicity to certain grounds on which the successful establishment of the proposed society of playwrights would render international legislation not only superfluous but positively objectionable.

The absence of such legislation means international Communism in the product of the dramatist's labor, which product is, I fully admit, quite as legitimate a subject of private property as land or capital. The genius of the dramatist is his monopoly; the profit he makes is the rent of that monopoly; and it is grossly unfair to him that his rent should not be secured to his private use in communities like England and America, where the rents of other far less defensible monopolies are secured to their holders by international laws enforced by the heaviest penalties, and where Communism is denounced as pernicious and detestable in principle. Having admitted this much, it will not, I hope, be assumed that I am insensible to the hardships which the present communistic conditions inflict on dramatists who live by their pens, when I declare my conviction that in this very Communism lies the sole hope of making the British drama intellectually serious. So abject is our present predicament in this respect that we look on French dramatists as bold grapplers with social problems because their heroines sometimes commit adultery. Some of our own critics and playwrights, when lauding the French drama, occasionally express themselves in a manner that indicates their conviction that a little adultery would purify and ennoble the British stage. For my own part, I do not see that the way in which the French dramatists snatch at a "success by scandal" under cover of expressing floating Parisian notions that the place of woman in society is now a widely reopened question, shews much more intellectual seriousness than the dull igno-

---

1. Archer (1856–1924), Scottish critic, Ibsen translator, and dramatist, was one of Shaw's best friends from their meeting in the British Museum's Reading Room c. 1883 until Archer's death.

rance of there being any open social questions at all which the British dramatist—worthy son of the British matron—habitually displays. Our drama is sinking for want, not of an Augier, but of an Ibsen.[2]

Now comes the point which concerns Mr Archer's scheme. Suppose our Ibsen comes, what manager will produce his plays? Absolutely not one. Why has the Doll's House (or Nora, as it is absurdly called in a recent translation)[3] not become as popular here as in Norway? Because no manager would produce it until its intellectual seriousness was deliberately extirpated by British "adapters."[4] Happily, the resultant elaborate frivolity failed. What, then, must the English Ibsen do when he comes? His sole chance is to write a play; publish it: n o t by Mr William Archer's proposed method; and wait for some American manager to seize it and produce it. Should it succeed, which—on the supposition of Ibsenic genius in the author—it would probably do if not too much adapted, its production in England, where the privileges of the author would be intact, would come about in time, and the British drama would obtain a much needed lift.

A complete international copyright treaty would bar this avenue to intellectual seriousness. It is a circuitous avenue, but it is the only one that remains open. Mr Archer's scheme has the great advantage of fitting it with a valve by means of which the English dramatist can keep the American pirate from his printed play when he is not counting on piracy to gain him the hearing that his manager-compatriots deny him. If you are a popular playwright, you will publish through Mr Archer's society for subscribers only, and defy piracy. If you are an Ibsen or a Shakespear, you will publish in the ordinary way, and invite piracy. Therefore I submit that Mr Archer's scheme, without fresh legislation, is what the British drama wants at present.

The disposition shewn by The Dramatic Review to recognize the social importance of the matters to which it is devoted has encouraged me to make this inroad on the space at its disposal.

2. (Guillaume Victor) Émile Augier (1820–89), French dramatist, supposedly dealt with social issues but actually wrote variants of the well-made play (drama constructed according to a formula for exposition, development, and conclusion) with such "social" subjects as adultery and fallen women. The Norwegian Henrik Ibsen (1828–1906) is the founder of modern drama.

3. A Doll's House (1879) by Ibsen; Nora (1882) by Henrietta Frances Lord.

4. English dramatists Henry Arthur Jones (1851–1929) and Henry Herman (1832–94), under the title Breaking a Butterfly (1884).

[LE MAÎTRE DE FORGES AND THE MONEY SPINNER]
C (*Our Corner*, August 1885)

At the theatres nothing very remarkable has occurred except the revival of Olivia which has been dealt with at great length by the daily papers, and the appearance of Madame Sarah Bernhardt here in Sardou's Théodora.[1] She was preceded by the Gymnase Company, whose performance of Ohnet's Maître de Forges was made interesting by the acting of Madame Jane Hading in a part that has been played in London by Miss Ada Cavendish and Mrs Kendal.[2] Le Maître de Forges is not a good play: not to be compared with Mr Robert Buchanan's version entitled Lady Clare.[3] Claire, the heroine, marries Philippe Derblay to spite the Duc de Bligny, who has jilted her. When Philippe discovers that his wife loathes him instead of loving him, he tells her that someday he will see her at his feet, imploring his pardon, and longing vainly for a word of pity from him. This settles his pretensions to be a hero as far as the audience is concerned; but Claire admires him for it; falls in love with him; and enables him to fulfil his spiteful threat to his heart's content. There is little scope for genuine acting in the piece; but it presents many opportunities for emotional display. The impression left by the whole performance was that Madame Jane Hading is an interesting and attractive woman, and that one would like to see her in a good play, in order to ascertain whether she can really act or not. M. Damala,[4] who impersonated the sham hero Philippe, is an actor of considerable natural force and dignity; and the skill with which he moves and speaks only needs to have the evidences of study worn off it to entitle him to be considered an adept in his own line. The remaining parts were all well played, M. Saint-Germain[5] achieving the feat of amusing an English audience by a vocal peculiarity which prevented most of them from understanding what he was saying.

1. *Olivia* (1878) by William Gorman Wills (1828–91), based on an episode in *The Vicar of Wakefield* (1766) by Oliver Goldsmith (1730–74). Sarah Henriette Rosine Bernhardt (née Bernard, 1845–1923), French actress who achieved worldwide popularity, in *Théodora* (1884).

2. *Le Maître de forges* (*The Ironmaster*, 1883) by Georges Ohnet (1848–1918); Jane Hading (1859–1941); Ada Cavendish (1839–95); Madge (later Dame Madge) Robertson Kendal (1848–1935).

3. *Lady Clare* (1843) by Robert Buchanan (1841–1901), Victorian poet, novelist, dramatist, and critic who would become an anti-Ibsenite.

4. Jacques Damala (1832–89).

5. François-Victor de Saint-Germain.

Mrs Kendal has been playing with consummate skill in Mr Pinero's Money Spinner,[6] a clever comedy which interests the audience until the curtain descends, when they go away rather disagreeably affected by the glimpse they have had of the household of a dishonest clerk married to a gambler's decoy, watched by a detective who is the most respectable character in the play, and visited by his father-in-law, an old gambling saloon keeper, who has retired from his profession in order to marry his remaining daughter to a foolish Scotch lord, who avowedly accepts her only because she occasionally reminds him of her married sister, his real love. Baron Croodle, with his brandy flask, and his opinion that "to eat without drinking is a doglike and revolting habit," is the only tolerable person introduced, because he is the only one that does not claim more sympathy than he deserves. After acting such a detestable character as Millicent Boycott, Mrs Kendal cannot again be accused of prudery as to the morals of the heroines she represents. An afterpiece entitled Castaways by Theyre Smith, the author of Uncle's Will,[7] serves only to waste the time of the audience and the talent of Mrs Kendal.

[HOODMAN BLIND]
C/Un (*The Dramatic Review*, 5 September 1885)

W.S.M., who writes to the Daily News on the subject of critical error in connection with Hoodman Blind,[1] is one of those amiable gentlemen who consider that everyone who does not agree with them is, *ipso facto*, a fool. It had been suggested that in connection with the gypsy fraud arranged by the villain there is a slight confusion in time. But according to the gentle W.S.M., everyone who holds that opinion is "absurd" or "ill-natured," or some rubbish of that kind. This is the sequence of time in the play:

(a) The villagers announce that they have seen a gypsy tramp kissing Mrs Yeulett, though, undisguised, it would be absolutely impossible

---

6. *The Money Spinner* (1880) by Arthur (later Sir Arthur) Wing Pinero (1855–1934), popular English dramatist.

7. *Castaways* (1885) and *Uncle's Will* (1870) by S. Theyre Smith.

1. (1885) by Henry Arthur Jones and Wilson Barrett (1847–1904), actor-manager and playwright.

for any sane villager to mistake the neat and buxom Nance for the ragged and woebegone Jess.

(b) Mark Lezzard sees the gypsy and his girl friend f o r   t h e   f i r s t   t i m e   as they are entering the village, is struck with the likeness, but does not dare to instigate the fraud until he has d i s g u i s e d   Jess in Mrs Yeulett's familiar shawl.

(c) The d i s g u i s e d   Jess is mistaken for Nance by her husband simply because she is disguised.

Would not the following sequence be more natural?

(a) The villain sees the tramp arriving, and suggests the fraud, immediately disguising Jess.

(b) The villagers see the d i s g u i s e d   Jess in Mrs Yeulett's familiar shawl.

(c) Jack, the husband, is caught in the same trap as the villagers, and is deceived by the stolen shawl.

The only other way out of the difficulty in order to preserve the present sequence of scenes would be to bring on Mr Willard[2] in the ale-house scene, and let him h e a r   of the mysterious likeness to Nance. From the ale-house he would go in search of Jess, and plan the fraud for the destruction of Jack's happiness. For my own part, I think that the interest taken in a clever play that leads to analyses is no bad compliment to the play itself. If the work were worthless it would not bear discussion, or, indeed, have the benefit of a discussion that is in itself no bad advertisement. Why should it be "carping criticism," and "ill-natured," and "absurd," and heaven knows what, to state in print what has occurred to hundreds of minds in the theatre? On the unheroic character of the hero Jack, there is just as much to be said—and fairly said—without the slightest suggestion of "ill-nature" or "absurdity." The merit of many plays consists in the interest they create in opposite minds. Is Hamlet a bad play because no two critics agree about his sanity? and are all the critics fools, absurd, ill-natured, and carpers because they discuss Hamlet as a hero, and as a man?

2. Edward S. Willard (1853–1915).

QUALIFICATIONS OF THE COMPLETE ACTOR
C (*The Dramatic Review*, 19 September 1885)

Since The Dramatic Review first appeared, the Editor has received regularly every week some such communication as this: Dear Sir, I write to ask whether you would advise me to adopt the stage as a profession, and how I should set to work to qualify myself for it. I am five feet eight high, with brown eyes and hair, and should be satisfied with a small salary to commence. I am, sir, yours truly, A Constant Subscriber.

If the Editor were an irresponsible private individual, he might reply that the only indispensable qualification for appearing on the stage is a sufficiency of the presumption born of ignorance, or, more briefly, cheek. When an audience has been lured past the checktaker, it will stand quite as much incompetence as the stupidest novice can find any satisfaction in displaying. Actors in their relation to their art are classified by Polonius as tragedians, comedians, &c., in eight divisions, all of which might be further subdivided; but stage players (not necessarily actors) in their relation to the public may be sorted into three only, as follows: 1. Actors, who are sought after by the public: who d r a w. 2. Professors of claptrap, who often gain more applause than those of the first class, but who do not draw. 3. Duffers, who are only tolerated. Into one of these classes the novice must fall, even at his first attempt. If a trembling aspirant inquire whether omission has not been made of the class that is hissed, pelted with gingerbeer bottles, and assailed by dead cats, the reply is that there is no such class. There have been riots in the theatre as there have been in other public places, and the drunk and disorderly occasionally wander into the gallery, and annoy actors and audience alike; but no such disturbance has ever been provoked by bad acting. Whenever an actor has been the subject of a tumult, he has been a famous actor, a Kean, a Macready, or a Forrest.[1] The novice may rely on his own insignificance to shield him. In England at least he will have to stir the nation very deeply before it will buy eggs or burden itself with heavy bottles and clammy cats on his account. Consequently, on our stage failure is purely negative: to fail is only not to succeed. And as the novice is usually entrusted with a part in

---

1. Edwin Forrest (1806–72), American tragic actor of the romantic school. His rivalry with William Charles Macready led in 1848 to fatal riots in Astor Place, New York (where the Public Theater is located at present).

which there is no opportunity for any particular success, the negative condition disappears with the positive one, and failure is practically impossible. Sometimes a success would be bad policy for the actor. When a starring Hamlet engages you to play Marcellus, Rosencrantz, Guildenstern, the priest, the sailor, and Osric all on the same night, you may take it for granted that he does not intend you to make a sensation as any of them.

The beginner then risks no direct aggression from the public if he or she can obtain an engagement. But to get before the public is one thing: to get the public before you is another. Nervousness apart, it is very easy to repeat a given number of lines, and to walk and stand where the manager tells you; but it is very difficult to become an accomplished actor. Once upon the stage, it may seem easy to learn your profession upon it at the expense of the public. Our public speakers as a rule learn their business on the platform at the expense of audiences who interrupt, cough, and groan in a manner unknown in the theatre. But a public speaker practises his whole art every time he speaks, whereas an inexperienced actor applies only a small portion of his art to such minor parts as he is likely to obtain at first. Repeating that minor part every night for six months will not advance him as a skilled actor as much as half a dozen public meetings on different subjects will advance a candidate for a redistributed seat at the East End. Let us suppose that a stagestruck young gentleman succeeds in getting cast for the County Paris in a revival of Romeo and Juliet. Any young man who can deliver blank verse intelligibly, and who can dance and fence, can play Paris gracefully enough to satisfy a public trained to expect the least and worst from representatives of minor parts in Shakespear's plays. Probably, however, the stagestruck young gentleman, though he may have enjoyed a sound commercial or classical education, knows neither dancing nor fencing. So he has to be coached in a minuet and a stage duel. Now, the repetition of the minuet for a hundred and fifty nights will not make him a dancer, nor that of the duel a fencer. For similar reasons the repetition of the part of Paris will not make him an actor, though it will teach him a little if he be capable of learning. By the time he has played twenty parts he will have a repertory; but he will still not be a fully qualified actor; and he will have spent ten years on the stage. Shakespear's remark that one man in his time plays many parts[2] is now much more a metaphor than it was. Mr Jefferson[3] is

2. *As You Like It*, II.vii.

3. The American actor Joseph Jefferson III (1829–1905) became so popular as and so associated with the role of Rip Van Winkle that he played virtually nothing else for over forty years.

an extreme instance of this. The number of parts played by many of our metropolitan actors in their time must be astonishingly small in proportion to the number of nights they have played.

The question now arises, what is a fully qualified actor? The answer is that he is a man who knows the visible symptoms of every human condition, and has such perfect command of his motor powers that he can reproduce with his own person all the movements which constitute such symptoms. Then, it may be said, no actor was ever yet fully qualified. This is, in fact, the case, and it only remains unperceived because the fully qualified critic, who should equally know the visible symptoms of every human condition (though he, of course, is exempt from all obligation to simulate them) is also nonexistent. The ideal standard of perfection has not yet been realized by the actor or the critic of the theatre any more than by the workers of any other class. But it is necessary to determine the standard in order to keep both actors and critics from going astray.

The next question of the oppressed novice will most likely be to this effect. How much knowledge of physical expression is now attainable; and how can I get perfect command of my motor powers? To the first part of the question the reply is: Very little, but more than Garrick knew. Fifty years ago the student-actor (if any such phenomenon existed) might have read Leonardo da Vinci, Le Brun, Raphael Mengs, Lavater, Engel,[4] and others, and might have profited by them as much as the illustrious George Frederick Cooke, who once, when "delineating" the passions with his countenance for the edification of the elder Mathews,[5] insisted, whilst apparently convulsed with rage, that he was accurately counterfeiting maternal affection. Today the subject is falling into shape; and the actor can derive a clear conception from the works of Sir Charles Bell, Herbert Spencer, Francis Galton, Francis Warner, and above all Charles Darwin,[6] of the nature and magnitude of the problems it is his profession to solve. From them he can also learn whatever has so far been ascertained as to the postures, changes of color, and visible actions which invariably accompany the workings of any emotion or the existence of any mental or bodily

4. Leonardo da Vinci (1452–1519), great Italian painter and universal genius. Charles Le Brun (1619–90), chief artistic adviser to King Louis XIV of France in rebuilding the palace of Versailles; Le Brun also decorated its Galérie de Glaces. Anton Raphael Mengs (1728–79), German painter and critic who planned the Villa Albani in Rome. Johann Kaspar Lavater (1741–1801), Swiss physiognomist, theologian, and poet. Johann Jakob Engel (1741–1802), writer of popular philosophical books and of novels.

5. George Frederick Cooke (1756–1812); Charles Mathews (1776–1835), father of Charles James Mathews (1803–1878), both actors.

6. Sir Charles Bell (1774–1842), Scottish anatomist; Herbert Spencer (1820–1903), philosopher and social scientist; Sir Francis Galton (1822–1911), biologist; Francis Warner (1847–1926), author of *Physical Expression: Its Modes and Principles* (1885); Charles Robert Darwin (1809–82), pioneer in the study of evolution.

condition in man, and which are therefore their appropriate physical expression. He will find, for instance, that Hamlet's normal attitude, as exhibited during his presence on the stage for the short time which elapses before he takes any part in the business of the play, depends, not on the actor's taste, but on his opinion of Hamlet's constitution and state of health. When once that is settled, the proper position and movements of the head, eyelids, fingers, and so on down to the smallest muscle follow with rigid scientific precision. As the list of movements and postures is far from complete, and as the savants of every civilized country add daily some valuable particular to it, the actor should not neglect to master all the modern languages—especially German—and to read all the proceedings of scientific societies, the physiological journals, &c., both English and foreign, with the utmost care and regularity.

The power of executing all the movements which constitute physical expression can only be acquired by a gymnastic training so thorough as not to leave a single muscle in his body involuntary. He should be able to move the various parts of his throat at will, as certainly and easily as he can move his thumb and forefinger. Even rudimentary or unstriped muscles should be cultivated, so that the ears can be wagged or the scalp agitated on occasion. The actor should be an accomplished wrestler, not only with a view to playing Orlando or Charles[7] to the satisfaction of a Cumberland or Westmoreland audience, but in order to be able to fall with impunity in all positions. His voice and articulation should be cultivated until he is able to communicate intelligibly and impressively with a thousand people without shouting. He should have all the arts and sciences at his fingers' ends, in order that he may become conversant with the ideas which determine the subtle shades of manner that mark off the lawyer from the doctor, the painter from the musician. He should be acquainted with the points at issue between the ritualist and the evangelical, so as to replace the oldfashioned "holy man" of the stage with at least half a dozen distinct varieties of parson. A thorough knowledge of political economy can alone qualify him to understand the relations between class and class which are concerned in the plots of so many romantic dramas. In order not to be dependent on textbooks and compilations for his information, he should be adept at statistical methods of inquiry. On points as to which there is no recorded testimony, personal experience alone can help him to attain to scientific truth of representation. If a reprieve at the last moment can possibly be arranged, he should commit a murder—or even several, on persons differing in sex, age, and degree of relationship to himself—and get condemned to death. Burglary and forgery are experiences which no actor should be without. But study of this kind may easily

7. They wrestle in *As You Like It*.

be overdone. It is useless to commit outrages that are never presented on the stage, such as assaults on bishops, and the like. Child-stealing, however, should not be omited.

This account of the qualifications of a complete actor is necessarily very imperfect; but it is probably sufficiently comprehensive for most inquirers. It has the root of the matter in it; and its purpose will be fulfilled should the facility with which correspondents can be referred to it result in a saving of time to my Editor.

[HOODMAN BLIND AND OLIVIA]
C (*Our Corner*, October 1885)

Hoodman Blind, the new play by Mr Henry A. Jones, which has succeeded The Silver King[1] at the Princess's Theatre, is inferior to it in interest, and the illusion produced by the performance is much weaker. The story, which has been compared with that of Othello, but which is at least as like that of The Comedy of Errors, is of the jealousy of a young farmer who, misled by a strong personal resemblance, mistakes what is called in the playbill "a waif" for his wife, and is confirmed in his error by a villain. Unlike Othello, however, Hoodman Blind has not only a story, but also that dramatic cancer, a plot. There is no plot in Othello. As we cannot know a man's character until we have seen him tried by circumstances, a set of circumstances are provided for the exhibition of the characters in Shakespear's tragedy. But Desdemona does not in the last act turn out to be Bianca's half-sister, and heiress to a large fortune left by Brabantio. Emilia does not interrupt her death-speech to inform Iago that Roderigo was their child, stolen in infancy by gypsies under circumstances known only to Cassio under seal of an oath of secrecy. Nor do the Cypriot police arrest Iago on a charge of having strangled Brabantio in order to obtain possession of a bond for forty thousand pounds, payable by the Turkish tourist at whose expense Othello so officiously displayed his mercenary patriotism at Aleppo. Hoodman Blind is full of this kind of childish make-believe, to make room for which the action of the drama is distorted, irrelevant and disagreeable incidents are introduced, and the spectators are pestered by suppressed wills, long lost relatives, documents hidden in safes, and other matters of no interest to them. As Mr Jones's

---

1. (1882), in collaboration with Henry Herman.

name is coupled, as usual, with that of a collaborator, he may not be wholly responsible for the ill-judged plot machinery; but the dialogue is evidently his; and this leaves him responsible for some "sentiments" which have been deliberately written down to the silliest level of British cant in order to please the gallery, and which are the most reprehensible features of the drama. In spite of these blemishes, there is enough power shewn in the play to sustain the reputation which Mr Jones founded by The Silver King. Like that play, Hoodman Blind contains many minor parts which are easy to act well, and effective when well acted. The leading parts are far less happily contrived. Mr Jones has not done his best for either Mr Willard or Mr Wilson Barrett; and they have revenged themselves by ill-treating their opportunities. Mr Wilson Barrett's acting is shallow and monotonous throughout. There is no reticence in his manner, and no variety in his elocution. Before the play is half over his presence on the stage becomes an affliction; and the scenes in which he does not appear assert themselves as the redeeming points in the play. It is but fair to add that this is partly the author's fault. Jack Yeulett, the hero, was evidently not intended to appear anything worse than a very hotheaded young farmer: a manly fellow in the main. But he is so ill-tempered, so vindictive, and so atrociously inconsiderate even when he is not in a rage, that he only needs to have the offensive side of his character accentuated to become intolerably disagreeable. This accentuation is the only effect produced by Mr Wilson Barrett's acting. Mr Willard's failure is more extraordinary. If his part were that of a righteous man in sore trouble, his acting would be a little triumph in its way. But Mark Lezzard, as created by Mr Jones, is a most sordid scoundrel. Consequently Mr Willard's griefstricken face, and his voice softened and saddened by emotion, are beside the mark: they only suggest that he fancies himself the Silver King, and that he would make a capital substitute for Mr Wilson Barrett in that part. One result of this has been that the retribution which overtakes Mark in the last act so revolted the audience on the first night that the scene had to be modified at the subsequent representations. Fortunately for Mr Willard, his acting, inappropriate as it is, is so clever and effective that his performance has been greatly admired and praised; and his share of the incongruity of the last act has been visited upon Mr Jones. The best part in the play, and one of the best acted, is Chibbles the blacksmith, by Mr George Barrett.[2] His speech at his wedding supper, where, in a desperate attempt to make light of his affection for his bride, he blunders into assuring the company that he has no particular affection for his bride, is the best stroke of comedy the piece contains; and it is the more keenly relished for occuring in the only scene in which there is a

2. George Edward Barrett (1849–94), Wilson's brother.

momentary relief from that pervading nuisance, the plot. Artistic honors, as far as the male characters are concerned, are divided between Mr George Barrett and Mr Charles Hudson,[3] who plays the small part of the gypsy. It is interesting to see Miss Eastlake,[4] as Nance the farmer's wife and Jess the waif, alternately playing at two different levels of habit and education. Both parts are easily within her powers. Her greatest effect is made in a scene in a public house, where Jess, worn out by illness, finds her lover with his arms about the neck of another woman, and makes a heartbroken effort to eclipse her rival's gaiety by attempting to dance.

The performances of Mr W. G. Wills's Olivia were resumed at the Lyceum Theatre on the 3rd September. The redecoration of the house during the recess by Mr Phipps[5] seems to indicate a reaction against the prevailing system of excluding the draughtsman from the auditorium, and merely setting the upholsterer and the paint-pot man to tint the lines of the building. The change is only partly successful. The ceiling, covered with a design of medallions and arabesques in the manner of the famous decoration of the Vatican *loggie* by Raffaello and Giovanni da Udine, is admirable, as is the design after Baldassare Peruzzi[6] on the panels of the dress circle. But the other circles are colored too garishly; the ceiling is marred by the chandelier and the centre piece from which it descends; and there is an excess of detail on too small a scale for the size of the theatre. The alternation is nevertheless in the right direction. The very worst ceiling that can result from the exercise of an artist's intelligence is likely to be better than a roof which seems like an ottoman upholstered in old gold brocade, and turned upside down over the British public.

The acting at the Lyceum unfortunately needs looking after more than the house did. Taking into account the representative position of the theatre, it is not too much to say that the playing of the minor parts in Olivia is deplorable. Moses is unnatural without being in the least amusing: Messrs Howe and Wenman,[7] as Flamborough and Burchell, are perfunctory to an inexcusable degree. Mrs Primrose, as represented by Miss L. Payne, is an undignified shrew who occasionally becomes ridiculous. Miss Winifred Emery,[8] as Sophia, does her best, and her best is very fair; but her pains are heavily discounted by Mr Wenman's mannerism, which seems to have even less thought than usual behind it, and by the

3. (d. 1897), actor and dramatist.
4. Mary Eastlake (d. 1911).
5. Charles John Phipps, architect (d. 1897).
6. Raphael (Raffaelo Santi, 1483–1520); Giovanni (c. 1487–1564); Peruzzi (1481–1536) built the Villa Farnesina, Rome (1508–1511).
7. Henry Howe (1812–96); Thomas Edmund Newman Wenman (1844–92).
8. Mrs Cyril Maude (1861–1924).

burlesque of Mr Norman Forbes and Miss L. Payne.[9] Judged even as burlesque, Mr Norman Forbes's Moses would appear crude even at the Gaiety or Toole's. Olivia is no longer the play that charmed London years ago at the Court Theatre. Mr Irving's make-up as the Vicar is capital; and his playing in the second act is not only remarkable—Mr Irving's acting is always that—but excellently to the purpose of acting. Nevertheless, he elsewhere sets the example of burlesque which some of his colleagues have followed; and the total effect of his impersonation is less than that made by Mr Hermann Vezin[10] in the same part. Miss Ellen Terry tries very hard to reproduce her old Olivia; but the very effort does away with the apparent spontaneity that was once so fascinating. It is inevitable that her representation of the dawn of womanood should be a little more artificial than it was; but there is no valid reason why such memorable points[11] in the old Court performance as the glimpse of Olivia's face as she passes the window in her flight should be replaced by the monstrous improbability of her opening the lattice widely and kissing her hand several times to her father. Playgoers who have never seen Miss Terry in this part should not lose the opportunity of doing so; but those who have tender recollections of the original Olivia will do well to keep away from the Lyceum. The spectacle of Miss Terry imitating herself, and overdoing it, would not compensate them for the disappointments which they would suffer in the course of the play. Mr Terriss[12] alone repeats his first success without abatement. His appearance and manner suit the part so happily that he has only to be his external self (the only part for which Mr Terriss has shewn any marked aptitude) to be Squire Thornhill to the life. At the conclusion of the performance Mr Irving made a brief speech. He did not say that his company were doing what they could to bring the run of Olivia to an end; but he promised that it should be succeeded by Mr Wills's Faust, with Mrs Stirling in the cast.[13]

9. Norman Forbes (1858/59–1936), brother of Sir Johnston Forbes-Robertson; Louisa Payne (d. 1887).

10. American actor (1829–1910).

11. A "point" is a word, phrase, action, piece of stage business, joke, or emotional moment in a play, which an actor would use to make a histrionic effect. If the play were well known, audiences would await the "point" and how the actor might make it.

12. William Charles James Lewin Terriss (1847–97), known as "Breezy Bill," would become manager of the Adelphi Theater, specializing in melodrama, and one of the most popular actors of his time.

13. Mary Anne Stirling (1813–95).

[HAMLET]
C/Un (*Pall Mall Gazette*, 30 October 1885)

Mr Gerard B. Finch[1] has taken a rise out of the New Shakespear Society: not a very difficult feat for a skilled metaphysician. The other night he undertook to deal with Hamlet from a Theosophic point of view. The society took a preliminary dip into the lore of Colonel Olcott, and prepared to have the Ghost presented to them in a novel light, as the astral self of Hamlet senior, with perhaps a hint of what Madame Blavatsky has to say to Mr Hodgson's revelations at the Psychical Society.[2] But Mr Finch ignored the thoughtless inference that the Theosophic point of view means the point of view of the Theosophical Society. In an orderly metaphysical way he coolly laid bare the conflicting principles in the play by abstracting all its phenomena. The Shakespeareans, being for the most part capable of nothing but the phenomena, gasped as they saw their pet play, all concrete as they knew it, fade into a nebulous region of Intuition and Aspiration, wherein the very Rosencrantz and Guildenstern became misty and allegorical. When they were told that Ophelia was Experience they turned and rent the metaphysician with chivalrous speeches.

[COLOMBE'S BIRTHDAY]
C/Un (*The Dramatic Review*, 21 November 1885)

The much-ridiculed Browning Society have made their enemies their footstool at last.[1] On Thursday, at St George's Hall, they gave a representation of their poet's five-act drama, Colombe's Birthday.[2] It is quite possible that the effect of this performance on dramatic art in England may be revolutionary. The Society's previous attempts with In a Balcony[3] at

1. Gerard Brown Finch (1835–1913) was a Cambridge lawyer.
2. Colonel Henry Steele Olcott (1832–1907) was an American theosophist and follower of Madame Helena Petrovna Blavatsky (1831–1891), founder of the Theosophical Society and author of *The Secret Doctrine*. In 1885, Richard Hodgson (1855–1905), an Australian, demonstrated that many of her miracles were fraudulent.
1. "The Lord said unto my Lord: Sit thou on my right hand, until I make thine enemies thy footstool."—*Prayer Book* (1662), 110:1.
2. Published 1844.
3. Published 1855.

Prince's Hall the season before last, and with the Blot on the 'Scutcheon last spring, were only partially successful. The first was lost in a large and unsuitable hall, the second was indifferently acted. But Colombe's Birthday has unexpectedly proved to be an acting drama of the first class. It has two cardinal elements of failure from the ordinary managerial point of view. It is full of long speeches, and it is persistently addressed to the higher faculties of an educated and thoughtful audience. Both of these features materially contributed on Thursday to its success, which was complete and unequivocal. Miss Alma Murray played Colombe, and thoroughly justified the faith which the Browning Society have placed in her since her performance of Constance in In a Balcony. Her playing in the second act was especially striking. Mr Leonard Outram,[4] whose theory of acting is familiar to readers of The Dramatic Review, shewed that his theory has borne fruit in practice. His playing of the very long and very difficult part of Valence was a remarkable achievement, and one that promises largely for his future career. Mr Foss as Guibert, and Mr B. Webster as the Prince,[5] did less justice to Browning than Miss Murray or Mr Outram; but they too proved that a new departure in drama need not be hindered by any lack of men ripe to enter upon a higher class of work than there is yet any demand for on the part of our managers. Mr Bernard Gould efficiently discharged a comparatively easy task as Melchior; and Messrs Bouverie and R. de Cordova deserve mention for their careful acting in the parts of Manfroy and Gaucelme.[6] A few more successes of this description, and it will become as fashionable to be ridiculed for seriousness as a member of the Browning Society as it has hitherto been to be reproached for frivolity as an uninitiated outsider.

[SHAKESPEAREAN VERSE]
C/Un (*Pall Mall Gazette*, 19 December 1885)

The latest Shakespearean disturbance is due to the veteran critic, Mr Watkiss Lloyd,[1] who declares that the passages printed as prose in the poet's works are not prose at all. In a bar of music, he argues, there may

4. Leonard S. Outram (d. 1901), actor and dramatist.
5. George R. Foss (1859–1938); Ben Webster (1864–1947).
6. Bernard Gould (1861–1945), the stage name of the *Punch* caricaturist Sir Bernard Partridge, would play Sergius in the first production of *Arms and the Man*, 1894; J.D. Bouverie; Rudolph de Cordova (1860–1941), actor and dramatist.
1. William Watkiss Lloyd (1813–93) was a classical and Shakespearean scholar.

be four notes in one bar and thirtytwo in the next, provided the thirtytwo be uttered eight times as fast as the four. Similarly, in a line of blank verse you may have eighteen or a couple of dozen syllables in a line, provided you speak them in the same time as the ordinary ten. The speeches of Falstaff are metrical, and should be printed in lines like the soliloquies in Hamlet. Mr Watkiss Lloyd is prepared to edit a new edition in this way. He frankly admits that as all previous editions will then be so much waste paper, he anticipates some opposition. His views were laid before the Royal Society of Literature[2] last Thursday in a paper which he supplemented by a reading of the gravedigger scene in Hamlet, as arranged by him in metre without the transposition of a single word. The experience seemed quite conclusive: against Mr Watkiss Lloyd's view. Sir Patrick de Colquhoun, who presided, read from the work of Gibbon,[3] and from a Dutch author, passages which were, as averred, as nearly hexameters as they could be. Proceeding to defend the practice of Latin verse making in schools, he said that Mr Watkiss Lloyd could not possibly have made his discovery but for his early classical training. The audience, having their own opinion of the value of the discovery, hardly drew the inference in favor of Latin verses pointed to by Sir Patrick. An interesting paper by Mr Sharpe[4] on the same subject, in which the consideration which determined Shakespear's changes from prose to metre were discriminated, was read at the last meeting of the New Shakespear Society, and proved much more convincing than the hopeless enterprise of Mr Watkiss Lloyd, who was unfortunately not present to break a lance with Mr Sharpe.

[MAYFAIR, IMPULSE, COLOMBE'S BIRTHDAY]
C (*Our Corner*, January 1886)

The managers of the St James's Theatre have withdrawn Mr Pinero's Mayfair, and substituted Impulse. This indicates a pretty state of things.

---

2. Established in 1823 for the purpose of sustaining what is best, whether old or new, in English letters, and to encourage the appreciation of literature, the Royal Society still exists.

3. Sir Patrick MacChombaich de Colquhoun (1815–91) was a lawyer and diplomat; Edward Gibbon (1737–94) was an English historian, whose *Decline and Fall of the Roman Empire* was published, ironically, in 1776.

4. On 11 December 1885, Henry Sharpe had addressed the New Shakespere Society on "Shakespeare's Prose."

Mayfair, an adaptation of Sardou's Maison Neuve,[1] is about thirty times as good a play as Impulse, and provides a correspondingly greater scope for the highest powers of the St James company. The morality of Impulse is the morality of Mr Pecksniff.[2] In one scene, an elderly British husband, catching his wife in the act of eloping with a Frenchman, gives her a sermon on her duties to her lord and master, which is a stronger indirect incitement to revolt against the institution of the family than a dozen Palais Royal farces. The play became popular because the spectacle of Mr Kendal[3] following his wife about the stage, and idiotically repeating the formula "You a r e: you really a r e," somehow tickled the public. The play, as a whole, was rather amusing. It contained nothing deep enough to puzzle even a downright fool; and it did not disparage the West End. Now Mr Pinero, in Mayfair, not only disparaged the West End, but attacked it directly and bitterly by exhibiting society as a tedious fraud. Society accordingly fled from the stalls; and to lure it back again Mr Kendal has had to suppress Mr Pinero, and to resume his assurances to Mrs Kendal that she is: she really is. The hero of Mayfair is a prosperous elderly stockbroker, who lives in an oldfashioned house in Bloomsbury, and declines to do speculative business. He proposes to take into partnership his nephew, a young stockbroker with a pretty and ambitious wife. The nephew, in a hurry to be rich, hankers after speculative business; is ashamed of living so far East as Bloomsbury; and secretly considers his uncle an old stick-in-the-mud (a compound epithet much used at present to describe a conscientious person). His wife is equally base in her aspirations, and is delighted when he tells her that he has secretly taken and furnished a house in Mayfair. But they are afraid to tell Uncle Nicholas; and the selfishness and cowardice with which, impatient to be in their new house, and not daring to face the unpleasantness of an explanation, they slip away from the Bloomsbury mansion at a moment when their desertion most wounds and disappoints the old man, are mercilessly emphasized. Mr Pinero has been blamed for not softening his point; but he could not have done so without spoiling the first act, and stultifying himself as a translator of M. Sardou. It is to be feared that the complainants saw nothing vile in the aspirations of Jeff and Agnes, and were therefore unable to see the consistency of their stupid cruelty. The rest of the play deals with the attainment of the paltry ambition of the young couple; the sort of friends they gain by their lavish expenditure; the entanglement of the weak husband in an intrigue with an adventuress who blackmails him; his wife's discovery of his faithlessness, and

1. *Mayfair* (1885); *Impulse* (1882) by Benjamin Charles Stephenson (d. 1906); *Maison neuve* (1866).

2. Seth Pecksniff is a character in *Martin Chuzzlewit* (1843–44) by Charles (John Huffham) Dickens (1812–70). His name has become synonymous with unctuous hypocrisy, selfishness, or corruption beneath a facade of goodness or sanctimoniousness.

3. William Hunter Kendal (1843–1917).

her characteristic revenge by inviting another man to degrade her; the collapse of Jeff's speculative stockbroking; and the rescue of the pair from the consequences of their folly by honest Uncle Nick. All this is as much the point in London today as Maison Neuve was in 1867 in Paris under the régime of Napoleon III and Haussmann.[4] Mr Pinero might have made the social contrast clearer by substituting for Bloomsbury one of the northern or eastern suburbs in which our oldfashioned city people dwell; for Russell Square is hardly so outlandish as a foreigner might infer it to be from witnessing a performance of Mayfair. But this does not seriously interfere with the effort of the play, which is interesting and witty all through its five acts. Mrs Kendal has acquired a few tricks lately which occasionally betray the unreality of her impersonations in the lighter scenes; but when she is thoroughly in earnest she displays a surer command than she has ever before attained of the varied resources she has developed so highly. Mr Brookfield's counterfeit of a broken man about town could not be bettered.[5] Mr Hare,[6] as the old stockbroker, divides with Mr Brookfield the artistic honors that fall to the men. Miss Linda Dietz,[7] as a French maid, is relieved for a while from the sentimental aspect in which she is usually condemned to appear; and she makes the most of her opportunity. The other parts are satisfactorily played, with the important exception of Lord Sulgrave, who, as enacted by Mr Cartwright,[8] does not fit into his place. Mr Cartwright does his best; but the part does not suit him, and the third and fourth acts suffer in consequence.

A very remarkable performance of one of Robert Browning's plays, Colombe's Birthday, took place at St George's Hall on the 19th of November. It was announced as "the fifth annual entertainment of the Browning Society." When it is proposed to put a work of Mr Browning's on the stage, doubts arise not so much as to the quality of the play as to the quality of the audience. The safe and usual course in theatres is to present the public with nothing above the mental capacity of children, although the incidents may be beyond childish experience. The result of this is that serious people, as a class, do not go to the theatre. When the manager declares that "the public" will not have this, that, or the other, he means that frivolous people will not have them. Point out to him that earnest people will have them, and prefer them, and he can reply that earnest

4. Following the 1848 revolts in Paris, the financier and town-planner Georges Eugène Haussmann (1809–91), under Louis-Napoléon, laid out parks and boulevards, built bridges, and so forth in the 1850s and 1860s. Because of enormous costs, he was dismissed in 1870.

5. Charles Hallam Brookfield (1857–1913), actor, dramatist, and later Examiner of Plays for the Lord Chamberlain's office.

6. John (later Sir John) Hare (1844–1921).

7. American actress and singer (d. 1920).

8. Charles Cartwright (1855–1916).

people never think of coming to his theatre; and that, if they did, there are not enough of them to keep a play running sufficiently long to pay for the initial expenditure on dresses and scenery. Much of that expenditure is, however, in itself a concession to frivolity. Again, the ordinary play has its run of so many hundred nights, after which it dies, and its dresses and scenery are of no further use. But Hamlet has enjoyed an intermittent run of nearly three hundred years: it wears out its audiences. The same man will go again and again to see Hamlet; but no reasonable man goes twice to a "popular" piece unless he happens to fall in love with one of the actresses, in which case he is, for the time, unreasonable. Earnest people—earnest enough, at least, to prefer Colombe's Birthday to a Gaiety burlesque—are not so scarce as the managers suppose. Enough of them could easily be lured back into the habit of playgoing to support at least one theatre, which would raise the standard of dramatic art and be a school for actors as well. It pays to issue shilling reprints of deep and weighty classics, enormous numbers of which are sold in London alone. At lectures and public meetings crowds of citizens sit out appalingly tedious orations in the hope of improving their minds. Yet the managers tell us that the public will not stand long speeches. That is all the managers know about it. If they can persuade the public that theatregoing is not a waste of valuable time, and that as much can be learnt by listening to a play as by reading a book, they will find that they have hitherto been taking a great deal of trouble to please the wrong people and to keep away the right people. The masterpieces of English dramatic poetry are surely not less likely to be appreciated than the masterpieces of classical music. Mr Browning's In a Balcony would not recommend itself to Mr Charles Wyndham[9] for the subject of his next enterprise at the Criterion Theatre; but it is much more popular than one of Beethoven's posthumous quartets. Yet these draw to St James's Hall people who are as unmistakably the intelligent public, as the majority of the frequenters of our theatres are unmistakably the silly or half-educated public. Let the managers go to the Monday Popular Concerts; consider their ways; and be wise.[10]

Colombe's Birthday proves more interesting in action than even Browning enthusiasts expected. The truth of the study of courtier nature in the group of envious timeservers who constitute the Duchess's court is amply verified by the numerous court memoirs with which retired palace lackeys from time to time favor us. It supplies just the necessary background to Guibert, the marshal, who cynically professes himself a Machiavellian scoundrel, but who invariably acts, when put to the proof, upon honorable

9. Charles (later Sir Charles) Wyndham (1837–1919), actor-manager.

10. "Go to the ant, thou sluggard; consider her ways, and be wise"—Proverbs 6:6. In *Man and Superman* (1902), Shaw has Tanner give Octavius this advice, substituting "bee" for "ant."

and generous impulses. The position of the Duchess between the ambitious prince who courts her from political motives, but will not simulate a
passion he does not feel, and the poor advocate who has failed somewhat
ignominiously to conceal his apparently desperate love for her, is more
interesting as Browning has treated it than any conventional dramatist
could have made it. The relief given to the ear of the jaded theatregoer by
the pregnant and pointed verse was beyond description. The acting
proved that we have still material for a company of players capable of
restoring dramatic poetry to the stage. Miss Alma Murray played Colombe
quite satisfactorily, which is equivalent to saying that she achieved an
arduous feat in the highest department of her profession. Mr Leonard
Outram did very well as Valence. The other gentlemen only require more
practice in the class of work required, to qualify them thoroughly for it.
The impression made by the performance was so favorable that the Browning Society was greatly pleased with itself; and Dr Furnivall, in a speech
between the first and second acts, promised a representation of Straf-
ford[11] for next year, possibly at the Lyceum Theatre.

[FAUST]
C/X (*Our Corner*, March 1886)

The Lyceum Faust, as Mr W. G. Wills's "adaptation" of the first part of
Goethe's tragedy[1] to Mr Henry Irving's purposes is now commonly called,
is very unsatisfactory. To save it from intolerable tediousness, the dialogue
has been pared to the slenderest possible thread. Although the curtain is
up for only two hours and eighteen minutes, there are eleven scenes; so
that there is, on an average, something new to look at every eleven and a
half minutes, without counting the changes of light, the eruptions of
subterranean fire, the visions, the apotheosis, the flights of witches on
broomsticks, the incandescent rain on the red-hot mountain at the
sabbat, and the magic wreaths of mist that proceed from a copper of
boiling water beneath the stage near the right upper entrance. Of the
illusion thus laboriously produced, about nine tenths is destroyed by the
acting and dialogue. Goethe's tragedy requires two actors of the highest

11. First produced 1837 by Macready, it ran only four nights.
   1. *Faust*, Part 1 (1806) by Johann Wolfgang von Goethe (1749–1832), German poet,
novelist, critic, dramatist, and director.

class, the better of the pair to play Faust, and the other to play the easier part of Mephistopheles. Faust and Mephistopheles are a dual present-ment of one character: the play is a one-part play; but the one personality has been decomposed by the author into what is popularly called its own good and evil angel, and so it has to be impersonated by two men. And unless there be a certain equation of power in these men, and a certain reflection of the one in the other, there can be no credible Faust. When a popular actor selects Mephistopheles as a show part, and engages a walk-ing gentleman to speak as many of Faust's lines as cannot well be left out, he courts failure and shews that he is not the man to grapple with Goe-the.[2] Mr Irving is not the first actor-manager who has been seduced into this error by the fascination of the scarlet coat and cock's feather of the fiend, in spite of the verdict on such attempts having always been that Goethe's masterpiece is not interesting on stage. That verdict will never be set aside by any attempt to present Faust with the part of Faust left out. In the Lyceum version, the philosopher is our old friend of Gounod's opera,[3] a senile pedant changed into a sentimental fop: his age overdone in the first phase, his youth in the second. As he sneaks irresolutely after the fiend, who bullies him, and threatens to tear him to pieces, and scatter his blood like rain on the blast, there is not a gleam in him of the Faust of whom Mephistopheles speaks as *der mir so kräftig wider-stand.*[4] The relations of Faust and Margaret are absurdly reversed. In-stead of the philosopher and the maiden, we have a refined and sensible woman, and an unripe youth whose passion for her is developing him into a dissolute young spark. The Mephistopheles is little more than the oper-atic Mephistopheles, a grotesque person posing in red limelight, and collapsing when a cross is flourished in his face. Mr Irving presents him as a malicious sorcerer with certain monstrous mental deficiencies, walk-ing the earth with the awkward strut of a creature made only to perch and fly. He inspires disgust rather than interest and awe, as if he were obvi-ously and continually the "abortion of fire and filth" that Faust sees in him in a moment of revulsion against his pessimism. Mr Irving seems to have forgotten that the same Mephistopheles who terrified and repeled poor Margaret because he was proof against the limited scale of simple emo-tions which was to her the whole of human feeling, was yet so genial in his intercourse with higher intelligences that Faust never became quite convinced that his companionship was an unmixed evil. God Omniscient

2. A walking gentleman is a male performer of minor roles; his female counterpart is a walking lady. Shaw is insulting the actor H. B. Conway (1850–1909), a major player, by saying he has not talent enough to play a lead.

3. *Faust* (1859) by Charles François Gounod (1818–93).

4. The one who so strongly resisted me. *Faust*, Part 2 (1832), line 11,590.

himself confessed to enjoying an occasional chat with him, and declared that without him human virtue would stagnate. Mephistopheles, as an eternal spirit, is incapable of temporal compromises, and absolutely indifferent to the death or the particular form of suffering endured by any mortal individual. To ordinary intelligences he therefore appears in emergencies as a monster devoid of pity, love, or fear. But he has interests and even passions to serve: they are the motive for his activity among men. He takes care to make himself agreeable, padding his cloven hoof with a false calf, and dressing himself sprucely. The Prince of Darkness becomes thus an interesting and accomplished gentleman[5] in his intercourse with human society. Mr Irving's devil is an unpresentable person, slow, deadly, sour, and sardonic in his graver moments, but dropping at other times into the manner of the eminent tragedian's impersonation of Alfred Jingle.[6] We get occasional glimpses of the medieval Satan; but they are few and far between. The scenes of purely mundane comedy with Martha are the best in the play, thanks to Mrs Stirling, whose acting is better than that of any of her colleagues, male or female. Miss Terry's Margaret is in no way memorable or remarkable, though one or two points in it suggest that with a thoroughly congenial opportunity she may, when freed from the unfavorable artistic conditions of the Lyceum Theatre, again do something to justify her great reputation. Mr Wills's part of the business has been badly done. He has flattened out the animated rhythms and rhymed endings of Goethe's pregnant lines into blank verse that is poor in ideas and commonplace in expression. As may be imagined, the altered verse form spoils the utterances of Margaret, Mephistopheles, and Valentine. The extensive omissions may not be Mr Wills's fault, as the pruning knife has been freely used since the manager discovered that the audience could not possibly have too little dialogue to please them. But the dilution of what is retained, and the changes and additions, are clearly the work of the "adapter and arranger." Even the prison scene, a page of dramatic literature which even Ducis[7] would have refrained from meddling with, has been hacked and cooked in such a fashion that the interest declines steadily from the first line to the last. Though the alterations, measured by a compositor's rule, are small, they are, as Mercutio says of his wound, "enough."[8] Mr Wills's "arrangement" will sooner or later go the way of Garrick's and Cibber's adaptations of

5. "The prince of darkness is a gentleman."—Shakespeare, *King Lear* (1605), III.iv.

6. A character in *Pickwick* by James Albery (1838–89), based on Charles Dickens's *Pickwick Papers* (1836–37). In 1878, Albery revised the play, *Pickwick* (1871), expanding Irving's role, and retitled it *Jingle*.

7. Jean François Ducis (1733–1816), the first adapter of Shakespeare for the French theater, tried to make Shakespeare's plays conform to the neoclassical mode then favored in France.

8. *Romeo and Juliet*, III.i: meaning enough to kill him.

Shakespear's plays, or Kalkbrenner's version of Don Giovanni.[9] The scenery partly compensates the spectator, though it by no means wholly indemnifies him, for the task of following the lines. The music presents no novelty (except that Mr Irving actually sings the serenade); and the orchestra is of fair quality, though feeble. Lindpaintner's[10] oldfashioned overture is played before the rising of the curtain. It might be replaced with advantage by Gounod's beautiful prelude, which is better suited to a small orchestra than any of the works to which Mr Meredith Ball's choice is limited by the subject.

A new play by Mr H.A. Jones, entitled The Lord Harry, has just been produced, too late for further notice here this month, at the Princess's Theatre. It will not seriously affect Mr Jones's reputation as a dramatist either favorably or otherwise.

[THE LORD HARRY, A BED OF ROSES, ANTOINETTE RIGAUD]
C (*Our Corner*, April 1886)

Two new plays by Mr H. A. Jones have been produced lately, and are still running. One, a comedietta entitled Bed of Roses, serves as "curtain raiser" at the St James's Theatre. The other is The Lord Harry, described in the playbill as "an entirely New and Original Romantic Play in Five Acts, by Henry Arthur Jones and Wilson Barrett." It is not, however, either new or original enough to bring anything more serious in question than the curious law of collaboration imposed upon dramatic authors at the Princess's Theatre. Apparently no play is accepted there unless somebody officially connected with the establishment has favored the dramatist with enough more or less judicious advice and more or less skilled assistance to justify the insertion of his name in the program as joint author. If this law may not be abrogated, it should be furnished with a clause excluding actors from collaboration. The temptation to insist as much as possible on their own parts is too likely to corrupt them as playwrights, forced as they are into perpetual self-assertion by the struggle for existence. Stagemanagers and scene painters should also be forbidden to bear on the play during its artistic growth. Not even the call boy or the check taker should be trusted; for the first might be tempted to

9. Frédéric Kalkbrenner (1785–1849), of Mozart's *Don Giovanni* (1787).
10. Peter Josef von Lindpaintner (1791–1856).

arrange the exits and entrances with a view to saving himself trouble rather than to perfecting the balance of the scenes; and the second might too easily make his post a sinecure by damaging the play to such an extent that no one could be induced to witness its performance. If someone connected with the theatre must collaborate, let him be the fireman, whose duties are invariable whether the play be good or bad. The Lord Harry is a flimsy play in comparison with Hoodman Blind; but it is much more agreeable. "Upon the tented field, and where castles mounted stand," we spend the hours more pleasantly than we did among the sanctimonious rustics of Abbots Creslow and the waterside refuse of London. Mr Wilson Barrett swaggers for God and King Charles. Mr Willard, the sticking-plaster gaps in whose front teeth gave a horrible jaggedness to his malicious smiles, is for the Parliament; though it soon appears that he is merely backing the winner, and is quite ready to change sides as the fortunes of war fluctuate. Miss Eastlake is the daughter of a Roundhead colonel; and of course she and Mr Wilson Barrett fall in love with oneanother. Duels, threats of the rack, sentences of death, the condemned in prison visited by his beloved, escapes, treacheries, faithful servants, alarums, and excursions relieve the wordiness of the persons concerned: the Lord Harry having a turn for description, and the colonel and his daughter being adepts at extemporaneous prayer. In the thrilling scene of the rising flood, Miss Eastlake all but raises a laugh by beginning, as she clings to a chimney stack, and looks in vain for a boat, "Oh thou, that walkedst on the waters," &c. The sole superiority of The Lord Harry to Mr Jones's previous works consists in its almost complete freedom from the incubus of a plot. Signs are not wanting in it that to be collaborated with by Mr Wilson Barrett means, in effect, to be crippled and stultified by the limited aims and personal interest of an actor-manager, who can act better than he can write, and who can manage much better than he can act. Perhaps the fact that The Lord Harry has had a narrow escape from failure may induce Mr Wilson Barrett to allow dramatic authors the same independence in their own department as he doubtless claims for himself in his. Of the acting little need be said. Mr Charles Coote's Shekeniah Pank, a minor comic part, is the most thorough feat of impersonation in the performance. Miss Eastlake plays very well: so do Miss Lottie Venne and Mr Willard. Mr Clyndes[1] plays Col Breane with his usual steadiness and emphasizes by contrast the want of method in Mr Wilson Barrett's more imaginative but unconvincing attempt to play the dashing cavalier. A stage battle, a flood, and a coast scene, at the ends of the third, fourth, and fifth acts respectively, are important factors in the success of the drama.

1. Charles Coote (1858–97); Lottie Venne (1852–1928); J. H. Clyndes (d. 1927).

At the St James's Theatre, Antoinette Rigaud, translated by Ernest Warren from the French of M. Deslandes,[2] is preceded nightly by A Bed of Roses. In this little play, Mr Jones, not having had to provide Mr Wilson Barrett with a part, acquits himself far more featly than in his vast works for the Princess's. The plan of the piece is slight and familiar. A couple of pairs of sweethearts are crossed in love for a while by a crusty old stage father, who soon winds up the business with the customary "Take her, Charles," which has superseded the oldfashioned "Bless you, my children. May you be happy." Miss [Annie] Webster, who is thrown away as a "walking lady" in Antoinette Rigaud, finds some worthier employment in the part of Dora Vellacott. Her recent exploit as the Maiden Queen in the performance by the Dramatic Students of Dryden's Secret Love,[3] has drawn due attention to her development from a stiff, joyless, laborious apprentice into an accomplished actress of serious parts. Only in representing lightheartedness are any traces of the heaviness of her novitiate now perceptible. In the pathetic passages of Mr Jones's comedietta, her acting was remarkably truthful and in the nicest taste.

Antoinette Rigaud is a string of tolerably interesting scenes, brought about on impossible pretexts. Mr Warren, the translator, has a bad ear for dialogue: he makes his characters converse, even at emotional crises, in the artificial periods of essayists and historians. "Filled with vague alarm, I hastened to her room" says General de Préfond. "Trembling and breathless I lay, not daring to stir" says his daughter Marie. Mr Warren may consider, like the novelists of the last century, that these inversions impart style to the remarks of his characters; but none—not even a professed pedant—ever did or ever will talk so in real life under the influence of emotion. Antoinette Rigaud is married to a jolly but jealous man of business. An artist, to whom she has written some compromising letters, meets her at General de Préfond's. She asks him to give up the letters; and he does so with such scrupulous haste that instead of waiting until morning to hand them to her safely at the railway station on her departure, he breaks into the general's house at night and presents himself in Antoinette's room. Whilst he is there, her husband unexpectedly arrives, making nothing of paying a midnight visit at the house of his friend the General. There is a terrible to-do to hide Sannoy (the artist) and get him off the premises unknown to Rigaud. At last he manages to slip out of Antoinette's chamber, but only to blunder into the bedroom of the General's daughter and scare her almost out of her senses. He then gets through the window; tears away the roses from the wall; tramples the

2. *Antoinette Rigaud* (1885) by Raimond (or Raymond) Deslandes (1828–90), trans. Ernest Warren (d. 1887).

3. *Secret Love, or The Maiden Queen* (1667) by John Dryden (1631–1700).

flower bed beneath; drops a medallion portrait of Antoinette; and makes off, leaving behind him much circumstantial evidence of his escapade. Next morning Antoinette's brother is accused of having broken into the room of Marie de Préfond, with whom he is admittedly in love; and he, suspecting the truth, saves Antoinette's honor by pleading guilty. The exasperated General is about to eject him from the premises when Antoinette confesses her folly. The General promptly produces his daughter and says "Take her, Henri." The jealous husband is apparently satisfied without receiving any explanation of this change of front; and the curtain descends on domestic bliss. The play requires for its acceptance rather more makebelieve than a Briton of average incredulity can afford; but it is saved from failure by the acting of Mrs Kendal as Antoinette, Mr Hare as General de Préfond, and Mr Barnes as Rigaud. Mr Kendal as Henri, the scapegoat, plays so much more in sorrow than in anger—which is just the reverse of what might be expected—that he becomes too lachrymose for robust tastes. Miss Linda Dietz's impersonation of Marie, the ingénue, is clever; and Mr Hendrie[4] hits off the martially disposed stockbroker very happily. But the weight of the play falls on Mrs Kendal, who begins badly by depending on a few effective mannerisms for the lighter phases of her part, but who addresses herself to the subsequent serious business with extraordinary variety and subtlety, reading whole chapters of psychology into the play between the lines. Her powers are deplorably wasted on the repertory of the St James's Theatre.

[THE CENCI]
C (*Our Corner*, June 1886)

The most remarkable event of last month with which I have any concern in this Corner is the performance of Shelley's tragedy The Cenci for the first time during the sixtyseven years which have elapsed since it was published in 1819. The Censor forbade the representation; and the Shelley Society could therefore do no more than engage a large theatre—the Grand at Islington—and have their play in strict technical privacy, which in this case meant in the presence of a crowded audience who were only distinguished from other audiences by the fact that they had not paid for their seats at the doors in the usual way. That tickets may, nevertheless,

4. Ernest Hendrie (1858–1929).

have changed hands for money is quite possible: I am myself a member of the Shelley Society; I received applications from people desirous of purchasing my tickets; and it was certainly not any sentiment of loyalty to the Lord Chamberlain that restrained me from meeting their wishes. The official licence was withheld on the ground that the performance of such a play would deprave the public. Yet the play has been performed; its attractions have been supplemented by the presence of a number of celebrated persons in the auditorium; and as many people as the theatre could hold have been not only admitted for nothing but invited and personally welcomed. So far, the anticipated depravation of the public seems not to have come off; for the conduct of the nation has not perceptibly altered for the worse since the afternoon of Friday, the 7th of May, 1886; whilst the attempt to drive theatregoers from the performances of the Shelley Society to such licensed alternatives as the Criterion Theatre, for example, has so accentuated the anomaly, folly, and hypocrisy of the censorship as to strengthen the hope that the institution may soon be as extinct as the Star Chamber,[1] to which, in point of obnoxiousness to all accredited political principle, it is exactly similar.

A performance of The Cenci must have come sooner or later, because Shelley, although he rushed into print before he was ripe for it, and often disgraced himself by doing very ordinary literary jobs in an unworkmanlike way, is yet, with the exception—under certain limitations—of Shakespear, the greatest of English poets; and The Cenci is the only work which he wrote with a view to actual representation on the stage. In indulging his whim to produce something in the obsolete and absurd form which Shakespear had done so much with, Shelley no doubt believed that he was engaged upon a solid and permanent composition. In reality he was only experimenting to find a suitable form for his efforts to "teach the human heart, through its sympathies and antipathies, the knowledge of itself; in proportion to the possession of which knowledge, every human being is wise, just, sincere, tolerant, and kind." This, he says, is the purpose of "the highest species of drama";[2] and it seems to me that such purpose makes all the difference between the writer of fiction and the ordinary imaginative liar. However that may be, Shelley, groping for the scientific drama which is yet in the future, and which alone could have reconciled his philosophic craving for truth to the unrealities of the stage, certainly got hold of the wrong vehicle when he chose the five-act

1. A notoriously oppressive court in England from the fifteenth century until 1641, when Parliament abolished it; meeting in camera in a Royal Palace of Westminster apartment that had a ceiling ornamented with stars, and using arbitrary procedures, the Star Chamber exercised wide civil and criminal jurisdiction.

2. A slight misquotation of Shelley's preface to the play.

tragedy in blank verse which had sufficed for Otway and Nicholas Rowe.[3] The obligations imposed on him by this form and its traditions were that he should imitate Shakespear in an unShakespearean fashion by attempting to write constantly as Shakespear only wrote at the extreme emotional crises in his plays; that his hero should have a dash of Richard III in him; that the tragedy should be raised to "the dignity of history" by the arbitrary introduction of incidents (mostly fictitious) mentioned in recondite historical manuscripts; and that the whole should be made sufficiently stagey to appear natural and suitable to actors and frequenters of the theatre, and outrageous and impossible to everyone else. Shelley, with the modesty of a novice, complied with these conditions. He produced a villain worse than Richard III, Macbeth, Iago, Antiochus, and Ireland's Vortigern[4] all rolled into one. He expanded Othello's "Put out the light; and then put out the light" into a whole scene. He wrote a father's curse compared to which Lear's on Goneril appears a mere petulance. He put Lady Macbeth's famous "Give me the daggers" into the mouth of a heroine urging her father's murder. He gave her a sad song to sing before her death, like Desdemona. Long tirades, thunder and lightning, a banquet, a castle, murders, tortures, and executions were not spared. The inevitable historical document was duly translated from the Italian original. And he wrote a preface in which he scrupulously stated that an idea in one of the speeches was suggested by a passage in Calderon's El Purgatorio de San Patricio.[5] This, he said, was the only plagiarism he had intentionally commited in the whole piece; a declaration which proves how unconsciously he had been guilty of all the secondhand Shakespear. The result furnishes an artistic parallel to Wagner's Rienzi. It is a strenuous but futile and never-to-be-repeated attempt to bottle the new wine in the old skins.

The Cenci, then, is a failure in the sense in which we call an experiment with a negative result a failure. But the powers called forth by it were so extraordinary that many generations of audiences will probably submit to have the experiment repeated on them, in spite of the incidental tedium. And if the play be ever adequately acted, the experiment will not be even temporarily fatiguing to witness, though it perhaps may prove at one or two points unendurably horrible. For Count Cenci, mere stage puppet, striking figure in Italian history, tragedy villain and so forth, as he is supposed to be, is really a personification of the Almighty Fiend of

3. Thomas Otway (1651/52–85) and Nicholas Rowe (1674–1718) both composed tragic dramas.

4. William Henry Ireland (1793–1835) forged "Shakespearean" plays, among them Vortigern (1796).

5. The Purgatory of St Patrick by Pedro Calderón de la Barca (1600–81).

Queen Mab,[6] the God whose attributes convicted the average evangelical
Briton in Shelley's eyes of being a devil worshiper. Cenci is ruthless,
powerful, and malignant; and, above all, there is no appeal and no relief
from his injustice. He identifies his cause with that of his God by the
appaling preface to his valediction against Beatrice:

> The world's Father
> Must grant a parent's prayer against his child.

Beatrice, too, banishes all mere stage heroism from our minds when she
absolutely despairs, and, without losing her self-possession, dies in her
despair. She withstands physical torture; but she succumbs, as she tells
her torturer,

> —with considering all the wretched life
> Which I have lived, and its now wretched end,
> And the small justice shewn by Heaven and Earth
> To me or mine; and what a tyrant thou art,
> And what slaves these; and what a world we make,
> The oppressor and the oppressed.

Those who have witnessed the agony and death of any innocent creature upon whom Nature has wantonly fastened a dreadful malady, will
recognize here a tragedy truer and deeper than that of any conventional
heroine whose lover dies in the fifth act. Shelley and Shakespear are the
only dramatists who have dealt in despair of this quality; and Shelley
alone has shewn it driven into the heart of a girl. The devil-god, incarnate
in a wicked human tyrant, is characteristically Shelleyan. He is of course
as pure a superstition as the benevolent *deus ex machina* of optimistic
religious playwrights; but both represent a real aspect of nature; and the
one is therefore as terribly real and effective as the other is delightfully
pleasant and useful.

The performance could not have been materially improved upon at any
other theatre in London. Miss Alma Murray played with remarkable
power—quite startlingly at some points—whilst her strength lasted.
When it began to fail (which occurred, it seemed to me, after the third
act), she husbanded it so skilfully, and managed her part with so much
tact, that her inability to give full breadth and intensity to the more
formidable passages in the last act only won additional sympathy for her
from the very few who felt the shortcoming. Shelley does not seem to
have thought of the limits to human endurance, and the possibility of

6. Poem (1813) in nine cantos by Shelley.

contriving intervals of rest and relief during the player's task, which he made about as arduous as three successive performances of Juliet or Pauline Deschappelles[7] on the same day would be. Not a line of the play was cut: only a few were forgotten. Mr Hermann Vezin did what he could with the part of Cenci, and did it very well considering the impossibility of such an impersonation to an actor who happily cannot make a monster of himself. Mr Leonard Outram had the most important of the really feasible parts: that of Orsino; and his treatment of it confirmed the high estimate of his ability which his performance as Valence, in Colombe's Birthday, caused the Browning Society and their guests to form last year at St George's Hall. Miss Maude Brennan's[8] appearance was surprisingly in accordance with the description of Lucretia in Shelley's historical document; but the effect was not quite satisfactory from the artistic point of view. Mr de Cordova and Mr Foss came off with credit as Giacomo and Marzio; and Mr Mark Ambient's[9] earnestness helped him through the self-sacrifice of playing the tragic boy Bernardo Cenci. A prologue by Mr John Todhunter,[10] in which Mr Browning, who was present, was pointedly apostrophized, was recited by Mr Outram. A rough-and-ready orchestra played the most sublime pieces in their repertory: the overture to Masaniello, Lucrezia Borgia,[11] and the like, with the best intentions.

[LOVE'S LABOR'S LOST]
(*Our Corner*, August 1886)

A performance of Love's Labor's Lost is a sort of entertainment to be valued rather for Shakespear's sake than for its own. The Dramatic Students did not tempt many people into the St James's Theatre on the sultry afternoon of the 2nd July by the experiment; and it is perhaps as well that they did not, for their efforts bore much the same relation to fine acting as the play does to Antony and Cleopatra. They failed not only in skill and finish, but in intelligence. Having gathered from their study of the play that they must all be very amusing and in desperately high spirits, they set to work to pro-

7. Title character of *The Lady of Lyons* (1838) by Edward Bulwer-Lytton (1803–73).

8. (1855–1915).

9. Dramatist and actor (1860–1937).

10. Irish dramatist (1839–1916).

11. *Masaniello Overture* by Daniel François Esprit Aubert (1782–1871); *Lucrezia Borgia* by Gaetano Donizetti (1797–1848).

duce that effect by being obstreperous in action, and in speech full of the unnatural archness by which people with no sense of humor betray their deficiency when they desire to appear jocund. Though they devoutly believed the play a funny one, they did not see the joke themselves, and so, ill at ease in their merriment, forgot that dignity and grace may be presumed to have tempered the wit of the gentlemen of the Court of Navarre, and the vivacity of the ladies of the Court of France. In some scenes, consequently, the performance was like an Elizabethan version of High Life Below Stairs.[1] I shall say nothing of the feminine parts, except that they were all unfortunately cast. The men were better. Mr. G. R. Foss as Boyet and Mr Frank Evans as Holofernes were quite efficient; and Mr Lugg[2] as Costard, though as yet a raw actor and prone to overdo his business, enlivened the performance considerably by his fun and mimetic turn. He sang When Icicles Hung by the Wall with commendable spirit, and with the recklessness of a man who has got the tune on his ear and considers that it is the conductor's business to keep the band with the singer, which poor Herr Schoening tried gallantly to do, with more or less success. Mr Bernard Gould and Mr de Cordova, as Biron[3] and Armado, were next best; but they made very little of their large share of the best opportunities of the afternoon. Mr Gould's gaiety lacked dignity and variety: he swaggered restlessly and frittered away all the music of his lines. His colleague looked Armado, but did not act him. Mr de Cordova is always picturesque; but his elocution, correct as far as it goes, is monotonous; and the adaptability and subtlety which go to constitute that impersonative power which is the distinctive faculty of the actor are not at present apparent in him. His qualifications, so far, are those of an artist's model: he has yet to make himself an actor.

The play itself shewed more vitality than might have been expected. Three hundred years ago, its would-be wits, with their forced smartness, their indecent waggeries, their snobbish sneers at poverty, and their illbred and ill-natured mockery of age and natural infirmity, passed more easily as ideal compounds of soldier, courtier, and scholar than they can nowadays. Among people of moderate culture in this century they would be ostracized as insufferable cads. Something of their taste survives in the puns and chaff of such plays as those of the late H. J. Byron, and even in the productions of so able a writer as Mr Gilbert, who seems to consider a comic opera incomplete without a middleaged woman in it to be ridiculed because she is no longer young and pretty.[4] Most of us, it is to be hoped,

1. (1759) by the Reverend James Townley (1714–78).
2. William Lugg (1852–1940).
3. The character's name is usually spelled Berowne.
4. Henry James Byron (1834–84); William (later Sir William) Schwenck Gilbert (1836–1911).

have grace enough to regard Ruth, Lady Jane, Katisha, and the rest as detestable blemishes on Mr Gilbert's works.[5] Much of Love's Labor's Lost is as objectionable and more tedious. Nothing, it seems to me, but a perverse hero-worship can see much to admire in the badinage of Biron and Rosaline. Benedick and Beatrice are better; and Orlando and Rosalind much better: still, they repeatedly annoy us by repartees of which the trivial ingenuity by no means compensates the silliness, coarseness, or malice. It is not until Shakespear's great period began with the XVII century that, in Measure for Measure, we find this sort of thing shewn in its proper light and put in its proper place in the person of Lucio, whose embryonic stages may be traced in Mercutio and Biron. Fortunately for Love's Labor's Lost, Biron is not quite so bad as Mercutio: you never absolutely long to kick him off the stage as you long to kick Mercutio when he makes game of the Nurse. And Shakespear, though a very feeble beginner then in comparison to the master he subsequently became, was already too far on the way to his greatness to fail completely when he set himself to write a sunny, joyous, and delightful play. Much of the verse is charming: even when it is rhymed doggerel it is full of that bewitching Shakespearean music which tempts the susceptible critic to sugar his ink and declare that Shakespear can do no wrong. The construction of the play is simple and effective. The only absolutely impossible situation was that of Biron hiding in the tree to overlook the king, who presently hides to watch Longaville, who in turn spies on Dumain; as the result of which we had three out of the four gentlemen shouting "asides" through the sylvan stillness, No. 1 being inaudible to 2, 3, and 4; No. 2 audible to No. 1, but not to 3 and 4; No. 3 audible to 1 and 2, but not to No. 4; and No. 4 audible to all the rest, but himself temporarily stone deaf. Shakespear has certainly succeeded in making this arrangement intelligible; but the Dramatic Students' stage manager did not succeed in making it credible. For Shakespear's sake one can make-believe a good deal; but here the illusion was too thin. Matters might have been mended had Biron climbed among the foliage of the tree instead of affixing himself to the trunk in an attitude so precarious and so extraordinarily prominent that Dumain (or perhaps it was Longaville), though supposed to be unconscious of his presence, could not refrain from staring at him as if fascinated for several seconds. On the whole, I am not sure that Love's Labor's Lost is worth reviving at this time of day; but I am bound to add that if it were announced tomorrow with an adequate cast, I should make a point of seeing it.

5. In *The Pirates of Penzance* (1879), *Patience* (1881), and *The Mikado* (1885), respectively.

[DELSARTISM][1]
C (*Our Corner*, September 1886)

On Saturday afternoon, the 31st July, Mr and Mrs Edmund Russell gave a lecture on what has been dubbed (though not by the lecturers) "del Sartism." Mrs Russell, a clever and interesting lady, had made her mark during the season in London society; and Mr Russell had played up to her, more or less intentionally, by wearing a colored silk neckcloth instead of the usual white tie, and taking himself and everyone else so seriously that he was soon described in newspaper paragraphs as "beautiful Edmund Russell" and compared to Mr Oscar Wilde: not the staid and responsible Mr Oscar Wilde of today, but the youth whose favorite freak it was to encourage foolish people to identify him with the imaginary "esthete" invented by Mr du Maurier.[2] Mr Russell was pointed out to me one evening as an American who had brought us over a new religion, or philosophy, or esthetic doctrine, or (the manner of my informant implied) some such tomfoolery. I had the pleasure of a brief conversation with him later on, and found him, apart from a certain not too oppressive gravity, as of a man with a mission of some sort, an unexceptionable young American gentleman, still full of the novelty of being in London, well mannered, with a characteristic transatlantic touch of formality occasionally recollected and put on with a certain degree of artistic method in Mr Russell's case, and that pleasant readiness to give and anxiety to get information which makes an American a conversational godsend in an English social gathering of well-to-do people. Subsequently I learned from a newspaper paragraph that Mr Russell was a professor of del Sartism. This probably conveyed no definite idea to more than two or three score people in London; but I was by chance one of the two or three score. The oddest acquaintance I ever formed was with an ex-opera singer, who, in searching throughout Europe for that phoenix, a perfect singing master, had fallen into the hands of del Sarte, and had recognized in him an artist of extraordinarily subtle perception and noble taste; a faultless teacher of elocution, deportment, and gesture; and a philosophic

1. François Delsarte (1811–71), widely infuential French acting teacher who aimed to codify external manifestations of speech and gesture with mathematical precision. In this article, and elsewhere, his surname would be written "del Sarte."

2. Oscar Fingal O'Flahertie Wills Wilde (1854–1900), known as a wit and aesthete, would write his brilliant comedies in the next decade. George (Louis Palmella Busson) du Maurier (1834–96), a satirist and cartoonist for *Punch*, would be author of the best-selling novel *Trilby* (1894).

student as well as a practical master of his profession. Whether del Sarte was actually all this or not, I of course cannot say; but it does not overstate the impression he produced upon my poor friend D.,[3] who was a trustworthy judge, having previously tried nearly every famous master in Europe. D.'s ambition, in fact, was to become an improved del Sarte himself, and he might perhaps have succeeded but for extreme thinskinnedness and an incorrigible infirmity of will, which left him, in spite of his considerable artistic gifts, his fine voice, lofty aspirations, and imposing person, a mere builder of castles in the air. Thus, although a knowledge of the English language would have been of the utmost value to him, he contrived to spend twelve years in London without learning to carry on a conversation in it. Indeed, properly speaking, he knew no language at all; for he had forgotten his native Alsatian dialect of German, and had adopted an unacademic French, which, though appalingly fluent, was seldom free from quaint Italian locutions and scraps of slang from all the countries in which he had sojourned. He told me a good deal about del Sarte; though to this day I do not exactly know how much of his theory of artistic training was del Sarte's and how much D.'s. On one point he was quite clear. Del Sarte's knowledge of singing (in the restricted sense of producing the voice) was limited to a shrewd suspicion of his own ignorance. He had broken his voice by sheer ill-usage long before D. knew him; but his skill in declamation, and his command of facial expression, enabled him nevertheless to sing certain airs with striking effect. Mr Russell admits that del Sarte's voice had failed, but ascribes the failure to extreme privation in early life. D., who knew better, no longer lives to dispute the point. He died in a London hospital of a complaint which to a man rich enough to command careful treatment and nursing in his own house would have been a trifle,[4] leaving implanted in me sufficient interest in del Sarte to induce me to pay a couple of shillings for admission to the pit of Drury Lane Theatre on the 31st July.

My impression of the lecture was that its delivery would not have satisfied del Sarte except at a few points, whilst its style was ill-adapted to engage the faith of a British audience. Mr Russell told anecdotes of del Sarte which neither I nor, I suspect, anyone else present, believed. The story about his being jocularly challenged by a manager to whom he applied for an engagement to go before the public dressed in rags as he was, and sing to them; his acceptance of the challenge; and his immediate success, is probably just as true as the romance of his refusing to

3. Richard Deck, d. 1882.
4. Inflammation of the prostate. His treatment at University Hospital, London, was so poorly handled that he was unable to rid himself of the fever caused by the passing of the catheter.

interrupt a train of thought in order to appear before an audience of three thousand people then waiting to hear him lecture. No doubt Mr Russell thinks these tales true; but he was wrong to repeat them without giving sufficient dates, authorities, and circumstances to convince sceptics that truth is sometimes stranger than fiction. Even when fortified in this way, the story would be impolitic; as the only effect of persuading the British public that del Sarte was a hero of romance will be to convince it that he was an unpractical one. Mr Russell's delivery lacks spontaneity. He is preoccupied with his method; betrays that he is repeating by rote a pre-pared address; and adopts as his normal facial expression a sort of tragic mask which may have been appropriate enough to del Sarte in the act of declaiming a recitative by Gluck, but which was extremely ill-chosen by a strange lecturer with a suspicious British audience to win over. A still greater error, and one into which Mrs Russell subsequently plunged, was that of acting the lecture as if it were a dramatic monologue, and even accompanying it with imitative gestures. Imagine a temperance lecturer quaffing imaginary goblets and reeling about the platform; or a Socialist orator enforcing the moral of the factory acts by imitating the motion of a power loom! How the people would laugh! How del Sarte's ghost, if present and capable of utterance, would unravel the confusion between representation and persuasion, concentration and irrelevance, which had led the speaker astray! Mrs Russell did even worse than this from a del Sartean point of view. Her normal attitude, instead of being one of perfect equilibrium, was not even upright. She constantly swayed and stooped, sometimes with a lateral movement which was distressing and unmean-ing; and she held her arms downwards, with the forearms turned out-ward at an ungraceful oblique angle which was exactly equal at both sides (a curiously elementary blunder). Further, she was draped and made up to so little advantage that I hardly recognized the remarkably interesting and attractive young lady who had been pointed out to me in private as Mr Russell's wife. I give, with some remorse, these unfavorable impressions for what they are worth, hoping that they may be at least as helpful as the no-criticism which the lecture has so far elicited. Now for the pleasanter duty of pointing out the qualities which convinced the little audience that there was something in del Sartism in spite of the mistakes of its exponents.

First, there was Mr Russell's excellent enunciation, unforced and per-fectly clear. A few obscure vowels were suppressed, as in galry for gal-lery; a final r introduced, as in arenar for arena; and an occasional Americanism—jahschoor for gesture, for example—let slip. But these are not defects of method. Del Sarte taught verbal enunciation with rigorous thoroughness; and Mr Russell fully justified his school by af-fording us the rare treat of publicly hearing without effort a gentleman

speaking without effort. Mrs Russell, being constitutionally restless, neither speaks nor stands so del Sarteanly as her husband; but she, too,
makes herself audible without the least effort. Perhaps the most striking
proof of the soundness of her master's method was the magic change in
her appearance when she left off her set speech and came to the real
business of her lecture. The set speech was not only—to be quite
frank—three parts bosh, but it was, as I have already complained,
treated as drama instead of as rhetoric. But when Mrs Russell proceeded
to practical illustration, she at once became graceful and expressive; and
the audience became interested and friendly.

If Mr Russell intends to settle in London as a teacher of artistic speech
and motion, he will at least find plenty of clumsy people to teach, on and off
the stage. Everyone who has compared Signor Salvini's Hamlet with Mr
Irving's or Mr Wilson Barrett's knows that the technique of these English
actors is, in comparison with that of the great Italian, violent, wasteful, and
futile.[5] Even Mrs Kendal, accomplished as she is, sometimes wavers and
proceeds tentatively in passages such as Madame Ristori treats with firmness and certainty.[6] It is true that there must always be bad actors: men
and women who honestly see nothing in classical acting, and rant because
they think ranting fine; but there will also be a large body of players
without sufficient insight to discover the laws of good acting for themselves, but quite well able to appreciate them when they are revealed by a
subtle and intelligent teacher such as del Sarte was. Acting and stage
business are based on the sciences of expression and esthetics: our knowledge of them grows and gives us trustworthy rules just as our knowledge of
arithmetic does. There are certain conditions of graceful motion which are
as much past debate, and as binding on the most original genius, as that
two and two make four; and these conditions should, without any reference to acting, be taught to every child by its dancing master, who ought,
by the bye, to be a highly educated artist with the social standing of a
university professor. If Mr and Mrs Russell will make a start in transform-
ing a nation of bad speakers, bad walkers, vile singers, and prematurely
stale athletes into healthy, lasting, and graceful creatures, I, for one, am
quite ready to take their mission seriously, believing, as I do, that what del
Sarte taught had an important bearing on moral, as popularly distinguished from physical, welfare. But I hope they will not be tempted to
make a mystery of their profession; or to deny that del Sarte's conclusions
have been arrived at independently before, during, and since his time in
various places by men who never heard of him; or in any way to claim a

5. Tommaso Salvini (1829–1916), Italian actor of worldwide fame, particularly in tragic
roles. In 1847 he joined the company of Ristori (see below), who was then starting her
successful career.

6. Adelaide Ristori (1822–1906), Italian tragic actress of worldwide fame.

monopoly of acute reasoning and cultivated taste in the arts of speech and gesture. Finally, I will place on record (perhaps it may prove useful to Mrs Russell) the polyglot precept which my unfortunate friend D. used to address to his sturdy British pupils when they set their teeth and clenched their fists in the face of a difficulty. "Ma non," he would exclaim: "il faut que tout çela vient absolument sans effort. Soyez sheepish, mon enfant: soyez sheepish."[7]

MACBETH AT THE OLYMPIC
C/Un (*Pall Mall Gazette*, 9 September 1886)

"This" says Mr Barnes to Mrs Conover every evening "is a sorry sight."[1] "A foolish thought, to say a sorry sight" retorts Mrs Conover. And she is right; since, whatever excuse there may be for Mr Barnes's remark, an honest and careful attempt to shew the people a great play at easy prices is by no means a sorry sight when the shortcomings, no matter how numerous, are unavoidable. "You are requested not to shoot at the performers, as they are doing their level best," is an appeal rarely disregarded among the pioneers of civilization. No such motto is exhibited at the Olympic; but the people do not hiss; for there too the performers are doing their level best. Mrs Conover could not play Lady Macbeth better than she does, though that is the least of her merits. Manageresses have ere now been stingy, slovenly, and disrespectful to Shakespear: she has been liberal and conscientious. The scenery, the dresses, and the musical arrangements have been provided by a hand that disdains the cheap and nasty. Under these circumstances the public is bound to be indulgent; and it certainly deserves credit for resisting all temptations to be otherwise. For, though the acting fulfils all the expectations that were formed when the play was announced, there is no denying that these expectations were not entirely favorable. As Signor Salvini, Mr Irving, Mr Wilson Barrett, Mr Hermann Vezin, and Mr Barry Sullivan[2] were engaged elsewhere, Mrs Conover had to depend for her Macbeth on Mr Barnes, an estimable actor, robust rather than subtle, and withal so colloquial in his

7. But no, all of that must come absolutely without effort. Be sheepish, my child, be sheepish.

1. Anna Conover, actress, lessee, manager.

2. Thomas Barry Sullivan (1821–91), romantic actor who specialized in Shakespearean roles, was better known in the English provinces and Ireland than in London. As a boy, Shaw saw him perform in Dublin; he remained one of Shaw's favorite actors.

delivery that when he demands of the witches why "upon this blasted heath" they stop his way, the unlettered gallery mistakes the adjective for a familiar but profane expletive, coming not incongruously from a hardy thane fresh from the rough life and free conversation of the camp. His pronunciation of "prologue" as "proloag" (instead of prolog) must be condemned, as its general adoption might lead to demagoag, cataloag, epiloag, and other unpleasantness. The only textual novelty introduced by him is the following:

> My way of life is fallen
> Into the sere, the yellow leaf, and that
> Which should accompany old age as honor.
> Love, obedience, troops of friends I must not,
> &c., &c.

On the whole, the more usual division of lines seems preferable. Mr. J. D. Beveridge, whose playing is manly and sympathetic, occasionally suggests that Macduff was an Irishman.[3]

> What! All me purty chickens an'dhr damn!

he exclaims. This, however, occurs when he is overpowered by emotion, and may be excused on that account, Diderot's paradox notwithstanding.[4] Banquo (Mr Dewhurst)[5] is best after his death. Duncan is an affable monarch, shrinking from ceremony and blank verse. Locke's music[6] goes off with great spirit, although "the echo of a hollow hill" comes back nearly quarter of a tone flat. Hecate, it subsequently appears, has learned her notes from this wild music of nature; for she is often even flatter than the echo. But the most exasperating musical feature of the performance is an undignified platitude of a trumpet flourish, which, after about forty noisy repetitions, inspires a detestation which the first cornet player has finally to appease by a stirring performance (encored) of The Lost Chord.[7]

Mrs Conover, perhaps arguing that one must walk before one can run, has learned to whisper before she can speak. Her voiceless "Come, come. To bed: to bed: to bed:" is almost her only satisfactorily audible utterance. Tone will develop by and bye; but the more distinctly she makes herself

---

3. James D. Beveridge (1844–1926), Irish actor.

4. *The Paradox of Acting* (c. 1773) by Denis Diderot (1713–84), editor of the first encyclopedia as well as playwright and critic of drama and theater: the actor himself is unmoved despite the emotion he reproduces.

5. Jonathan Dewhurst (d. 1913).

6. Matthew Locke (1632?–77), English composer.

7. By Sir Arthur Sullivan (1842–1900).

heard, the more careful must she be not to call Banquo "Bonco," catch "ketch," spent "spannt," safer "say for," or bellman "bellmin." As yet she is so occupied with the precepts of her instructors in elocution and deportment that she has but little attention to spare for Lady Macbeth. When she has thoroughly assimilated her lessons, she will be able to walk and will speak without constant consideration, and then her impersonative talent will have unhindered way. Meanwhile, her personal attractions, her taste in costume, and her devotion to Shakespear recommend her to the forbearance of the public. In judging her ambitious sally, it should not be forgotten that actresses who aspire to poetic tragedy must, pending the establishment of a school, not only learn their business on the stage, but take a theatre for the purpose. One result of this state of things is that a few months' practice will cure Mrs Conover, as far as Shakespear is concerned, of all the ineptitudes which she does not share with the experienced actors who support her. When she learns to make herself heard, to correct a few doubtful vowels, and to avoid walking pointedly to the footlights and delivering soliloquies straight across them at the audience, besides bowing at her first entrance, she will be no worse technically than the others, and will consequently be able to command full credit for any superiority she may enjoy as a player.

Mr Bruce Smith has made the moon full in the scene of the witches' cauldron.[8] This does not accord with the text, wherein Hecate expressly mentions the corner of the moon, which should therefore be new. If not, where is the corner of a full moon?

MISS ALMA MURRAY AS BEATRICE CENCI
C (Speech at Shelley Society Meeting, 9 March 1887)[1]

Mr G. Bernard Shaw said that in his opinion The Cenci was a play unworthy of the genius of Shelley. It was simply an abomination, an accumulation of horrors partaking of the nature of a *tour de force*, and probably written by Shelley merely to satisfy his ambition of producing something for the stage. He considered it as bad a piece of work as a man

---

8. Scenic artist (1855?-1942).

1. B. L. Mosely, *Miss Alma Murray as Beatrice Cenci* (1887). Stenographic report in third person, but proofread and revised by Shaw.

of Shelley's genius could be capable of, so bad indeed that it was hardly worth discussion. In his opinion excision would not remedy the fault of the play after the third act.

With regard to Miss Murray's acting, he could not regard it, great as it undoubtedly was, as an entirely perfect and adequate performance. He did not see, in the absence of a National Theatre, where she could have got the requisite experience, but he had no doubt that, after a measure of training at such an institution, Miss Murray's Beatrice would be all that Mr Mosely described it.[2] He thought the physical strain of the part beyond what any actress could completely bear, and he believed that after the third act he detected signs of exhaustion in Miss Murray which prevented her giving full effect to some of the more formidable passages, notably the one in which she turns on the judge and her guards thus:

> and what a tyrant thou art,
> And what slaves these; and what a world we make,
> The oppressor and the oppressed.

He attributed it to her admirable method alone that she was enabled to conceal this fact from her audience.

As a whole he thought the Cenci performance could not have been improved upon by the company of any London theatre.

[HELD BY THE ENEMY (I)][1]
C/Un (*Manchester Guardian*, 4 April 1887)

Mr C. Overton's[2] matinée at the Princess's Theatre yesterday was the means of introducing to the London public a popular American melodrama which is likely soon to be familiar to English playgoers. The scene is laid in a Southern city occupied by Northern forces during the Civil War, the conflicting interests and passions of which enable the author to dispense with the usual mechanical villainy. The first act is pleasant and

2. Benjamin L. Mosely (1845?-1916), who had lectured on Alma Murray's acting, was a Browningite, Shelleyite, and Wagnerite.

1. *Held by the Enemy* (1886) by William Gillette (1855–1937), American actor and dramatist.

2. Charles Overton (d.1898), actor and dramatist.

interesting; the second short and very exciting; the third—the weakest in the play—noisy and full of trashy heroics; and the fourth contains a highly novel situation. It is brought about by an attempt to have a wounded man (condemned to death as a spy) carried out of his captors' hands as a corpse. The plot is discovered, but when the ambulance is stopped and examined it is found that the occupant is indeed dead. The fifth act resembles the first, and reaches a happy and natural ending. On the whole the performance was successful. Miss Alma Murray impresses one more and more with her ability as an emotional actress, and Mr Charles Warner[3] impersonated the hero in his usual effective manner.

[HELD BY THE ENEMY (II)]
C/Un (*Scottish Leader* [Edinburgh], 11 April 1887)

Mr William Gillette's drama, Held by the Enemy, was produced tonight at the Princess['s] Theatre with the same decided success that attended its trial at a matinée on the 2nd inst. This second performance was by no means an improvement on the first. All kinds of mishaps occurred throughout the evening. The Clockmaker's Hat,[1] which served as a "curtain raiser" for the occasion, was played in such a fashion as to provoke cries of "Shut up" and "Ring down the curtain" from the occupants of the pit. Ill-humor was thus, unfortunately, established before the business of the evening began, and it soon became apparent that the expectations roused by the success of the previous Saturday had made the performers nervous. Mr Yorke Stephens,[2] who, as the impudent special artist at the seat of war, was all fluency and self-possession on the 2nd, had to turn to the prompter for help in one of his first speeches, and subsequently found several of his colleagues in the same predicament to keep him thoroughly in countenance. At the end of the second act, which produced such a sensation before, Mr Gardiner[3] became so excited that he lost his self-

3. (1846–1909).
1. (1855), adapted by Thomas William Robertson (1829–71) from *Le chapeau d'un horloger* (1854) by Emelie Delphine Gay de Girardin (1804–55).
2. Stephens (1860–1937) would play Bluntschli in the first production of *Arms and the Man*, 1894.
3. E. W. Gardiner (d. 1899).

command, and had much reason to be thankful that his inadvertent substitution of nature for art proved as effective as it did. Mr Calhaem's[4] impersonation of the aged black servant was, indeed, the only one in which no falling-off was perceptible. Even behind the scenes matters went wrong. The phenomena attending the explosion in the third act, where the scene is wrecked by the bursting of a shell, were curiously inverted. First a barrel in the middle of the stage spontaneously and noiselessly fell to pieces. A little later some splintered rafters appeared in the doorway. A decent interval ensued, and finally the cause of these effects followed with a thundering report, with much fire and smoke. It is not to be wondered at that after these hitches the players were somewhat disconcerted and hesitating. Nevertheless the success of the play was confirmed. It is only a clever popular melodrama of no special literary excellence, and conventional enough in its assumptions as to character and motive; but the judgment with which the author has turned to account the serious interest of the American Civil War, the tact with which the more distressing scenes are relieved and varied, and the welcome elimination of the customary villain, with his vulgar and tiresome mechanism of rejected love, revenge, forged documents, murders of which the blame falls on the hero, and so forth, all tend to raise Held by the Enemy out of the ruck of commonplace melodrama, and to secure for it a wider popularity than any play of the kind since The Silver King. The acting will leave little to be desired when the scare of the first night is over. Miss Alma Murray has gained ground by her Rachel M'Creery, and Mr Charles Warner has lost none by his Colonel Prescott. Miss Annie Hughes[5] and Mr Yorke Stephens have made a hit in the passages of comedy between Thomas Henry Bean and Susan M'Creery. Mr Calhaem's Uncle Rufus could hardly be improved upon. Mr E. W. Gardiner allows his part to run away with him, but his sincerity is not ineffective in its way. Mrs Canninge, Mr William Rignold,[6] and Mr C. Overton give due weight to the more important subsidiary characters. It may be added that the play is not given exactly as in America, where it has for some time been popular. In the original version Lieutenant Hayne, the spy, was wounded in the first act, and did not appear in the third. In response to a call for the author, Mr Warner informed the audience that Mr Gillette sailed for the United States last Thursday.

4. Stanislaus Calhaem (d. 1901).
5. Mrs Edmund Maurice (1869–1954).
6. Mrs George Canninge; William Rignold (d. 1904).

[LA DOCTORESSE]
C/Un (*Pall Mall Gazette*, 11 July 1887)

After many postponements, Mr Burnand's adaptation of La Doctoresse[1] has got through its first night at the Globe Theatre: got through by the skin of its teeth. So far, it is impossible to say what its fate will be. On Saturday the interest of the play and the patience of the audience were repeatedly on the point of flickering out. The first act was lively and promising; the second disappointing; the third so placidly dull that Mr Penley, in despair, gave up the part of Alfred Blossom and relapsed into the Rev Robert Spalding,[2] at whom the audience were content to laugh goodhumoredly at intervals until the curtain fell, when the pent-up weariness relieved itself in a little hissing, too languid to put Mr Burnand out of countenance as he responded to the applause of his friends. Still the play is not past praying for. The pleasant and novel character of the lady doctor, capitally played in the manner of Mrs Kendal by Miss Fanny Carson, would alone suffice to keep it on the stage but for the last act, in which she is supposed to return to womanly virtue by deliberately degrading herself to the level of the paltry fop to whom she is married. This is too bad even for farcical comedy, but there is no reason why it should not be remedied by the excision of a few silly speeches, and of the ineffective scene with the lad Bertie Cameron. Mr Penley, as the husband, was of course ludicrous; the part, however, is an acting part; and acting is not Mr Penley's forte. Mr Kemble's overdone make-up, and Miss Victor's desperately unsuccessful attempt to speak with an Irish brogue were the only unacceptable points in their important share of the proceedings.[3] Miss Cissy Grahame and Mr Hill[4] did what they could with somewhat barren parts that, like the whole play, promised well and turned out poorly. Fifteen other characters frequented the stage in the course of the performance without provoking serious inquiry as to who they were and what they were there for.

---

1. Francis Cowley Burnand (1836–1917); *La doctoresse* (The Lady Doctor, 1885) by Henri Bocage (1835–1917) and Paul Ferrier (1843–1920).

2. William Sydney Penley (1861/62–1912); Rev. Spalding is a character in *The Private Secretary* (1883) by Charles (later Sir Charles) Henry Hawtrey (1858–1923).

3. Henry Kemble (1848–1907); Mary Anne Victor (d. 1907).

4. Grahame (b. 1862); William J. Hill (1834–88).

IN FIVE ACTS AND IN BLANK VERSE
Un (*Pall Mall Gazette*, 14 July 1887)

This is the sort of thing we have all done. We hardly know what blank verse is; and of the nature of an "act" we are utterly ignorant; yet we do it to give expression to the Shakespear in us. Nobody reads it when it is done: not even the reviewer who makes merry over it: there is always enough in the first page he chances on to inspire as many gibes as we are worth. No matter: gibe as he may, he has done it himself. In his bureau, pushed to the back of the drawer over-littered and dusty, is his Cromwell, or Raleigh, or Caracatacus, or Timur, "an historical tragedy, in five acts and in blank verse." If it was not published, that proves only that the author was poor. Had he possessed the needful spare cash, some book-seller of the High Street, Oxford, would have been the richer and the British Museum catalogue the longer for him. The present writer was poor, and gave in before the third act was finished.[1] What is he that he should sit in judgment on others? Yet there were some fine lines in it: finer than any he has since reviewed.

What is blank verse?

ESTHER. Place a light in my uncle's study.

Is that blank verse? The author of Wiclif[2] says it is. But "be it not said, thought, understood"; for no actor that ever mouthed could make blank verse of it. It should run:

ESTHER. A light place in mine uncle's study.

Or, better still, to save the ambiguity and lack of distinction:

> Yare, yare, good Esther;
> Pour thou the petrol oil: snip thou the wick:
> Light up the study.

This at least cannot be mistaken for sane prose. Mr David Graham,[3] the author of King James the First, an Historical, &c., understands the matter

---

1. Shaw refers to his *Passion Play*, written in 1878. Actually, he gave in before the third act was begun.

2. Charles Edward Sayle (1864–1924), English poet, who published *Wiclif*, his only play, anonymously.

3. (b. 1854).

better than the author of Wiclif. He featly turns the phrase "Italian-minuet" into blank verse, thus:

> A minuet
> Straight from the sunny land of Italy.

This is the true blank manner. Mr Graham's characters even laugh in blank verse:

> QUEEN. And the tenth General Council would break up.
>   With—No decision come to. Ha! ha!
> ABBOTT.   Ha! ha! ha!

Here the measured cachinnation preserves the stately march of tragedy. There is one dangerous line in King James the First; and that, significantly enough, adorns a scene in which the author soars into prose. The King, early in the third act, says:

> This is of interest: go on.

In actual performance that line might bring down the house, very much as it was brought down by Kemble's[4] delivery of

> And when this solemn mockery is o'er—

in Ireland's Vortigern, which, by the bye, was really not a bad historical tragedy as such works go. Vortigern was a well intended blend of what most people like in Macbeth and Cibber's Richard III. Should any of our popular plagiarists need a benefit Mr Irving might find a worse play to revive for the occasion. The Elizabethan lymph does not seem to have taken satisfactorily with the author of Wiclif. The late R. H. Horne would have thought him a poor creature.[5] His metaphors lack immensity; and his language is too little magniloquent. A successor of Chapman and Marlowe cannot afford to play the gentle student, avoid hyperbole, and treat history in the modern sociological spirit. Nor must he so delude himself as to hope that moderate prose, cut into lengths, will pass as even Byronic blank verse. The following is a sample of Wiclif:

> Yet had I wished a little more of life,
> A little longer still to ply the oar,

4. John Philip Kemble (1757–1823), actor-manager.
5. Richard Henry Hengist Horne (1803–84), poet who wrote *Orion* (1843).

> To carry still yet further [still yet further is
>   really too bad][6] on her way
> The ship we sail by. We shall sleep at last
> Beneath the bunkers when our work is done,
> And go unconsciously to our longed haven.

Now, in cold blood, was this worth doing? Is the thought beyond the capacity of a well educated poodle? Is the expression specially apt, harmonious, forcible, suggestive, or in any way interesting? Is the metaphor not fitted to Tom Tug[7] rather than to Wiclif? Were bunkers known years before steam navigation? and are dead shipmen buried in them? Is the power to write such lines any excuse for the error of thinking them worth writing? Above all, does the consciousness of having written an historical tragedy compensate one for the publisher's bill, and the unpleasantness of being publicly asked such questions as the foregoing?

Mr W. W. Aldred, in his "drama of an Ancient Democracy"[8] has lain low for his reviewers in a singular fashion. We have all heard of the gentlemen who send rolls of blank paper to theatrical managers, and receive them again with neat notes to the effect that "their play" has been read attentively, but is not suitable for presentation on the boards. Mr Aldred, having so poor an opinion of human nature as to suspect that reviewers, lost to all professional honor, criticize dramas in blank verse without having anxiously scrutinized every line, has laid a trap. On page 176, in the middle of the fifth act, the scene being ancient Rome, the time 82 B.C., and the personages Sulla, Pompey, Cæsar, Cato, &c., he has interpolated, without connection, warning, or explanation, a ballad, as follows:

> POMPEIUS. Ah, do not jest, Tullius. I am too
>   anxious in mind to laugh with you.
>   Ballad.
> The last shots are growing more distant,
>   Hushed is the cannon's roar.
> And he lies with his soldiers around him,
>   All silent for evermore. &c., &c., &c.

In the flush of triumph at having escaped this ambush, one may magnanimously admit that there are gleams of nature, of wit, of observation, and even of verse, in The Love Affair. The style is free from mere verbiage and line padding; and it changes with freedom from the old and stately to the modern and familiar. For example:

---

6. Shaw's brackets.
7. *Tom Tug, or The Regatta* (1816), a burletta, author unknown.
8. Subtitle of *The Love Affair* (publ 1887).

Oh, now methinks the Fates look at the clock
And wait the hour which is to change the world

is Marlovian. But the following smacks of our own time:

CENTURION (*to soldiers*) Halt! Shoulder arms! Fall out!
SPY. You understand?
CENTURION. No; I'm damned if I do. But I will carry out the
orders. Fall in! Dress your ranks! Left wheel! Quick march!

LOYAL LOVE AT THE GAIETY
C/Un (*Pall Mall Gazette*, 15 August 1887)

Mrs Brown Potter[1] is getting on. That is, she is continuing her course of
practical dramatic training before the eyes of the critical London public,
with its long memory for anything savoring of failure, and despite the
great unwisdom of the proceeding, she is undoubtedly adding to her
personal charms, the ability which comes only from experience. Her bad
luck, however, or bad management or bad judgment, still pursues her,
and Man and Wife and Civil War[2] are now followed by a play in its
essentials less possible than either of them. Loyal Love is a piece of the
most thoroughgoing oldfashioned romance than has been attempted in
London for a long time. The Lady of Lyons is commonplace and workaday
beside it. It is written to begin with in blank verse; the scene is carefully
laid nowhere in particular; the most clearly specified place to which the
reader is introduced is called "The Garden in the Mountains"; the sentiment is the most superfine and the tragedy of the most approved, not to
say trite, character; Shakespear has been ransacked for some of the
leading ideas and the form of not a few of the verses, the first two acts
being Hamlet with Iago added, and the conclusion being Romeo and
Juliet with a reviving heroine. Such speeches as "All may be well"[3] are
taken bodily; the Count di Luna is transferred straight from Trovatore,
and even the ultra-familiar "Is this a dream?—Then waking would be

1. Mrs (James) Brown Potter (Cora Urquhart Potter, 1859–1936), American actress and
celebrated beauty of the stage.
2. *Man and Wife* (1885) by D. S. James; *Civil War* (1887) by Herman C. Merivale.
3. The last line of Claudius's soliloquy in *Hamlet*, III.iii.

pain"[4] is placed almost in these identical words, at a critical moment, in the mouth of the heroine. Ross Neil is understood to be the name of a lady who has written many plays, published some, and had one or two produced,[5] and while a good deal of her blank verse refuses so uncompromisingly to scan that the actors wisely recited it as downright prose, other parts are really not without considerable merit. "To watch until the sun with his bright shield first touched the western waves," and

> Now praised be Heaven that gives me to thy sight
> And my starved soul from darkness into light;

And

> Rest assured that I will shortly find
> What lies beyond that ivy mantled wall,

are chiefly rubbish, but on the other hand "Speak what you will, you speak it to the air," and "What should we fear that threatens not our love," and "together always, you and I and love," and a man "that has no rotten spot of pity in his heart," and the curtain of the second act

> How fair! how fair!
> I never saw a woman fair til now,

are lines good in themselves, and proved very effective in their delivery.

Mrs Brown Potter is peculiarly unfortunate in this play because the part is exactly suited by nature to her personality. She is preeminently a heroine of high-pitched romance. Her face, her hair, her voice, and evidently her temperament fit her exactly to wander in the wood where Knights of the Round Table are straying in search of beautiful and fancy-taught and hapless maidens; and hand in hand with Sir Galahad, or perhaps more accurately with Sir Launcelot, Mrs Brown Potter would be ideally situated. But Iñez—not Inez as they all called it—has no chance in Loyal Love. It is all too absurd even to be romantic. Nevertheless Mrs Brown Potter has not been seen before to such advantage as on Saturday night, and the novel compliment of a genuinely enthusiastic double recall must have been a welcome balm to heal the wounds of previous neglect, and a still more welcome presage of the future when not only the actress but the play shall find favor. She is becoming more at home on the stage, more natural, more

4. From "Let Me Dream Again" (1875) by Arthur Sullivan and B. C. Stephenson, a song that was immensely popular for a long time.
5. Isabella Harwood (c. 1840–88).

forcible without approaching rant, and on several occasions on Saturday, at the moment of taking the cold poison for instance, she exhibited excellent self-control and saved an otherwise absurd situation. Her charms and her pluck will ultimately carry her through. One may be fairly sure of that now, but we would once more strongly urge upon her to practise for the present only before provincial eyes.

Mr Kyrle Bellew[6] always makes a suitable hero of romance, and he plays quite up to his best form in this one. Several times on Saturday, when the audience was just slipping into laughter at the inherent absurdity of the action and the verse, his sincerity and vigor rescued the piece. Mr Willard seems curiously misplaced at the Gaiety Theatre, but he was thoroughly at home in the Iago-like part provided for him, and as he is one of our best actors, he did everything that was possible with it. The audience was on the whole very well disposed, and Mrs Brown Potter would have no difficulty in seeing that she is growing in the appreciation of the public. The two or three ill-conditioned persons of the counter-jumping species who stayed behind and howled for a long time, are a familiar nuisance by this time, and before long they may well be personally recognized and treated as they so richly deserve.

MOLIÈRE'S THINGS
C/Un (*Pall Mall Gazette*, 1 December 1887)

"I like seeing Molière's things: it's education, isn't it?" said an English gentleman, rather more publicly than he intended, perhaps, to an English lady last night at Tartuffe.[1] It was not only education, but amusement— wonderfully fresh, too, considering its age. M. Fébvre,[2] though he has one or two fine moments, is not an interesting Tartuffe; he is incorrigibly dry and dignified. The honors of the evening were carried off by M. Talbot,[3] who played Orgon with extraordinary unction, and, with the help of Madame de Sevry's tact as Elmire, and Lefevre's[4] spirit and grace as Dorine, kept the house alert and in good humor until the curtain fell. Decidedly, Molière is not dead yet.

6. Harold Kyrle Bellew (1855–1911), actor and dramatist.
1. (1664).
2. Alexandre Fréderic Fébre (1835–1916).
3. Denis Talbot (Denis-Stanislas Montalant, 1824–1904).
4. Aline (?) Lefevre.

PLAYS AND PLAYERS
C/Un (*The Pioneer*, Allahabad, India, 7 February [written 13 January] 1888)

If there is a man in England with a good play in him, now is his time. The theatres are ready; the actors are ready; the money is ready; the public is ready; and yet the man does not turn up. At the same time, nobody with the gift of assurance objects to putting himself up for the vacancy, just to oblige an expectant world. One can do no worse than fail; and, after all, failure does not mean a shower bath of dead cats and bottles, but only a bow before the curtain to the goodnatured applause of your friends in the stalls who are used to you, whilst the pit and gallery stare, perplexed but dumb, at the futile personality from whose visions they have been striving to extract some entertainment and edification. Instantaneous photographs should be taken of authors responding to curtain calls; and composites should be made for the guidance of managers of the unsuccessful ones. I am afraid that the successful ones are not numerous enough to make a useful composite. For many are called, but few are chosen.[1]

Although I must immediately proceed to deal with an essay in dramatic authorship made on Wednesday afternoon (January 11th) by Mr Hamilton Aïdé,[2] I by no means class him with the astonishing persons who inspired the above, and whose ineffectual afternoon flittings behind the footlights sometimes make me wonder at the presumption which offers for a journeyman one who has not yet begun his apprenticeship. Mr Hamilton Aïdé has proved his adroitness in many of the lighter departments of art; and if there was no reason on Wednesday morning to believe him an able dramatist, there was at least no strong case prima facie to the contrary. The performance took place at the Haymarket Theatre for the benefit of the Actors' Benevolent Fund, and began with The Ballad Monger, which has disappeared from the nightly bill since the production of Mr Buchanan's Partners; Miss Marion Terry was ill; and her part, Loyse, was taken by a novice, Miss Beatrice Lamb, who came off with unexpected honors.[3] At the end of the little play, Mr Beerbohm Tree,[4] still in

---

1. Matthew 22:14.
2. (1826–1906), French-English dramatist.
3. *The Ballad Monger* (1887) by Walter (later Sir Walter) Besant (1836–1901), novelist and dramatist, and W. H. Pollock (d. 1887), actor and dramatist; *Partners* (1888); Marion Terry (1853–1930); Beatrice Lamb (b. 1866).
4. Herbert (later Sir Herbert) Beerbohm Tree (1853–1917).

the costume of Gringoire, came upon the stage to announce that the fund would gain "considerably above £100" by the performance. Then came Mr Hamilton Aïdé's Incognito. With Miss Geneviève Ward in the cast, one might have expected an Incognito on the model of Forget-Me-Not;[5] and, indeed, except that that adventuress had changed her sex and been consequently taken in hand by Mr Beerbohm Tree, there was not much difference.

The action takes place at Nice, where Mrs Mordaunt (Miss Geneviève Ward) is staying with her son Eric. His mentor is one Smith, gifted with good sense and correct morals, but otherwise unattractive. Now, Mrs Mordaunt is the wife of Cracroft, a rascal who, having absconded years ago after killing Smith's father (for which, somehow, one does not feel disposed to be too hard on him), is supposed to have been drowned. Of course, he was not drowned; and equally of course, he turns up at Nice and undertakes the instruction of his son, whom he meets but does not recognize, in the arts of gambling and of nomadic high life generally.

Now, it so happens that Mlle de Florian (Mrs Beerbohm Tree),[6] whose sister young Eric is going to marry, is also there. She is fascinated by Cracroft, *alias* Vincent (Mr Beerbohm Tree); for he, with all his faults, is extremely well dressed, and not badly preserved considering his age. It is as her suitor that he is introduced to his widow (if one may use that expression); and Mrs Mordaunt is immediately struck with terror at the thought of his evil influence coming between her and their son; still she feels that she must not, by remaining silent, allow him to contract a bigamous marriage with the sister of his own son's wife. As the introduction of Mrs Mordaunt to Cracroft is the climax of the first act, the means of getting her rid of him is the problem of the second. She asks him—they are supposed not to have recognized oneanother—to call upon her. He does so, and behaves in a way which she describes as heartless, but which strikes the dispassionate spectator as full of candor and reasonableness. When with a tragic air she reveals her identity, he assures her quietly that he knew her all along, but did not wish to intrude on her under the circumstances. He does not affect emotions which, however they might become him in the eyes of the gallery, he is far from feeling; and when he addresses her, after a slight natural hesitation, as "Margaret," he adds, very prettily, "I think your name w a s Margaret, if I recollect aright." Mrs Mordaunt makes a scene; calls him "Man, man" and "Monster," and so forth; and finally offers him half her fortune to leave Nice and sign a written engagement never to cross her path again. To this

5. Geneviève (later Dame Geneviève, Countess de Guerbel) Ward (1838–1922); *Forget-Me-Not* (1879) by Herman Merivale and F. Crawford Grove (d. 1902).
6. Maud (Holt) Beerbohm Tree (1863–1937).

proposition he replies that he believes both halves of her fortune are legally his already. The written engagement he properly ignores as an absurdity. Mrs Mordaunt does not seem to know that his legal claims are obsolete; and she can give him no good reason for renouncing Mlle de Florian and going about his business. At last she tells the young lady that Mr Vincent is a rascal. Mademoiselle, offended, stands up for her admirer, and demands explanations. None being forthcoming, she declines to believe the aspersion; and Vincent-Cracroft is getting the best of it when Smith enters and demolishes him by a reference to his murdered father. The adventurer agrees to leave Nice, and, as the curtain falls, politely expresses his determination to be even with Smith someday.

In the third act, Cracroft tries to induce Mlle de Florian to follow him to Paris, and explains that his lips are sealed to the necessity for his flight for a regard for Mrs Mordaunt's honor. Mrs Mordaunt overhears this; and it is too much for her. She comes forward and tells the whole truth to Mlle de Florian, who spurns her suitor conclusively, and leaves the room. Thereupon his annoyance carries him to the length of strangling Mrs Mordaunt; but he is interrupted by the entry of Eric, who, after contemplating the operation for a moment in grieved surprise, proceeds to strangle Cracroft. On Cracroft's gasping out "I am your—" Mrs Mordaunt interferes and stops the revelation by stopping the parricide. Smith then appears and tells Cracroft that he is wanted by the police for a recent swindle. He flies, and is presently seen from the balcony struggling with the police. Presently he reenters as a fugitive and throws himself on the mercy of his wife, who hides him behind the window curtain. The police enter and proceed to search the premises. Eric sees the curtain stir and directs attention to it. Bang! A terrific scream from Mrs Mordaunt; and Eric drags aside the curtain. Cracroft, a ghastly figure, is seen standing for a moment: then he sways sullenly and falls dead on the carpet. His suicide is extremely opportune for everybody but himself; and it is with some vague sense of this that somebody—Smith, I think—says: "He is before a Judge where there is no *incognito*," an idiotic remark which brings the curtain down on him.

It would take a very original view of these materials to make a strong or fresh play out of them; and Mr Hamilton Aïdé's view is certainly not original. The moment Mrs Mordaunt declared that she was Cracroft's "wife in the sight of God," as if the Divine view of the situation were necessarily the unreasonable and cruel one, it was evident that the play was to proceed on the usual lines, and that the persons of the drama would spend a couple of hours in thinking stale thoughts and uttering stale speeches about stale incidents. The public enjoyed it more than they would have done if they went to the theatre as often as I have to go. Mr Hamilton Aïdé is a gentleman with an artistic turn and some address; and

I congratulate him on having risked nothing, lost nothing, and gained a surer foothold on the stage. As to the performance, I suspect that it included much improvisation; for the minor characters occasionally shewed a disposition to interrupt oneanother, to speak all at once, and to make suspiciously weak remarks. Mr and Mrs Beerbohm Tree and Miss Geneviève Ward had evidently left the unimportant scenes in which they took no part to the more precarious opportunities of rehearsal. Miss Ward's cooperation with the Haymarket company was part of the novelty of the occasion. She played with reassuring breadth and firmness: a little monotonously, perhaps, but still satisfactorily. Mrs Beerbohm Tree had the only part that shewed any power of characterization; and she played it very cleverly indeed. Mr Beerbohm Tree's Cracroft could hardly have been improved on; but it would be paying him a poor compliment to imply that the impersonation made any great demand on his powers. None of the other parts was of sufficient weight to need comment.

The death of Mr W. H. Chippendale[7] is no loss to the contemporary stage, for he has for years been unable to act, but it seems like a personal sorrow to many playgoers throughout the country—to more, perhaps, in the provinces than in London. "Old Chip" was always good—at least I never saw him play badly, though I have seen him in parts which did not in the least suit him. The characters in which he was really incomparable, however, were those three delightful old gentlemen, Sir Peter Teazle, Sir Anthony Absolute, and Mr Hardcastle.[8] I cannot believe that these parts were ever played better than by "Old Chip" at his best. Other actors may have extracted different and equally good effects from them, but none can have incarnated them more thoroughly or more amiably. He had not much opportunity of playing these parts in London, for the old comedies did not appear very frequently in the Haymarket bill, but on the provincial tours of the Haymarket company they were the most popular comedies in the repertory. The School for Scandal was, indeed, admirably cast with Chippendale as Sir Peter, Mrs Kendal as Lady Teazle, Mr Kendal as Charles Surface, Compton as Crabtree, Buckstone as Backbite, Howe as Joseph Surface, and Mrs Chippendale as Mrs Candour.[9] As You Like It, too, was altogether delightful with Mrs Kendal as Rosalind, Mr Kendal as Orlando, Compton as Touchstone, and Chippendale as Adam. This was one of his most beautiful performances. Mr Kendal told me the other day that, often as he had played Orlando to Chippendale's Adam, the old

7. William H. Chippendale (1801–88).

8. In·The School for Scandal (1777) and The Rivals (1775) by Richard Brinsley Sheridan (1751–1816) and Goldsmith's She Stoops to Conquer (1773), respectively.

9. Henry Compton (1805–77); John Baldwin Buckstone (1802–79), also a dramatist; Mary Jane Chippendale (1837?-88).

man's acting always brought tears to his eyes: and I can well believe it. He died at the age of 87, having made his first appearance in 1819 and his last in 1879. It is said that he was a "reader" in Ballantyne's printing office when Waverley[10] was passing through the press, but as he was then only thirteen this is scarcely credible. There is no doubt, however, that he was connected with the Ballantynes in some capacity or other, and that he attracted the notice of Sir Walter Scott, who had known his father, also an actor in his day. Perhaps he was the "printer's devil" who carried to the "great unknown" the proofs of his unacknowledged bantling, first-born of so great a race.

Mr J. L. Toole, it appears, does not lose with advancing years his taste for practical jokes. One Sunday evening some weeks ago Mr Thomas Thorne gave a farewell dinner party in honor of Mr Charles Warner, then on the point of starting for Australia. There were present, besides Mr Toole and the guest of the evening, Mr David James, Mr Clement Scott, Mr Joseph Knight, Mr Pettitt, Mr Alport (acting manager at the Vaudeville Theatre), and some others.[11] It so happened that Mr Pettitt had that day met, in a restaurant, a well known dramatist (I shall call him Mr A.), who being of an irascible turn of mind, was declaiming very violently against another well known dramatist, Mr X., whom he accused of having stolen from him the comic scenes of a certain play. As Mr Thorne's guests were sitting over their dessert Mr X. came in, and the conversation turned on another plagiarism supposed to have been commited by Mr X., who vehemently protested his innocence. Now, Mr Pettitt, who does not love Mr X., saw in this an opportunity of annoying him. "I dont know about that, X.," he said, "but this I can tell you, that youll have some trouble with A—. He vows you stole the idea of your stableboy from his groom, and he's going about swearing he'll have your blood. He's mad, you know: I met him today positively raving." Mr X. was thunderstruck at this fresh accusation (a preposterous one, I may say) and the annoyance he shewed prompted Mr Toole to carry the joke a step further. Half an hour passed, nothing more having been said of the matter, when a thundering knock was heard at the front door. Presently Mr Thorne's butler entered the room and loudly announced "Mr A!" Up jumped Mr Thorne in a state of grievous perplexity. "I cannot possibly see Mr A. just now" he said. "Tell him that I am entertaining a party of friends, and that I shall be greatly obliged if he will call again some other time." Exit the butler, to return immediately with the news that Mr A. insisted on seeing Mr Thorne. "Alport," said Mr

10. (1814) by Sir Walter Scott.
11. John Lawrence Toole (1830–1906), actor-manager; Thomas Thorne (1841–1918), actor; David James (1839–93), actor; Clement William Scott (1841–1904), drama critic and playwright; Joseph Knight (1829–1907), theater historian and drama critic; Henry Pettitt (b. 1881), actor and dramatist; Sydney Alport (d. 1906), manager.

Thorne, "wont you go and try to get rid of him?" Off went Mr Alport, and before long a noise of furious altercation was heard outside; then the front door was heard to close and all breathed more freely. Mr Alport soon reentered, panting and pale, to report that A. declared that he knew X. was there, that he had come determined to wreak summary vengeance upon him, and had only departed on his (Alport's) solemn assurance that he had been misinformed and X. was n o t there. Poor X. was naturally a good deal discomposed by all this; for without anything approaching to physical cowardice, one may very well shrink from an unseemly brawl with an infuriated playwright, and A. is notorious as at once a powerful and a passionate man. Conviviality was resumed and all went merrily for an hour or so, when once more there came a thunder peal on the knocker; the bell was rung violently; and the butler, in great perturbation, appeared to announce "Mr A. come again, sir." "Alport," said Mr Thorne, "you must tackle him again." Out went Mr Alport, and this time a noise like the furious banging about of furniture was heard. Presently Mr Alport reappeared, very much out of breath, to state that A. had somehow assured himself of Mr X.'s presence, and had returned more violent than ever, having meanwhile been inflaming his wrath at a public house round the corner. By dint of much diplomacy, Mr Alport had persuaded him to cool himself down for the moment, in the back garden. Mr X. was now concerting measures for flight; but Mr Toole reassured him. "No, no " he said. "You stay here. Youll be all right. Warner and I will go out and get rid of him." Accordingly Mr Toole and Mr Warner set off on their forlorn hope, and, before long, sounds of a terrific struggle were heard outside. Then, once more, the front door slammed, and Mr Toole and Mr Warner rushed in, Mr Toole with his necktie on one side and his waistcoat torn open, Mr Warner holding his hand to his head as though he had received a severe blow. They had to expel the savage A. by main force, and reported that he was now lying in wait for his victim in the street outside. By this time, however, the joke had been carried far enough, and Mr X. was informed that he had been the victim of a hoax. Such are the entertainments of our entertainers!

[THE BLOT IN THE 'SCUTCHEON]
C/Un (*The Star*, 16 March 1888)

The Browning Society's performance of The Blot in the 'Scutcheon at the Olympic Theatre yesterday afternoon was better than its first attempt at

St George's Hall a couple of years ago, by just as much as Miss Alma
Murray is better than the lady amateur who attempted the part of Mildred
on that occasion. It was, indeed, a case of Miss Alma Murray first and the
rest nowhere. The experiments of the Browning Society and the Dramatic Students have shewn that there is a public ready for the poetic
drama as soon as ever the poetic drama be ready for its public. But that
millennium will not be until we have actors capable of speaking verse.
Browning, when the mere action of his play flags, lifts and prolongs
apparently exhausted situations by bursts of poetry, sometimes of rare
melody and grandeur. Spoken as these invariably are nowadays, with
deplorable poverty of emphasis and without variety of pitch or tone color,
they lose both music and meaning; and Browning is voted a bore by
everybody present, except Dr Furnivall and the sworn Browningites. Dr
Furnivall is so far right in that it is not Browning's fault; it is rather the
misfortune of the actors. But the tedium remains; for one Miss Alma
Murray cannot make a whole cast any more than one swallow can make a
summer. However, let the Browning Society keep at it by all means. It is
only by venturing into deep water that one learns to swim.

THE TAMING OF THE SHREW
Ps (To the Editor, *Pall Mall Gazette*,
8 June 1888, signed Horatia Ribbonson)

They say that the American woman is the most advanced woman to be
found at present on this planet. I am an Englishwoman, just come up,
frivolously enough, from Devon to enjoy a few weeks of the season in
London, and at the very first theatre I visit I find an American woman
playing Katherine in The Taming of the Shrew: a piece which is one vile
insult to womanhood and manhood from the first word to the last. I think
no woman should enter a theatre where that play is being performed; and
I should not have stayed to witness it myself, but that, having been told
that the Daly company[1] had restored Shakespear's version to the stage, I
desired to see with my own eyes whether any civilized audience would
stand its brutality. Of course it was not Shakespear: it was only Garrick
adulterated by Shakespear. Instead of Shakespear's coarse, thick-skinned
money hunter, who sets to work to tame his wife exactly as brutal people
tame animals or children—that is, by breaking their spirit by domineer-

1. Augustin Daly (1839–99), American dramatist and manager.

ing cruelty—we had Garrick's fop who tries to "shut up" his wife by behaving worse than she: a plan which is often tried by foolish and ill-mannered husbands in real life, and one which invariably fails ignominiously, as it deserves to. The gentleman who plays Petruchio at Daly's—I neither know nor desire to know his name[2]—does what he can to persuade the audience that he is not in earnest, and that the whole play is a farce, just as Garrick before him found it necessary to do; but in spite of his fine clothes, even at the wedding, and his winks and smirks when Katharine is not looking, he cannot make the spectacle of a man cracking a heavy whip at a starving woman otherwise than disgusting and unmanly. In an age when a woman was a mere chattel, Katherine's degrading speech about

> Thy husband is thy lord, thy life, thy keeper,
> Thy head, thy sovereign: one that cares for thee
>   (with a whip),
> And for thy maintenance commits his body
> To painful labor both by sea and land, &c.

might have passed with an audience of bullies. But imagine a parcel of gentlemen in the stalls at the Gaiety Theatre, half of them perhaps living idly on their wives' incomes, grinning complacently through it as if it were true or even honorably romantic. I am sorry that I did not come to town earlier that I might have made a more timely protest. In the future I hope all men and women who respect oneanother will boycott The Taming of the Shrew until it is driven off the boards.

ROYALTY THEATRE . . . FRENCH V. ENGLISH HISTRIONICS
C/Ps (To Mr Spectator,[1] *The Star*, 1 February 1889, signed Julius Floemmochser)

The reinforcements at the Royalty Theatre having set you spectating at the French plays, I am glad to find that your powerful mind is shaking off the illusion that French acting is better than English. There is a welcome

2. John Drew (1853–1927), founder of an acting family that included the Barrymores; Ada Rehan (Ada Crehan, 1860–1916), played Katherine.
   1. Arthur Bingham Walkley (1855–1926), drama critic of *The Star* under the pseudonym "Spectator." Shaw's *Man and Superman* contains an Epistle Dedicatory to him.

hedge-note in your last utterance. The French players are still "unapproachable," but only when "judged by their own standard, their own system: that Gallic system of histrionics which holds illusion and naturalness subservient to perfect elocution and consummate finish of style." In short, Mr Spectator, you are beginning to find them out; and you instinctively prepare us for your discovery that the French actor is no actor at all, but only that horrible speaking automaton, an elocutionist, and that his proceedings on the stage represent not life, but that empty simulacrum called a style. In genuine Art, *le style, c'est l'homme.*[2] On the French stage, *l'homme, c'est le style.*

Let us consider the theory of French acting for a moment. What does a man do on the stage? According to the Conservatoire, he stands, sits, walks, kneels, and speaks: Talma's[3] acting consisted in these things; so does Mr Bandmann's.[4] Good. What is art? The pursuit of the beautiful. What then is artistic acting? Obviously, standing, sitting, walking, kneeling, and speaking in the most beautiful way. How is the most beautiful way to be ascertained? Simply by experiment; but the question is practically idle; for the most beautiful way h a s been ascertained at the Comédie Française, the traditions of which are complete. Hence, to become a perfect classical actor, you have now only to go to the Conservatoire and learn the most beautiful way of standing, sitting, walking, kneeling, pronouncing all the vowels and consonants of which plays are mere permutations and combinations; and there you are. It is not difficult. After a little practice, you become accustomed to shaking a man's right hand with your left (an action ideally beautiful in profile); to kneeling on the left knee when you are on the *coté cour,* and your right when you are on the *coté jardin;*[5] to picking up a handkerchief as if you had a knee-joint in one leg only; to walking as if you had no knees at all; and to doing a number of other things in the perfectly beautiful way in which nobody ever does or ever will do them off the stage. And when you get an engagement, everyone else in the company will do them in the same way, thereby producing a classic unity of effect, whilst the critics, who always like to know exactly what to look for, will be delighted. It saves them the trouble. So much for the theory of French acting.

2. *"Le style c'est l'homme même"* (The style is the man himself)—Georges Louis Leclerc, Comte de Buffon (1707–88), *Discourse on Style* (1753).

3. François Joseph Talma (1763–1826), French actor of the romantic period who, despite Shaw's observation to the contrary, is credited with having substituted historically accurate and realistically natural acting for the dignified repose of classical acting, and for realistically portraying passion and horror.

4. Daniel E. Bandmann (1840–1905), German tragedian.

5. After the French Revolution, the terms for, respectively, "stage left" (literally, the court side: toward the Court of the Carousel monument in Paris) and "stage right" (literally, the garden side: toward the Tuileries Gardens in Paris).

Now for the practice. If—but seriously, Mr Spectator, do you think this is worth wasting ink and paper on? Inimitable *farceur* as you are in your whimsical moments, dare even you assert that the Court company or the American Daly company would be permitted by the public to adopt for a single night the imbecile conventions of the French stage, or its childish stage business, or its brutal thumping signals? Imagine Mr John Drew standing stock still, with his nose carefully in profile, to declaim the part of Petruchio! Imagine the whole cast of Mamma[6] drawn up in a straight line across the proscenium at Sloane Square, waiting for their cues like a family standing to be photographed. Imagine, if you can, even the roughest provincial English company making Hernani[7] as like a superior Madame Tussaud's as the Comédie Française did in spite of the passion of Sarah Bernhardt and the conviction of Malvau.[8] Imagine an English actor coming on the stage, walking straight to the footlights, and beginning instantly, music hall style, to spout a soliloquy pointedly at the audience! The truth is that the French players have everything to learn from us: even the greatest of them, M. Coquelin, plays Mascarille[9] better perhaps than any English comedian could. If he had to play it by accident with his arm in a sling, he would do it better; but would any sane critic attribute the superiority to the sling, and complain of the English actor's habit of leaving his arms free? Can you not see, Mr Spectator, that whether M. Coquelin be a better or worse actor on the whole than either Mr Hare or Mr Joseph Jefferson, yet his acting is hampered by pedantic formalities from which both Mr Hare and Mr Jefferson are completely emancipated? The ordinary French actor is not merely hampered by these formalities; he is galvanized by them. In the words of Partridge,[10] anyone can see that he is an actor, because he has only one way—the French actor's way—of doing and saying everything on the stage. We have as many ways as we have actors, as many styles as we have actors, as many individuals as we have actors. A truce then to your flatteries[11] of this rococo "Gallic system of histrionics": to your compliments about "perfect elocution" (not one in 20 of them speaks decent French) and "consummate finish," which— pardon me—is only your incorrigible politeness to foreigners. Bid them rather come to the English, consider their ways, and be wise.

6. (1888) by Sydney Grundy (1848–1914), adapted from *Les surprises de divorce* (1880) by Alexandre Bisson (1848–1912) and Antony Mars (1861–1915).

7. (1830) by Victor Hugo (1802–85).

8. Jeanne Adèle Andrée Malvau (b. 1862).

9. Benoît Constant Coquelin (1841–1909); character in *Les Précieuses ridicules* (1659) by Molière.

10. Character in the novel *Tom Jones* (1749) by Henry Fielding (1707–54).

11. "A truce to this light conversation"—Bulwer-Lytton, *Rienzi* (novel, 1835).

ACTING, BY ONE WHO DOES NOT BELIEVE IN IT; OR THE PLACE OF THE STAGE IN THE FOOL'S PARADISE OF ART
F (Paper read at a meeting of the Reverend Stewart D. Headlam's Church and Stage Guild, 5 February 1889)[1]

[U:] I have chosen an aggressive title for my paper today because I wanted to attract one or two people who do not take a serious view of the Church and Stage Guild, and who would not have come if they did not think that I intended to have what is called a lark at the Guild's expense. As I have no such design, the lark will be entirely at the expense of those—if there be any such—who expect to hear me poking fun and paradox at my hosts. I take the Guild very seriously indeed; and if I fail to come to a harmonious understanding with them this afternoon—which is possible—it will be because I take them more seriously than they are as yet prepared to take themselves. I shall not be surprised if they dismiss questions I wish to raise, with the remark that it will be time enough to trouble about them when the stage player has his or her right to be buried in consecrated ground; to be received at the Lord's table; and to be admitted everywhere as the social equal of the Mincing Lane man,[2] his respectable wife, and his innocent daughter. These ambitions, however, do not strongly appeal to me. Not only actors, but even nonconformists are now buried in consecrated ground as a rule; but so far as feeling that a point has been gained thereby, I strongly object, in the interests of the living, to their being buried at all. However, let that pass: it is the House of Life, not the House of Death, that really matters. As to the Lord's table, I can speak only as an outsider; but if I thoroughly comprehend the theory of it, the exclusion, on class grounds, of any Christian from it, instantly destroys its special character and reduces it to the level of an ordinary supper at Willis's Rooms.[3] It seems to me that it will be safer to

---

1. Conflation of unpublished H at BL and report drafted by Shaw in the *Church Reformer*, March 1889, rpt. PP. The Rev. Stewart D. Headlam (1847–1924) was a Christian Socialist minister.

2. One who auctioned tea, coffee, sugar, and other commodities in an auction room situated in the London street of this name.

3. A famous London club and assembly rooms until 1890, when they became a restaurant.

be the stage dancer turned away from the altar rails than the participant in the blasphemy of a spurious communion, when the question comes up for final settlement, a contingency which both parties regard as certain. On the question of social ostracism, I can only say to those who are shut out from the reunions paid for out of the profits of Mincing Lane, that I congratulate them on the privilege. The actress's independence of what calls itself "society" is the most enviable feature in her lot; and I could wish her nothing worse than a visiting list and a basketful of at-home cards. I have noticed that the leaders of the London stage, who can now lionize when and where they please, very soon voluntarily restrict their social excursions to circles in which there never at any time seems to have been any prejudice against them.

Today I propose to pass over all the stock grievances of the players, and to start from the ground occupied by a very considerable class in the community—including perhaps everyone in this room—[to] whom the excommunication and outlawry of the actor are senseless superstitions. These enlightened persons go to the theatre, read dramatic criticism, and buy photographs of Miss Ellen Terry, which they exhibit in fancy frames on their mantelpieces without causing scandal among their elder relatives. In their lives the latest Shakespearean revival at the Lyceum Theatre is an event of quite perceptible magnitude. At the approach of winter, they wonder what Mr Irving will open his theatre with. They never wonder what the unemployed will fill their stomachs with. They can therefore hardly be accused of underrating the social importance of the stage. [:U]

One of the questions I came here to ask is: Would the Church and Stage Guild be satisfied if it could bring the whole nation, including the Bishop of London and his Puritanic following, into the same frame of mind with the theatre-loving folk? If so, then certainly it does not take itself so seriously as I take it; for my own feeling is that the attitude of the Puritan towards the actor is to be prefered to that of the "first-nighter" by just as much superstitious horror as is easier to bear than contempt. [U:] The majority of stage fanciers, having no occasion to make up their minds on the subject, are not conscious of any serious view of the actor as a man at all. But one section of them has to make up its mind, and that pretty definitely, in order to earn its living. I allude, of course, to the dramatic critics. All able critics despise actors. Garrick ranks as the greatest of English actors; and no piece of theatrical criticism in the language bears a higher stamp than Johnson's description of Garrick. He did not say "Punch has no feelings"; but he did say Punch, and he thought Punch.[4] A

4. The voice of Samuel Johnson (1709–84), coming from the wings, annoyed David Garrick while he was trying to concentrate on his role. When someone backstage asked Johnson to be silent out of consideraton for the actor's feelings, Johnson supposedly responded, "Punch has no feelings."

few years ago, one of the ablest and most conscientious of our critics, in a book about the theatre,[5] expressed a strong disparagement of actors as men, and justified it with unsparing directness. Not one of his colleagues took up arms on the other side: all tacitly agreed with him, though probably some of them held it not honesty to have it thus set down.[6] Again, when Mr William Archer, in collecting materials for his recently published and important criticism of Diderot's famous paradox, applied to an acute French critic for help in getting information from French actors, the acute one replied that it would be useless, as the actors had neither the intelligence to understand the questions nor the candor to answer them seriously.[7] All the critics have had something to say about Mr Archer's book; but none of them have taken exception to the French writer's estimate of French actors. It is to be considered, too, that since actors are better paid than their critics, it is certain that if the latter believed the profession of acting to be a thoroughly worthy one, it is one of the very first they would think of for their sons. The fact that it is usually the last one they can endure the thought of, seems to me a striking proof of the depth of their mistrust and contempt for the men and women who are merely players. Little as they esteem their own profession, even that is prefered by them for their boys to the sham career of the stage. Salvini's critic?—yes, if nothing better is to be had; but Salvini himself?—no, not on any terms. [:U]

The ground of this contempt is obvious. The dramatic critic believes in acting, and regards the man on the stage as an actor. In English, acting means shamming. The critic, then, despises the stage as a sham, and the actor as a wretched imposter, disguised in the toga of Cæsar, and spouting the words of Shakespear—a creature with the trappings and the language of a hero, but with the will of a vain mummer—a fellow that fights without courage, dares without danger, is eloquent without ideas, commands without power, suffers without self-denial, loves without passion, and comes between the author and the stalls much as a plaster of colored earths and oil comes between Raphael and the Cook's tourist.[8]

Now, even if the actor admitted that he is no more than this, which no actor does, he could retort with terrible effect on his literary censor. "Granted" he might say "that I am incapable of doing the deeds I play at, pray do you practise what you write about? If it takes no real courage to

5. *About the Theatre*, by William Archer (London, 1886), 211–38. [G.B.S.]

6. *Hamlet*, II.ii.

7. *Masks or Faces?* (1888). The French critic, whose reply but not his name Archer cites in his Introduction, is Jules Lemaître (1853–1914), also a dramatist, short-story writer, and novelist.

8. Cook's Tours is an international travel agency founded in England by Thomas Cook (1808–92).

fight a duel on the stage, does it take any more to write the scene in which that duel occurs, or to criticize my fencing? If I have not the will of Cæsar, had Shakespear, or have you? Is the inventor of the sham scene, or the actor, or the delighted spectator the most futile and ridiculous from your point of view? Are the real virtues and the real trials of the actor at all different from those of the men who condemn him without being intelligent enough to see that they must plead guilty themselves to every count of their indictment?" The reason that this retort is not actually made is that it satisfies neither the enthusiastic actor, who generally does suppose that he only needs opportunity to become all that he pretends to be on the stage, nor even the cynical actor, who at least knows that, in proportion to the opportunities, competent actors of Cæsar are much scarcer than real Cæsars, the inevitable conclusion being that, for any given man whatsoever, it is much easier to be Cæsar than to act Cæsar. And, indeed, if we consider how the achievements for which we honor Cæsar are really the achievements of many thousands typified in one; if we could subtract from his reputation the fame of the things he never did, and of those which fell out quite otherwise than he intended them; if we make due allowance, in calculating his stature, for the height of the wave of fortune on whose crest he came to his throne, then, considering on the other hand how absolutely individual and unaided is the task of the great actor, we begin to perceive why no actor has any consciousness of paradox when he hears it claimed that the first Napoleon was a commonplace person in comparison with Talma. I might go on to make some amends to the critic by pointing out that he may with some color claim to be the rarest of all species in his highest development, but such a process would be endless and idle. I have said enough to bear the trite moral that the contempt of one for another, whether it be the contempt of the historian for the statesman, the critic for the actor, or the virtuous person for the vicious, is as a hood to the eyes and a wired lawn to the feet of the seeker for justice.

But there is a contempt that is harder to escape than any of these: the contempt of a man for himself. The most terrible doubt that can come into the mind of a man is a doubt as to the utility of his profession. No class of men—not even doctors—can be more subject to that sort of doubt than artists. All art is play; and all play is make-believe. How, then, be an artist without being a rogue and a vagabond? Make a few thousand a year and the thing is done, as far as the opinion of others is concerned. But self-opinion, what of that? Must the novelist know himself a liar, the sculptor an image-man, the actor an illusion, a simulacrum, a glittering sword that will not cut, a burnished hydrant that will not extinguish anything? The eternal cry of the artist's soul is for salvation in this matter: the claim which he most vehemently urges is the claim for the reality of what he plays at. When Mr Archer, in a methodical, coldblooded way, asked Signor Salvini whether his stage tears came unbidden; whether his voice broke of its own accord; whether he deliberately simulated affections without physically experiencing them; whether, to put it shortly, he was anything more than an elaboration of the doll which says "mamma," and shuts its eyes when it is placed in a horizontal position, the great actor replied, with the roar of a wounded lion: "If you do not weep in the agony of grief; if you do not blush with shame, glow with love, tremble with terror; if your eyes do not become bloodshot with rage; if you yourself do not intimately experience whatever befits the diverse characters and passions you represent, you can never thoroughly transfuse into the hearts of your audience the sentiment of the situation." No protest could be more passionate than this. The greatest actor of the day proclaims with all his force that he is no actor at all; that there is no such thing as acting; that he is no sham, no puppet, no simulacrum, but in real earnest all that he pretends to be; that Othello, Hamlet, and Samson are not merely aped by him, but live and suffer in his person; that he throws himself into them because in them he realizes himself as he never could realize himself in the prosaic parts that are played off the stage, such as those of the stockbroker, the lawyer, the painter, or the dust contractor.

M. Coquelin, on the other hand, renounces his professional reality in the temper in which Diderot renounced the prospect of a hereafter. He shakes his head at the tragedian, and says: "No, my friend: you are not Samson, not Othello, not Hamlet: you are Salvini." It is in vain for the tragedian to accept the statement and declare that Othello is Salvini simply because Salvini is Othello; the comedian has too good a digestion to confuse himself with metaphysics. When Mr Archer interviews him, he replies to the question about the sincerity of the break in his voice by then and there breaking it in a heartrending manner as if it were a walnut. And in this action we have the clue to the citadel of Coquelin's self-respect, which he has maintained in spite of his confession that he is a sham: that is, an actor. He has to depend for his salvation on the pride of the craftsman in his skill, the delight of doing a very difficult thing consummately. That M. Coquelin adds to this the moral satisfaction of believing that the thing he does is beneficial to his fellows we need not doubt: therein alone could consist his superiority to the skilful burglar; but for my part, though I cannot but relish the humorous side of M. Coquelin's theory that Mascarille is nothing but a cleverly worked marionet, I am not imposed on by it for a moment. For if it were sound, what a contemptibly shiftless and limited automaton he would be! Salvini's reason for not impersonating Mascarille is clear. Mascarille is not Salvini; and therefore Salvini cannot be Mascarille. But what is Coquelin's reason for not acting Othello or Hamlet? On his own theory there can be none except that he is an inefficient puppet. I will not insult you by pleading what have been called "physical limitations," and concluding that M. Coquelin is debarred from heroic characters by the upward turn of the tip of his nose. M. Coquelin's presence and voice are far more imposing than those of many actors who have made their mark in tragedy. Avoiding odious comparisons with contemporary players, I would refer you to the photographs of Charles Kean and Ronconi,[9] and to the ample testimony accessible concerning them; and then ask whether you can doubt that M. Coquelin is at least as well fitted for heroic parts by his face, his figure, his voice, and his stage acquirements as either of these tragedians. If M. Coquelin is really an actor, he ought to be able to pass from Mascarille to Hamlet with no more difficulty than Artemus Ward's wax figures passed from the sacred parts they played in New England to the murderers whom they represented in the Wild West.[10]

The truth is, of course, that M. Coquelin is less an actor than any other comedian on the stage. So far from being a mere mask with no individuality, to be put on by Shakespear, Molière, or any other author, he is one of the few points in the human mass at which individuality is concentrated, fixed, gripped in one exceptionally gifted man, who is, consequently, what we call a personality, a man preeminently himself, impossible to disguise, the very last man who could under any circumstances be an actor. Yet this is just what makes him the stage player *par excellence*. We go to see him because we know he will always be Coquelin, because every new part he plays will be some new side of Coquelin or some new light on a familiar side of him, because his best part will be that which shews all sides of him and realizes him wholly to us and to himself. If no such part exists in dramatic literature, then the want of it is the great sorrow and unfulfilment of his life. If he finds such a part, he seizes on it as oxygen seizes on certain metallic bases. In it he becomes for the first time completely real: he has achieved the aspiration of the hero of Ibsen's fantastic play[11] and become himself at last. This is not acting: it is the final escape from acting, the ineffable release from the conventional mask which must be resumed as the artist passes behind the wing, washes off the paint, and goes down into the false lights and simulated interests and passions of the street.

[U:] It must not, however, be inferred that the line which divides fully realized existence from stunted and baffled existence coincides with the

9. Charles Kean (1811–68), son of Edmund; Domenico Ronconi (1772–1839).

10. Artemus Ward was the pen name of Charles Farrar Browne (1834–67), a satirical American writer and lecturer who traveled throughout the country, including the West. A New Englander, he looked like a caricature of the rural Yankee, but he also appeared on stage as hoosiers, blacks, and other American types.

11. *Peer Gynt* (1867).

line which divides the stage from the ordinary world. We are all striving to get cast for the part which most fully realizes us. That strife consists in an attempt to elude certain circumstances or conditions which are fatal to our full play, and the securing of certain other circumstances or conditions which are essential to them. Let us glance at some examples, on the stage and off. In London, where the professional man who begins life in a desperately needy and harassed condition, and rises to a position of comparative affluence, is commoner than elsewhere, we have opportunities of seeing how a character may be lost for want of a few hundred pounds a year.[12] When the professional man is at his lowest ebb: when his patrimony is spent and his practice not yet on a remunerative footing, he usually takes advantage of the lull in his affairs to get married. If his wife is impatient of small economics, fond of society, ambitious, luxurious, and clever, she is unable to realize herself under the conditions of a narrow income; and the pair live a cat-and-dog existence: he cynical and disillusioned; she contemptuous and tired of the whole business. She is set down as a bad wife; and the unhappy marriage is held up as a warning to others craving after the married stage. But the man in the course of time achieves some thousands a year, and so rids his wife of the economic conditions which are unendurable to her, and opens up to her a social career in which at last she can be fully herself. Thus realized, she becomes a delightful person; and her husband falls in love with her again and finds her a perfect wife: so far as human frailty will permit. Whereas if she had been a good cheap housekeeper, and a domesticated and helpful spouse in the poor days, she would probably not know how to spend an income of four figures, and would be uncomfortable, regretful, exacting, and out of place on the higher scale of expenditure. In the one case, the actress's best part is the rich man's wife, in the other the poor man's wife; and whilst the husband of the one remains poor and of the other rich, the public will never know what they are capable of, nor cease to reproach them with, acting their parts badly. [:U]

Let us take another instance. A man has a strong sense of mischievous humor, and a certain mercurial vivacity and agility which make rapid and riotous movement essential to his complete satisfaction. His sense of the ludicrous feeds on his veneration and eats it up. Nevertheless, he is a goodnatured man and possibly a timid one. When he sees a cripple painfully traversing the streets, he is sorry for him, but cannot resist laughing at the notion of knocking his crutches from under him and flying, pur-

---

12. Allusion to George Herbert (1593–1633), *Jacula Prudentum* (1651), No. 499: "For want of a nail the shoe is lost, for want of a shoe the horse is lost, for want of a horse the rider is lost" or to Benjamin Franklin (1706–90), preface (1758) to *Poor Richard's Almanac*, which repeats the statement.

sued by a policeman, only to lie down unexpectedly in his pursuer's path, and upset him, too, in the mud. But he does not do these things, because the cripple would be hurt, and the policeman would make him pay too dearly for his jest. In order to give the fullest expression to the craving of his whimsical side for action and exhibition, he must find a scene where these restraining conditions do not exist. He finds it on the stage or in the circus ring as a clown. This instance is an extremely improbable one, because although to a schoolboy of twelve a career of mischievous trickery without moral responsibility or ulterior risk may seem the fullest self-realization, to the adult man, with his passions and ambitions, it appeals very feebly and intermittently. As far as can be gathered at present, there has never been but one genuine clown: Grimaldi.[13] I myself have never seen one who was not an obvious sham; and I observe that, though everybody agrees that a good harlequinade would be delightful, an actual harlequinade is seldom witnessed except by novices. Still, we all have a clown in us somewhere; and Garrick's Petruchio, Lemaître's Macaire, and Mr Irving's Jingle and Jeremy Didler may be regarded as the outcome of the impulse felt by these actors to realize for a moment the clown in themselves.[14] This, of course, is a realization of only a side of themselves; but there are very few parts in drama which will hold an entire man or woman.

The ordinary actor realizes himself for the most part off the stage in his private character; and only the unrealized residue, which may be the unworthiest part of him, finds its expression on the boards. Sometimes it is a part of him which he would be quite content to leave unrealized if he could afford to drop his profession. The walking gentleman in us does not crave for realization; but if the manager is already provided with a Macbeth, we must place the walking gentleman at his service or else starve. On our way up to Macbeth, we must perforce allow many sides of us to be turned to the footlights which we would fain hide. Embryologists tell us that we have been many strange things in our time. Had you and I been arrested in the early stages of our career, and exhibited, as some of our fellow creatures have been, in bottles of spirits of wine, we must have figured as mere ascidians, or a little later as rudimentary fishes, or reptiles, or birds; for we passed through all these stages on our way to our present vertebrate dignity; and we have still not merely a bone or two and

13. Joseph Grimaldi (1779–1837), traditionally regarded as the funniest English pantomime clown.

14. Frédéric Lemaître (1800–76), French romantic actor. The character are in, respectively, *L'auberge des Adrets* (1823) by Benjamin Antier (1787–1870), Paulyanthe (Alexandre Chapponier), and Saint-Amante (Jean Amand Lacoste), anglicized by Charles Selby (1802?–63) as *Robert Macaire* (1835); *Pickwick* or *Jingle* by Albery; and *Raising the Wind* (1803), by James Kenney (1780–1849).

certain muscles and even organs quite irrelevant to our humanity, but we have even some tastes and habits which seem referable rather to our winged or finned stage than to our sober citizenship. And beyond a doubt, each of us has not only the bird and fish in him, but also—and how much more strongly!—the savage, the barbarian, the hunter and slayer, the warrior, the murderer, the thief, the coward, and the fanatic. How often must the actor, to serve a purpose not his own, but imposed on him by public, author, and manager on pain of starvation, night after night realize in his part the murderer and the coward in him until such realization becomes a mere trick of simulation, and his pleasure in acting becomes a combination of the mere craftsman's pleasure in the cleverness with which he does it, the frail mortal's delight in applause, and the economic man's appreciation of a large salary and a steady engagement!

[U:] One would like to have a candid opinion on the subject from Mr Willard. I feel confident that if he ever takes a theatre for himself, he may attempt Richard or Macbeth, or even Count Cenci; but not the spider.[15] [:U] Next to the plot of a melodrama, the silliest convention in it is the villain. [U:] Some time ago I saw a melodrama entitled Held by the Enemy, and I actually enjoyed it and believed it. It had no plot; it had no villain; and it was a success. It violated the critics' convention, founded on the puppet theory of acting, that a melodrama is successful in proportion as it is melodramatic; and that therefore [:U] a plot must be substituted for a story, and actors and actresses for human beings. [U:] I call these critics' conventions, for I have not done with the dramatic critic yet. [:U] Dramatic criticism is the quintessence of art criticism, which is itself the essence of human folly and ignorance; [U:] so I prefer to approach this part of my subject by a word about Art generally. My own history is, I believe, typical on this point; and I shall not scruple to give it to you with a brevity as severe as the fascination of the subject permits. [:U]

When I was a boy, I was taken to church, to the theatre, to the concert room, and to the public picture gallery. Church proved so unpleasant that I have never gone since, except once when my friend the Warden[16] induced me to go to hear a Bishop, who struck me as excellent material for a dramatic critic. In the theatre, the concert room, and the picture gallery, however, I was happier than anywhere else indoors, and out of mischief. [U:] After this, I need hardly say that I read all the fiction I could lay hands on. I also read anything about Art that came in my way; and it delighted me the more because I could then profusely imagine

15. In *The Silver King* by Jones and Herman, Captain Herbert Skinner is known as "The Spider."
16. The Reverend Stewart Headlam.

pictures from descriptions. I read Vasari[17] with the greatest relish; and bookmakers' books about the opera, or biographies of painters, and composers, actors, singers, or volumes of anecdotes about them not only interested me deeply, but gave me a sense of elevated tone which I never derived from works avowedly of edification. I soon became an accomplished art critic after the fashion of the period to which my books belonged. My authors held for the most part that the figures in a picture should be arranged so as to form a pyramid; and they looked on a foreshortening as a work of piety, honorable in itself. [:U]

I was capable of looking at a picture then, and, if it displeased me, immediately considering whether the figures formed a pyramid, so that, if they did not, I could prove the picture defective because the composition was wrong. And if I saw a picture of a man foreshortened at me in such a way that I could see nothing but the soles of his feet and his eyes looking out between his toes, I marveled at it and almost revered the painter, though veneration was at no time one of my strong points. I did not read dramatic or literary criticism much, and therefore I never explained the failure of a play on the ground that the fourth act was longer than the third, or ascribed the superiority of Great Expectations to Dombey and Son[18] to the effect produced on Dickens by the contemplation of Mr Wilkie Collins's plots;[19] but I said things quite as idiotic, and I can only thank my stars that my sense of what was real in works of art somehow did survive my burst of interest in irrelevant critical conventions and the pretensions of this or that technical method to be absolute.

But the main thing was that this cloud of silly illusions which I supposed to be Art was still my refuge from real life, my asylum from the squalor and snobbery outside, from the bewilderment of a world in which, as in church, everybody was pretending to enjoy what he disliked, and praising one course of conduct whilst pursuing another; above all, from the irksomeness of the struggle for bread and butter. When at last I made a plunge into London, I soon found out that the artistic people were the shirkers of the community. They ran away from their political duties to portfolios of etchings; from their social duties to essays on the delicacies of their culture; and from their religious duties to the theatre. They were doing exactly what I had done myself, in short: keeping up a Fool's Paradise in order to save themselves the trouble of making the real world

17. *Lives of the Artists* (1550) by Giorgio Vasari (1511–74).

18. (1860–61) and (1848).

19. (William) Wilkie Collins (1824–89), who wrote sensational novels of mystery, suspense, and crime, also wrote articles and short stories for *Household Words*, a weekly started by Dickens in 1850, and *All the Year Round*, which incorporated it in 1859 and which Dickens edited until his death in 1870.

any better. Naturally, they hated reality; and this involved some awkward consequences for them. For since the climaxes of Art are brought about by the successful effort of some powerful individuality or idea to realize itself in an act of some kind, whether picture, book, or stage imperson- ation, these artistic skulkers had to be continually dodging great works of art, or else devising ways of discussing and enjoying their accidental methods, conditions, and qualities so as to ward off their essential pur- pose and meaning. And they, or rather we, did this so effectually that I might have remained in my Fool's Paradise of Art with the other fools to this day, had I not, to preserve myself from the dry rot of idleness, at- tempted to realize myself in works of Art.

[U:] In short, I wrote novels.[20] Now, [:U] as it happens, I have an incorrigible propensity for preaching. In conversation this did not make me so unpopular as might have been expected; for I have some uncon- scious and unintentional infirmity of expression which often leads people to doubt whether I am serious in my sermons. [U:] But there was no doubt about the seriousness of the novels. They were sermons; and they were unreadable, not in the least because, as my critical friends assured me, they lacked this or that convention or form, or plot, or incident, or what not, but simply because they were [:U] bad sermons, which failed because I, thanks to my skulking in picture galleries, was a nonentity; and the realization of a nonentity in a novel is not interesting. [U:] So I gave up novel writing, and took to oral sermonizing at street corners, workmen's clubs, and the like, where I learned a great deal, and where they always took me seriously, not being such idiots, I suppose, as to suspect me of throwing away my start in life in order to keep up a bad joke, which was the polite view of my conduct. From my own point of view, I was of course simply making a start in life; and it presently brought me into contact with our friend Mr Stewart Headlam. [:U]

He, not being a dramatic critic, saw what none of the dramatic critics could see, that the world behind the footlights was a real world, peopled with men and women instead of with despicable puppets. He proclaimed the solidarity of the stage with the stalls by founding the Church and Stage Guild. The critics stared, laughed, and promptly set up a conven- tion that the Guild was a ludicrous combination of parson and ballet. Mr Headlam affected them on just one point. He disclosed to them the fact that the ballet is the richest mine of idiotic conventions that exists: it is practically dying of them. The critics are now eagerly learning the jargon of these conventions, in order that their minds, hitherto a blank on the subject of dancing, may be filled with a basketful of irrelevancies to it.

20. *Immaturity* (1879), *The Irrational Knot* (1880), *Love Among the Artists* (1881), *Cashel Byron's Profession* (1882), *An Unsocial Socialist* (1883).

As to any chance of reforming these gentlemen, or obtaining help from them in reforming the drama, I am inclined to think it would be less trouble to undertake the work without them. They never learn anything, never discuss anything, never believe anything, never doubt that they are heading the march that is really leaving them almost out of sight. They cannot tell you anything about a play or an actor that is of the smallest consequence, though they will tell you a dozen things that are quite beside the point. They can write as good a notice of a perfectly hollow play as it is worth; but confront them with a great piece of acting and they will astonish you by the ingenuity with which they will evade the main point, and, like cuttlefish, conceal their bonelessness in a cloud of ink. Salvini startles them by his Othello; and the town rings with their opinions as to the exact length to which a man should go in pretending to cut his throat. Not long ago, the true relation of the actor to the dramatist was thrust before them by a French playwright, who, having to write plays expressly for Madame Sarah Bernhardt, could not help seeing that his task was to provide her with a vehicle for the expression of herself and not with a mask and domino. Under these circumstances, what did this much admired dramatist do? He deliberately took that part of Madame Bernhardt's nature which she shares with any tigress, and he exploited that to the uttermost farthingsworth. Finding that it paid, he did it again. The critics had not a word to say, except to protest against their nerves being shaken by the exhibition on the stage of implements of torture and of the bowstring at full stretch. This was what they called "realism," save the mark. But after two years of Théodora and La Tosca,[21] they began to complain that their actress was vulgarized. Sarah was *encanaillée* [debased]. Having at last discovered a fact, the next thing was to find a wrong and ridiculous reason for it. But the true reason was so obvious that even the coincidence that Madame Bernhardt had grown a little older and stouter did not suffice to take its place. Some of the better critics did see plainly enough that somehow M. Sardou had been playing it rather low down. But why did they not see that in time? Why did they make much of this abominable Théodora on its first night, instead of at once protesting against it as a vile degradation of the actress, of the stage, of the drama, and of the playgoing public? Simply because the whole affair was not real enough to be worth troubling about. After all, the play was a sham, the woman a puppet: why should you expect a cultivated man to make a fuss about these things, and incidentally to make himself ridiculous? Besides, such considerations disturb the Fool's Paradise. It is a deliberate planting of the Tree of the Knowledge of Good and Evil[22]

21. (1887) by Sardou.
22. Genesis, 2:17.

there: a part of that infernal conspiracy to make art didactic which the great writers of the past fell into because they were not up to modern "form."

I do not propose to bring further evidence against the critics now; they will perhaps supply it themselves in the course of the discussion. I have said enough to make myself thoroughly misunderstood; and I will conclude by restating the views upon which I base my respect for the actor and the stage, and my despair of the critics. 1. That acting, in the common use of the word, is self-falsification, forgery, and fraud. 2. That the true goal of the stage player is self-realization, expression, and exhibition. 3. That the drama can only progress by making higher and higher demands on the players' powers of self-development and realization. 4. That the critic who rejects this view lapses into a vicious contempt for the player, and, having no valid standard, is compelled to coin conventions which will not circulate anywhere outside his own circle of accomplices. These are the points on which I invite you to enlighten me by a frank discussion.

[NOTE ON NEW SHAKESPEAR SOCIETY READING OF TWELFTH NIGHT] C/Un (*The Star*, 21 February 1889)

Last night the lecture theatre at the London Institution was glorious with flowers and "indispensable evening dress." It was the Shakespear Society's annual reading, and Twelfth Night was the play selected. In the focus of the semicircle of readers sat Mr William Poel, the master spirit and conductor of the recital.[1] On his right appeared the "Corno di Bassetto,"[2] deep in Shakespearean thought, and looking every inch an Italian noble. On Mr Poel's left Mr Frederick Wedmore[3] made studies for his forthcoming monograph on Edmund Kean. At the back of the stage Dr J. T. Furnivall looked delightedly over Olivia's head, and was confidently supposed by the foreigners present to be the divine William in person.

1. (1852–1934), actor and director who pioneered the production of Shakespeare's plays under conditions as close as possible to the Elizabethan stage. To help achieve this end, he would found the Elizabethan Stage Society in 1894.
2. Shaw's pen name as music critic for *The Star*.
3. Frederick (later Sir Frederick) Wedmore (1844–1921), author, editor, and art critic.

The success of the reading shewed how possible it is to enjoy a poetic drama without the intervention of the theatre proprietor and stage manager. The readers acquitted themselves very fairly, especially Miss Hannah Hall (Olivia) and Miss Florence Bourne, who would have beaten all recorded Violas if she could possibly have read the part as perfectly as she looked it.

[A DOLL'S HOUSE]
Ps/SI ("Asides," *Penny Illustrated Paper,* 1 June 1889, signed N. G. [for No Gentleman])

Talking of the theatre reminds me of the experiment Mr Charrington and Miss Achurch are going to try at the Novelty Theatre by producing Ibsen's Doll's House.[1] My own opinion is that if Mr Charrington approves of this play he, too, is no gentleman; therefore, I hope he will succeed. It may follow, however, that he will play the hero badly; for he, like all heroes, is a perfect gentleman. The drama takes place in a charming little household, the home of a rising young man of business (the gentleman aforesaid), who works hard to get on in the world, and finds relaxation, recreation, and pure domestic joy in the attachment of his wife, Nora. Her good looks are so precious to him that he not only will not let the winds of heaven visit her face too harshly, but he objects to her eating lollipops lest they should spoil her teeth. An ideal husband, dear reader: a type of steady, hearth-and-home, healthy, middleclass chivalry.

But what, do you suppose, comes of it all? The young wife suddenly begins to wake up to the fact that the arrangement narrows her life to a mere functioning as his plaything and nurserymaid, a view which strikes him as extremely unladylike, but which he is unable to deny when she makes him face it fairly. So she, there and then, walks out of the house which is nothing but his nursery and harem, and vanishes. Rather an unsatisfactory ending for a play, you will say. Do not be too sure of that. I saw it once, in Amsterdam;[2] and I never saw a play listened to with closer

1. Charles Charrington (d. 1926) and his wife Janet Achurch (1864–1916) would produce *A Doll's House* on 7 June—the first untampered-with English production of the play; she would play Nora; he, Dr Rank, not "the hero," as Shaw says below.
2. 21 April 1889, under the title *Nora,* in nearby Haarlem.

attention. Even a knot of noisy young Dutch bloods, who had evidently paid at the doors under a quite mistaken notion of the character of the entertainment, got interested, and eventually quite absorbed. The applause had a specially earnest tone; and at the close, the performers were called three times before the curtain. Yet—mark this, Mr Charrington, if it should meet your eye!—not a word of the play was altered except so far as was necessary to turn it from Norwegian into Dutch; and the final situation was presented exactly as Ibsen conceived it.

It cannot be denied, however, that gentlemen of the type of the master of the Doll's House may be involved in a domestic crash by the influence of the play. It set women thinking hard in Norway, and it will set them thinking equally hard here, where the break-up of the doll's-house conception of woman's sphere has gone further than in Norway. Do I surprise any country reader by going on in this cool way? Well, you see, if you w i l l read a column written by no gentleman you have yourself to thank!

A PLAY BY HENRIK IBSEN IN LONDON
Un (*Manchester Guardian*, 8 June 1889)

A Doll's House, a translation by Mr William Archer of Et Dukkehjem, one of the best known plays of the Norwegian poet Henrik Ibsen, was produced last evening at the Novelty Theatre. This is the first time that a play of Ibsen's has been presented in an English theatre exactly as the author wrote it. Nine years ago Mr Archer produced at a Gaiety matinée a version of The Pillars of Society[1] called Quicksands, which followed the original pretty closely save that the first act was in a measure reconstructed. Messrs Jones and Herman, again, founded on Et Dukkehjem a play which they called Breaking a Butterfly, produced six years ago[2] at the present Prince of Wales' Theatre, but they so entirely reversed the idea of Ibsen's play that their work could scarcely be called even an adaptation. A short time afterwards a company of daring amateurs at a charity performance went through a literal version of A Doll's House: they can scarcely be said to have acted it; and no other attempt has been made until yesterday to acclimatize Ibsen on the English stage. The study of his works,

1. (1877).
2. Actually, five years ago.

however, has been rapidly spreading of late years, and there has been some talk of giving subscription performances of more than one of his modern plays. For the present these schemes have come to nothing, and the production at the Novelty is an entirely unsubsidized enterprise of Mr Charles Charrington's. To those present who knew what was coming the development of the play was intensely interesting, and the process of watching its effect on the audience not a little anxious. The result was never in doubt. It is true that throughout the first act the house unsuspiciously accepted the husband, Helmer (Mr Herbert Waring),[3] as a fine, manly fellow. But in the second act, when the crucial line comes wherein he says to his wife "Your father, to say the least, was not unimpeachable, but *I* a m," the shock was perceptible, but the situation was seized with wonderful intelligence by the gallery, who thenceforth saw plainly that Helmer and not Krogstad (Mr R. Carleton)[4] is the true "villain" of the piece, and when the same discovery flashes on the wife in the last act they were in perfect sympathy with the situation and with Miss Achurch. It would of course be absurd to pretend that Nora's assertion of her intention to leave her husband and home in obedience to an impulse of duty to herself before which all the institutions and prejudices of society must yield was felt to have the irresistible power of an awakening social force behind it. Audiences are not yet trained in the dynamics of the "will to live," and when Miss Achurch said "I m u s t, I m u s t," the audience, not having studied Schopenhauer, did not quite see it. It is all the more significant that they submitted to Ibsen on the point without a murmur. Miss Achurch as Nora achieved a success of a high order. With the single exception, perhaps, of Miss Ada Rehan, no other English-speaking actress could have brought to the part Miss Achurch's charm, her magnetism, and her instinctive intelligence. Mr Charrington's Dr Rank, though marred by a melodramatic exit at the end, was a fine piece of acting. The scene with the children quite carried away the audience.

It should be added that the play as performed was textually complete, with the exception of a few quite unimportant curtailments. It will be played for a week only: such, at least, is the present arrangement. But after so striking and significant a result of an unprecedented dramatic experiment, it is possible that Mr Charrington may change his plans very materially.

3. (real name Herbert Waring Rutty, 1857–1932).
4. Royce Carleton (Colin Campbell, 1860–95), Scottish actor.

IS MR BUCHANAN A CRITIC WITH A WOODEN HEAD?
SI (*Pall Mall Gazette*, 13 June 1889)[1]

I make no apology for the unmannerliness of the question with which I head this article. I wish to put Mr Buchanan at his ease with me by falling frankly into his vein, and foregoing all the rebukeful advantage which I might derive by adopting a severely becoming tone. We have the most entire contempt for oneanother's opinions; and it would be a pity to blur that sharply-defined position by any affectation of the mere politeness of controversy. Besides, I have no intention of arguing with Mr Buchanan: I merely wish to attack him in order to discredit his verdict on Ibsen's great play. It happens that the dramatic critics of London have had this month the great chance that comes once in the lifetime of every critic: the chance that Wagner, not so long ago, offered to the musical critics. Most of them have missed it most miserably. To them, in their disgrace, comes Mr Buchanan, and voluntarily concentrates all that is blind and puerile in their notices into one intense half-column, which he signs with his own name, taking all their sins upon his shoulders without even the assurance that with his stripes they shall be healed. That is Mr Buchanan's situation: now for mine.

I represent that section of the community which is almost cut off from the enjoyment of dramatic art because theatrical managers refuse to provide entertainment for it, and insist on providing entertainment for Mr Buchanan. Mr Buchanan's plays bore me; and his views do not interest me in the least: I had grown out of them before I was born. His description of A Doll's House as a play in which we are presented with a maundering physician, a cashier who has been cashiered (mark the pun!), the unpleasant widow of an unpleasant husband, &c., &c., is exactly the sort of work a Texan cowboy produces when he turns "dramatic editor," and begins by being smart at the expense of Shakespear. Mr Buchanan has not the Texan felicity of epigram; but he has the Texan inadequacy. Now, since I have always let Mr Buchanan alone, and refrained from writing to the papers to spoil his sport by declaring, whenever a play after his own heart was produced, that to me the whole performance was an idle twaddling, in which mere spite against unconventional conduct was held up

---

1. A reply to a letter to the editor ("Is Ibsen a Zola with a Wooden Leg?" *Pall Mall Gazette*, 11 June) from Robert Buchanan. Emile Zola (1840–1902) was the leading French naturalistic novelist.

as morality, in which the most serious problems of life and conduct were either glozed or shirked, in which marriage was treated as the end instead of the beginning of life, in which the underlying assumptions were known by everyone in the theatre to be hypocrisies, and in which the whole action was devitalized by a mechanical stagecraft. I say, since I have held my peace under all this provocation, why cannot Mr Buchanan do the same when, for once in a way, I get a chance of seeing a play which suits me? I saw the Doll's House on the first night. I went again on Tuesday; I shall go again if I can get another night free before the piece is withdrawn.[2] I find people enjoying themselves there who have been practically driven from the other theatres by the intolerable emptiness of the ordinary performances. I miss the conventional lies of the stage there; and I do not droop, wither, and protest I am being poisoned for want of them. I escape from foolish Egyptian magician's tricks of "delineating character" and see a vital truth searched out and held up in a light intense enough to dispel all the mists and shadows that obscure it in actual life. I see people silent, attentive, thoughtful, startled: struck to the heart, some of them. I see an unprecedented dramatic progression, in which a domestic story which is word for word the true story of half our households, first deepens to tragedy, and then sublimates and vanishes, leaving its two figures no longer the Helmer and Nora of the story, but the types of Man and Woman at the point where they now stand, she revealing the new Will in her before which must yield all institutions hostile to it: his harem, his nursery, his lust and superstition, in their established forms of home duties, family ties, and chivalry: he dimly beginning to see that in giving this irresistible Will its way he is not losing her, since he never really possessed her, but standing at last to win her for the first time. And then I come home to my Pall Mall Gazette, and find Mr Buchanan hovering skittishly over the Ibsen ocean, like the sprite in Mr Watts's picture in the New Gallery,[3] dropping his plummet in to the full fathom of his three foot string, and then assuring us that it is not his habit to discuss writings with which he has only a superficial acquaintance. I can in turn assure Mr Buchanan that his acquaintance with Ibsen is just as deep as himself: no more and no less; and how deep that is may be ascertained by his published works and plays, especially from those letters of his to the press which contain his direct contributions to the social problems of the age.

In conclusion, let me say that I do not blame Mr Buchanan for fighting Ibsen as Krogstad in The Doll's House declares that he will fight for his position at the bank: "fight as if for life itself." There are many people who

2. He *had* seen it twice and would see it twice more.
3. "Good Luck to Your Fishing," by George Frederick Watts (1817–1904), a fashionable painter then at the height of his reputation. The New Gallery was in Regent Street, London.

have never admitted any merit in Wagner's music; but they cannot stand Donizetti's operas after it, for all that. There are more people who laugh at Mr Whistler's "impressions" and rage at M. Monet's;[4] but when they go back to their pet pictures they find, to their dismay, that there is no art in the landscapes and no light—except studio light—on the figures. The London playgoer has now seen a play of Ibsen's acted. I do not claim that he likes it—perhaps he is only pretending—but let him just try a Buchanan play after it!

PROOF
C/Ps (*The Star*, 13 August 1889, signed C. Di B. [for Corno di Bassetto])

I must begin this notice by an apology for my appearance in the capacity of dramatic critic. The truth is, Spectator has been missing for some time, and as the search for him had yielded no result up to yesterday afternoon, I had to take his place for the moment. It was, of course, no trouble for me to do so, for to a musical critic dramatic criticism is child's play. The first thing that struck me at the Princess's was the inferiority of the band to the Bayreuth orchestra. The music is under the direction of Michael Conolly; and if he will kindly direct his drum, piccolo, and cornet to play at some distance from the audience—say about the middle of Wimbledon Common—he may rely on my assurance that the effect of their performance will be much improved. Proof, Mr Burnand's translation of Une Cause Célèbre,[1] is one of those plays in which the author gets an innocent man into trouble for the sake of getting him out again without any ulterior motives whatsoever. This, though it exercises the sympathies, is not, in my opinion, worth the necessary effort of makebelieve without considerable assistance from actors and stage manager. Consequently, when Mr Vernon,[2] on murder bent, groped blindly about for his victim on a stage sufficiently illuminated for anything short of taking a photograph, my blood refused to curdle, and when Mr Barnes stood outside his child's

---

4. Impressionist painters James Abbott McNeill Whistler (1834–1903), American, and Claude Monet (1840–1926), French.

1. *Proof* (1878), from *Une Cause célèbre* (1877) by Adolphe Philippe d'Ennery (1811–99).

2. W. H. Vernon (d. 1905).

bedroom, and, with the moving observation "She sleeps; it would be cruel to wake her," bolted the door with a clatter that would have startled an opium eater, the unbidden tear remained safely inside my eye. But I can hardly blame the actors for not carrying conviction to me when they were obviously not themelves convinced. In the third act there was a fine opportunity for scenic effect when the gang of convicts entered from the dusty, baking road to snatch a moment's rest on the cool green sward under the shady trees of the park of the Count d'Aubeterre. I remember once seeing a finely painted avenue of elms help Ristori to make a memorable effect of this kind as Marie Stuart[3] in the scene where she is allowed for a moment from her prison walls into the open air. But last night there was no green sward, no shade; and when Miss Illington[4] said they were both there, the audience not unnaturally laughed. Stage managers who throw away such little chances do not grasp the importance of their business. In extenuation of these oversights I am given to understand that though it is generally admitted at the theatre that if a melodrama is worth doing at all it is worth doing well, this rule is suspended in August. However, as a reference to the playbill shews that the special autumnal conditions do not apply to the prices charged for admission, I altogether decline to make any allowances. It is enough to have to accept the childish plot, and to listen gravely to the tedious and impossible explanations, which, after all, have to be supplemented by supernatural inspirations on the part of all the young ladies concerned before a final understanding is come to. The additional burden of easily-avoidable shortcomings in the performance is hard to bear. I must in justice add that these shortcomings were confined to the first seven or eight acts. Towards the middle of the play, as the business devolved more and more on Mr Vernon, who was quite in earnest, and on Miss Illington, whose pathos has all the piquancy of her light comedy, matters improved considerably; Miss Grace Hawthorne, in ravishing Lutetian confections, played Valentine, and reminded me strongly of Lucia di Lammermoor.[5] The piece must have been very extensively rehearsed, for I noticed that most of the "new scenery by Mr Richard C. Durant" was already surprisingly the worse for wear.

P.S. If this should meet the eye of Spectator, he is requested to return in time for the next melodrama. All will be forgiven.

---

3. Title character in play (1800) by Friedrich von Schiller (1759–1805).
4. Marie Illington (d. 1927).
5. Hawthorne (1860?-1922); *Lucia di Lammermoor* (1835) by Donizetti.

THE GOLD CRAZE
C/Un (*Manchester Guardian*, 2 December 1889)

The extraordinarily elaborate melodrama just produced at the Princess's Theatre, London, demonstrates the reverse of what the author, Mr Brandon Thomas,[1] seems to have set himself to demonstrate: namely, that it is impossible to overdo this department of stage art. It would be hard to point out an incident in any known melodrama that does not occur in the Gold Craze. Forgery, suicide, murder, the accession of a poor man to a large fortune, an exchange of letters, the imprisonment of an innocent man, his interview with his wife in gaol, a plan of escape, complicated by an adjournment to Africa, a battle with lawless goldminers, a sentimental ballad, a plot to murder the fugitive: all these are but episodes in the four acts, involving twelve changes of scene, which began at eight and ended at twelve on Saturday night. An ominous ending it was! Not one of the performers, much less the author, ventured to face the stamping and shouting, which were kept up until the lights were lowered. The play, however, is not decisively condemned. The third act, mainly occupied by the episode of the hero's imprisonment and escape, may be fairly said to have succeeded, though at the crisis of it the house was set in a roar by the unlucky announcement that the muskets of the sentinels were "loaded with false bullets." This was only one out of dozens of maladroit speeches. In the second act the appearance of Miss Roselle[2] trailing a robe of white China silk about an African hut was only eclipsed by the subsequent entry of Mr Barnes disguised by a golden beard considerably more than a foot long, a spotless broad leather belt with several minor straps fresh from the saddler's, and a pair of high boots equally suggestive of the costumier's window. The working of the scenery, too, led to several ludicrous mishaps, poor Miss Roselle being twice baffled in her attempts to leave the stage by doors which ought to have been, but were not, practicable. The heroine's undeniable failure to look her part in the earlier scenes did not improve the extravagant absurdity of the first act, but the audience were not disposed to complain of that. In the third act Miss Roselle played with great courage and skill in spite of the most daunting influences. Miss Fanny Brough, Miss Dairolles, Mr Girardot, Mr Sant Matthews, and Mr Pateman also rendered valuable but unavailing help.[3] It remains to be seen whether Mr Brandon Thomas can mend the play sufficiently to secure it a prolonged hearing.

1. (1864–1914), actor and dramatist.
2. Amy Roselle (1854–95).
3. Fanny Whiteside Brough (1854–1914); Adrienne Dairolles; Etienne Girardot (1856–1939); Sant Matthews (d. 1896); Robert Pateman (1840–1924).

IBSEN IN DIFFICULTIES
(To the Editor, *Pall Mall Gazette*, 9 January 1891)

I have an appeal of rather an unusual nature to make to you on behalf of
the English stage. Have you any experience as an actor? Could you and
the members of your talented staff manage to fill up the casts of The
Doll's House and Rosmersholm any time this month that would be most
convenient to you? The theatre shall be forthcoming; your wardrobes
shall be of the best; all expenses are provided for; and your own critic will
probably do every justice to your creation of Rosmer: which is the part
you would help us best by doing. If you refuse, there is no more chance of
the current generation becoming acquainted with the works of the greatest living dramatic poet than there seems to be of their hearing the latest
masterpieces of Richard Wagner in an English opera-house. You must
not suppose that so unreasonable an application would be made to you
had not every other means of putting Ibsen on the stage been tried
without success. You will say—and truly—that the production of great
plays is neither your business nor mine, but that of Mr Irving and his
fellows and rivals in management. But Mr Irving is content to have done
for Goethe and Sir Walter Scott what the Gaiety management has done
for Carmen: he finds Casimir Delavigne's Louis XI more to his taste than
Bishop Nicholas in The Pretenders.[1] The other managers follow Mr Irving's example. But, you will ask, are there not actors to be found both
able and willing to play Rosmer, Helmer, and so on, if it be indeed true
that the theatre is ready and the money in hand? So there are; but they
are all fulfiling engagements with Messrs Irving and Co., who refuse to
allow them to appear at the projected Ibsen matinées. The managers will
neither play Ibsen themselves nor allow anyone else to play him. In 1889
Mr Charrington and Miss Janet Achurch had to go into management
themselves at a heavy risk to put on The Doll's House. As managers they
were able to offer Mr Waring, for example, a regular engagement as well
as the enviable chance of "creating" the part of Helmer. At present we
naturally turn to Mr Waring to "create" the part of Rosmer at an experimental matinée; but the management of the Shaftesbury Theatre vetoes
the proposition. Mr Forbes-Robertson, at the Garrick, is suggested; but

1. Irving had Herman Merivale adapt Scott's *The Bride of Lammermoor* (1819) as *Ra-
venswood* (1890). *Carmen Up to Data* (1890) by George Robert Sims (1847–1922), Henry
Pettitt, and W. Meyer Lutz (1829–1903) was adapted from the story "Carmen" (1845) by
Prosper Mérimée (1803–70) and the opera *Carmen* (1875) by Georges Bizet (1835–75).
Louis XI (1832) is a tragedy by Casimir-Jean-François Delavigne. Bishop Nicholas is a
character in Ibsen's *The Pretenders* (1864).

Mr Hare will not hear of it. Mr Thalberg, at the Adelphi, is approached; but the Messrs Gatti are inexorable, perhaps mistrusting the reaction of Ibsen on the popular taste for Adelphi melodrama.[2] The result is that the performance of Rosmersholm which Miss Florence Farr all but formally announced for the 15th inst. must be postponed unless you, Mr Editor, will play Rosmer.[3] And Miss Marie Fraser's undertaking to produce The Doll's House on the 27th is in jeopardy[4] because Mr Wyndham has nipped one proposed Dr Rank in the bud; and Mr Alexander[5] has done the like by another; whilst an obvious one at the Shaftesbury is likely to share Mr Waring's fate. It is useless to look to the Lyceum: Mr Irving's veto is a foregone conclusion. Mrs John Wood[6] is equally hardhearted on the subject of matinées. In desperation I have suggested that the part of Rosmer be offered to Mr Robert Buchanan; but it is very doubtful whether his conscience would permit him to contribute in any way to the diffusion of Ibsenism. Hence my last card, an appeal to you personally. Even if you refuse, something will have been gained if the public know definitely whom they have to thank for the exclusion from the stage of the best of modern dramatic literature. Perhaps, too, the managers may be roused to render a reason for their opposition to an experiment which interests them so directly that they ought to be well pleased at escaping an invitation to contribute funds as well as "kind permissions." Surely artists of their eminence cannot be jealous of the reputations which might grow out of performances of Ibsen's plays. Still, that hypothesis is sufficiently plausible to make it advisable for them either to relent, to explain, or to come forward and play the unfilled rôles themselves. Mr Irving as Rosmer, Mr Wyndham as Dr Rank, Mr Hare as Krogstad would be welcomed as warmly by the public as by the Ibsen *entrepreneurs* and by yours truly,

G. Bernard Shaw.

2. Johnston (later Sir Johnston) Forbes-Robertson (1853–1937), for whom Shaw would write *Cæsar and Cleopatra*, 1898, but who would not play it until 1906 in New York; T. B. Thalberg (1864–1947); Agostino Gatti (1842?-97) and Stefano Gatti (d. 1906).

3. Florence Farr, wife of the actor Edward Emery (1861–1938), who was Winifred Emery's brother, opened the play on 23 February, with Francis Robert ("Frank," later Sir Frank) Benson (1858–1939) as Rosmer and herself as Rebecca West. Farr, with whom Shaw had a love affair, would play Blanche Sartorius in the first production of his first play, *Widower's Houses*, 1892, and Louka in the first *Arms and the Man*, 1894.

4. However, it opened as scheduled, with Fraser as Nora and William Herbert (1844–96) as Dr. Rank.

5. George (later Sir George) Alexander (1858–1918).

6. Mrs Wood (Matilda Charlotte Vining, 1833?-1915).

THE QUINTESSENCE OF IBSENISM
(First Edition, September 1891)

PREFACE

In the spring of 1890, the Fabian Society, finding itself at a loss for a course of lectures to occupy its summer meetings, was compelled to make shift with a series of papers put forward under the general heading Socialism in Contemporary Literature. The Fabian Essayists,[1] strongly pressed to do "something or other," for the most part shook their heads; but in the end Sydney Olivier consented to "take Zola"; I consented to "take Ibsen"; and Hubert Bland undertook to read all the Socialist novels of the day, an enterprise the desperate failure of which resulted in the most amusing paper of the series. William Morris,[2] asked to read a paper on himself, flatly declined, but gave us one on Gothic Architecture. Stepniak[3] also came to the rescue with a lecture on modern Russian fiction; and so the Society tided over the summer without having to close its doors, but also without having added anything whatever to the general stock of information on Socialism in Contemporary Literature. After this I cannot claim that my paper on Ibsen, which was duly read at the St James's Restaurant on the 18th July 1890, under the presidency of Mrs Annie Besant, and which was the first form of this little book, is an original work in the sense of being the result of a spontaneous internal impulse on my part. Having purposely couched it in the most provocative terms (of which traces may be found by the curious in its present state), I did not attach much importance to the somewhat lively debate that arose upon it; and I had laid it aside as a *pièce d'occasion* which had served its turn, when the production of Rosmersholm at the Vaudeville Theatre by Miss Farr, the inauguration of the Independent Theatre by Mr. J. T. Grein with a performance of Ghosts, and the sensation created by the experiment of Miss

1. Contributors to *Fabian Essays in Socialism* (1889), edited by Shaw: Shaw himself; Sydney (later Baron) Olivier (1859–1943), lifelong friend of Shaw and Webb; Sidney James Webb (1859–1947, later Lord Passfield), whom Shaw met in 1880, of whom he became a lifelong friend, and with whom he was instrumental in building the Fabian Society (founded 1884) into one of the most significant Socialist organizations in Britain; Annie Besant (1847–1933), a freethinker and a theosophist; William Clarke (1852–1901); Graham Wallas (1858–1932); and Hubert Bland (1856–1914), one of the Fabian Society's founders.

2. (1834–96), influential artist, designer, poet, printer, arts-and-crafts entrepreneur, socialist.

3. Sergius Stepniak (pseudonym of Sergei Mikhailovich Kravchinski, 1852–95), Russian nihilist who had settled in London and was active in the Socialist movement.

Robins and Miss Lea with Hedda Gabler,[4] started a frantic newspaper controversy, in which I could see no sign of any of the disputants having ever been forced by circumstances, as I had, to make up his mind definitely as to what Ibsen's plays meant, and to defend his view face to face with some of the keenest debaters in London. I allow due weight to the fact that Ibsen himself has not enjoyed this advantage; but I have also shewn that the existence of a discoverable and perfectly definite thesis in a poet's work by no means depends on the completeness of his own intellectual consciousness of it. At any rate, the controversialists, whether in the abusive stage, or the apologetic stage, or the hero worshiping stage, by no means made clear what they were abusing, or apologizing for, or going into ecstasies about; and I came to the conclusion that my explanation might as well be placed in the field until a better could be found.

With this account of the origin of the book, and a reminder that it is not a critical essay on the poetic beauties of Ibsen, but simply an exposition of Ibsenism, I offer it to the public to make what they can of.

LONDON, *June 1891.*

THE QUINTESSENCE OF IBSENISM

THE TWO PIONEERS

That is, pioneers of the march to the plains of heaven (so to speak).

The second, whose eyes are in the back of his head, is the man who declares that it is wrong to do something that no one has hitherto seen any harm in.

The first, whose eyes are very longsighted and in the usual place, is the man who declares that it is right to do something hitherto regarded as infamous.

The second is treated with great respect by the army. They give him testimonials; name him the Good Man; and hate him like the devil.

The first is stoned and shrieked at by the whole army. They call him all

---

4. Jacob Thomas Grein (1852–1935), a theater critic born in Holland, founded the Independent Theater in 1891, modeled on the Théâtre Libre (founded 1887 by André Antoine [1858–1943]), with Ibsen's *Ghosts* (1881) as its first production; it would produce Shaw's first play, *Widowers' Houses*, in 1892. *Hedda Gabler* (1890) opened 20 April 1891, with Elizabeth Robins (1862–1952) as Hedda and Marion Lea (1864–1944), wife of American dramatist Langdon Mitchell (1862–1933), as Thea.

manner of opprobrious names; grudge him his bare bread and water; and secretly adore him as their savior from utter despair.

Let me take an example from life of my pioneers. Shelley was a pioneer and nothing else; he did both first and second pioneer's work.

Now compare the effect produced by Shelley as abstinence preacher with that which he produced as indulgence preacher or first pioneer. For example:

SECOND PIONEER PROPOSITION: It is wrong to kill animals and eat them.

FIRST PIONEER PROPOSITION: It is not wrong to take your sister as your wife.[1]

Here the second pioneer appears as a gentle humanitarian, and the first as an unnatural corrupter of public morals and family life. So much easier is it to declare the right wrong than the wrong right in a society with a guilty conscience, to which as to Dickens's detective,[2] "Any possible move is a probable move provided it's in a wrong direction." Just as the liar's punishment is, not in the least that he is not believed, but that he cannot believe anyone else, so a guilty society can more easily be persuaded that any apparently innocent act is guilty than that any apparently guilty act is innocent.

The English newspaper which best represents the guilty conscience of the middleclass, or dominant factor in society today, is The Daily Telegraph. If we can find The Daily Telegraph speaking of Ibsen as The

---

1. "The curious persistence of this proposition in the higher poetry of the XIX century is not easy to account for now that it sounds both unimportant and oldfashioned. It is as if one said 'It is not wrong to stand on one's head.' The reply is 'You may be very right; but as nobody wants to, why bother about it?' Yet I think this sensible way of treating the matter—obviously more healthy than the old morbid horror—has been produced largely by the refusal of poets like Shelley and Wagner to accept the theory of natural antipathy as the basis of the tables of Consanguinity, and by the subsequent publication of masses of evidence by sociologists, from Herbert Spencer to [Edward Alexander] Westermarck [1862–1939], shewing that such tables are entirely conventional and that all our prohibitions have been either ignored or actually turned into positive obligations at one time or another without any shock to human instincts. The consequence is that our eyes are now opened to the practical social reasons for barring marriage between Laon and Cythna [eponymous hero and heroine, brother and sister, in Shelley's poem (1817)], Siegmund and Sieglinda [brother and sister, groom and bride, in Wagner's Die Walküre (1870)]; and the preaching of incest as something poetic in itself has lost all its morbid interest and ceased. Also we are beginning to recognize the important fact that the absence of romantic illusion as beween persons brought up together, which undoubtedly exists, and which used to be mistaken for natural antipathy, cannot be depended on as between strangers, however close their consanguinity, and that any domestic or educational system which segregates the sexes produces romantic illusion, no matter how undesirable it may be. It will be seen later on in the chapter dealing with the play Ghosts, that Ibsen took this modern view that consanguinity does not count between strangers. I have accepted it myself in my play Mrs Warren's Profession." [G.B.S., 1912]

2. Mr Bucket in Bleak House (1853).

Quarterly Review used to speak of Shelley, it will occur to us at once that there must be something of the first pioneer about Ibsen.

Mr Clement Scott, dramatic critic to The Daily Telegraph, a goodnatured gentleman, not a pioneer, but emotional, impressionable, zealous, and sincere, accuses Ibsen of dramatic impotence, ludicrous amateurishness, nastiness, vulgarity, egotism, coarseness, absurdity, uninteresting verbosity, and suburbanity, declaring that he has taken ideas that would have inspired a great tragic poet, and vulgarized and debased them in dull, hateful, loathsome, horrible plays. This criticism, which occurs in a notice of the first performance of Ghosts in England, is to be found in The Daily Telegraph for the 14th March 1891, and is supplemented by a leading article which compares the play to an open drain, a loathsome sore unbandaged, a dirty act done publicly, or a lazar house with all its doors and windows open. Bestial, cynical, disgusting, poisonous, sickly, delirious, indecent, loathsome, fetid, literary carrion, crapulous stuff, clinical confessions: all these epithets are used in the article as descriptive of Ibsen's work. "Realism" says the writer "is one thing; but the nostrils of the audience must not be visibly held before a play can be stamped as true to nature. It is difficult to expose in decorous words the gross and almost putrid indecorum of this play." As the performance of Ghosts took place on the evening of the 13th March, and the criticism appeared next morning, it is evident that Mr Scott must have gone straight from the theatre to the newspaper office, and there, in an almost hysterical condition, penned his share of this extraordinary protest. The literary workmanship bears marks of haste and disorder, which, however, only heighten the expression of the passionate horror produced in the writer by seeing Ghosts on the stage. He calls on the authorities to cancel the licence of the theatre, and declares that he has been exhorted to laugh at honor, to disbelieve in love, to mock at virtue, to distrust friendship, and to deride fidelity.

If this document were at all singular, it would rank as one of the curiosities of criticism, exhibiting, as it does, the most seasoned playgoer in the world thrown into convulsions by a performance which was witnessed with approval, and even with enthusiasm, by many persons of approved moral and artistic conscientiousness. But Mr Scott's criticism was hardly distinguishable in tone from hundreds of others which appeared simultaneously. His opinion was the vulgar opinion. Mr Alfred Watson, critic to The Standard, the leading Tory daily paper, proposed that proceedings should be taken against the theatre under Lord Campbell's Act for the suppression of disorderly houses.[3] Clearly Mr Scott and his editor Sir Edwin Arnold,[4] with whom rests the responsibility for the

3. Alfred Edward Thomas Watson (1849–1922).
4. (1832–1904).

article which accompanied the criticism, may claim to represent a considerable party.

How then is it that Ibsen, a Norwegian playwright of European celebrity, attracts one section of the English people so strongly that they hail him as the greatest living dramatic poet and moral teacher, whilst another section is so revolted by his works that they describe him in terms which they themselves admit are, by the necessities of the case, all but obscene? This phenomenon, which has occurred throughout Europe whenever Ibsen's plays have been acted, as well as in America and Australia, must be exhaustively explained before the plays can be described without danger of reproducing the same confusion in the reader's own mind. Such an explanation, therefore, must be my first business.

Understand, at the outset, that the explanation will not be an explaining away. Mr Clement Scott's judgment has not misled him in the least as to Ibsen's meaning. Ibsen means all that most revolts his critic. For example, in Ghosts, the play in question, a clergyman and a married woman fall in love with oneanother. The woman proposes to abandon her husband and live with the clergyman. He recalls her to her duty, and makes her behave as a virtuous woman. She afterwards tells him that this was a crime on his part. Ibsen agrees with her, and has written the play to bring you round to his opinion. Mr Clement Scott does not agree with her, and believes that when you are brought round to her opinion you will be morally corrupted. By this conviction he is impelled to denounce Ibsen as he does, Ibsen being equally impelled to propagate the convictions which provoke the attack. Which of the two is right cannot be decided until it is ascertained whether a society of persons holding Ibsen's opinions would be higher or lower than a society holding Mr Clement Scott's.

There are many people who cannot conceive this as an open question. To them a denunciation of any of the recognized virtues is an incitement to unsocial conduct; and every utterance in which an assumption of the eternal validity of these virtues is not implicit is a paradox. Yet all progress involves the beating of them from that position. By way of illustration, one may rake up the case of Proudhon, who nearly half a century ago denounced property as theft.[5] This was thought the very maddest paradox that ever man hazarded: it seemed obvious that a society which countenanced such a proposition would speedily be reduced to the condition of a sacked city. Today schemes for the confiscation by taxation of mining royalties and ground rents are commonplaces of social reform; and the honesty of the relation of our big property holders to the rest of the community is challenged on all hands. It would be easy to multiply in-

5. In Qu'est-ce que la propriété? (What Is Property? [1840]), Pierre Joseph Proudhon (1809–65), a French socialist, stated, "Property is theft!"

stances, though the most complete are now ineffective through the triumph of the original paradox having obliterated all memory of the opposition it first had to encounter. The point to seize is that social progress takes effect through the replacement of old institutions by new ones; and since every institution involves the recognition of the duty of conforming to it, progress must involve the repudiation of an established duty at every step. If the Englishman had not repudiated the duty of absolute obedience to his king, his political progress would have been impossible. If women had not repudiated the duty of absolute submission to their husbands, and defied public opinion as to the limits set by modesty to their education, they would never have gained the protection of the Married Women's Property Act[6] or the power to qualify themselves as medical practitioners. If Luther[7] had not trampled on his duty to the head of his Church and on his vow of chastity, our priests would still have to choose between celibacy and profligacy. There is nothing new, then, in the defiance of duty by the reformer: every step of progress means a duty repudiated, and a scripture torn up. And every reformer is denounced accordingly, Luther as an apostate, Cromwell as a traitor, Mary Wollstoncraft[8] as an unwomany virago, Shelley as a libertine, and Ibsen as all the things enumerated in The Daily Telegraph.

This crablike progress of social evolution, in which the individual advances by seeming to go backward, continues to illude us in spite of all the lessons of history. To the pious man the newly made freethinker, suddenly renouncing supernatural revelation, and denying all obligation to believe the Bible and obey the commandments as such, appears to be claiming the right to rob and murder at large. But the freethinker soon finds reasons for not doing what he does not want to do; and these reasons seem to him to be far more binding on the conscience than the precepts of a book of which the divine inspiration cannot be rationally proved. The pious man is at last forced to admit—as he was in the case of the late Charles Bradlaugh, for instance—that the disciples of Voltaire and Tom Paine do not pick pockets or cut throats oftener than your even Christian: he actually is driven to doubt whether Voltaire himself really screamed and saw the devil on his deathbed.[9]

6. Passed into law in 1882, it gave married women the right to own property separately from their husbands.

7. Martin Luther (1483–1546).

8. Oliver Cromwell (1599–1658); Mary Wollstoncraft (Godwin, 1759–97), author of *A Vindication of the Rights of Women* (1792).

9. Bradlaugh (1833–91), founder of the National Secular Society, was an outspoken atheist. Although he was elected to the House of Commons in 1880, he was prevented, until 1886, from being seated because he refused to take the oath of allegiance in its religious form. Voltaire (pseudonym of François Marie Arouet, 1694–1778) and the American Thomas Paine (1737–1809), author of *Common Sense* (1776), were also freethinkers.

This experience by no means saves the rationalist[10] from falling into the same conservatism when the time comes for his own belief to be questioned. No sooner has he triumphed over the theologian than he forthwith sets up as binding on all men the duty of acting logically with the object of securing the greatest good of the greatest number, with the result that he is presently landed in vivisection, Contagious Diseases Acts,[11] dynamite conspiracies, and other grotesque but strictly reasonable abominations. Reason becomes Dagon, Moloch, and Jehovah[12] rolled into one. Its devotees exult in having freed themselves from the old slavery to a collection of books written by Jewish men of letters. To worship such books was, they can prove, manifestly as absurd as to worship sonatas composed by German musicians, as was done by the hero of Wagner's novelette, who sat up on his deathbed to say his creed, beginning "I believe in God, Mozart, and Beethoven."[13] The Voltairean freethinker despises such a piece of sentiment; but is it not much more sensible to worship a sonata constructed by a musician than to worship a syllogism constructed by a logician, since the sonata may at least inspire feelings of awe and devotion? This does not occur to the votary of reason; and rationalist "freethinking" soon comes to mean syllogism worship with rites of human sacrifice; for just as the rationalist's pious predecessor thought that the man who scoffed at the Bible must infallibly yield without resistance to all his criminal propensities, so the rationalist in turn becomes convinced that when a man once loses his faith in Mr Herbert Spencer's Data of Ethics,[14] he is no longer to be trusted to keep his hands off his neighbor's person, purse, or wife.

In process of time the age of reason had to go its way after the age of faith. In actual experience, the first shock to rationalism came from the observation that though nothing could persuade women to adopt it, their inaptitude for reasoning no more prevented them from arriving at right conclusions than the masculine aptitude for it saved men from arriving at wrong ones.[15] When this generalization had to be modified in view of the

10. "I had better here warn students of philosophy that I am speaking of rationalism, not as classified in the books, but as apparent in men." [G.B.S., 1891]

11. The Contagious Diseases Acts, passed in the 1860s, included the compulsory examination of prostitutes; they were repealed in 1886.

12. Gods of, respectively, the Philistines, the Canaanites, and the Old Testament Jews.

13. *An End in Paris* (1841). The creed of Shaw's artist, Dubedat, in *The Doctor's Dilemma* (1906), which begins "I believe in Michael Angelo, Velasquez, and Rembrandt," derives from this.

14. (1879); it aimed to establish a secular basis for ethics.

15. Shaw revised the sentence for the 1913 edition: "In actual experience, the first shock to rationalism comes from the observation that though nothing can persuade women to adopt it, their impatience of reasoning no more prevents them from arriving at right conclusions than the masculine belief in it (never a very deeply rooted faith in England, by the way, whatever it may have been in France or Greece) saves men from arriving at wrong ones."

fact that some women did at last begin to try their skill at ratiocination, reason was not reestablished on the throne; because the result of Woman's reasoning was that she began to fall into all the errors which men are just learning to mistrust. From the moment she set about doing things for reasons instead of merely finding reasons for what she wanted to do, there was no saying what mischief she would be at next; since there are just as good reasons for burning a heretic at the stake as for rescuing a shipwrecked crew from drowning: in fact, there are better.

One of the first and most famous utterances of rationalism would have condemned it without further hearing had its full significance been seen at the time. Voltaire, taking exception to the trash of some poetaster, was met with the plea "One must live." "I dont see the necessity " replied Voltaire.[16] The evasion was worthy of the Father of Lies himself; for Voltaire was face to face with the very necessity he was denying; must have known, consciously or not, that it was the universal postulate; would have understood, if he had lived today, that since all human institutions are constructed to fulfil man's will, and that his will to live even when his reason teaches him to die, logical necessity, which was the sort Voltaire meant (the other sort being visible enough) can never be a motor in human action, and is, in short, not necessity at all. But that was not brought to light in Voltaire's time; and he died impenitent, bequeathing to his disciples that most logical of agents, the guillotine, which also "did not see the necessity."

In our own century the recognition of the will as distinct from the reasoning machinery began to spread. Schopenhauer was the first among the moderns[17] to appreciate the enormous practical importance of the distinction, and to make it clear to amateur metaphysicians by concrete instances. Out of his teaching came the formulation of the dilemma that Voltaire shut his eyes to. Here it is. Rationally considered, life is only worth living when its pleasures are greater than its pains. Now to a

16. In Voltaire's Preliminary Discourse to his tragedy *Alzire, or The Americans* (1736), Abbot Guyot Desfontaines pleads, "One must live," to which Count D'Argenson replies, "I do not see the necessity."

17. "I say the moderns, because the will is our old friend the soul or spirit of man; and the doctrine of justification, not by works, but by faith, clearly derives its validity from the consideration that no action, taken apart from the will behind it, has any moral character: for example, the acts which make the murderer and incendiary infamous are exactly similar to those which make the patriotic hero famous. 'Original sin' is the will doing mischief. 'Divine grace' is the will doing good. Our fathers, unversed in the Hegelian dialectic, could not conceive that these two, each the negation of the other, were the same. [Arthur] Schopenhauer's [1788–1860] philosophy, like that of all pessimists, is really based on the old view of the will as original sin, and on the 1750–1850 view that the intellect is the divine grace that is to save us from it. It is as well to warn those who fancy that Schopenhauerism is one and indivisible, that acceptance of its metaphysics by no means involves endorsement of its philosophy." [G.B.S., 1891]

generation which has ceased to believe in heaven, and has not yet learnt that the degradation by poverty of four out of every five of its numbers is artificial and remediable, the fact that life is not worth living is obvious. It is useless to pretend that the pessimism of Koheleth,[18] Shakespear, Dryden, and Swift can be refuted if the world progresses solely by the destruction of the unfit, and yet can only maintain its civilization by manufacturing the unfit in swarms of which that appaling proportion of four to one represents but the comparatively fit survivors. Plainly, then, the reasonable thing for the rationalists to do is to refuse to live. But as none of them will commit suicide in obedience to this demonstration of "the necessity" for it, there is an end of the notion that we live for reasons instead of in fulfilment of our will to live. Thus we are landed afresh in mystery; for positive science gives no account whatever of this will to live. Indeed the utmost light that positive science throws is but feeble in comparison with the illumination that was looked forward to when it first began to dazzle us with its analyses of the machinery of sensation: its researches into the nature of sound and the construction of the ear, the nature of light and the construction of the eye, its measurement of the speed of sensation, its localization of the functions of the brain, and its hints as to the possibility of producing a homunculus presently as the fruit of its chemical investigation of protoplasm. The fact remains that when Darwin, Haeckel, Helmholtz, Young, and the rest, popularized here among the middle class by Tyndall and Huxley, and among the proletariat by the lectures of the National Secular Society, have taught you all they know, you are still as utterly at a loss to explain the fact of consciousness as you would have been in the days when you were satisfied with Chambers's Vestiges of Creation.[19] Materialism, in short, only isolated the great mystery of consciousness by clearing away several petty mysteries with which we had confused it; just as rationalism isolated the great mystery of the will to live. The isolation made both more conspicuous than before. We thought we had escaped forever from the cloudy region of metaphysics; and we were only carried further into the heart of them.[20]

18. Ecclesiastes, or The Preacher (Ecclesiastes is the Greek form of the Hebrew word Koheleth).

19. Ernst Heinrich Haeckel (1834–1919), German author of *Natural History of Creation* (1868); Hermann von Helmholtz (1821–94), German physicist and physiologist; Thomas Young, (1773–1829) English physicist; John Tyndall (1820–93), Irish physicist; Thomas Henry Huxley (1825–95), English author of *Evidence as to Man's Place in Nature* (1863). *Vestiges of Creation* (1844) by Robert Chambers (1802–71) was a pre-Darwinian scientific primer on evolution. In 1913, Shaw substituted Fanny Umphelby's *The Child's Guide to Knowledge* (1825, still in print and popular in 1891) for the Chambers reference.

20. "The correlation between rationalism and materialism in this process has some immediate practical importance. Those who give up materialism whilst clinging to rationalism

We have not yet worn off the strangeness of the position to which we have now been led. Only the other day our highest boast was that we were reasonable human beings. Today we laugh at that conceit, and see ourselves as wilful creatures. Ability to reason accurately is as desirable as ever, since it is only by accurate reasoning that we can calculate our actions so as to do what we intend to do: that is, to fulfil our will; but faith in reason as a prime motor is no longer the criterion of the sound mind, any more than faith in the Bible is the criterion of righteous intention.

At this point, accordingly, the illusion as to the retrogressive movement of progress recurs as strongly as ever. Just as the beneficent step from theology to rationalism seems to the theologist a growth of impiety, does the step from rationalism to the recognition of the will as the prime motor strike the rationalist as a lapse of common sanity, so that to both theologist and rationalist progress at last appears alarming, threatening, hideous, because it seems to tend towards chaos. The deists Voltaire and Tom Paine were, to the divines of their day, predestined devils, tempting mankind hellward.[21] To deists and divines alike Ferdinand Lassalle,[22] the godless self-worshiper and man-worshiper, would have been a monster. Yet many who today echo Lassalle's demand that economic and political institutions should be adapted to the poor man's will to eat and drink his fill out of the product of his own labor, are revolted by Ibsen's acceptance of the impulse towards greater freedom as sufficient ground for the repudiation of any customary duty, however sacred, that conflicts with it. Society, were it even as free as Lassalle's Social-Democratic republic, m u s t, it seems to them, go to pieces when conduct is no longer regulated by inviolable covenants.

For what, during all these overthrowings of things sacred and things infallible, has been happening to that preeminently sanctified thing, Duty? Evidently it cannot have come off scatheless. First there was man's

---

generally either relapse into abject submission to the most paternal of the Churches, or are caught by the attempts, constantly renewed, of mystics to found a new faith by rationalizing on the hollowness of materialism. The hollowness has nothing in it; and if you have come to grief as a materialist by reasoning about something, you are not likely, as a mystic, to improve matters by reasoning about nothing." [G.B.S., 1891]

21. "This is not precisely true. Voltaire was what we should now call an advanced Congregationalist: in fact, modern Dissent, on its educated side, is sound Voltaireanism. Voltaire was for some time on very friendly terms with the Genevese pastors. But what with his jests at the expense of Bible worship, and the fact that he could not formally cut himself off from the Established Church of France without placing himself in its power, the pastors had finally to conceal their agreement with him." [G.B.S., 1912]

22. A German Socialist leader, Lassalle (1825–64) wrote on politics, economics, and philosophy; he was also a dramatist.

duty to God, with priest as assessor. That was repudiated; and then came Man's duty to his neighbor, with Society as assessor. Will this too be repudiated, and be succeeded by Man's duty to himself, assessed by himself? And if so, what will be the effect on the conception of Duty in the abstract? Let us see.

I have just called Lassalle a self-worshiper. In doing so I cast no reproach on him; for this is the last step in the evolution of the conception of duty. Duty arises at first, a gloomy tyranny, out of man's helplessness, his self-mistrust, in a word, his abstract fear. He personifies all that he abstractly fears as God, and straightway becomes the slave of his duty to God. He imposes that slavery fiercely on his children, threatening them with hell, and punishing them for their attempts to be happy. When, becoming bolder, he ceases to fear everything, and dares to love something, this duty of his to what he fears evolves into a sense of duty to what he loves. Sometimes he again personifies what he loves as God; and the God of Wrath becomes the God of Love: sometimes he at once becomes a humanitarian, an altruist, acknowledging only his duty to his neighbor. This stage is correlative to the rationalist stage in the evolution of philosophy and the capitalist phase in the evolution of history. But in it the emancipated slave of God falls under the dominion of Society, which, having just reached a phase in which all the love is ground out of it by the competitive struggle for money, remorselessly crushes him until, in due course of the further growth of his spirit or will, a sense at last arises in him of his duty to himself. And when this sense is fully grown, which it hardly is yet, the tyranny of duty is broken; for now the man's God is himself; and he, self-satisfied at last, ceases to be selfish. The evangelist of this last step must therefore preach the repudiation of duty. This, to the unprepared of his generation, is indeed the wanton masterpiece of paradox. What! after all that has been said of man by men of noble life as to the secret of all right conduct being only "Duty, duty, duty," is he to be told now that duty is the primal curse from which we must redeem ourselves before we can advance another step on the road along which, as we imagine (having forgotten the repudiations made by our fathers) duty and duty alone has brought us thus far? But why not? God was once the most sacred of our conceptions; and he had to be denied. Then Reason became the Infallible Pope, only to be deposed in turn. Is Duty more sacred than God or Reason?

Having now arrived at the prospect of the repudiation of duty by Man, I shall make a digression on the subject of ideals and idealists, as treated by Ibsen. I shall go round in a loop, and come back to the same point by way of the repudiation of duty by Woman; and then at last I shall be in a position to describe the plays without risk of misunderstanding.

IDEALS AND IDEALISTS

We have seen that as Man grows through the ages, he finds himself bolder by the growth of his spirit (if I may so name the unknown) and dares more and more to love and trust instead of to fear and fight. But his courage has other effects: he also raises himself from mere consciousness to knowledge by daring more and more to face facts and tell himself the truth. For in his infancy of helplessness and terror he could not face the inexorable; and facts being of all things the most inexorable, he masked all the threatening ones as fast as he discovered them; so that now every mask requires a hero to tear it off. The king of terrors, Death, was the Arch-Inexorable: Man could not bear the dread of that thought. He must persuade himself that Death could be propitiated, circumvented, abolished. How he fixed the mask of immortality on the face of Death for this purpose we all know. And he did the like with all disagreeables as long as they remained inevitable. Otherwise he must have gone mad with terror of the grim shapes around him, headed by the skeleton with the scythe and hourglass. The masks were his ideals, as he called them; and what, he would ask, would life be without ideals? Thus he became an idealist, and remained so until he dared to begin pulling the masks off and looking the spectres in the face: dared, that is, to be more and more a realist. But all men are not equally brave; and the greatest terror prevailed whenever some realist bolder than the rest laid hands on a mask which they did not yet dare to do without.

We have plenty of these masks around us still: some of them more fantastic than any of the Sandwich islanders' masks in the British Museum. In our novels and romances especially we see the most beautiful of all the masks: those devised to disguise the brutalities of the sexual instinct in the earlier stages of its development, and to soften the rigorous aspect of the iron laws by which Society regulates its gratification. When the social organism becomes bent on civilization, it has to force marriage and family life on the individual, because it can perpetuate itself in no other way whilst love is still known only by fitful glimpses, the basis of sexual relationship being in the main mere physical appetite. Under these circumstances men try to graft pleasure on necessity by desperately pretending that the institution forced upon them is a congenial one, making it a point of public decency to assume always that men spontaneously love their kindred better than their chance acquaintances, and that the woman once desired is always desired: also that the family is woman's proper sphere, and that no really womanly woman ever forms an attachment, or even knows what it means, until she is requested to do so by a man. Now if anyone's childhood has been embittered by the dislike of his mother and the ill-temper of his father; if his wife has ceased to care for him and he is heartily tired of his wife; if his brother is going to law with him over the division of the family property, and his son acting in studied defiance of his plans and wishes, it is hard for him to persuade himself that passion is eternal and that blood is thicker than water. Yet if he tells himself the truth, all his life seems a waste and a failure by the light of it. It comes then to this, that his neighbors must either agree with him that the whole system is a mistake, and discard it for a new one, which cannot possibly happen until social organization so far outgrows the institution that Society can perpetuate itself without it; or else they must keep him in countenance by resolutely making believe that all the illusions with which it has been masked are realities.

For the sake of precision, let us imagine a community of a thousand persons, organized for the perpetuation of the species on the basis of the British family as we know it at present. Seven hundred of them, we will suppose, find the British family arrangement quite good enough for them. Two hundred and ninetynine find it a failure, but must put up with it since they are in a minority. The remaining person occupies a position to be explained presently. The 299 failures will not have the courage to face the fact that they are failures: irremediable failures, since they cannot prevent the 700 satisfied ones from coercing them into conformity with the marriage law. They will accordingly try to persuade themselves that, whatever their own particular domestic arrangements may be, the family is a beautiful and holy natural institution. For the fox not only declares that the grapes he cannot get are sour: he also insists that the sloes he c a n get are sweet. Now observe what has happened. The family as it really is is a conventional arrangement, legally enforced, which the majority, because it happens to suit them, think good enough for the minority, whom it happens not to suit at all. The family as a beautiful and holy natural institution is only a fancy picture of what every family would have to be if everybody was to be suited, invented by the minority as a mask for the reality, which in its nakedness is intolerable to them. We call this sort of fancy picture an Ideal; and the policy of forcing individuals to act on the assumption that all ideals are real, and to recognize and accept such action as standard moral conduct, absolutely valid under all circumstances, contrary conduct or any advocacy of it being discountenanced and punished as immoral, may therefore be described as the policy of Idealism. Our 299 domestic failures are therefore become idealists as to marriage; and in proclaiming the ideal in fiction, poetry, pulpit and platform oratory, and serious private conversation, they will far outdo the 700 who comfortably accept marriage as a matter of course, never dreaming of calling it an "institution," much less a holy and beautiful one, and being pretty plainly of opinion that idealism is a crackbrained fuss about nothing. The idealists, hurt by this, will retort by calling them Philistines. We then have our society classed as 700 Philistines and 299 idealists, leaving one man unclassified. He is the man who is strong enough to face the truth that the idealists are shirking. He says flatly of marriage "This thing is a failure for many of us. It is insufferable that two human beings, having entered into relations which only warm affection can render tolerable, should be forced to maintain them after such affections have ceased to exist, or in spite of the fact that they have never arisen. The alleged natural attractions and repulsions upon which the family ideal is based do not exist; and it is historically false that the family was founded for the purpose of satisfying them. Let us provide otherwise for the social ends which the family subserves, and then abolish its compulsory character altogether." What will be the attitude of the rest to this outspoken man? The Philistines will simply think him mad. But the idealists will be terrified beyond measure at the proclamation of their hidden thought—at the presence of the traitor among the conspirators of silence—at the rending of the beautiful veil they and their poets have woven to hide the unbearable face of truth. They will crucify him, burn him, violate their own ideals of family affection by taking his children away from him, ostracize him, brand him as immoral, profligate, filthy, and appeal against him to the despised Philistines, specially idealized for the occasion as Society. How far they will proceed against him depends on how far his courage exceeds theirs. At his worst, they call him cynic and paradoxer: at his best they do their utmost to ruin him if not to take his life. Thus, purblindly courageous moralists like Mandeville and Larochefoucauld,[1] who merely state unpleasant facts without denying the validity of current ideals, and who indeed depend on those ideals to make their statements piquant, get off with nothing worse than this name of cynic, the free use of which is a familiar mark of the zealous idealist. But take the case of the man who has already served us as an example: Shelley. The idealists did not call Shelley a cynic: they called him a fiend until they invented a new illusion to enable them to enjoy the beauty of his lyrics, said illusion being nothing less than the pretence that since he was at bottom an idealist himself, his ideals must be identical with those of Tennyson and Longfellow,[2] neither of whom ever wrote a line in which some highly respectable ideal was not implicit.[3]

1. Bernard de Mandeville (1670–1733), author of *Fable of the Bees* (1714); François Alexandre Frédéric, Duc de La Rochefoucauld-Liancourt (1613–80), author of *Maxims* (1665). The latter's 113th Maxim is, "There are good marriages, but no delightful ones."
2. Alfred, Lord Tennyson (1809–92); Henry Wadsworth Longfellow (1807–82), American.
3. "The following are examples of the two stages of Shelley criticism:
'We feel as if one of the darkest of the fiends had been clothed with a human body to enable him to gratify his enmity against the human race, and as if the supernatural atrocity

Here the admission that Shelley, the realist, was an idealist too, seems to spoil the whole argument. And it certainly spoils its verbal consistency. For we unfortunately use this word ideal indifferently to denote both the institution which the ideal masks and the mask itself, thereby producing desperate confusion of thought, since the institution may be an effete and poisonous one, whilst the mask may be, and indeed generally is, an image of what we would fain have in its place. If the existing facts, with their masks on, are to be called ideals, and the future possibilities which the masks depict are also to be called ideals; if, again, the man who is defending existing institutions by maintaining their identity with their masks is to be confounded under one name with the man who is striving to realize the future possibilities by tearing the mask and the thing masked asunder, then the position cannot be intelligibly described by mortal pen: you and I, reader, will be at cross purposes at every sentence unless you allow me to distinguish pioneers like Shelley and Ibsen from the idealists of my imaginary community of one thousand. If you ask why I have not allotted the terms the other way, and called Shelley and Ibsen idealists and the conventionalists realists, I reply that Ibsen himself, though he has not formally made the distinction, has so repeatedly harped on conventions and conventionalists as ideals and idealists that if I were now perversely to call them realities and realists, I should confuse readers of The Wild Duck[4] and Rosmersholm more than I should help them. Doubtless I shall be reproached for puzzling people by thus limiting the meaning of the term ideal. But what, I ask, is that inevitable passing perplexity compared to the inextricable tangle I must produce if I follow the custom, and use the word indiscriminately in its two violently incompatible senses? If the term realist is objected to on account of some of its modern associations, I can only recommend you, if you must associate it with something else than my own description of its meaning (I do not deal in definitions), to associate it, not with Zola and Maupassant, but with Plato.[5]

---

of his hate were only heightened by his power to do injury. So strongly has this impression dwelt upon our minds that we absolutely asked a friend, who had seen this individual, to describe him to us: as if a cloven hoof, or horns, or flames from the mouth, must have marked the external appearance of so bitter an enemy of mankind.' (Literary Gazette, 19th May 1821.)

'A beautiful and ineffectual angel, beating in the void his luminous wings in vain.' (MATTHEW ARNOLD [1812–88], in his preface to the selection of poems by [George Gordon, Lord] Byron [1788–1824], dated 1881.)

The 1881 opinion is much sillier than the 1821 opinion. Further samples will be found in the articles of Henry Salt [1851–1939], one of the few writers on Shelley who understood his true position as a social pioneer." [G.B.S., 1891]

4. (1884).

5. Guy de Maupassant (1850–93), French short story and novel writer; Plato (c. 427–c. 347 B.C.), Greek philosopher.

Now let us return to our community of 700 Philistines, 299 idealists, and 1 realist. The mere verbal ambiguity against which I have just provided is as nothing beside that which comes of any attempt to express the relations of these three sections, simple as they are, in terms of the ordinary systems of reason and duty. The idealist, higher in the ascent of evolution than the Philistine, yet hates the highest and strikes at him with a dread and rancor of which the easygoing Philistine is guiltless. The man who has risen above the danger and the fear that his acquisitiveness will lead him to theft, his temper to murder, and his affections to debauchery: this is he who is denounced as an arch-scoundrel and libertine, and thus confounded with the lowest because he is the highest. And it is not the ignorant and stupid who maintain this error, but the literate and the cultured. When the true prophet speaks, he is proved to be both rascal and idiot, not by those who have never read of how foolishly such learned demonstrations have come off in the past, but by those who have themselves written volumes on the crucifixions, the burnings, the stonings, the headings and hangings, the Siberia transportations, the calumny and ostracism which have been the lot of the pioneer as well as of the camp follower. It is from men of established literary reputation that we learn that William Blake was mad, that Shelley was spoiled by living in a low set, that Robert Owen was a man who did not know the world, that Ruskin is incapable of comprehending political economy,[6] that Zola is a mere blackguard, and that Ibsen is "a Zola with a wooden leg."[7] The great musician, accepted by the unskilled listener, is vilified by his fellow-musicians: it was the musical culture of Europe that pronounced Wagner the inferior of Mendelssohn and Meyerbeer.[8] The great artist finds his foes among the painters, and not among the men in the street: it is the Royal Academy which places Mr Marcus Stone, not to mention Mr Hodgson, above Mr Burne-Jones.[9] It is not rational that it should be so; but it is so, for all that.

The realist at last loses patience with ideals altogether, and sees in them only something to blind us, something to numb us, something to

6. Blake (1757–1827), poet and artist; Owen (1771–1858), self-made Welsh industrialist who paternalistically instituted reforms to improve the social, intellectual, and moral conditions of his workers at his mills in Scotland, established a cooperative experiment in Indiana, and remained a significant figure in the labor and cooperative movements in England; John Ruskin (1819–1900), English writer and critic of art and architecture.

7. Said Robert Buchanan; see Shaw's response, 13 June 1889.

8. Felix Mendelssohn-Bartholdy (1809–47); Giacomo Meyerbeer (1791–1864).

9. Stone (1840–1921), historical genre painter and book illustrator; John Evan Hodgson (1831–95), genre, historical, and landscape painter; Sir Edward Burne-Jones (1833–98), English painter of the Royal Academy, leader of the second phase of the Pre-Raphaelite movement. For the 1913 edition, Shaw revised the phrase: "the Royal Academy [. . .] placed forgotten nobodies above Burne-Jones."

murder self in us, something whereby, instead of resisting death, we can disarm it by commiting suicide. The idealist, who has taken refuge with the ideals because he hates himself and is ashamed of himself, thinks that all this is so much the better. The realist, who has come to have a deep respect for himself and faith in the validity of his own will, thinks it so much the worse. To the one, human nature, naturally corrupt, is only held back from the excesses of the last years of the Roman empire by self-denying conformity to the ideals. To the other these ideals are only swaddling clothes which man has outgrown, and which insufferably impede his movements. No wonder the two cannot agree. The idealist says "Realism means egotism; and egotism means depravity." The realist declares that when a man abnegates the will to live and be free in a world of the living and free, seeking only to conform to ideals for the sake of being, not himself, but "a good man," then he is morally dead and rotten, and must be left unheeded to abide his resurrection, if that by good luck arrive before his bodily death.[10] Unfortunately, this is the sort of speech that nobody but a realist understands. It will be more amusing as well as more convincing to take an actual example of an idealist criticizing a realist.

THE WOMANLY WOMAN

Everybody remembers the Diary of Marie Bashkirtseff.[1] An outline of it, with a running commentary, was given in The Review of Reviews (June 1890) by its editor, Mr William Stead, a sort of modern Julian the Apostate,[2] who, having gained an immense following by a public service in rendering which he had to perform a realistic feat of a somewhat scandalous character, entered upon a campaign with the object of establishing the ideal of sexual "purity" as a condition of public life. As he retains his best qualities—faith in himself, wilfulness, conscientious unscrupulousness—he can always make himself heard. Prominent among his ideals is an ideal of womanliness. In support of that ideal he will, like all idealists, make and believe any statement, however obviously and grotesquely un-

10. "The above was written in 1890, ten years before Ibsen, in When We Dead Awaken, fully adopted its metaphor without, as far as I know, having any knowledge of my essay. Such an anticipation is a better proof than any mere argument that I found the right track of Ibsen's thought." [G.B.S., 1912] Although When We Dead Awaken was first produced in 1900, it was written and published in 1899.

1. A Russian painter (1860–84) whose Journal was published in English in 1890.

2. Stead (1849–1912) was a crusading journalist interested in religion, society, and international peace. It is unclear whether Shaw refers to the historical Julian or to the Julian who is the protagonist of Ibsen's Emperor and Galilean (1873). Shaw deleted this phrase from the 1913 edition.

real. When he found Marie Bashkirtseff's account of herself utterly incompatible with the account of a woman's mind given to him by his ideal,
he was confronted with the dilemma that either Marie was not a woman
or else his ideal did not correspond to nature. He actually accepted the
former alternative. "Of the distinctively womanly" he says "there is in her
but little trace. She was the very antithesis of a true woman." Mr Stead's
next difficulty was, that self-control, being a leading quality in his ideal,
could not have been possessed by Marie: otherwise she would have been
more like his ideal. Nevertheless he had to record that she, without any
compulsion from circumstances, made herself a highly skilled artist by
working ten hours a day for six years. Let anyone who thinks that this is
no evidence of self-control just try it for six months. Mr Stead's verdict
nevertheless was "No self-control." However, his fundamental quarrel
with Marie came out in the following lines. "Marie" he said "was artist,
musician, wit, philosopher, student, anything you like but a natural
woman with a heart to love, and a soul to find its supreme satisfaction in
sacrifice for love or for child." Now of all the idealist abominations that
make society pestiferous, I doubt if there be any so mean as that of forcing
self-sacrifice on a woman under pretence that she likes it; and, if she
ventures to contradict the pretence, declaring her no true woman. In
India they carried this piece of idealism to the length of declaring that a
wife could not bear to survive her husband, but would be prompted by her
own faithful, loving, beautiful nature to offer up her life on the pyre which
consumed his dead body. The astonishing thing is that women, sooner
than be branded as unsexed wretches, allowed themselves to be stupefied
with drink, and in that unwomanly condition burnt alive. British Philistinism put down widow idealizing with the strong hand; and suttee is abolished in India. The English form of it still survives; and Mr Stead, the
rescuer of the children,[3] is one of its high priests. Imagine his feelings on
coming across this entry in a woman's diary: "I love myself." Or this: "I
swear solemnly—by the Gospels, by the passion of Christ, by MYSELF—
that in four years I will be famous." The young woman was positively
proposing to exercise for her own sake all the powers that were given her,
in Mr Stead's opinion, solely that she might sacrifice them for her lover or
child! No wonder he is driven to exclaim again "She was very clever, no
doubt; but woman she was not."

Now observe this notable result. Marie Bashkirtseff, instead of being a
less agreeable person than the ordinary female conformer to the ideal of
womanliness, was conspicuously the reverse. Mr Stead himself wrote as

3. "It was to force the Government to take steps to suppress child prostitution that Stead
resorted to the desperate expedient already alluded to. He succeeded." [G.B.S., 1912]

one infatuated with her mere diary, and pleased himself by representing her as a person who fascinated everybody, and was a source of delight to all about her by the mere exhilaration and hope-giving atmosphere of her wilfulness. The truth is, that in real life a self-sacrificing woman, or, as Mr Stead would put it, a womanly woman, is not only taken advantage of, but disliked for her pains. No m a n pretends that his soul finds its supreme satisfaction in self-sacrifice: such an affectation would stamp him as a coward and weakling: the manly man is he who takes the Bashkirtseff view of himself. But men are not the less loved on this account. No one ever feels helpless by the side of the self-helper; whilst the self-sacrificer is always a drag, a responsibility, a reproach, an everlasting and unnatural trouble with whom no really strong soul can live. Only those who have helped themselves know how to help others, and to respect their right to help themselves.[4]

Although romantic idealists generally insist on self-surrender as an indispensable element in true womanly love, its repulsive effect is well known and feared in practice by both sexes. The extreme instance is the reckless self-abandonment seen in the infatuation of passionate sexual desire. Everyone who becomes the object of that infatuation shrinks from it instinctively. Love loses its charm when it is not free; and whether the compulsion is that of custom and law, or of infatuation, the effect is the same: it becomes valueless. The desire to give inspires no affection unless there is also the power to withhold; and the successful wooer, in both sexes alike, is the one who can stand out for honorable conditions, and, failing them, go without. Such conditions are evidently not offered to either sex by the legal marriage of today; for it is the intense repugnance inspired by the compulsory character of the legalized conjugal relation that leads, first to the idealization of marriage whilst it remains indispensable as a means of perpetuating society; then to its modification by divorce and by the abolition of penalties for refusal to comply with judicial orders for restitution of conjugal rights; and finally to its disuse and

4. "Shortly after the publication of this passage, a German lady told me that she knew 'where I had got it from,' evidently not meaning from Ibsen. She added 'You have been reading Nietzsche's [1844–1900] Through Good and Evil and Out at the Other Side [1886].' That was the first I ever heard of Nietzsche. I mention this fact, not with the ridiculous object of vindicating my 'originality' in XIX century fashion, but because I attach great importance to the evidence that the movement voiced by Schopenhauer, Wagner, Ibsen, Nietzsche, and [August] Strindberg [1849–1912], was a world movement, and would have found expression if every one of these writers had perished in his cradle. I have dealt with this question in the preface [1907] to my play Major Barbara [1905]. The movement is alive today in the philosophy of [Henri] Bergson [1859–1941] and the plays of [Maxim] Gorki [1868–1936], [Anton Pavlovich] Tchekov [1860–1904], and the post-Ibsen English drama." [G.B.S., 1912] In that preface, Shaw identifies the German lady as Miss Borchardt, a mathematician.

disappearance as the responsibility for the maintenance and education of the rising generation is shifted from the parent to the community.[5]

Although the growing repugnance to face the Church of England marriage service has led many celebrants to omit those passages which frankly explain the object of the institution, we are not likely to dispense with legal ties and obligations, and trust wholly to the permanence of love, until the continuity of society no longer depends on the private nursery. Love, as a practical factor in society, is still a mere appetite. That higher development of it which Ibsen shews us occuring in the case of Rebecca West in Rosmersholm is only known to most of us by the descriptions of great poets, who themselves, as their biographies prove, have often known it, not by sustained experience, but only by brief glimpses. And it is never a first fruit of their love affairs.[6] Tannhäuser[7] may die in the conviction that one moment of the emotion he felt with St Elizabeth was fuller and happier than all the hours of passion he spent with Venus; but that does not alter the fact that love began for him with Venus, and that its earlier tentatives towards the final goal were attended with relapses. Now Tannhäuser's passion for Venus is a development of the humdrum fondness of the bourgeois Jack for his Jill, a development at once higher and more dangerous, just as idealism is at once higher and

5. "A dissertation on the anomalies and impossibilities of the marriage law at its present stage would be too far out of the main course of my argument to be introduced in the text above; but it may be well to point out in passing to those who regard marriage as an inviolable and inviolate institution, that necessity has already forced us to tamper with it to such an extent that at this moment the highest court in the kingdom is face to face with a husband and wife, the one demanding whether a woman may saddle him with all the responsibilities of a husband and then refuse to live with him, and the other asking whether the law allows her husband to commit abduction, imprisonment, and rape upon her. If the court says Yes to the husband, marriage is made intolerable for men; if it says Yes to the wife, marriage is made intolerable for women; and as this exhausts the possible alternatives, it is clear that provision must be made for the dissolution of such marriages if the institution is to be maintained at all, which it must be until its social function is otherwise provided for. Marriage is thus, by force of circumstances, compelled to buy extension of life by extension of divorce, much as if a fugitive should try to delay a pursuing wolf by throwing portions of his own heart to it." [G.B.S., 1891] "The court decided against the man; but England still lags behind the rest of Protestant Europe in the necessary readjustment of the law of divorce. See the preface [1911] to my play Getting Married [1908], which supplies the dissertation crowded out of the forgoing note." [G.B.S., 1912] In Weldon v. Weldon (1883), the Court ruled that the husband must live with his wife even though he does not want to. In Regina v. Jackson (1891), the Court ruled that the husband could not force his wife to live with him if she does not want to.

6. Shaw omitted this sentence from the 1913 edition and inserted: "Dante [1265–1321] loved Beatrice with the higher love; but neither during her life nor after her death was he 'faithful' to her or to the woman he actually married. And he would be a bold bourgeois who would pretend to a higher mind than Dante."

7. Title character of opera (1845) by Wagner.

more dangerous than Philistinism. The fondness is the germ of the passion: the passion is the germ of the more perfect love. When Blake told men that through excess they would learn moderation,[8] he knew that the way for the present lay through the Venusberg, and that the race would assuredly not perish there as some individuals have, and as the Puritan fears we all share unless we find a way round. Also he no doubt foresaw the time when our children would be born on the other side of it, and so be spared that fiery purgation.

But the very facts that Blake is still commonly regarded as a crazy visionary, and that the current criticism of Rosmersholm entirely fails even to notice the evolution of Rebecca's passion for Rosmer into her love for him, much more to credit the moral transfiguration which accompanies it, shew how absurd it would be to pretend, for the sake of edification, that the ordinary marriage of today is a union between a William Blake and a Rebecca West, or that it would be possible, even if it were enlightened policy, to deny the satisfaction of the sexual appetite to persons who have not reached that stage. An overwhelming majority of such marriages as are not purely *de convenance* [for convenience], are entered into for the gratification of that appetite either in its crudest form or veiled only by those idealistic illusions which the youthful imagination weaves so wonderfully under the stimulus of desire, and which older people indulgently laugh at.

This being so, it is not surprising that our society, being directly dominated by men, comes to regard Woman, not as an end in herself like Man, but solely as a means of ministering to his appetite. The ideal wife is one who does everything that the ideal husband likes, and nothing else. Now to treat a person as a means instead of an end is to deny that person's right to live. And to be treated as a means to such an end as sexual intercourse with those who deny one's right to live is insufferable to any human being. Woman, if she dares face the fact that she is being so treated, must either loathe herself or else rebel. As a rule, when circumstances enable her to rebel successfully—for instance, when the accident of genius enables her to "lose her character" without losing her employment or cutting herself off from the society she values—she does rebel; but circumstances seldom do. Does she then loathe herself? By no means: she deceives herself in the idealist fashion by denying that the love which her suitor offers her is tainted with sexual appetite at all. It is, she declares, a beautiful, disinterested, pure, sublime devotion to another by which a man's life is exalted and purified, and a woman's rendered blest. And of all the cynics, the filthiest to her mind is the one who sees, in the man

8. One of the "Proverbs of Hell" in *The Marriage of Heaven and Hell* (1790–93): "The road of excess leads to the palace of wisdom."

making honorable proposals to his future wife, nothing but the human male seeking his female. The man himself keeps her confirmed in her illusion; for the truth is unbearable to him too: he wants to form an affectionate tie, and not to drive a degrading bargain. After all, the germ of the highest love is in them both, though as yet it is no more than the appetite they are disguising so carefully from themselves. Consequently every stockbroker who has just brought his business up to marrying point woos in terms of the romantic illusion; and it is agreed between the two that their marriage shall realize the romantic ideal. Then comes the breakdown of the plan. The young wife finds that her husband is neglecting her for his business; that his interests, his activities, his whole life except that one part of it to which only a cynic ever referred before her marriage, lies away from home; and that her business is to sit there and mope until she is wanted. Then what can she do? If she complains, he, the self-helper, can do without her; whilst she is dependent on him for her position, her livelihood, her place in society, her home, her name, her very bread.[9] All this is brought home to her by the first burst of displeasure her complaints provoke. Fortunately, things do not remain forever at this point: perhaps the most wretched in a woman's life. The self-respect she has lost as a wife she regains as a mother, in which capacity her use and importance to the community compare favorably with those of most men of business. She is wanted in the house, wanted in the market, wanted by the children; and now, instead of weeping because her husband is away in the city,[10] thinking of stocks and shares instead of his ideal woman, she would regard his presence in the house all day as an intolerable nuisance. And so, though she is completely disillusioned on the subject of ideal love, yet, since it has not turned out so badly after all, she countenances the illusion still from the point of view that it is a useful and harmless means of getting boys and girls to marry and settle down. And this conviction is

9. "I should have warned my male readers to be very careful how they presume on this position. In actual practice marriage reduces the man to a greater dependence on the woman than is good for either party. But the woman can tyrannize only by misconduct or threats of misconduct, whilst the man can tyrannize legally, though it must be added that a good deal of the makeshift law that has been set up to restrain this tyranny is very unfair to the man. The writings of Belfort Bax are instructive on this point." [G.B.S., 1912] The books of Ernest Belfort Bax (1854–1926), who wrote on socialism, philosophy, and feminism, and who dealt with women's legal privileges, include *Outspoken Essays on Social Subjects* (1897) and *The Legal Subjection of Men* (1908). In 1913, the year Shaw's revised *Quintessence of Ibsenism* appeared, Bax published *The Fraud of Feminism*. In the preface to *Major Barbara*, Shaw says that Bax's treatment of feminism would spark romantic protests even from Strindberg. In *Getting Married*, one of Bax's essays prompts a prospective bridegroom to reconsider marriage.

10. The business and financial center of London (its American equivalent would be Wall Street.

the stronger in her because she feels that if she had known as much about marriage the day before her wedding as she did six months after, it would have been extremely hard to induce her to get married at all.

This prosaic solution is satisfactory only within certain limits. It depends altogether upon the accident of the woman having some natural vocation for domestic management and the care of children, as well as on the husband being fairly goodnatured and livable-with. Hence arises the idealist illusion that a vocation for domestic management and the care of children is natural to women, and that women who lack them are not women at all, but members of the third, or Bashkirtseff sex. Even if this were true, it is obvious that if the Bashkirtseffs are to be allowed to live, they have a right to suitable institutions just as much as men and women. But it is not true. The domestic career is no more natural to all women than the military career is natural to all men; although it may be necessary that every ablebodied woman should be called on to risk her life in childbed just as it may be necessary that every man should be called on to risk his life in the battlefield. It is of course quite true that the majority of women are kind to children and prefer their own to other people's. But exactly the same thing is true of the majority of men, who nevertheless do not consider that their proper sphere is the nursery. The case may be illustrated more grotesquely by the fact that the majority of women who have dogs are kind to them, and prefer their own dogs to other people's; yet it is not proposed that women should restrict their activities to the rearing of puppies. If we have come to think that the nursery and the kitchen are the natural sphere of a woman, we have done so exactly as English children come to think that a cage is the natural sphere of a parrot: because they have never seen one anywhere else. No doubt there are Philistine parrots who agree with their owners that it is better to be in a cage than out, so long as there is plenty of hempseed and Indian corn there. There may even be idealist parrots who persuade themselves that the mission of a parrot is to minister to the happiness of a private family by whistling and saying Pretty Polly, and that it is in the sacrifice of its liberty to this altruistic pursuit that a true parrot finds the supreme satisfaction of its soul. I will not go so far as to affirm that there are theological parrots who are convinced that imprisonment is the will of God because it is unpleasant; but I am confident that there are rationalist parrots who can demonstrate that it would be a cruel kindness to let a parrot out to fall a prey to cats, or at least to forget its accomplishments and coarsen its naturally delicate fibres in an unprotected struggle for existence. Still, the only parrot a free-souled person can sympathize with is the one that insists on being let out as the first condition of its making itself agreeable. A selfish bird, you may say: one that puts its own gratification before that of the family which is so fond of it: before even the greatest happiness of the greatest number: one that, in aping the independent spirit of a man, has unparroted itself and become a creature that has neither the home-loving nature of a bird nor the strength and enterprise of a mastiff. All the same, you respect that parrot in spite of your conclusive reasoning; and if it persists, you will have either to let it out or kill it.

The sum of the matter is that unless Woman repudiates her womanli-ness, her duty to her husband, to her children, to society, to the law, and to everyone but herself, she cannot emancipate herself. But her duty to herself is no duty at all, since a debt is cancelled when the debtor and creditor are the same person. Its payment is simply a fulfilment of the individual will, upon which all duty is a restriction, founded on the con-ception of the will as naturally malign and devilish. Therefore Woman has to repudiate duty altogether. In that repudiation lies her freedom; for it is false to say that Woman is now directly the slave of Man: she is the immediate slave of duty; and as man's path to freedom is strewn with the wreckage of the duties and ideals he has trampled on, so must hers be. She may indeed mask her iconoclasm by proving in rationalist fashion, as Man has often done for the sake of a quiet life, that all these discarded idealist conceptions will be fortified instead of shattered by her emancipa-tion. To a person with a turn for logic, such proofs are as easy as playing the piano is to Paderewski.[11] But it will not be true. A whole basketful of ideals of the most sacred quality will be smashed by the achievement of equality for women and men. Those who shrink from such a clatter and breakage may comfort themselves with the reflection that the replace-ment of the broken goods will be prompt and certain. It is always a case of "The ideal is dead: long live the ideal!" And the advantage of the work of destruction is that every new ideal is less of an illusion than the one it has supplanted; so that the destroyer of ideals, though denounced as an en-emy of society, is in fact sweeping the world clear of lies.

My digression is now over. Having traversed my loop as I promised, and come back to Man's repudiation of duty by way of Woman's, I may at last proceed to give some more particular account of Ibsen's work without further preoccupation with Mr Clement Scott's protest, or the many oth-ers of which it is the type. For we now see that the pioneer must necessar-ily provoke such outcry as he repudiates duties, tramples on ideals, pro-fanes what was sacred, sanctifies what was infamous, always driving his plough through gardens of pretty weeds in spite of the laws made against trespassers for the protection of the worms which feed on the roots, letting in light and air to hasten the putrefaction of decaying matter, and everywhere proclaiming that "the old beauty is no longer beautiful, the

11. Ignace Jan Paderewski (1860–1941), Polish pianist and composer.

new truth no longer true."[12] He can do no less; and what more and what else he does it is not given to all of his generation to understand. And if any man does not understand, and cannot foresee the harvest, what can he do but cry out in all sincerity against such destruction, until at last we come to know the cry of the blind like any other street cry, and to bear with it as an honest cry, albeit a false alarm?

THE PLAYS

Brand, 1866[1]

We are now prepared to learn without misgiving that a typical Ibsen play is one in which the leading lady is an unwomanly woman, and the villain an idealist. It follows that the leading lady is not a heroine of the Drury Lane type;[2] nor does the villain forge or assassinate, since he is a villain by virtue of his determination to do nothing wrong. Therefore readers of Ibsen—not playgoers—have sometimes so far misconceived him as to suppose that his villains are examples rather than warnings, and that the mischief and ruin which attend their actions are but the tribulations from which the soul comes out purified as gold from the furnace. In fact, the beginning of Ibsen's European reputation was the edification with which the pious of Scandinavia received his great dramatic poem Brand.[3]

Brand the priest is an idealist of heroic earnestness, strength, and courage.[4] He declares himself the champion, not of things as they are, nor of things as they can be made, but of things as they ought to be. Things as they ought to be mean for him things as ordered by men conformed to his ideal of the perfect Adam, who, again, is not man as he is or can be, but man conformed to all the ideals: man as it is his duty to be.

---

12. *Emperor and Galilean*, Part 1, act II.

1. Shaw added the dates in the 1913 edition. Although *Brand* was published in 1886, it was written and produced in 1885.

2. That is, a heroine of melodrama, in which the Drury Lane Theatre specialized.

3. In the 1913 edition, Shaw added: "Brand is not his first play; indeed it is his seventh; and of its six forerunners all are notable and some splendid; but it is in Brand that he definitely, if not yet quite consciously, takes the field against idealism and, like another Luther, nails his thesis to the door of the Temple of Morality. With Brand therefore we must begin, lest we should be swept into an eddy of mere literary criticism, a matter altogether beside the purpose of this book." Actually, *Brand* is Ibsen's eleventh play.

4. In the 1913 edition, Shaw added: "Conventional, comfortable, sentimental church-going withers into selfish snobbery and cowardly weakness before his terrible word. 'Your God' he cries 'is an old man: mine is young'; and all Europe, hearing him, suddenly realizes that it has so far forgotten God as to worship an image of an elderly gentleman with a well-trimmed beard, an imposing forehead, and the expression of a headmaster."

In insisting on this conformity, Brand spares neither himself nor anyone else. Life is nothing: self is nothing: the perfect Adam is everything. The imperfect Adam does not fall in with these views. A peasant whom he urges to cross a glacier in a fog because it is his duty to visit his dying daughter, not only flatly declines, but endeavors forcibly to prevent Brand from risking his own life. Brand knocks him down, and sermonizes him with fierce earnestness and scorn. Presently Brand has to cross a fiord in a storm to reach a dying man who, having commited a series of murders, wants "consolation" from a priest. Brand cannot go alone: someone must hold the rudder of his boat whilst he manages the sail. The fisher folk, in whom the old Adam is strong, do not adopt his estimate of the gravity of the situation, and refuse to go. A woman, fascinated by his heroism and idealism, goes. That ends in their marriage, and in the birth of a child to whom they become deeply attached. Then Brand, aspiring from height to height of devotion to his ideal, plunges from depth to depth of murderous cruelty. First the child must die from the severity of the climate because Brand must not flinch from the post of duty and leave his congregation exposed to the peril of getting an inferior preacher in his place. Then he forces his wife to give the clothes of the dead child to a gypsy whose baby needs them. The bereaved mother does not grudge the gift; but she wants to hold back only one little garment as a relic of her darling. But Brand sees in this reservation the imperfection of the imperfect Eve. He forces her to regard the situation as a choice between the relic and his ideal. She sacrifices the relic to the ideal, and then dies, brokenhearted. Having killed her, and thereby placed himself beyond ever daring to doubt the idealism upon whose altar he has immolated her; having also refused to go to his mother's deathbed because she compromises with his principles in disposing of her property, he is hailed by the people as a saint, and finds his newly built church too small for his congregation. So he calls upon them to follow him to worship God in His own temple, the mountains. After a brief practical experience of this arrangement, they change their minds, and stone him. The very mountains themselves stone him, indeed; for he is killed by an avalanche.

PEER GYNT, 1867

Brand dies a saint, having caused more intense suffering by his saintliness than the most talented sinner could possibly have done with twice his opportunities. Ibsen does not leave this to be inferred. In another dramatic poem he gives us an accomplished rascal named Peer Gynt, an idealist who avoids Brand's errors by setting up as his ideal the realization of himself by the utter satisfaction of his own will. In this he would seem to be on the path to which Ibsen himelf points; and indeed all who know the two plays will agree that whether or no it was better to be Peer Gynt than Brand, it was beyond all question better to be the mother or the sweetheart of Peer, scapegrace and liar as he was, than mother or wife to the saintly Brand. Brand would force his ideal on all men and women: Peer Gynt keeps his ideal for himself alone: it is indeed implicit in the ideal itself that it should be unique: that he alone should have the force to realize it. For Peer's first boyish notion of the self-realized man is not the saint, but the demigod whose indomitable will is stronger than destiny, the fighter, the master, the man whom no woman can resist, the mighty hunter, the knight of a thousand adventures, the model, in short, of the lover in a lady's novel, or the hero in a boy's romance. Now, no such person exists, or ever did exist, or ever can exist. The man who cultivates an indomitable will and refuses to make way for anything or anybody, soon finds that he cannot hold a street crossing against a tram car, much less a world against the whole human race. Only by plunging into illusions to which every fact gives the lie can he persuade himself that his will is a force that can overcome all other forces, or that it is less conditioned by circumstances than is a wheelbarrow. However, Peer Gynt, being imaginative enough to conceive his ideal, is also imaginative enough to find illusions to hide its unreality, and to persuade himself that Peer Gynt, the shabby countryside loafer, is Peer Gynt, Emperor of Himself, as he writes over the door of his hut in the mountains. His hunting feats are invented; his military genius has no solider foundation than a street fight with a smith; and his reputation as an adventurous daredevil he has to gain by the bravado of carrying off the bride from a wedding at which the guests snub him. Only in the mountains can he enjoy his illusions undisturbed by ridicule; yet even in the mountains he finds obstacles which he cannot force his way through, obstacles which withstand him as spirits with voices, telling him that he must go round. But he will not: he will go forward: he will cut his path sword in hand, in spite of fate. All the same, he has to go round; for the world-will is without Peer Gynt as well as within him.

Then he tries the supernatural, only to find that it means nothing more than the transmogrifying of squalid realities by lies and pretences. Still, like our amateurs of thaumaturgy, he is willing to enter into a conspiracy of makebelieve up to a certain point. When the Trold king's daughter appears as a repulsive ragged creature riding on a pig, he is ready to accept her as a beautiful princess on a noble steed, on condition that she accepts his mother's tumbledown farmhouse, with the broken window panes stopped up with old clouts, as a splendid castle. He will go with her among the Trolds, and pretend that the gruesome ravine in which they hold their orgies is a glorious palace; he will partake of their filthy food and declare it nectar and ambrosia; he will applaud their obscene antics as exquisite dancing, and their discordant din as divine music; but when they finally propose to slit his eyes so that he may see and hear these things, not as they are, but as he has been pretending to see and hear them, he draws back, resolved to be himself even in self-deception. He leaves the mountains and becomes a prosperous man of business in America, highly respectable and ready for any profitable speculation: Bible trade, whisky trade, missionary trade, anything! In this phase, he takes to piety, and persuades himself, like Mr Stanley,[5] that he is under the special care of God. This opinion is shaken by an adventure in which he is marooned on the African coast; and it is not restored until the treacherous friends who marooned him are destroyed before his eyes by the blowing-up of the steam yacht they have just stolen from him, when he utters his celebrated exclamation "Ah, God is a Father to me after all; but economical he certainly is not." He finds a white horse in the desert, and is accepted on its account as the Messiah by an Arab tribe, a success which moves him to declare that now at last he is really worshipped for himself, whereas in America people only respected his breastpin, the symbol of his money. In commerce, too, he reflects, his eminence was a mere matter of chance, whilst as a prophet he is eminent by pure natural fitness for the post. This is ended by his falling in love with a dancing girl, who, after leading him into every sort of undignified and ludicrous extravagance, ranging from his hailing her as the Eternal Feminine of Goethe[6] to the more practical folly of giving her his white horse and all his prophetic finery, runs away with the spoil, and leaves him once more helpless and alone in the desert. He wanders until he comes to the great Sphinx, beside which he finds a German gentleman in great perplexity as to who the Sphinx is. Peer Gynt, seeing in that impassive, immovable, majestic figure, a symbol of his own ideal, is able to tell the German gentleman at once that the Sphinx is itself. This explanation dazzles the German, who, after some further discussion of the philosophy of self-realization, invites Peer Gynt to accompany him to a club of learned men in Cairo, who are ripe for enlightenment on this very question. Peer, delighted, accompanies the German to the club, which turns out to be a madhouse in which the lunatics have broken loose and locked up their keepers. It is in this madhouse, and by these madmen, that Peer Gynt is at last crowned Emperor of Himself. He receives their homage as he lies in the dust fainting with terror.

5. Sir Henry Morton Stanley (1841–1904), African explorer. In the 1913 edition, Shaw rewrote this sentence: "His commercial success in this phase persuades him that he is under the special care of God."

6. *Faust*, Part 2 (1832), act V, final two lines: "The Eternal Feminine / draws us upward."

As an old man, Peer Gynt, returning to the scenes of his early adventures, is troubled with the prospect of meeting a certain button moulder who threatens to make short work of his realized self by melting it down into buttons in his crucible with a heap of other button material. Immediately the old exaltation of the self realizer is changed into an unspeakable dread of the button moulder Death, to avoid whom Peer Gynt will commit any act, even to pushing a drowning man from the spar he is clinging to in a shipwreck lest it should not suffice to support two.[7] At last he finds a deserted sweetheart of his youth still waiting for him and still believing in him. In the imagination of this old woman he finds the ideal Peer Gynt; whilst in himself, the loafer, the braggart, the confederate of sham magicians, the Charleston speculator, the false prophet, the dancing girl's dupe, the bedlam emperor, the selfish thruster of the drowning man into the waves, there is nothing heroic: nothing but commonplace self-seeking and shirking, cowardice and sensuality, veiled only by the romantic fancies of the born liar. With this crowningly unreal realization he is left to face the button moulder as best he can.[8]

Peer Gynt has puzzled a good many people by Ibsen's fantastic and subtle treatment of its thesis. It is so far a difficult play, that the ideal of self-realization, however familiar its suggestions may be to the ambitious reader, is not at all understood by him, much less formulated as a proposition in metaphysics. When it is stated to him by someone who does understand it, he unhesitatingly dismisses it as idiotic; and it is because he is perfectly right in doing so—because it is idiotic in the most accurate sense of the term—that he finds such difficulty in recognizing it as the common ideal of his own prototype, the pushing, competitive, success-loving man who is the hero of the modern world.

There is nothing novel in Ibsen's dramatic method of reducing these

7. Shaw corrected this error in the 1913 edition: "Peer Gynt has already pushed a drowning man [. . .]."

8. "Miss [Isabelle M.] Pagan [(1867–1960), theosophist and astrologer], who has produced scenes from Peer Gynt in Edinburgh and London (which, to its shame, has not yet seen a complete public performance of Peer Gynt), regards the death of Peer as occuring in the scene where all the wasted possibilities of his life drift about him as withered leaves and fluffs of bog-cotton. He picks up an onion, and, playing with the idea that it is himself, and that its skins are the phases of his own career wrapped round the kernel of his real self, strips them off one after another only to discover that there is no kernel. 'Nature is ironical' says Peer bitterly; and that discovery of his own nothingness is taken by Miss Pagan as his death, the subsequent adventures being those of his soul. It is impossible to demur to so poetic an interpretation; though it assumes, in spite of the onion, that Peer had not wholly destroyed his soul. Still, as the button moulder (who might be Brand's ghost) does respite Peer 'until the next cross roads,' it cannot be said that Ibsen leaves Peer definitely scrapped." [G.B.S., 1912]

ideals to absurdity. Exactly as Cervantes took the old ideal of chivalry, and shewed what came of a man attempting to act as if it were real,[9] so Ibsen takes the ideals of Brand and Peer Gynt, and treats them in the very same manner. Don Quixote acts as if he were a perfect knight in a world of giants and distressed damsels instead of a country gentleman in a land of innkeepers and farm wenches; Brand acts as if he were the perfect Adam in a world where, by resolute rejection of all compromise with imperfection, it was immediately possible to change the rainbow "bridge between flesh and spirit" into as enduring a structure as the tower of Babel was intended to be, thereby restoring man to the condition in which he walked with God in the garden; and Peer Gynt tries to act as if he had in him a special force that could be concentrated so as to prevail over all other forces. They ignore the real: ignore what they are and where they are, not only, like Nelson, shutting their eyes to the signals that a brave man may disregard,[10] but insanely steering straight on the rocks that no resolution can prevail against. Observe that neither Cervantes nor Ibsen is incredulous, in the Philistine way, as to the power of ideals over men. Don Quixote, Brand, and Peer Gynt are, all three, men of action seeking to realize their ideals in deeds. However ridiculous Don Quixote makes himself, you cannot dislike or despise him, much less think that it would have been better for him to have been a Philistine like Sancho [Panza]; and Peer Gynt, selfish rascal as he is, is not unlovable. Brand, made terrible by the consequences of his idealism to others, is heroic. Their castles in the air are more beautiful than castles of brick and mortar; but one cannot live in them; and they seduce men into pretending that every hovel is such a castle, just as Peer Gynt pretended that the Trold king's den was a palace.

EMPEROR AND GALILEAN, 1873

When Ibsen, by merely giving the rein to the creative impulse of his poetic nature, had produced Brand and Peer Gynt, he was nearly forty. His will, in setting his imagination to work, had produced a great puzzle for his intellect. In no case does the difference between the will and the intellect come out more clearly than in that of the poet, save only that of the lover. Had Ibsen died in 1867, he, like many another great poet, would have gone to his grave without having ever rationally understood his own meaning. Nay, if in that year an intellectual expert—a commenta-

9. Miguel de Cervantes Saavedra (1547–1616), Spanish novelist and dramatist, in his novel *Don Quixote* (1605–15).

10. At the battle of Copenhagen (1801), when his commander-in-chief signaled Lord Horatio Nelson (1758–1805) to withdraw, he held his telescope to his blind eye. "I have only one eye, I have a right to be blind sometimes," he said. "I really do not see the signal."

tor, as we call him—had gone to Ibsen and offered him the explanation of Brand which he himself must have arrived at before he constructed Ghosts and The Wild Duck, he would perhaps have repudiated it with as much disgust as a maiden would feel if anyone were brutal enough to give her the physiological *rationale* of her dreams of meeting a fairy prince. It is only the naïf who goes to the creative artist with absolute confidence in receiving an answer to his "What does this passage mean?" That is the very question which the poet's own intellect, which had no part in the conception of the poem, may be asking him. And this curiosity of the intellect, this restless life in it which differentiates it from dead machinery, and which troubles our lesser artists but little, is one of the marks of the greater sort. Shakespear, in Hamlet, made a drama of the self-questioning that came upon him when his intellect rose up in alarm, as well it might, against the vulgar optimism of his Henry V, and yet could mend it to no better purpose than by the equally vulgar pessimism of Troilus and Cressida. Dante took pains to understand himself: so did Goethe. Richard Wagner, one of the greatest poets of our own day, has left us as many volumes of criticism of art as he has left musical scores; and he has expressly described how the intellectual activity which he brought to the analysis of his music dramas was in abeyance during their creation. Just so do we find Ibsen, after composing his two great dramatic poems, entering on a struggle to become intellectually conscious of what he had done.

We have seen that with Shakespear such an effort became itself creative and produced a drama of questioning. With Ibsen the same thing occurred: he harked back to an abandoned project of his, and wrote two huge dramas on the subject of the apostasy of the Emperor Julian. In this work we find him at first preoccupied with a piece of oldfashioned freethinking: the dilemma that moral responsibility presupposes free will, and that free will sets man above God. Cain, who slew because he willed, willed because he must, and must have willed to slay because he was himself, comes upon the stage to claim that murder is fertile, and death the ground of life, though he cannot say what is the ground of death. Judas, who betrayed under the same necessity, wants to know whether, since the Master chose him, he chose him foreknowingly. This part of the drama has no very deep significance. It is easy to invent conundrums which dogmatic evangelicalism cannot answer; and no doubt, whilst it was still a nine days' wonder that evangelicalism could not solve all enigmas, such invention seemed something much deeper than the mere intellectual chess-play which it is seen to be now that the nine days are past. In his occasional weakness for such conundrums, and later on in his harping on the hereditary transmission of disease, we see Ibsen's active intellect busy, not only with the problems peculiar to his own plays, but with the fatalism and pessimism of the middle of our century, when the typical advanced culture was attainable by reading Strauss's Leben Jesu,[11] the popularizations of Helmholtz and Darwin by Tyndall and Huxley, and George Eliot's novels, vainly protested against by Ruskin as peopled with "the sweepings of a Pentonville omnibus."[12] The traces of this period in Ibsen's writings shew how well he knew the crushing weight with which the sordid cares of the ordinary struggle for money and respectability fell on the world when the romance of the creeds was discredited, and progress seemed for the moment to mean, not the growth of the spirit of man, but an effect of the survival of the fittest brought about by the destruction of the unfit, all the most frightful examples of this systematic destruction being thrust into the utmost prominence by those who were fighting the Church with Mill's[13] favorite dialectical weapon, the incompatibility of divine omnipotence with divine benevolence. His plays are full of evidence of his overwhelming sense of the necessity for rousing the individual into self-assertion against this numbing fatalism; and yet he never seems to have freed his intellect wholly from an acceptance of its scientific validity. That it only accounted for progress at all on the hypothesis of a continuous increase in the severity of the conditions of existence—that is, on an assumption of just the reverse of what was actually taking place—appears to have escaped Ibsen as completely as it has escaped Professor Huxley himself. It is true that he did not allow himself to be stopped by this gloomy fortress of pessimism and materialism: his genius pushed him past it, but without intellectually reducing it; and the result is, that as far as one can guess, he believes to this day that it is impregnable, not dreaming that it has been demolished, and that too with ridiculous ease, by the mere march behind him of the working class, which, by its freedom from the characteristic bias of the middle classes, has escaped their characteristic illusions, and solved many of the enigmas which they found insoluble because they wished to find them so.[14] His prophetic belief in the spontaneous growth of the will makes him a meliorist without reference to the operation of Natural Selection; but his impression of the light thrown by physical and biological science on the facts of life seems to be the gloomy one of the period at which he must have received his education in these departments. External nature often plays her most ruthless and destructive part in his works, which have an extraordinary fascination for the pessimists of that school, in spite of the incompati-

11. *The Life of Jesus* (1835) by David Friedrich Strauss (1808–74), German theologian.
12. Ruskin's *Fiction, Fair and Foul* (1880–81), on *The Mill on the Floss* (1860) by Eliot (1819–80).
13. John Stuart Mill (1806–73), writer on philosophy, economy, and sociey.
14. In the 1913 edition, Shaw replaced the passage from "That it only accounted for" to here with a long section on Darwinism, including its criticism by Samuel Butler (1835–1902, whom he likened to Ibsen), and a rephrasing of the class conflict theme.

bility of his individualism with that mechanical utilitarian ethic of theirs which treats Man as the sport of every circumstance, and ignores his will altogether.

Another inessential but very prominent feature in Ibsen's dramas will be understood easily by anyone who has observed how a change of religious faith intensifies our concern about our own salvation. An ideal, pious or secular, is practically used as a standard of conduct; and whilst it remains unquestioned, the simple rule of right is to conform to it. In the theological stage, when the Bible is accepted as the revelation of God's will, the pious man, when in doubt as to whether he is acting rightly or wrongly, quiets his misgivings by searching the Scripture until he finds a text which endorses his action.[15] The rationalist, for whom the Bible has no authority, brings his conduct to such tests as asking himself, after Kant, how it would be if everyone did as he proposes to do; or by calculating the effect of his action on the greatest happiness of the greatest number; or by judging whether the liberty of action he is claiming infringes the equal liberty of others, &c., &c. Most men are ingenious enough to pass examinations of this kind successfully in respect to everything they really want to do. But in periods of transition, as, for instance, when faith in the infallibility of the Bible is shattered, and faith in that of reason not yet perfected, men's uncertainty as to the rightness and wrongness of their actions keeps them in a continual perplexity, amid which casuistry seems the most important branch of intellectual activity. Life, as depicted by Ibsen, is very full of it. We find the great double drama of Emperor and Galilean occupied at first with Julian's case regarded as a case of conscience. It is compared, in the manner already described, with the cases of Cain and Judas, the three men being introduced as "cornerstones under the wrath of necessity," "great freedmen under necessity," and so forth. The qualms of Julian are theatrically effective in producing the most exciting suspense as to whether he will dare to choose between Christ and the imperial purple; but the mere exhibition of a man struggling between his ambition and his creed belongs to a phase of intellectual interest which Ibsen had passed when he wrote his Kongs Emnerne or The Pretenders.[16] Emperor and Galilean might have been appropriately, if prosaically, named The Mistake of Maximus the Mystic. It is Maximus who forces the choice on Julian, not as between ambition and principle; between Paganism and Christianity; between "the old beauty that is no longer beautiful and the new truth that is no longer true," but

15. "As such misgivings seldom arise except when the conscience revolts against the contemplated action, an appeal to Scripture to justify a point of conduct is generally found in practice to be an attempt to excuse a crime." [G.B.S., 1891]

16. (1863).

between Christ and Julian himself. Maximus knows that there is no going back to "the first empire" of pagan sensualism. "The second empire," Christian or self-abnegatory idealism, is already rotten at heart. "The third empire" is what he looks for: the empire of Man asserting the eternal validity of his own will. He who can see that not on Olympus, not nailed to the cross, but in himself is God: he is the man to build Brand's bridge between the flesh and the spirit, establishing this third empire in which the spirit shall not be unknown, nor the flesh starved, nor the will tortured and baffled. Thus throughout the first part of the double drama we have Julian prompted step by step to the stupendous conviction that he and not the Galilean[17] is God. His final resolution to seize the throne is expressed in his interruption of the Lord's prayer, which he hears intoned by worshipers in church as he wrestles in the gloom of the catacombs with his own fears and the entreaties and threats of his soldiers urging him to take the final decisive step. At the cue "Lead us not into temptation; but deliver us from evil" he rushes to the church with his soldiers, exclaiming "For mine is the kingdom." Yet he halts on the threshold, dazzled by the light, as his follower Sallust points the declaration by adding "and the power, and the glory."

Once on the throne Julian becomes a mere pedant-tyrant, trying to revive Paganism mechanically by cruel enforcement of external conformity to its rites. In his moments of exaltation he half grasps the meaning of Maximus, only to relapse presently and pervert it into a grotesque mixture of superstition and monstrous vanity. We have him making such speeches as this, worthy of Peer Gynt at his most ludicrous: "Has not Plato long ago enunciated the truth that only a god can rule over men? What did he mean by that saying? Answer me: what did he mean? Far be it from me to assert that Plato, incomparable sage though he was, had any individual, even the greatest, in his prophetic eyes," &c. In this frame of mind Christ appears to him, not as the prototype of himself, as Maximus would have him feel, but as a rival god over whom he must prevail at all costs. It galls him to think that the Galilean still reigns in the hearts of men whilst the emperor can only extort lip honor from them by brute force; for in his wildest excesses of egotism he never so loses his saving sense of the realities of things as to mistake the trophies of persecution for the fruits of faith. "Tell me who shall conquer," he demands of Maximus, "the emperor or the Galilean?"

"Both the emperor and the Galilean shall succumb" says Maximus. "Whether in our time or in hundreds of years I know not; but so it shall be when the right man comes."

"Who is the right man?" says Julian.

17. In the 1913 edition, Shaw revised the phrase: "he no less than the Galilean."

"He who shall swallow up both emperor and Galilean" replies the
seer.[18] "Both shall succumb; but you shall not therefore perish. Does not
the child succumb in the youth and the youth in the man: yet neither
child nor youth perishes. You know I have never approved of your policy
as emperor. You have tried to make the youth a child again. The empire of
the flesh is fallen a prey to the empire of the spirit. But the empire of the
spirit is not final, any more than the youth is. You have tried to hinder the
youth from growing: from becoming a man. Oh fool, who have drawn
your sword against that which is to be: against the third empire, in which
the twin-natured shall reign. For him the Jews have a name. They call
him Messiah, and are waiting for him."

Still Julian stumbles on the threshold of the idea without entering into
it. He is galled out of all comprehension by the rivalry of the Galilean, and
asks despairingly who shall break his power. Then Maximus drives the
lesson home.

> MAXIMUS. Is it not written "Thou shalt have none other gods but
> me"?
> JULIAN. Yes—yes—yes.
> MAXIMUS. The seer of Nazareth did not preach this god or that:
> he said "God is I: I am God."
> JULIAN. And that is what makes the emperor powerless? The
> third empire? The Messiah? Not the Jews' Messiah, but the
> Messiah of the two empires, the spirit and the world?
> MAXIMUS. The God-Emperor.
> JULIAN. The Emperor-God.
> MAXIMUS. Logos in Pan, Pan in Logos.
> JULIAN. How is he begotten?
> MAXIMUS. He is self-begotten in the man who wills.

But it is of no use. Maximus's idea is a synthesis of relations in which not
only is Christ God in exactly the same sense as that in which Julian is God,
but Julian is Christ as well. The persistence of Julian's jealousy of the
Galilean shews that he has not comprehended the synthesis at all, but only
seized on that part of it which flatters his own egotism. And since this part
is only valid as a constituent of the synthesis, and has no reality when
isolated from it, it cannot by itself convince Julian. In vain does Maximus
repeat his lesson in every sort of parable, and in such pregnant questions as
"How do you know, Julian, that you were not in him whom you now
persecute?" He can only wreak him to utter commands to the winds, and to
exclaim, in the excitement of burning his fleet on the borders of Persia,

18. "Or, as we should now say, the Superman." [G.B.S., 1912]

"The third empire is here, Maximus. I feel that the Messiah of the earth lives within me. The spirit has become flesh and the flesh spirit. All creation lies within my will and power. More than the fleet is burning. In that glowing, swirling pyre the crucified Galilean is burning to ashes; and the earthly empire is burning with the Galilean. But from the ashes shall arise, phoenix-like, the God of earth and the Emperor of the spirit in one, in one, in one." At which point he is informed that the Persian refugee whose information has emboldened him to burn his ships, has fled from the camp and is a manifest spy. From that moment he is a broken man. In his next and last emergency, when the Persians fall upon his camp, his first desperate exclamation is a vow to sacrifice to the gods. "To what gods, oh fool?" cries Maximus. "Where are they; and what are they?" "I will sacrifice to this god and that god: I will sacrifice to many" he answers desperately. "One or other must surely hear me. I m u s t c a l l o n s o m e t h i n g w i t h o u t m e a n d a b o v e m e." A flash of lightning seems to him a response from above; and with this encouragement he throws himself into the fight, clinging, like Macbeth, to an ambiguous oracle which leads him to suppose that only in the Phrygian regions need he fear defeat. He imagines he sees the Nazarene in the ranks of the enemy; and in fighting madly to reach him he is struck down, in the name of Christ, by one of his own soldiers. Then his one Christian general, Jovian, calls on his "believing brethren" to give Cæsar what is Cæsar's. Declaring that the heavens are open and the angels coming to the rescue with their swords of fire, he rallies the Galileans of whom Julian has made slave-soldiers. The pagan free legions, crying out that the god of the Galileans is on the Roman side, and that he is the strongest, follow Jovian as he charges the enemy, who fly in all directions whilst Julian, sinking back from a vain effort to rise, exclaims "Thou hast conquered, oh Galilean."

Julian dies quietly in his tent, averring, in reply to a Christian friend's inquiry, that he has nothing to repent of. "The power which circumstances placed in my hands" he says "and which is an emanation of divinity, I am conscious of having used to the best of my skill. I have never wittingly wronged anyone. If some should think that I have not fulfiled all expectations, they should in justice reflect that there is a mysterious power outside us, which in a great measure governs the issue of human undertakings." He still does not see eye to eye with Maximus, though there is a flash of insight in his remark to him, when he learns that the village where he fell is called the Phrygian region, that "the world-will has laid an ambush for him." It was something for Julian to have seen that the power which he found stronger than his individual will was itself will; but inasmuch as he conceived it, not as the whole of which his will was but a part, but as a rival will, he was not the man to found the third empire. He had felt the godhead in himself, but not in others. Being only able to say, with half conviction, "The kingdom of heaven is within ME," he had been utterly vanquished by the Galilean who had been able to say "The kingdom of heaven is within YOU." But he was on the way to that full truth. A man cannot believe in others until he believes in himself; for his conviction of the equal worth of his fellows must be filled by the overflow of his conviction of his own worth. Against the spurious Christianity of asceticism, starving that indispensable prior conviction, Julian rightly rebelled; and Maximus rightly incited him to rebel. But Maximus could not fill the prior conviction even to fulness, much less to overflowing; for the third empire was not yet, and is not yet.

Still the tyrant dies with a peaceful conscience; and Maximus is able to tell the priest at the bedside that the world-will shall answer for Julian's soul. What troubles the mystic is his having misled Julian by encouraging him to bring upon himself the fate of Cain and Judas. As water can be boiled by fire, man can be prompted and stimulated from without to assert his individuality; but just as no boiling can fill a half-empty well, no external stimulus can enlarge the spirit of man to the point at which he can self-beget the Emperor-God in himself by willing. At that point "to will is to have to will"; and it is with these words on his lips that Maximus leaves the stage, still sure that the third empire is to come.

It is not necessary to translate the scheme of Emperor and Galilean into terms of the antithesis between idealism and realism. Julian, in this respect, is a reincarnation of Peer Gynt. All the difference is that the subject which was instinctively projected in the earlier poem, is intellectually constructed in the later history, Julius plus Maximus the Mystic being Peer plus one who understands him better than Ibsen did when he created him.

The current interest of Ibsen's interpretation of original Christianity is obvious. The deepest sayings recorded in the gospels are now nothing but eccentric paradoxes to most of those who reject the superstitious view of Christ's divinity. Those who accept that view often consider that such acceptance absolves them from attaching any sensible meaning to his words at all, and so might as well pin their faith to a stock or stone. Of these attitudes the first is superficial, and the second stupid. Ibsen's interpretation, whatever may be its validity, will certainly hold the field long after the current "Crosstianity," as it has been aptly called,[19] becomes unthinkable.

19. By Captain Frederick J. Wilson, pamphleteer and editor of *The Comprehensionist* (1872), "a journal of ideas and thinker's manual," of whch two issues appeared. Shaw alludes to the term in his preface to *Major Barbara*.

THE OBJECTIVE ANTI-IDEALIST PLAYS[1]

Ibsen had now written three immense dramas, all dealing with the effect of idealism on individual egotists of exceptional imaginative excitability. This he was able to do whilst his intellectual consciousness of this theme was yet incomplete, by simply portraying sides of himself. He has put himself into the skin of Brand, of Peer Gynt, and of Julian;[2] and these figures have accordingly a certain direct vitality which belongs to none of his subsequent creations of the male sex.[3] There are flashes of it in Relling, in Lövborg, in Ellida's stranger from the sea; but they are only flashes: henceforth[4] all his really vivid and solar figures are women. For, having at last completed his intellectual analysis of idealism, he could now construct methodical illustrations of its social working, instead of, as before, blindly projecting imaginary personal experiences which he himself had not yet succeeded in interpreting. Further, now that he understood the matter, he could see plainly the effect of idealism as a social force on people quite unlike himself: that is to say, on everyday people in everyday life: on shipbuilders, bank managers, parsons, and doctors, as well as on saints, romantic adventurers, and emperors. With his eyes thus opened, instances of the mischief of idealism crowded upon him so rapidly that he began deliberately to inculcate their moral by writing realistic prose plays of modern life, abandoning all production of art for art's sake. His skill as a playwright and his genius as an artist were thenceforth used only to secure attention and effectiveness for his detailed attack on idealism. No more verse, no more tragedy for the sake of tears or comedy for the sake of laughter, no more seeking to produce specimens of art forms in order that literary critics might fill the public belly with the east wind. The critics, it is true, soon declared that he had ceased to be an artist; but he, having something else to do with his talent than to fulfil critics' definitions, took no notice of them, not thinking their ideal sufficiently important to write a play about.

The League of Youth, 1869

The first of the series of realistic prose plays is called Pillars of Society; but before describing this, a word must be said about a previous work

1. Shaw added this heading in the 1913 edition.
2. In the 1913 edition, Shaw revised the last phrase: "He has divided himself between Maximus and Julian."
3. In the 1913 edition, Shaw added: "until it reappears under the shadow of death, less as vitality than as mortality putting on immortality, in the four great plays with which he closed and crowned his life's work."
4. In the 1913 edition, Shaw added: "for many years, indeed until his warfare against vulgar idealism is accomplished and a new phase entered upon in The Master Builder [.]"

which seems to have determined the form which the later series took. Between Peer Gynt and Emperor and Galilean, Ibsen had let fall an amusing comedy called The League of Youth (De Unges Forbund) in which the imaginative egotist reappears farcically as an ambitious young lawyer-politician who, smarting under a snub from a local landowner and county magnate, relieves his feelings with such a passionate explosion of Radical eloquence that he is cheered to the echo by the progressive party. Intoxicated with this success, he imagines himself a great leader of the people and a wielder of the mighty engine of democracy. He narrates to a friend a dream in which he saw kings swept helplessly over the surface of the earth by a mighty wind. He has hardly achieved this impromptu when he receives an invitation to dine with the local magnate, whose friends, to spare his feelings, have misled him as to the person aimed at in the new demagogue's speech. The invitation sets the egotist's imagination on the opposite tack: he is presently pouring forth his soul in the magnate's drawing room to the very friend to whom he related the great dream.

"My goal is this: in the course of time I shall get into Parliament, perhaps into the Ministry, and marry happily into a rich and honorable family. I intend to reach it by my own exertions. I must and shall reach it without help from anyone. Meanwhile I shall enjoy life here, drinking in beauty and sunshine. Here there are fine manners: life moves gracefully here: the very floors seem laid to be trodden only by lacquered shoes: the armchairs are deep; and the ladies sink exquisitely into them. Here the conversation goes lightly and elegantly, like a game at battledore; and no blunders come plumping in to make an awkward silence. Here I feel for the first time what distinction means. Yes: we have indeed an aristocracy of culture; and to it I will belong. Dont you yourself feel the refining influence of the place," &c., &c.

For the rest, the play is an ingenious comedy of intrigue, clever enough in its mechanical construction to entitle the French to claim that Ibsen owes something of his technical education as a playwright in the school of Scribe, although it is hardly necessary to add that the difference between The League of Youth and the typical "well-made play" of Scribe is like the difference between a human being and a marionette. One or two episodes in the last two acts contain germs of later plays; and it was the suitability of the realistic prose comedy form to these episodes that no doubt confirmed Ibsen in his choice of it. Therefore The League of Youth would stand as the first of the realistic plays in any classification which referred to form alone. In a classification by content, with which we are here alone concerned, it must stand in its chronological place as a farcical member of the group of heroic plays beginning with The Pretenders and ending with Emperor and Galilean.

PILLARS OF SOCIETY, 1877

Pillars of Society, then, is the first play in which Ibsen writes as one who has intellectually mastered his own didactic purpose, and no longer needs to project himself into his characters. It is the history of one Karsten Bernick, a "pillar of society" who, in pursuance of the duty of maintaining the respectability of his father's famous firm of shipbuilders (to shatter which would be to shatter one of the ideals of commercial society and to bring abstract respectability into disrepute), has averted a disgraceful exposure by allowing another man to bear the discredit not ony of a love affair in which he himself had been the sinner, but of a theft which was never commited at all, having been merely alleged as an excuse for the firm being out of funds at a critical period. Bernick is an abject slave to the idealizings of a certain schoolmaster Rörlund about respectability, duty to society, good example, social influence, health of the community, and so on. When he falls in love with a married actress, he feels that no man has a right to shock the feelings of Rörlund and the community for his own selfish gratification. However, a clandestine intrigue will shock nobody, since nobody need know of it. He accordingly adopts this method of satisfying himself and preserving the moral tone of the community at the same time. Unluckily, the intrigue is all but discovered; and Bernick has either to see the moral security of the community shaken to its foundations by the terrible scandal of his exposure, or else to deny what he did and put it on another man. As the other man happens to be going to America, where he can easily conceal his imputed shame, Bernick's conscience tells him that it would be little short of a crime against society to neglect such an opportunity; and he accordingly lies his way back into the good opinion of Rörland and company at the emigrant's expense.

There are three women in the play for whom the schoolmasters's ideals have no attractions. First, there is the actress's daughter, who wants to get to America because she hears that people there are not good; and she is heartily tired of good people, since it is part of their goodness to look down on her because of her mother's disgrace. The schoolmaster, to whom she is engaged, condescends to her for the same reason. The second has already sacrificed her happiness and wasted her life in conforming to Mr Stead's ideal of womanliness; and she earnestly advises the younger woman not to commit that folly, but to break her engagement with the schoolmaster, and elope promptly with the man she loves. The third is a naturally free woman who has snapped her fingers at the current ideals all her life; and it is her presence that at last encourages the liar to break with the ideals by telling the truth about himself.

The comic personage of the piece is a useless hypochondriac whose function in life, as described by himself, is "to hold up the banner of the ideal." This he does by sneering at everything and everybody for not resembling the heroic incidents and characters he reads about in novels and tales of adventure. But in his obvious peevishness and folly, he is much less dangerous than the pious idealist, the earnest and respectable Rörlund. The play concludes with Bernick's admission that the spirits of Truth and Freedom are the true pillars of society, a phrase which sounds so like an idealistic commonplace that it is necessary to add that Truth in this passage does not mean the nursery convention of truthtelling satirized by Ibsen himself in a later play, as well as by Labiche[5] and other comic dramatists. It means the unflinching recognition of facts, and the abandonment of the conspiracy to ignore such of them as do not bolster up the ideals. The idealist rule as to truth dictates the recognition only of those facts or idealistic masks of facts which have a respectable air, and the mentioning of these on all occasions and at all hazards. Ibsen urges the recognition of all facts; but as to mentioning them, he wrote a whole play, as we shall see presently, to shew that you must do that at your peril, and that a truthteller who cannot hold his tongue on occasion may do as much mischief as a whole university full of trained liars. The word Freedom, I need hardly say, means freedom from slavery to the Rörlund ideals.

A Doll's House, 1879

Unfortunately, Pillars of Society, as a propagandist play, is disabled by the circumstance that the hero, being a fraudulent hypocrite in the ordinary police court sense of the phrase, is not accepted[6] as a typical pillar of society by the class which he represents. Accordingly, Ibsen took care next time to make his idealist irreproachable from the standpoint of the ordinary idealist morality. In the famous Doll's House, the pillar of society who owns the doll is a model husband, father, and citizen. In his little household, with the three darling children and the affectionate little wife, all on the most loving terms with oneanother, we have the sweet home, the womanly woman, the happy family life of the idealist's dream. Mrs Nora Helmer is happy in the belief that she has attained a valid realization of all these illusions; that she is an ideal wife and mother; and that Helmer is an ideal husband who would, if the necessity arose, give his life to save her reputation. A few simply contrived incidents disabuse her effectually on all these points. One of her earliest acts of devotion to her husband has been the secret raising of a sum of money to enable him to make a tour which was necessary to restore his health. As he would have

5. Eugène Marin Labiche (1815–88).
6. In the 1913 edition, Shaw revised this phrase: "would hardly be accepted [.]"

broken down sooner than go into debt, she has had to persuade him that the money was a gift from her father. It was really obtained from a moneylender, who refused to make her the loan unless she induced her father to endorse the promisory note. This being impossible, as her father was dying at the time, she took the shortest way out of the difficulty by writing the name herself, to the entire satisfaction of the moneylender, who, though not at all duped, knows that forged bills are often the surest to be paid. Then she slaves in secret at scrivener's work until she has nearly paid off the debt.

At this point Helmer is made manager of the bank in which he is employed; and the moneylender, wishing to obtain a post there,[7] uses the forged bill to force Nora to exert her influence with Helmer on his behalf. But she, having a hearty contempt for the man, cannot be persuaded by him that there was any harm in putting her father's name on the bill, and ridicules the suggestion that the law would not recognize that she was right under the circumstances. It is her husband's own contemptuous denunciation of a forgery formerly commited by the moneylender himself that destroys her self-satisfaction and opens her eyes to her ignorance of the serious business of the world to which her husband belongs: the world outside the home he shares with her. When he goes on to tell her that commercial dishonesty is generally to be traced to the influence of bad mothers, she begins to perceive that the happy way in which she plays with the children, and the care she takes to dress them nicely, are not sufficient to constitute her a fit person to train them. In order to redeem the forged bill, she resolves to borrow the balance due upon it from a friend of the family. She has learnt to coax her husband into giving her what she asks by appealing to his affection for her: that is, by playing all sorts of pretty tricks until he is wheedled into an amorous humor. This plan she has adopted without thinking about it, instinctively taking the line of least resistance with him. And now she naturally takes the same line with her husband's friend. An unexpected declaration of love from him is the result; and it at once explains to her the real nature of the domestic influence she has been so proud of.

All her illusions about herself are now shattered: she sees herself as an ignorant and silly woman, a dangerous mother, and a wife kept for her husband's pleasure merely; but she only clings the harder to her illusion about him: he is still the ideal husband who would make any sacrifice to rescue her from ruin. She resolves to kill herself rather than allow him to destroy his own career by taking the forgery on himself to save her reputa-

---

7. An error uncorrected in later editions: since Krogstad has a subordinate post at the bank, from which Helmer's hiring of Mrs Linden would displace him, Krogstad wishes to *retain* it.

tion. The final disillusion comes when he, instead of at once proposing to pursue this ideal line of conduct when he hears of the forgery, naturally enough flies into a vulgar rage and heaps invective on her for disgracing him. Then she sees that their whole family life has been a fiction: their home a mere doll's house in which they have been playing at ideal husband and father, wife and mother. So she leaves him then and there in order to find out the reality of things for herself, and to gain some position not fundamentally false, refusing to see her children again until she is fit to be in charge of them, or to live with him until she and he become capable of a more honorable relation to oneanother than which they have hitherto stood. He at first cannot understand what has happened, and flourishes the shattered ideals over her as if they were as potent as ever. He presents the course most agreeable to him—that of staying at home and avoiding a scandal—as her duty to her husband, to her children, and to her religion; but the magic of these disguises is gone; and at last even he understands what has really happened, and sits down alone to wonder whether that more honorable relation can ever come to pass between them.

Ghosts, 1881

In his next play, Ibsen returned to the charge with such an uncompromising and outspoken attack on marriage as a useless sacrifice of human beings to an ideal, that his meaning was obscured by its very obviousness. Ghosts, as it is called, is the story of a woman who has faithfully acted as a model wife and mother, sacrificing herself at every point with selfless thoroughness. Her husband is a man with a huge capacity and appetite for sensuous enjoyment. Society, prescribing ideal duties and not enjoyment for him, drives him to enjoy himself in underhand and illicit ways. When he marries his model wife, her devotion to duty only makes life harder for him; and he at last takes refuge in the caresses of an undutiful but pleasure-loving housemaid, and leaves his wife to satisfy her conscience by managing his business affairs whilst he satisfies his cravings as best he can by reading novels, drinking, and flirting, as aforesaid, with the servants. At this point even those who are most indignant with Nora Helmer for walking out of the doll's house, must admit that Mrs Alving would be justified in walking out of h e r house. But Ibsen is determined to shew you what comes of the scrupulous line of conduct you were so angry with Nora for not pursuing. Mrs Alving feels that her place is by her husband for better for worse, and by her child. Now the ideal of wifely and womanly duty which demands this from her also demands that she should regard herself as an outraged wife, and her husband as a scoundrel. The family ideal again requires that she should suffer in silence, and, for her son's sake, never shatter his faith in the purity of home life by letting him know the truth about his father. It is her duty to conceal that truth from the world and from him. In this she only falters for one moment. Her marriage has not been a love match: she has, in pursuance of her duty as a daughter, contracted it for the sake of her family, although her heart inclined to a highly respectable clergyman, a professor of her own idealism, named Manders. In the humiliation of her first discovery of her husband's infidelity, she leaves the house and takes refuge with Manders; but he at once leads her back to the path of duty, from which she does not again swerve. With the utmost devotion she now carries out a tremendous scheme of lying and imposture. She so manages her husband's affairs and so shields his good name that everybody believes him to be a public-spirited citizen of the strictest conformity to current ideals of respectability and family life. She sits up of nights listening to his lewd and silly conversation, and even drinking with him, to keep him from going into the streets and betraying what she considers his vices. She provides for the servant he has seduced, and brings up his illegitimate daughter as a maid in her own household. And as a crowning sacrifice, she sends her son away to Paris to be educated there, knowing that if he stays at home the shattering of his ideals must come sooner or later.

Her work is crowned with success. She gains the esteem of her old love the clergyman, who is never tired of holding up her household as a beautiful realization of the Christian ideal of marriage. Her own martyrdom is brought to an end at last by the death of her husband in the odor of a most sanctified reputation, leaving her free to recall her son from Paris and enjoy his society, and his love and gratitude, in the flower of his early manhood.

But when he comes home, the facts refuse as obstinately as ever to correspond to her ideals. Oswald, the son, has inherited his father's love of enjoyment; and when, in dull rainy weather, he returns from Paris to the solemn, strictly ordered house where virtue and duty have had their temple for so many years, his mother sees him first shew the unmistakable signs of boredom with which she is so miserably familiar from of old; then sit after dinner killing time over the bottle; and finally—the climax of anguish—begin to flirt with the maid who, as his mother alone knows, is his own father's daughter. But there is this worldwide difference in her insight to the cases of the father and the son. She did not love the father; she loves the son with the intensity of a heart-starved woman who has nothing else left to love. Instead of recoiling from him with pious disgust and Pharisaical consciousness of moral superiority, she sees at once that he has a right to be happy in his own way, and that she has no right to force him to be dutiful and wretched in hers. She sees, too, her injustice to the unfortunate father, and the iniquity of the monstrous fabric of lies and false appearances which she has wasted her life in manufacturing. She resolves that the son's life, at least, shall not be sacrificed to joyless and unnatural ideals. But she soon finds that the work of the ideals is not to be undone quite so easily. In driving the father to steal his pleasures in secrecy and squalor, they had brought upon him the diseases bred by such conditions; and her son now tells her that those diseases have left their mark on him, and that he carries poison in his pocket against the time, foretold to him by a Parisian surgeon, when he shall be struck down with softening of the brain. In desperation she turns to the task of rescuing him from this horrible apprehension by making his life happy. The house shall be made as bright as Paris for him: he shall have as much champagne as he wishes until he is no longer driven to that dangerous resource by the dulness of his life with her: if he loves the girl he shall marry her if she were fifty times his half-sister.[8] But the half-sister, on learning the state of his health, leaves the house; for she, too, is her father's daughter, and is not going to sacrifice her life in devotion to an invalid. When the mother and son are left alone in their dreary home, with the rain still falling outside, all she can do for him is to promise that if his doom overtakes him before he can poison himself, she will make a final sacrifice of her natural feelings by performing the dreadful duty, the first of all her duties that has any real basis. Then the weather clears up at last; and the sun, which the young man has so longed to see, appears. He asks her to give it to him to play with; and a glance at him shews her that the ideals have claimed their victim, and that the time has come for her to save him from a real horror by sending him from her out of the world, just as she saved him from an imaginary one years before by sending him out of Norway.

The last scene of Ghosts is so appallingly tragic that the emotions it excites prevent the play from being seized and discussed like that of A Doll's House. In England nobody, as far as I know, seems to have perceived that Ghosts is to A Doll's House what Mr Walter Besant intended his own sequel[9] to that play to be. Mr Besant attempted to shew what might come of

8. An ironic allusion to *Hamlet*, III.ii: Hamlet agrees to obey the Queen's desire "were she ten times our mother."

9. "An astonishing production, which will be found in the English Illustrated Magazine for January 1890. Mr Besant makes the moneylender, as a reformed man, and a pattern of all the virtues, repeat his old tactics by holding a forged bill *in terrorem* over Nora's grown-up daughter, who is engaged to his son. The bill has been forged by her brother, who has inherited a tendency to this sort of offence from his mother. Helmer having taken to drink after the departure of his wife, and forfeited his social position, the moneylender tells the girl that if she persists in disgracing him by marrying the son, he will send her brother to gaol. She evades the dilemma by drowning herself. An exquisite absurdity is given to this *jeu d'esprit* by the moral, which is, that if Nora had never run away from her husband her daughter would never have drowned herself; and a l s o by the writer's naïve unconscious-

Nora's repudiation of that idealism of which he is one of the most popular professors. But the effect made on Mr Besant by A Doll's House was very faint compared to that produced on the English critics by the first performance of Ghosts in this country. In the earlier part of this essay I have shewn that since Mrs Alving's early conceptions of duty are as valid to ordinary critics as to Pastor Manders, who must appear to them as an admirable man, endowed with Helmer's good sense without Helmer's selfishness, a pretty general disapproval of the moral of the play was inevitable. Fortunately, the newspaper press went to such bedlamite lengths on this occasion that Mr William Archer, the well known dramatic critic and translator of Ibsen, was able to put the whole body of hostile criticism out of court by simply quoting its excesses in an article entitled Ghosts and Gibberings, which appeared in The Pall Mall Gazette of the 8th of April 1891. Mr Archer's extracts, which he offers as a nucleus for a Dictionary of Abuse

---

ness of the fact that he has represented the moneylender as doing over again what he did in the play, with the difference that, having become eminently respectable, he has also become a remorseless scoundrel. Ibsen shews him as a goodnatured fellow at bottom." [G.B.S., 1891] "I wrote a sequel to this sequel. Another sequel was written by Eleanor, the youngest daughter of Karl Marx. I forget where they appeared." [G.B.S., 1913] Besant's short story was titled "The Doll's House—and after"; Shaw's, "Still After the Doll's House," appeared in *Time*, a Socialist journal edited by Ernest Belfort Bax, in February 1890. In collaboration with Israel Zangwill (1864–1926), novelist and dramatist, Eleanor Marx-Aveling (1865–98) wrote not a sequel but a revised ending that parodied the objections of the play's hostile English critics. Eleanor was the common-law wife of Edward Bibbins Aveling (1851–98), who translated Marx's *Capital* and would be a model for the artist-scoundrel Louis Dubedat in Shaw's *The Doctor's Dilemma* (1906). Eleanor had published the first English translations of Ibsen's *An Enemy of the People* under the title *An Enemy of Society* (1888) and *The Lady from the Sea* (1890). The Zangwill–Marx parody, called "*A Doll's House* Repaired," appeared in *Time*, March 1891. According to the authors, their repairs, which include giving Ibsen's dialogue to different speakers, "adhere to English commonsense." In their conclusion, Helmer persuades Krogstad to prevent his future wife from working but instead, as Krogstad puts it, "make her my true helpmate by making her dependent upon me." Happy that Krogstad is "awakening to a higher ideal of life and its duties," Helmer pays off Nora's debt and returns the bank job to Krogstad. After Krogstad leaves, it is Helmer who points out to Nora that in all their married life they have never had a serious discussion as husband and wife should; tells her that he was never really happy and that his home "has been nothing but a playhouse" with her an actress who trained their children to be actors; asserts that he could have found the means to go to a warmer climate without her interference; determines that she needs education; tells her he no longer loves her and will sleep in the spare room; and proposes to ask Pastor Manders to recommend a good boarding school for the children, where Nora cannot exert her malign influence on them, though if she changes he may let them come home for holidays. She hopes to become his little squirrel and songbird again, in which case, he says, their "living together will be a true marriage." He leaves, whereupon she hopes for "the miracle of miracles!"

modelled upon the Wagner Schimpf-Lexicon,[10] are worth reprinting here as samples of contemporary idealist criticism of the drama.

DESCRIPTIONS OF THE PLAY

"Ibsen's positively abominable play entitled Ghosts . . . This disgusting representation . . . Reprobation due to such as aim at infecting the modern theatre with poison after desperately inoculating themselves and others . . . An open drain; a loathsome sore unbandaged; a dirty act done publicly; a lazar-house with all its doors and windows open . . . Candid foulness . . . Kotzebue[11] turned bestial and cynical. Offensive cynicism . . . Ibsen's melancholy and malodorous world . . . Absolutely loathsome and fetid . . . Gross, almost putrid indecorum . . . Literary carrion . . . Crapulous stuff . . . Novel and perilous nuisance." *Daily Telegraph* (leading article). "This mass of vulgarity, egotism, coarseness, and absurdity." *Daily Telegraph* (criticism). "Unutterably offensive . . . Prosecution under Lord Campbell's Act . . . Abominable piece . . . Scandalous." *Standard.* "Naked loathsomeness . . . Most dismal and repulsive production." *Daily News.* "Revoltingly suggestive and blasphemous . . . Characters either contradictory in themselves, uninteresting, or abhorrent." *Daily Chronicle.* "A repulsive and degrading work." *Queen.* "Morbid, unhealthy, unwholesome, and disgusting story . . . A piece to bring the stage into disrepute and dishonor with every right-thinking man and woman." *Lloyd's.* "Merely dull dirt long drawn out." *Hawk.* "Morbid horrors of the hideous tale . . . Ponderous dulness of the didactic talk . . . If any repetition of this outrage be attempted, the authorities will doubtless wake from their lethargy." *Sporting and Dramatic News.* "Just a wicked nightmare." *The Gentlewoman.* "Lugubrious diagnosis of sordid impropriety . . . Characters are prigs, pedants, and profligates . . . Morbid caricatures . . . Maunderings of nookshotten Norwegians . . . It is no more of a play than an average Gaiety burlesque." W. St Leger in *Black and White.* "Most loathsome of all Ibsen's plays . . . Garbage and offal." *Truth.* "Ibsen's putrid play called Ghosts . . . So loathsome an enterprise." *Academy.* "As foul and filthy a concoction as has ever been allowed to disgrace the boards of an English theatre . . . Dull and disgusting . . . Nastiness and malodorousness laid on thickly as with a trowel." *Era.* "Noisome corruption." *Stage.*

10. *A Dictionary of Impoliteness, Containing Rude, Sneering, Malicious, Slanderous Expressions Which Were Used by Enemies and Mockers against Meister Richard Wagner, His Works, and His Followers* (1877), compiled by Wilhelm Tappert.
11. August Friedrich Ferdinand von Kotzebue (1761–1819), internationally popular dramatist who wrote over two hundred plays.

DESCRIPTIONS OF IBSEN

"An egotist and a bungler." *Daily Telegraph.* "A crazy fanatic . . . A crazy, cranky being . . . Not only consistently dirty but deplorably dull." *Truth.* "The Norwegian pessimist *in petto*" (*sic*). W. St Leger in *Black and White.* "Ugly, nasty, discordant, and downright dull . . . A gloomy sort of ghoul, bent on groping for horrors by night, and blinking like a stupid old owl when the warm sunlight of the best of light dances into his wrinkled eyes." *Gentlewoman.* "A teacher of the estheticism of the Lock Hospital."[12] *Saturday Review.*

DESCRIPTIONS OF IBSEN'S ADMIRERS

"Lovers of prurience and dabblers in impropriety who are eager to gratify their illicit tastes under the pretence of art." *Evening Standard.* "Ninety-seven percent of the people who go to see Ghosts are nasty-minded people who find the discussion of nasty subjects to their taste in exact proportion to their nastiness." *Sporting and Dramatic News.* "The sexless . . . The unwomanly woman, the unsexed females, the whole army of unprepossessing cranks in petticoats . . . Educated and muck-ferreting dogs . . . Effeminate men and male women . . . They all of them—men and women alike—know that they are doing not only a nasty but an illegal thing . . . The Lord Chamberlain[13] left them alone to wallow in Ghosts . . . Outside a silly clique, there is not the slightest interest in the Scandinavian humbug or all his works . . . A wave of human folly." *Truth.*[14]

12. Located in London's West End, it specialized in the treatment of venereal diseases.

13. From 1737 to 1969, the office of the Lord Chamberlain issued or withheld licenses for the public performance of plays, thus making him, acting on the recommendations of his readers, censor for the English theater. Under the guise of private clubs, whose members might see nonpublic performances, censorship restrictions were sometimes evaded. Thus, the Shelley Society produced *The Cenci* and the Independent Theatre *Ghosts*, both of which had been refused licenses by the Lord Chamberlain's office.

14. "Outrageous as the above extracts now seem, I could make them appear quite moderate by setting beside them the hue and cry raised in New York in 1905 against a play of my own entitled Mrs Warren's Profession [1893]. But there was a commercial reason for that. My play exposed what has since become known as the White Slave Traffic: that is, the organization of prostitution as a regular commercial industry yielding huge profits to capital invested in it, directly or indirectly, by 'pillars of society.' The attack on the play was so corrupt that the newspaper that took the lead in it was heavily fined shortly afterwards for trading in advertisements of the traffic. But the attack on Ghosts was, I believe, really disinterested and sincere on its moral side. No doubt Ibsen was virulently hated by some of the writers quoted, as all great and original artists are hated by contemporary mediocrity, which needs must hate the highest when it sees it. [Parody of Tennyson, "Idylls of the King" (1842–85), "Guinivere," 1.655: "We needs must love the highest when we see it."] Our own mediocrities would abuse Ibsen as heartily as their fathers did if they were not young enough to have started with an entirely unculcated and unintelligent assumption that he is a classic, like Shakespear and Goethe, and therefore must not be abused and need not be

AN ENEMY OF THE PEOPLE, 1882

After this, the reader will understand the temper in which Ibsen set about his next play, An Enemy of the People, in which, having done sufficient execution among the ordinary social, domestic, and puritanic ideals, he puts his finger for a moment on political ideals. The play deals with a local majority of middleclass people who are pecuniarily interested in concealing the fact that the famous baths which attract visitors to their town and customers to their shops and hotels are contaminated by sewage. When an honest doctor insists on exposing this danger, the townspeople immediately disguise themselves ideally. Feeling the disadvantage of appearing in their true character as a conspiracy of interested rogues against an honest man, they pose as Society, as The People, as Democracy, as the solid Liberal Majority, and other imposing abstractions, the doctor, in attacking them, of course being thereby made an enemy of The People, a danger to Society, a traitor to Democracy, an apostate from the great Liberal party, and so on. Only those who take an active part in politics can appreciate the grim fun of the situation, which, though it has an intensely local Norwegian air, will be at once recognized as typical in England, not, perhaps, by the professional literary critics, who are for the most part *fainéants* as far as liberal life is concerned, but certainly by everyone who has got as far as a seat on the committee of the most obscure caucus.

As An Enemy of the People contains one or two references to democracy which are anything but respectful, it is necessary to define Ibsen's criticism of it with precision. Democracy is really only an arrangement by which the whole people are given a certain share in the control of the government.[15] It has never been proved that this is ideally the best arrangement: it became necessary because the people willed to have it; and it has been made effective only to the very limited extent short of which the dissatisfaction of the majority would have taken the form of actual violence. Now when men had to submit to kings, they consoled themselves by making it an article of faith that the king was always right: idealized him as a Pope, in fact. In the same way we who have to submit

---

understood. But we have only to compare the frantic and indecent vituperation quoted above with the mere disparagement and dislike expressed towards Ibsen's other plays at the same period to perceive that here Ibsen struck at something much deeper than the fancies of critics as to the proper way to make plays. An ordinary farcical comedy ridiculing Pastor Manders and making Alving out to be a good fellow would have enlisted their sympathy at once, as their tradition was distinctly 'Bohemian.' Their horror at Ghosts is a striking proof of the worthlessness of mere Bohemianism, which has all the idle sentimentality and idolatry of conventionality without any of its backbone of contract and law." [G.B.S., 1912]

15. In the 1913 edition, Shaw revised the definition: "an arrangement by which the governed are allowed to choose (as far as any choice is possible, which in capitalistic society is not saying much) the members of the representative bodies which control the executive."

to majorities set up Voltaire's pope, Monsieur Tout le Monde,[16] and make it blasphemy against Democracy to deny that the majority is always right, although that, as Ibsen says, is a lie. It is a scientific fact that the majority, however eager it may be for the reform of old abuses, is always wrong in its opinion of new developments, or rather is always unfit for them (for it can hardly be said to be wrong in opposing developments for which it is not yet fit). The pioneer is a tiny minority of the force he heads; and so, though it is easy to be in a minority and yet be wrong, it is absolutely impossible to be in the majority and yet be right as to the newest social prospects. We should never progress at all if it were possible for each of us to stand still on democratic principles until we saw whither all the rest were moving, as our statesmen declare themselves bound to do when they are called upon to lead. Whatever clatter we may make for a time with our filing through feudal serf collars and kicking off rusty capitalistic fetters, we shall never march a step forward except at the heels of "the strongest man, he who is able to stand alone" and to turn his back on "the damned compact Liberal majority." All of which is no disparagement of adult suffrage, payment of members, annual parliaments, and so on, but simply a wholesale reduction of them to their real place in the social economy as pure machinery: machinery which has absolutely no principles except the principles of mechanics, and no motive power in itself whatsoever. The idealization of public organizations is as dangerous as that of kings or priests. We need to be reminded that though there is in the world a vast number of buildings in which a certain ritual is conducted before crowds called congregations by a functionary called a priest who is subject to a central council controling all such functionaries on a few points, there is not therefore any such thing in reality as the ideal Catholic Church, nor ever was, nor ever will be. There may, too, be a highly elaborate organization of public affairs; but there is no such thing as the ideal State. All abstractions invested with collective consciousness or collective authority, set above the individual, and exacting duty from him on pretence of acting or thinking with greater validity than he, are man-eating idols red with human sacrifices.

This position must not be confounded with Anarchism, or the idealization of the repudiation of Governments. Ibsen does not refuse to pay the tax collector, but may be supposed to regard him, not as an emissary of something that does not exist and never did, called THE STATE, but simply

16. An error for Talleyrand (Prince Charles Maurice de Talleyrand-Périgort, 1754–1838): "There is someone smarter than Voltaire, smarter than Bonaparte, smarter than each of the directors, than each of the past, present, and future ministers: it is Everybody"—speech against the continuation of censorship, 24 July 1821. Shaw would continue this mistake, for example, *Saturday Review*, 2 March 1895 and 8 February 1896, below, and preface to *Getting Married*.

as the man sent round by the committee of citizens (mostly fools as far as "the third empire" is concerned) to collect the money for the police or the paving and lighting of the streets.

THE WILD DUCK, 1884

After An Enemy of the People, Ibsen, as I have said, left the vulgar ideals for dead, and set about the exposure of those of the choicer spirits, beginning with the incorrigible idealists who had idealized his very self, and were becoming known as Ibsenites. His first move in this direction was such a tragicomic slaughtering of sham Ibsenism that his astonished victims plaintively declared that The Wild Duck, as the new play was called, was a satire on his former works; whilst the pious, whom he had disappointed so severely by his interpretation of Brand, began to think that he had come back repentant to the fold. The household to which we are introduced in The Wild Duck is not, like Mrs Alving's, a handsome one made miserable by superstitious illusions, but a shabby one made happy by romantic illusions. The only member of it who sees it as it really is is the wife, a goodnatured Philistine who desires nothing better. The husband, a vain, petted, spoilt dawdler, believes that he is a delicate and high-souled man, devoting his life to redeeming his old father's name from the disgrace brought on it by an imprisonment for breach of the forest laws. This redemption he proposes to effect by making himself famous as a great inventor someday when he has the necessary inspiration. Their daughter, a girl in her teens, believes intensely in her father and in the promised invention. The disgraced grandfather cheers himself by drink whenever he can get it; but his chief resource is a wonderful garret full of rabbits and pigeons. The old man has procured a number of secondhand Christmas trees; and with these he has turned the garret into a sort of toy forest, in which he can play at bear hunting, which was one of the sports of his youth and prosperity. The weapons employed in the hunting expeditions are a gun which will not go off, and a pistol which occasionally brings down a rabbit or a pigeon. A crowning touch is given to the illusion by a wild duck, which, however, must not be shot, as it is the special property of the girl, who reads and dreams whilst the woman cooks and washes, besides carrying on the photographic work which is supposed to be the business of her husband. She does not appreciate his highly strung sensitiveness of character, which is constantly suffering agonizing jars from her vulgarity; but then she does not appreciate that other fact that he is a lazy and idle imposter. Downstairs there is a disgraceful clergyman named Molvik, a hopeless drunkard; but even he respects himself and is tolerated because of a special illusion invented for him by another lodger, a doctor—the now famous Dr Relling—upon whom the lesson of the household above has not been thrown away. Molvik, says the doctor, must break out into drinking fits because he is daimonic, an interesting explanation which completely relieves the reverend gentleman from the imputation of vulgar tippling.

Into this domestic circle there comes a new lodger, an idealist of the most advanced type. He greedily swallows the daimonic theory of the clergyman's drunkenness, and enthusiastically accepts the photographer as the high-souled hero he supposes himself to be; but he is troubled because the relations of the man and his wife do not constitute an ideal marriage. He happens to know that the woman, before her marriage, was the cast-off mistress of his own father; and because she has not told her husband this, he conceives her life as founded on a lie, like that of Bernick in Pillars of Society. He accordingly sets himself to work out the woman's salvation for her, and establish ideally frank relations between the pair, by simply blurting out the truth, and then asking them, with fatuous self-satisfaction, whether they do not feel much the better for it. This wanton piece of mischief has more serious results than a mere domestic scene. The husband is too weak to act on his bluster about outraged honor and the impossibility of his ever living with his wife again; and the woman is merely annoyed with the idealist for telling on her; but the girl takes the matter to heart and shoots herself. The doubt cast on her parentage, with her father's theatrical repudiation of her, destroy her ideal place in the home, and make her a source of discord there; so she sacrifices herself, thereby carrying out the ideal of the idealist mischief-maker, who has talked a good deal to her about the duty and beauty of self-sacrifice, without foreseeing that he might be taken in mortal earnest. The busybody thus finds that people cannot be freed from their failings from without. They must free themselves. When Nora is strong enough to live out of the doll's house, she will go out of it of her own accord if the door stands open; but if before that period you take her by the scruff of the neck and thrust her out, she will only take refuge in the next establishment of the kind that offers to receive her. Woman has thus two enemies to deal with: the oldfashioned one who wants to keep the door locked, and the newfashioned one who wants to thrust her into the street before she is ready to go. In the cognate case of a hypocrite and liar like Bernick, exposing him is a mere police measure: he is nonetheless a liar and hypocrite when you have exposed him. If you want to make a sincere and truthful man of him, all that you can do is to remove what you can of the external obstacles to his exposing himself, and then wait for the operation of his internal impulse to confess. If he has no such impulse, then you must put up with him as he is. It is useless to make claims on him which he is not yet prepared to meet. Whether, like Brand, we make such claims because to refrain would be to compromise with evil, or, like Gregers Werle, because we think their moral beauty must recommend them at sight to everyone, we shall alike incur Relling's impatient assurance that "life would be quite tolerable if we could only get rid of the confounded duns that keep on pestering us in our poverty with the claims of the ideal."

ROSMERSHOLM, 1886

Ibsen did not in The Wild Duck exhaust the subject of the danger of forming ideals for other people, and interfering in their lives with a view to enabling them to realize those ideals. Cases far more typical than that of the meddlesome lodger are those of the priest who regards the ennobling of mankind as a sort of trade process of which his cloth gives him a monopoly, and the clever woman who pictures a noble career for the man she loves, and devotes herself to helping him to achieve it. In Rosmersholm, the play with which Ibsen followed up The Wild Duck, there is an unpractical country parson, a gentleman of ancient stock, whose family has been for many years a centre of social influence. The tradition of that influence reinforces his priestly tendency to regard the ennoblement of the world as an external operation to be performed by himself; and the need of such ennoblement is very evident to him; for his nature is a fine one: he looks at the world with some dim prevision of "the third empire." He is married to a woman of passionately affectionate nature, who is very fond of him, but does not regard him as a regenerator of the human race. Indeed she does not share any of his dreams, and only acts as an extinguisher on the sacred fire of his idealism. He, she, her brother Kroll the headmaster, Kroll's wife, and their set form a select circle of the best people in the place, comfortably orbited in the social system, and quite planetary in ascertained position and unimpeachable respectability. Into the orbit comes presently a wandering star, one Rebecca Gamvik, an unpropertied orphan, who has been allowed to read advanced books, and is a Freethinker and a Radical: all things that disqualify a poor woman for admission to the Rosmer world. However, one must live somewhere; and as the Rosmer world is the only one in which an ambitious and cultivated woman can find powerful allies and educated companions, Rebecca, being both ambitious and cultivated, makes herself agreeable to the Rosmer circle with such success that the affectionate and impulsive but unintelligent Mrs Rosmer becomes wildly fond of her, and is not content until she has persuaded her to come and live with them. Rebecca, then a mere adventuress fighting for a foothold in polite society (which has hitherto shewn itself highly indignant at her thrusting herself in where nobody has thought of providing room for her), accepts the offer all the more readily because she has taken the measure of Parson Rosmer, and formed the idea of playing upon his aspirations, and making herself a leader in politics and society by using him as a figurehead.

But now two difficulties arise. First, there is Mrs Rosmer's extinguishing effect on her husband: an effect which convinces Rebecca that nothing can be done with him whilst his wife is in the way. Second—a contingency quite unallowed for in her provident calculations—she finds herself passionately enamored of him. The poor parson, too, falls in love with her; but he does not know it. He turns to the woman who understands him like a sunflower to the sun, and makes her his real friend and companion. The wife feels this soon enough; and he, quite unconscious of it, begins to think that her mind must be affected, since she has become so intensely miserable and hysterical about nothing: nothing that he can see. The truth is that she has come under the curse of the ideal too: she sees herself standing, a useless obstacle, between her husband and the woman he really loves, the woman who can help him to a glorious career. She cannot even be the mother in the household; for she is childless. Then comes Rebecca, fortified with a finely reasoned theory that Rosmer's future is staked against his wife's life, and says that it is better for all their sakes that she should quit Rosmersholm. She even hints that she must go at once if a grave scandal is to be avoided. Mrs Rosmer, regarding a scandal in Rosmersholm as the most terrible thing that can happen, and seeing that it could be averted by the marriage of Rebecca and Rosmer if she were out of the way, writes a letter secretly to Rosmer's bitterest enemy, the editor of the local Radical paper, a man who has forfeited his moral reputation by an intrigue which Rosmer has pitilessly denounced. In this letter she implores him not to believe or publish any stories that he may hear about Rosmer, to the effect that he is in any way to blame for anything that may happen to her. Then she sets Rosmer free to marry Rebecca, and to realize his ideals, by going out into the garden and throwing herself into the millstream that runs there.

Now follows a period of quiet mourning at Rosmersholm. Everybody except Rosmer suspects that Mrs Rosmer was not mad, and guesses why she commited suicide. Only it would not do to compromise the aristocratic party by treating Rosmer as the Radical editor was treated. So the neighbors shut their eyes and condole with the bereaved clergyman; and the Radical editor holds his tongue because Radicalism is getting respectable, and he hopes, with Rebecca's help, to get Rosmer over to his side presently. Meanwhile the unexpected has again happened to Rebecca. Her passion is worn out; but in the long days of mourning she has found the higher love; and it is now for Rosmer's own sake that she urges him to become a man of action, and brood no more over the dead. When his friends start a Conservative paper and ask him to become editor, she induces him to reply by declaring himself a Radical and Freethinker. To his utter amazement, the result is, not an animated discussion of his views, but just such an attack on his home life and private conduct as he had formerly made on those of the Radical editor. His friends tell him plainly that the compact of silence is broken by his defection, and that there will be no mercy for the traitor to the party. Even the Radical editor not only refuses to publish the fact that his new ally is a Freethinker (which would destroy all his social weight as a Radical recruit), but brings up the dead woman's letter as a proof that the attack is sufficiently well founded to make it unwise to go too far. Rosmer, who at first had been simply shocked that men whom he had always honored as gentlemen should descend to such hideous calumny, now sees that he really did love Rebecca, and is indeed guilty of his wife's death. His first impulse is to shake off the spectre of the dead woman by marrying Rebecca; but she, knowing that the guilt is hers, puts that temptation behind her and refuses. Then, as he thinks it all over, his dream of ennobling the world slips away from him: such work can only be done by a man conscious of his own innocence. To save him from despair, Rebecca makes a great sacrifice. She "gives him back his innocence" by confessing how she drove his wife to kill herself; and, as the confession is made in the presence of Kroll, she ascribes the whole plot to her ambition, and says not a word of her passion. Rosmer, confounded as he realizes what helpless puppets they have all been in the hands of this clever woman, for the moment misses the point that unscrupulous ambition, though it explains her crime, does not account for her confession. He turns his back on her and leaves the house with Kroll. She quietly packs up her trunk, and is about to vanish from Rosmersholm without another word when he comes back alone to ask why she confessed. She tells him why, offering him her self-sacrifice as a proof that his power of ennobling others was no vain dream, since it is his companionship that has changed her from the selfish adventuress she was to the devoted woman she has just proved herself to be. But he has lost his faith in himself, and cannot believe her. The proof is too subtle, too artful: he cannot forget that she duped him by flattering this very weakness of his before. Besides, he knows now that it is not true: that people are not ennobled from without. She has no more to say; for she can think of no further proof. But he has thought of an unanswerable one. Dare she make all doubt impossible by doing for his sake what the wife did? She asks what would happen if she had the heart and will to do it. "Then" he replies "I should have to believe in you. I should recover my faith in my mission. Faith in my power to ennoble human souls. Faith in the human soul's power to attain nobility." "You shall have your faith again" she answers. At this pass the inner truth of the situation comes out; and the thin veil of a demand for proof, with its monstrous sequel of asking the woman to kill herself in order to restore the man's good opinion of himself, falls away. What has really seized Rosmer is the old fatal ideal of expiation by sacrifice. He sees that when Rebecca goes into the millstream he must go too. And he speaks his real mind in the words "There is no judge over us: therefore we must do justice upon ourselves." But the woman's soul is free of this to the end; for when she says "I am under the power of the Rosmersholm view of life n o w. What I have sinned it is fit I should expiate," we feel in that speech a protest against the Rosmersholm view of life: the view that denied her right to live and be happy from the first, and now at the end, even in denying its God, exacts her life as a vain blood offering for its own blindness. The woman has the higher light: she goes to her death out of fellowship with the man who is driven thither by the superstition which has destroyed his will. The story ends with his taking her solemnly as his wife, and casting himself with her into the millstream.

It is unnecessary to repeat here what is said on pages 134–35 as to the vital part played in this drama by the evolution of the lower into the higher love. Peer Gynt, during the prophetic episode in his career, shocks the dancing girl Anitra into a remonstrance by comparing himself to a cat. He replies, with his wisest air, that from the standpoint of love there is perhaps not so much difference between a tomcat and a prophet as she may imagine. The number of critics who have entirely missed the point of Rebecca's transfiguration seem to indicate that the majority of men, even among critics of dramatic poetry, have not got beyond Peer Gynt's opinion in this matter. No doubt they would not endorse it as a definitely stated proposition, aware, as they are, that there is a poetic convention to the contrary. But if they fail to recognize the only possible alternative proposition when it is not stated in so many words by Rebecca West, but when without it her conduct dramatically contradicts her character—when they even complain of the contradiction as a blemish on the play—I am afraid there can be no further doubt that the extreme perplexity into which the first performance of Rosmersholm in England plunged the Press was due entirely to the prevalence of Peer Gynt's view of love among the dramatic critics.

THE LADY FROM THE SEA, 1888

Ibsen's next play, though it deals with the old theme, does not insist on the power of ideals to kill, as the two previous plays do. It rather deals with the origin of ideals in unhappiness, in dissatisfaction with the real. The subject of The Lady from the Sea is the most poetic fancy imaginable. A young woman, brought up on the seacoast, marries a respectable doctor, a widower, who idolizes her and places her in his household with nothing to do but dream and be made much of by everybody. Even the housekeeping is done by her stepdaughter: she has no responsibility, no care, and no trouble. In other words, she is an idle, helpless, utterly dependent article of luxury. A man turns red at the thought of being such a thing; but he thoughtlessly accepts a pretty and fragile-looking woman in the same position as a charming natural picture. The lady from the sea feels an indefinite want in her life. She reads her want into all other lives, and comes to the conclusion that man once had to choose whether he would be a land animal or a creature of the sea; and that having chosen the land, he has carried about with him ever since a secret sorrow for the element he has forsaken. The dissatisfaction that gnaws her is, as she interprets it, this desperate longing for the sea. When her only child dies and leaves her without the work of a mother to give her a valid place in the world, she yields wholly to her longing, and no longer cares for her husband, who, like Rosmer, begins to fear that she is going mad.

At last a seaman appears and claims her as his wife on the ground that they went years before through a rite which consisted of their marrying the sea by throwing their rings into it. This man, who had to fly from her in the old time because he killed his captain, and who fills her with a sense of dread and mystery, seems to her to embody the attraction which the sea has for her. She tells her husband that she must go away with the seaman. Naturally the doctor expostulates: declares that he cannot for her own sake let her do so mad a thing. She replies that he can only prevent her by locking her up, and asks him what satisfaction it will be to him to have her body under lock and key whilst her heart is with the other man. In vain he urges that he will only keep her under restraint until the seaman goes: that he must not, dare not, allow her to ruin herself. Her argument remains unanswerable. The seaman openly declares that she will come; so that the distracted husband asks him does he suppose he can force her from her home. To this the seaman replies that, on the contrary, unless she comes of her own free will there is no satisfaction to him in her coming at all: the unanswerable argument again. She echoes it by demanding her freedom to choose. Her husband must cry off his law-made and Church-made bargain; renounce his claim to the fulfilment of her vows; and leave her free to go back to the sea with her old lover. Then the doctor, with a heavy heart, drops his prate about his heavy responsibility for her actions, and throws the responsibility on her by crying off as she demands. The moment she feels herself a free and responsible woman, all her childish fancies vanish: the seaman becomes simply an old acquaintance whom she no longer cares for; and the doctor's affection produces its natural effect. In short, she says No to the seaman, and takes over the housekeeping keys from her stepdaughter without any further speculations concerning that secret sorrow for the abandoned sea.

It should be noted here that Ellida, the Lady from the Sea, appears a much more fantastic person to English readers than to Norwegian ones. The same thing is true of many other characters drawn by Ibsen, notably Peer Gynt, who, if born in England, would certainly not have been a poet and metaphysician as well as a blackguard and a speculator. The extreme type of Norwegian, as depicted by Ibsen, imagines himself doing wonderful things, but does nothing. He dreams as no Englishman dreams, and drinks to make himself dream the more, until his effective will is destroyed, and he becomes a brokendown, disreputable sot, carrying about the tradition that he is a hero, and discussing himself on that assumption. Although the number of persons who dawdle their life away over fiction in England must be frightful, and is probably increasing, yet we have no Ulric Brendels, Rosmers, Ellidas, Peer Gynts, nor anything at all like them; and it is for this reason that I am disposed to fear that Rosmersholm and The Lady from the Sea will always be received much more incredulously by English audiences than A Doll's House and the plays in which the leading figures are men and women of action.

Hedda Gabler, 1890

Hedda Gabler, the heroine after whom the last of Ibsen's plays (so far) is named, has no ideals at all. She is a pure skeptic,[17] a typical XIX century figure, falling into the abyss between the ideals which do not impose on her and the realities which she has not yet discovered. The result is that she has no heart, no courage, no conviction: with great beauty and great energy she remains mean, envious, insolent, cruel in protest against others' happiness, a bully in reaction from her own cowardice. Hedda's father, a general, is a widower. She has the traditions of the military caste about her; and these narrow her activities to the customary hunt for a socially and pecuniarily eligible husband. She makes the acquaintance of a young man of genius who, prohibited by an ideal-ridden society from taking his pleasures except where there is nothing to restrain him from excess, is going to the bad in search of his good, with the usual consequences. Hedda is intensely curious about the side of life which is forbidden to her, and in which powerful instincts, absolutely ignored and condemned by the society with which intercourse is permitted to her, steal their satisfaction. An odd intimacy springs up between the inquisitive girl and the rake. Whilst the general reads the paper in the afternoon, Lövborg and Hedda have long conversations in which he describes to her all his disreputable adventures. Although she is the questioner, she never dares to trust him: all the ques-

17. In the 1913 edition, Shaw deleted this phrase and revised the preceding sentence: "Hedda Gabler has no ethical ideals at all, only romantic ones."

tions are indirect; and the responsibility for his interpretations rests on him alone. Hedda has no conviction whatever that these conversations are disgraceful; but she will not risk a fight with society on the point: hypocrisy, the homage that truth pays to falsehood, is easier to face, as far as she can see, than ostracism. When he proceeds to make advances to her, Hedda has again no conviction that it would be wrong for her to gratify his instinct and her own; so that she is confronted with the alternative of sinning against herself and him, or sinning against social ideals in which she has no faith. Making the coward's choice, she carries it out with the utmost bravado, threatening Lövborg with one of her father's pistols, and driving him out of the house with all that ostentation of outraged purity which is the instinctive defence of women to whom chastity is not natural, much as libel actions are mostly brought by persons concerning whom libels are virtually, if not technically, justifiable.

Hedda, deprived of her lover, now finds that a life of conformity without faith involves something more terrible than the utmost ostracism: to wit, boredom. This scourge, unknown among revolutionists, is the curse which makes the security of respectability as dust in the balance against the unflagging interest of rebellion, and which forces society to eke out its harmless resources for killing time by licensing gambling, gluttony, hunting, shooting, coursing, and other vicious distractions for which even idealism has no disguise. These licences, however, are only available for people who have more than enough money to keep up appearances with; and as Hedda's father is too poor to leave her much more than the case of pistols, her boredom is only mitigated by dancing, at which she gains much admiration, but no substantial offers of marriage.

At last she has to find someone to support her. A goodnatured mediocrity of a professor is all that is to be had; and though she regards him as a member of an inferior class, and despises almost to loathing his family circle of two affectionate old aunts and the inevitable general servant who has helped to bring him up, she marries him *faute de mieux*, and immediately proceeds to wreck this prudent provision for her livelihood by accommodating his income to her expenditure instead of accommodating her expenditure to his income. Her nature so rebels against the whole sordid transaction that the prospect of bearing a child to her husband drives her almost frantic, since it will not only expose her to the intimate solicitude of his aunts in the course of a derangement of her health in which she can see nothing that is not repulsive and humiliating, but will make her one of his family in earnest.

To amuse herself in these galling circumstances, she forms an underhand alliance with a visitor who belongs to her old set, an elderly gallant who quite understands how little she cares for her husband, and proposes a *ménage à trois* to her. She consents to his coming there and talking to her as he pleases behind her husband's back; but she keeps her pistols in reserve in case he becomes seriously importunate. He, on the other hand, tries to get some hold over her by placing her husband under pecuniary obligations, as far as he can do it without being out of pocket. And so Hedda's married life begins, with only this gallant as a precaution against the most desperate tedium.

Meanwhile Lövborg is drifting to disgrace by the nearest way: through drink. In due time he descends from lecturing at the university on the history of civilization to taking a job in an out-of-the-way place as tutor to the little children of Sheriff Elvsted. This functionary, on being left a widower with a number of children, marries their governess, finding that she will cost him less and be bound to do more for him as his wife. As for her, she is too poor to dream of refusing such a settlement in life. When Lövborg comes, his society is heaven to her. He does not dare to tell her about his dissipations; but he tells her about his unwritten books. She does not dare to remonstrate with him for drinking; but he gives it up as soon as he sees that it shocks her. Just as Mr Fearing, in Bunyan's story,[18] was in a way the bravest of the pilgrims, so this timid and unfortunate Mrs Elvsted trembles her way to a point at which Lövborg, quite re-formed, publishes one book which makes him celebrated for the moment and completes another, faircopied in her handwriting, to which he looks for a solid position as an original thinker. But he cannot now stay tutoring Elvsted's children; so off he goes to town with his pockets full of the money the published book has brought him. Left once more in her old lonely plight, knowing that without her Lövborg will probably relapse into dissipation, and that without him her life will not be worth living, Mrs Elvsted is now confronted, on her own higher plane, with the same alternative which Hedda encountered. She must either sin against her-self and him or against the institution of marriage under which Elvsted purchased his housekeeper. It never occurs to her even that she has any choice. She knows that her action will count as "a dreadful thing"; but she sees that she must go; and accordingly Elvsted finds himself without a wife and his children without a governess, and so disappears unpitied from the story.

Now it happens that Hedda's husband, Jörgen Tesman, is an old friend and competitor (for academic honors) of Lövborg, and also that Hedda was a schoolfellow of Mrs Elvsted, or Thea, as she had better now be called. Thea's first business is to find out where Lövborg is; for hers is no preconcerted elopement: she has hurried to town to keep Lövborg away from the bottle, a design which she dare not hint at to himself. Accord-

---

18. John Bunyan (1628–88), *Pilgrim's Progress*, Part 2 (1684).

ingly, the first thing she does is to call on the Tesmans, who have just returned from their honeymoon, to beg them to invite Lövborg to their house so as to keep him in good company. They consent, with the result that the two pairs are brought together under the same roof, and the tragedy begins to work itself out.

Hedda's attitude now demands a careful analysis. Lövborg's experience with Thea has enlightened his judgment of Hedda; and as he is, in his gifted way, an arrant *poseur* and male coquet, he immediately tries to get on romantic terms with her—for have they not "a past"?—by impressing her with the penetrating criticism that she is and always was a coward. She admits that the virtuous heroics with the pistol were pure cowardice; but she is still so void of any other standard of conduct than conformity to the conventional ideals, that she thinks her cowardice consisted in not daring to be wicked. That is, she thinks that what she actually did was the right thing; and since she despises herself for doing it, and feels that he also rightly despises her for doing it, she gets a passionate feeling that what is wanted is the courage to do wrong. This unlooked-for reaction of idealism, this monstrous but very common setting-up of wrongdoing as an ideal, and of the wrongdoer as a hero or heroine *qua* wrongdoer, leads Hedda to conceive that when Lövborg tried to seduce her he was a hero, and that in allowing Thea to reform him he has played the recreant. In acting on this misconception, she is restrained by no consideration for any of the rest. Like all people whose lives are valueless, she has no more sense of the value of Lövborg's or Tesman's or Thea's lives than a railway shareholder has of the value of a shunter's. She gratifies her intense jealousy of Thea by deliberately taunting Lövborg into breaking loose from her influence by joining a carouse at which he not only loses his manuscript, but finally gets into the hands of the police through behaving outrageously in the house of a disreputable woman whom he accuses of stealing it, not knowing that it has been picked up by Tesman and handed to Hedda for safe keeping.[19] Now to Hedda this bundle of paper in another woman's handwriting is the fruit of Lövborg's union with Thea: he himself speaks of it as "their child." So when he turns his despair to romantic account by coming to the two women and making a tragic scene, telling Thea that he has cast the manuscript, torn into a thousand pieces, out upon the fiord; and then, when she is gone, telling Hedda that he has brought "the child" to a house of ill fame and lost it there, she, deceived by his posing, and thirsting to gain faith in human nobility[20]

19. In the 1913 edition, Shaw added: "Now Hedda's jealousy of Thea is not jealousy of her bodily fascination: at that Hedda can beat her. It is jealousy of her power of making a man of Lövborg, of her part in his life as a man of genius."

20. In the 1913 edition, Shaw revised the phrase: "to gain faith in the beauty of her own influence over him [. . .]."

from a heroic deed of some sort, makes him a present of one of her pistols, only begging him to "do it beautifully," by which she means that he is to kill himself without spoiling his appearance.[21] He takes it unblushingly, and leaves her with the air of a man who is looking his last on earth. But the moment he is out of sight of his audience, he goes back to the house where he still supposes that the manuscript was lost, and there renews the wrangle of the night before, using the pistol to threaten the woman, with the result that he gets shot in the abdomen, leaving the weapon to fall into the hands of the police. Meanwhile Hedda deliberately burns "the child." Then comes her elderly gallant to tell her the true story of the heroic deed which Lövborg promised her to do so beautifully, and to make her understand that he himself has now got her into his power by his ability to identify the pistol. She has either to be the slave of this man, or else to face the scandal of the connection of her name at the inquest with a squalid debauch ending in a murder. Thea, too, is not crushed by Lövborg's death. Ten minutes after she has received the news with a cry of heartfelt loss, she sits down with Tesman to reconstruct "the child" from the old notes which she has preserved. Over the congenial task of collecting and arranging another man's ideas Tesman is perfectly happy, and forgets his beautiful Hedda for the first time. Thea the trembler is still mistress of the situation, holding the dead Lövborg, gaining Tesman, and leaving Hedda to her elderly admirer, who smoothly remarks that he will answer for Mrs Tesman not being bored whilst her husband is occupied with Thea in putting the pieces of the book together. However, he has again reckoned without General Gabler's second pistol. She shoots herself then and there; and so the story ends.

THE MORAL OF THE PLAYS[1]

In following this sketch of the plays written by Ibsen to illustrate his thesis that the real slavery of today is slavery to ideals of virtue, it may be that readers who have conned Ibsen through idealist spectacles have wondered that I could so pervert the utterances of a great poet. Indeed I know already that many of those who are most fascinated by the poetry of the plays will plead for any explanation of them rather than that given by Ibsen himself in the plainest terms through the mouths of Mrs Alving, Relling, and the rest. No great writer uses his skill to conceal his meaning. There is a tale by a famous Scotch storyteller which would have

21. In the 1913 edition, Shaw revised the phrase: "to kill himself in some manner that will make his suicide a romantic memory and an imaginative luxury to her forever."

1. In the 1913 edition, Shaw changed the heading to "The Lesson of the Plays."

suited Ibsen exactly if he had hit on it first. Jeanie Deans sacrificing her sister's life on the scaffold to her own ideal of duty is far more horrible than the sacrifice in Rosmersholm; and the *deus ex machina* expedient by which Scott makes the end of his story agreeable is no solution of the moral problem raised, but only a puerile evasion of it. He undoubtedly believed that it was right that Effie should hang for the sake of Jeanie's ideals.[2] Consequently, if I were to pretend that Scott wrote The Heart of Midlothian[3] to shew that people are led to do as mischievous, as unnatural, as murderous things by their religious and moral ideals as by their envy and ambition, it would be easy to confute me from the pages of the book itself. But Ibsen has made his meaning no less plain than Scott's. If anyone attempts to maintain that Ghosts is a polemic in favor of indissoluble monogamic marriage, or that The Wild Duck was written to inculcate that truth should be told for its own sake, they must burn the text of the plays if their contention is to stand. The reason that Scott's story is tolerated by those who shrink from Ghosts is not that it is less terrible, but that Scott's views are familiar to all well-brought-up ladies and gentlemen, whereas Ibsen's are for the moment so strange as to be almost unthinkable. He is so great a poet that the idealist finds himself in the dilemma of being unable to conceive that such a genius should have an ignoble meaning, and yet equally unable to conceive his real meaning as otherwise than ignoble. Consequently he misses the meaning altogether in spite of Ibsen's explicit and circumstantial insistence on it, and proceeds to interpolate a meaning which conforms to his own ideal of nobility.

Ibsen's deep sympathy with his idealist figures seems to countenance this method of making confusion. Since it is on the weaknesses of the higher types of character that idealism seizes, his examples of vanity, selfishness, folly, and failure are not vulgar villains, but men who in an ordinary novel or melodrama would be heroes. His most tragic point is reached in the destinies of Brand and Rosmer, who drive those whom they love to death in its most wanton and cruel form. The ordinary Philistine commits no such atrocities: he marries the woman he likes and lives more or less happily ever after; but that is not because he is greater than

2. "The commonsense solution of the moral problem has often been delivered by acclamation in the theatre. Some sixteen or seventeen years ago I witnessed a performance of a melodrama founded on this story. After the painful trial scene, in which Jeanie Deans condemns her sister to death by refusing to swear to a perfectly innocent fiction, came a scene in the prison. 'If it had been me' said the jailor 'I wad ha sworn a hole through an iron pot.' The roar of applause which burst from the pit and gallery was thoroughly Ibsenite in sentiment. The speech, by the way, was a gag of the actor's, and is not to be found in the acting edition of the play." [G.B.S., 1891] In the 1913 edition Shaw revised the sentence in the text: "He dared not, when it came to the point, allow Effie to be hanged for the sake of Jeanie's ideals."
3. (1818).

Brand or Rosmer, but because he is less. The idealist is a more dangerous animal than the Philistine just as a man is a more dangerous animal than a sheep. Though Brand virtually murdered his wife, I can understand many a woman, comfortably married to an amiable Philistine, reading the play and envying the victim her husband. For when Brand's wife, having made the sacrifice he has exacted, tells him that he was right; that she is happy now; that she sees God face to face; but reminds him that "whoso sees Jehovah dies," he instinctively clasps his hands over her eyes; and that action raises him at once far above the criticism that sneers at idealism from beneath, instead of surveying it from the clear ether above, which can only be reached through its mists.

If, in my account of the plays, I have myself suggested false judgments by describing the errors of the idealists in the terms of the life they had risen above rather than in that of the life they fell short of, I can only plead, with but a moderate disrespect to a large section of my readers, that if I had done otherwise I should have failed wholly to make the matter understood. Indeed the terms of the realist morality have not yet appeared in our living language; and I have already, in this very distinction between idealism and realism, been forced to insist on a sense of these terms which, had not Ibsen forced my hand, I should perhaps have conveyed otherwise, so strongly does it conflict in many of its applications with the vernacular use of the words.

This, however, was a trifle compared to the difficulty which arose when personal characters had to be described from our inveterate habit of labeling men with the names of their moral qualities without the slightest reference to the underlying will which sets these qualities in action. At a recent anniversary celebration of the Paris Commune of 1871, I was struck by the fact that no speaker could find a eulogy for the Federals which would not have been equally appropriate to the peasants of La Vendée who fought for their tyrants against the French revolutionists, or to the Irishmen and Highlanders who fought for the Stuarts at the Boyne or Culloden.[4] Nor could the celebrators find any other adjectives for their favorite leaders of the Commune than those which had recently been liberally applied by all the journals to an African explorer[5] whose achievements were just then held in the liveliest abhorrence by the whole meeting. The statements that the slain members of the Commune were heroes who died for a noble ideal woud have left a stranger quite as much in the

4. The Paris Commune, an uprising of the workers of Paris against the regime of Napoleon III after his defeat during the Franco-Prussian War, was abolished in 1874. In 1690, the Protestant King William III of Orange defeated the Catholic James II, deposed king of England whom his coreligionists backed, at the Battle of the Boyne; in 1746, Charles Edward Stuart, the "Young Pretender," was defeated at the Battle of Culloden.
    5. Sir Henry Morton Stanley.

dark about them as the counter statements, once common enough in middleclass newspapers, that they were incendiaries and assassins. Our obituary notices are examples of the same ambiguity. Of all the public men lately deceased, none have been made more interesting by strongly marked personal characteristics than the late Charles Bradlaugh. He was not in the least like any other notable member of the House of Commons. Yet when the obituary notices appeared, with the usual string of qualities: eloquence, determination, integrity, strong commonsense, and so on, it would have been possible by merely expunging all names and other external details from these notices, to leave the reader entirely unable to say whether the subject of them was Mr Gladstone, Mr Morley, Mr Stead, or anyone else no more like Mr Bradlaugh than Garibaldi or the late Cardinal Newman,[6] whose obituary certificates of morality might nevertheless have been reprinted almost verbatim for the occasion without any gross incongruity. Bradlaugh had been the subject of many sorts of newspaper notices in his time. Ten years ago, when the middle classes supposed him to be a revolutionist, the string of qualities which the press hung upon him were all evil ones, great stress being laid on the fact that as he was an atheist it would be an insult to God to admit him to Parliament. When it became apparent that he was a conservative force in politics, he, without any recantation of his atheism, at once had the string of evil qualities exchanged for a rosary of good ones; but it is hardly necessary to add that neither the old badge nor the new will ever give any inquirer the least clue to the sort of man he actually was: he might have been Oliver Cromwell or Wat Tyler or Jack Cade, Penn or Wilberforce or Wellington, the late Mr Hampden of flat-earth-theory notoriety[7] or Proudhon or the Archbishop of Canterbury, for all the distinction that such labels could give him one way or the other. The worthlessness of these accounts of individuals is recognized in practice every day. Tax a stranger before a crowd with being a thief, a coward, and a liar; and the crowd will suspend its judgment until you answer the question "What's he done?" Attempt to make a collection for him on the ground that he is an upright, fearless, high-principled hero; and the same question must be answered before a penny goes into the hat.

6. William Ewart Gladstone (1809–98), Conservative Prime Minister; John, later Lord Morley (1838–1923), Liberal politician; Giuseppe Garibaldi (1807–82), Italian patriot who unified Italy; John Henry Newman (1801–90), English theologian who converted from the Anglican to the Catholic Church.

7. Wat Tyler (d. 1381), leader of the Peasants' Revolt; John (Jack) Cade (d. 1450) led a popular revolt against the king (and is a character in Shakespeare's 2 *Henry VI*); William Penn (1644–1718), Quaker and founder of Pennsylvania; William Wilberforce (1759–1833) antislavery activist; Arthur Wellesley, Duke of Wellington (1769–1852) defeated Napoleon; John Hampden (d. 1891) lectured and wrote, sometimes under the pseudonym Parallax.

The reader must therefore discount those partialities which I have permitted myself to express in telling the stories of the plays. They are as much beside the mark as any other example of the sort of criticism which seeks to create an impression favorable or otherwise to Ibsen by simply pasting his characters all over with good or bad conduct marks. If any person cares to describe Hedda Gabler as a modern Lucretia[8] who prefered death to dishonor, and Thea Elvsted as an abandoned, perjured strumpet who deserted the man she had sworn before her God to love, honor, and obey until her death, the play contains conclusive evidence establishing both points. If the critic goes on to argue that as Ibsen manifestly means to recommend Thea's conduct above Hedda's by making the end happier for her, the moral of the play is a vicious one, that, again, cannot be gainsaid. If, on the other hand, Ghosts be defended, as the dramatic critic of Piccadilly lately did defend it, because it throws into divine relief the beautiful figure of the simple and pious Pastor Manders, the fatal compliment cannot be parried. When you have called Mrs Alving an emancipated woman or an unprincipled one, Alving a debauchee or a victim of society, Nora a fearless and noble-hearted woman or a shocking little liar and an unnatural mother, Helmer a selfish hound or a model husband and father, according to your bias, you have said something which is at once true and false, and in either case perfectly idle.

The statement that Ibsen's plays have an immoral tendency, is, in the sense in which it is used, quite true. Immorality does not necessarily imply mischievous conduct: it implies conduct, mischievous or not, which does not conform to current ideals. Since Ibsen has devoted himself almost entirely to shewing that the spirit or will of Man is constantly outgrowing his ideals, and that therefore conformity to them is constantly producing results no less tragic than those which follow the violation of ideals which are still valid, the main effect of his plays is to keep before the public the importance of being always prepared to act immorally, to remind men that they ought to be as careful how they yield to a temptation to tell the truth as to a temptation to hold their tongues, and to urge upon women that the desirability of their preserving their chastity depends just as much on circumstances as the desirability of taking a cab instead of walking. He protests against the ordinary assumption that there are certain supreme ends which justify all means used to attain them; and insists that every end shall be challenged to shew that it justifies the means.[9] Our ideals, like the gods of old, are constantly de-

8. In sixth-century B.C. Rome, Lucretia, wife of Lucius Tarquinius Collatinus, killed herself after Sextus Tarquinius had raped her. See, e.g., Shakespeare's *The Rape of Lucrece*.

9. In the 1913 edition, Shaw, changing the final phrase, added: "insists that the supreme end shall be the inspired, eternal, ever growing one, not the external, unchanging, artificial

manding human sacrifices. Let none of them, says Ibsen, be placed above the obligation to prove that they are worth the sacrifices they demand; and let everyone refuse to sacrifice himself and others from the moment he loses his faith in the reality of the ideal. Of course it will be said here by incorrigibly slipshod readers that this, so far from being immoral, is the highest morality; and so, in a sense, it is; but I really shall not waste any further explanation on those who will neither mean one thing or another by a word nor allow me to do so. In short, then, among those who are not ridden by current ideals no question as to the morality of Ibsen's plays will ever arise; and among those who are so ridden his plays will seem immoral, and cannot be defended against the accusation.

There can be no question as to the effect likely to be produced on an individual by his conversion from the ordinary acceptance of current ideals as safe standards of conduct, to the vigilant openmindedness of Ibsen. It must at once greatly deepen the sense of moral responsibility. Before conversion the individual anticipates nothing worse in the way of examination at the judgment bar of his conscience than such questions as Have you kept the commandments? Have you obeyed the law? Have you attended church regularly; paid your rates and taxes to Cæsar; and contributed, in reason, to charitable institutions? It may be hard to do all these things; but it is still harder not to do them, as our ninetynine moral cowards in the hundred well know. And even a scoundrel can do them all and yet live a worse life than the smuggler or prostitute who must answer No all through the catechism. Substitute for such a technical examination one in which the whole point to be settled is Guilty or Not Guilty? one in which there is no more and no less respect for chastity than for incontinence, for subordination than for rebellion, for legality than for illegality,

---

one; not the letter but the spirit; not the contract but the object of the contract; not the abstract law but the living will. And because the will to change our habits and thus defy morality arises before the intellect can reason out any racially beneficent purpose in the change, there is always an interval during which the individual can say no more than that he wants to behave immorally because he likes, and because he will feel constrained and unhappy if he acts otherwise. For this reason it is enormously important that we should 'mind our business' and let other people do as they like unless we can prove some damage beyond the shock to our feelings and prejudices. It is easy to put revolutionary cases in which it is so impossible to draw the line that they will always be decided in practice more or less by physical force; but for all ordinary purposes of government and social conduct the distinction is a commonsense one. The plain working truth is that it is not only good for people to be shocked occasionally, but absolutely necessary to the progress of society that they should be shocked pretty often. But it is not good for people to be garotted occasionally, or at all. That is why it is a mistake to treat an atheist as you treat a garotter, or to put 'bad taste' on the footing of theft and murder. The need for freedom of evolution is the sole basis of toleration, the sole valid argument against Inquisitions and Censorships, the sole reason for not burning heretics and sending every eccentric person to the madhouse."

for piety than for blasphemy, in short, for the standard virtues than for the standard vices, and immediately, instead of lowering the moral standard by relaxing the tests of worth, you raise it by increasing their stringency to a point at which no mere Pharisaism or moral cowardice can pass them.

Naturally this does not please the Pharisee. The respectable lady of the strictest Christian principles, who has brought up her children with such relentless regard to their ideal morality that if they have any spirit left in them by the time they arrive at years of independence they use their liberty to rush deleriously to the devil: this unimpeachable woman has always felt it unjust that the respect she wins should be accompanied by deepseated detestation, whilst the latest spiritual heiress of Nell Gwynne, whom no respectable person dare bow to in the street, is a popular idol.[10] The reason is—though the virtuous lady does not know it—that Nell Gwynne is a better woman than she; and the abolition of the idealist test which brings her out a worse one, and its replacement by the realist test which would shew the true relation between them, would be a most desirable step forward in public morals, especially as it would act impartially, and set the good side of the Pharisee above the bad side of the Bohemian as ruthlessly as it would set the good side of the Bohemian above the bad side of the Pharisee.[11] For as long as convention goes counter to reality in these matters, people will be led into Hedda Gabler's error of making an ideal of vice. If we maintain the convention that the distinction between Catherine of Russia and Queen Victoria,[12] between Nell Gwynne and Mrs Proudie,[13] is the distinction between a bad woman and a good woman, we need not be surprised when those who sympathize with Catherine and Nell conclude that it is better to be a bad woman than a good one, and go on recklessly to conceive a prejudice against teetotalism and monogamy, and a prepossession in favor of alcoholic excitement and promiscuous amours. Ibsen himself is kinder to the man who has gone his own way as a rake and a drunkard than to the man who is

10. Eleanor (Nell) Gwyn or Gwynne (1650–87), actress and one of the mistresses of King Charles II (1630–85).

11. "The warning implied in this sentence is less needed now than it was twenty years ago. The association of Bohemianism with the artistic professions and with revolutionary political views has been weakened by the revolt of the children of the Bohemians against its domestic squalor and social outlawry. Bohemianism is now rather one of the stigmata of the highly conservative 'smart sets' of the idle rich than of the studio, the stage, and the Socialist organizations." [G.B.S., 1912]

12. Queen Catherine II (the Great) of Russia (1729–96), who had numerous love affairs (and is the title character of Shaw's *Great Catherine*, 1913); Queen Victoria of England (1819–1901).

13. The stern Evangelical wife of the Bishop of Barchester, a leading character in the "Barsetshire novels" (1855–67) by Anthony Trollope (1815–82).

respectable because he dare not be otherwise. We find that the franker and healthier a boy is, the more certain is he to prefer pirates and highwaymen, or Dumas musketeers,[14] to pillars of society as his favorite heroes of romance. We have already seen both Ibsenites and anti-Ibsenites who seem to think that the cases of Nora and Mrs Elvsted are meant to establish a golden rule for women who wish to be "emancipated," the said golden rule being simply Run away from your husband. But in Ibsen's view of life, that would come under the same condemnation as the conventional golden rule Cleave to your husband until death do you part. Most people know of a case or two in which it would be wise for a wife to follow the example of Nora or even of Mrs Elvsted. But they must also know cases in which the results of such a course would be as tragicomic as those of Gregers Werle's attempt in The Wild Duck to do for the Ekdal household what Lona Hessel did for the Bernick household. What Ibsen insists on is that there is no golden rule; that conduct must justify itself by its effect upon happiness and not by its conformity to any rule or ideal. And since happiness consists in the fulfilment of the will, which is constantly growing, and cannot be fulfiled today under the conditions which secured its fulfilment yesterday, he claims afresh the old Protestant right of private judgment in questions of conduct as against all institutions, the so-called Protestant Churches themselves included.

Here I must leave the matter, merely reminding those who may think that I have forgotten to reduce Ibsenism to a formula for them, that its quintessence is that there is no formula.

APPENDIX

I have a word or two to add as to the difficulties which Ibsen's philosophy places in the way of those who are called on to impersonate his characters on the stage in England. His idealist figures, at once higher and more mischievous than ordinary Philistines, puzzle by their dual aspect the conventional actor, who persists in assuming that if he is to be selfish on the stage he must be villainous; that if he is to be self-sacrificing and scrupulous he must be a hero; and that if he is to satirize himself unconsciously he must be comic. He is constantly striving to get back to familiar ground by reducing his part to one of the stage types with which he is familiar, and which he has learnt to present by rule of thumb. The more experienced he is, the more certain is he to de-Ibsenize the play into a melodrama or a farcical comedy of the common sort. Give him Helmer to

14. *The Three Musketeers* (1845) by Alexandre Dumas *père* (1802–70).

play, and he begins by declaring that the part is a mass of "inconsistencies," and ends by suddenly grasping the idea that it is only Joseph Surface[1] over again. Give him Gregers Werle, the devotee of Truth, and he will first play him in the vein of George Washington, and then, when he finds that the audience laughs at him instead of taking him respectfully, rush to the conclusion that Gregers is only his old friend the truthful milkman in A Phenomenon in a Smock Frock,[2] and begin to play for the laughs and relish them. That is, if there are only laughs enough to make the part completely comic. Otherwise he will want to omit the passages which provoke them. To be laughed at when playing a serious part is hard upon an actor, and still more upon an actress: it is derision, than which nothing is more terrible to those whose livelihood depends on public approbation, and whose calling produces an abnormal development of self-consciousness. Now Ibsen undoubtedly does freely require from his artists that they shall not only possess great skill and power on every plane of their art, but that they shall also be ready to make themselves acutely ridiculous sometimes at the very climax of their most deeply felt passages. It is not to be wondered at that they prefer to pick and choose among the lines of their parts, retaining the great professional opportunities afforded by the tragic scenes, and leaving out the touches which complete the portrait at the expense of the model's vanity. If an actress of established reputation were asked to play Hedda Gabler, her first impulse would probably be to not only turn Hedda into a Brinvilliers, or a Borgia, or a Forget-Me-Not,[3] but to suppress all the meaner callosities and odiousnesses which detract from Hedda's dignity as dignity is estimated on the stage. The result would be about as satisfactory to a skilled critic as that of the retouching which has made shop window photography the most worthless of the arts. The whole point of an Ibsen play lies in the exposure of the very conventions upon which are based those by which the actor is ridden. Charles Surface or Tom Jones may be very effectively played by artists who fully accept the morality professed by Joseph Surface and Blifil.[4] Neither Fielding nor Sheridan forces upon either actor or audience the dilemma that since Charles and Tom are lovable, there must be something hopelessly inadequate in the commercial and sexual morality which condemns them as a pair of blackguards. The ordinary actor will tell you

1. Character in Sheridan, *The School for Scandal.*
2. A one-act farce (1852) by William Brough (1826–70), in which the character causes difficulties by telling the truth.
3. That is, an evil woman in a melodrama, such as the title characters of *La Marquise de Brinvilliers* (1831) by Eugène Scribe, *Lucretia Borgia* (1833) by Victor Hugo, and *Forget-Me-Not* (1879) by Herman Merivale and F. C. Grove.
4. Master Blifil is a character in *Tom Jones*, by Henry Fielding.

that the authors "do not defend their heroes' conduct," not seeing that making them lovable is the most complete defence of their conduct that could possibly be made. How far Fielding and Sheridan saw it, how far Molière or Mozart were convinced that the statue had right on his side when he threw Don Juan into the bottomless pit, how far Milton went in his sympathy with Lucifer:[5] all these are speculative points which no actor has hitherto been called upon to solve. But they are the very subjects of Ibsen's plays: those whose interest and curiosity are not excited by them find him the most puzzling and tedious of dramatists. He has not only made "lost" women lovable; but he has recognized and avowed that this is a vital justification for them, and has accordingly explicitly argued on their side and awarded them the sympathy which poetic justice grants only to the righteous. He has made the terms "lost" and "ruined" in this sense ridiculous by making women apply them to men with the most ludicrous effect. Hence Ibsen cannot be played from the conventional point of view: to make that practicable the plays would have to be rewritten. In the rewriting, the fascination of the parts would vanish, and with it their attraction for the performers. A Doll's House was adapted in this fashion, though not at the instigation of an actress; but the adaptation fortunately failed. Otherwise we might have to endure in Ibsen's case what we have already endured in that of Shakespear, many of whose plays were supplanted for centuries by incredibly debased versions, of which Cibber's Richard III and Garrick's Catharine and Petruchio[6] have lasted to our own time.

Taking Talma's estimate of eighteen years as the apprenticeship of a completely accomplished stage artist,[7] there is little encouragement to offer Ibsen's parts to our finished actors and actresses. They do not understand them, and would not play them in their integrity if they could be induced to attempt them. In England only two women in the full maturity of their talent have hitherto meddled with Ibsen. One of these, Miss Geneviève Ward, who "created" the part of Lona Hessel in the English version of Pillars of Society, had the advantage of exceptional enterprise and intelligence, and of a more varied culture and experience of life and art than are common in her profession. The other, Mrs Theodore Wright, the first English Mrs Alving, was hardly known to the dramatic critics, though her personality and her artistic talent as an amateur reciter and actress had been familiar to the members of most of the advanced social

5. Molière in *Dom Juan, ou Le festin de pierre* (1665); Milton in *Paradise Lost* (1667).
6. (1754), an adaptation of Shakespeare's *Taming of the Shrew*.
7. In "Réflexions sur Lekain, et sur l'art théâtrale," included in the 1825 edition of *Mémoirs de Lekain*, François Joseph Talma (1763–1826), French actor, estimated twenty, not eighteen, years.

and political bodies in London since the days of the International.[8] It was precisely because her record lay outside the beaten track of newspaper criticism that she was qualified to surprise its writers as she did. In every other instance, the women who first ventured upon playing Ibsen hero- ines were young actresses whose ability had not before been fully tested and whose technical apprenticeships were far from complete. Miss Janet Achurch, though she settled the then disputed question of the feasibility of Ibsen's plays on the English stage by her impersonation of Nora in 1889, which still remains the most complete artistic achievement in the new *genre*, had not been long enough on the stage to secure a unanimous admission of her genius, though it was of the most irresistible and irre- pressible kind. Miss Florence Farr, who may claim the palm for artistic courage and intellectual conviction in selecting for her experiment Rosmersholm, incomparably the most difficult and dangerous, as it is also the greatest, of Ibsen's later plays, had almost relinquished her profession from lack of interest in its routine, after spending a few years in acting farcical comedies. Miss Elizabeth Robins and Miss Marion Lea, to whose unaided enterprise we owe our early acquaintance with Hedda Gabler on the stage, were, like Miss Achurch and Miss Farr, juniors in their profes- sion. All four were products of the modern movement for the higher education of women, literate, in touch with advanced thought, and com- ing by natural predilection on the stage from outside the theatrical class, in contradistinction to the senior generation of inveterately sentimental actresses, schooled in the old fashion if at all, born into their profession, quite out of the political and social movement around them: in short, intellectually naïve to the last degree. The new school says to the old: You cannot play Ibsen because you are ignoramuses. To which the old school retorts: You cannot play anything because you are amateurs. But taking amateur in its sense of unpractised executant, both schools are amateur as far as Ibsen's plays are concerned. The old technique breaks down in the new theatre; for though in theory it is a technique of general applica- tion, making the artist so plastic that he can mould himself to any shape designed by the dramatist, in practice it is but a stock of tones and attitudes out of which, by appropriate selection and combination, a cer-

8. Those days began two years earlier, when the Second (or Socialist) International, a loose federation of national socialist parties and trade unions, was founded at the Interna- tional Working Men's Congress held in Paris in 1889. It stood for parliamentary democracy but reaffirmed Marxist views of class warfare. In 1896, reasserting the inevitability of revolution, it rejected the theory, held by the Fabian Society, of gradually achieving social- ism through cooperation with nonsocialist parties in office. The Second International ended in 1919. Karl Marx had founded the first International (the International Working Men's Association) in London in 1864; it formally disbanded in 1876. Alice (Mrs Theodore) Wright (c. 1845–1922) was a member of the Fabian Society.

tain limited number of conventional stage figures can be made up. It is no more possible to get an Ibsen character out of it than to contrive a Greek costume out of an English wardrobe; and some of the attempts already made have been so grotesque, that at present, when one of the more specifically Ibsenian parts has to be filled, it is actually safer to entrust it to a novice than to a competent and experienced actor.

A steady improvement may be expected in the performances of Ibsen's plays as the young players whom they interest gain the experience needed to make mature artists of them. They will gain this experience not only in plays by Ibsen himself, but in the works of dramatists who have been largely influenced by Ibsen. Playwrights who formerly only compounded plays according to the received prescriptions for producing tears or laughter, are already taking their profession seriously to the full extent of their capacity, and venturing more and more to substitute the incidents and catastrophes of spiritual history for the swoons, surprises, discoveries, murders, duels, assassinations, and intrigues which are the commonplaces of the theatre at present. Others, who have no such impulse, find themselves forced to raise the quality of their work by the fact that even those who witness Ibsen's plays with undisguised weariness and aversion, find, when they return to their accustomed theatrical fare, that they have suddenly become conscious of absurdities and artificialities in it which never troubled them before. In just the same way the painters of the Naturalist school reformed their opponents much more extensively than the number of their own direct admirers indicates: for example, it is still common to hear the most contemptuous abuse and ridicule of Monet and Whistler from persons who have nevertheless had their former tolerance of the unrealities of the worst type of conventional studio picture wholly destroyed by these painters. Until quite lately, too, musicians were to be heard extoling Donizetti in the same breath with which they vehemently decried Wagner. They would make wry faces at every chord in Tristan und Isolde, and never suspected that their old faith was shaken until they went back to La Favorita, and found that it had become as obsolete as the rhymed tragedies of Lee[9] and Otway. In the drama then, we may depend on it that though we shall not have another Ibsen, yet nobody will write for the stage after him as most playwrights wrote before him. This will involve a corresponding change in the technical stock in trade of the actor, whose ordinary training will then cease to be a positive disadvantage to him when he is entrusted with an Ibsen part.

No one need fear on this account that Ibsen will gradually destroy melodrama. It might as well be assumed that Shakespear will destroy music hall entertainments, or the prose romances of William Morris su-

9. Nathaniel Lee (1649?–92).

persede The Illustrated Police News. All forms of art rise with the culture and capacity of the human race; but the forms rise together: the higher forms do not return upon and submerge the lower. The wretch who finds his happiness in setting a leash of greyhounds on a hare or in watching a terrier killing rats in a pit, may evolve into the mere blockhead who would rather go to a "free and easy"[10] and chuckle over a dull, silly, obscene song; but such a step will not raise him to the level of the frequenter of music halls of the better class, where, though the entertainment is administered in small separate doses or "turns,"[11] yet the turns have some artistic pretension. Above him again is the patron of that elementary form of sensational drama in which there is hardly any more connection between the incidents than the fact that the same people take part in them and call forth some very simple sort of moral judgment by being consistently villainous or virtuous throughout. As such a drama would be almost as enjoyable if the acts were played in the reverse of their appointed order, no inconvenience except that of a back seat is suffered by the playgoer who comes in for half price[12] at nine o'clock. On a higher plane we have dramas with a rational sequence of incidents, the interest of any one of which depends on those which have preceded it; and as we go up from plane to plane we find this sequence becoming more and more organic until at last we come to a class of play in which nobody can understand the last act who has not seen the first also. Accordingly, the institution of half price at nine o'clock does not exist at theatres devoted to plays of this class. The highest type of play is completely homogeneous, often consisting of a single very complex incident; and not even the most exhaustive information as to the story enables a spectator to receive the full force of the impression aimed at in any given passage if he enters the theatre for that passage alone. The success of such plays depends upon the exercise by the audience of powers of memory, imagination, insight, reasoning, and sympathy, which only a small minority of the playgoing public at present possesses. To the rest the higher drama is as disagreeably perplexing as the game of chess is to a man who has barely enough capacity to understand skittles. Consequently, just as we have the chess club and the skittle alley prospering side by side, we shall have the theatre of Shakespear, Molière, Goethe, and Ibsen prospering alongside that of Henry Arthur Jones and Gilbert; of Sardou, Grundy, and Pinero; of Buchanan and Ohnet, as naturally as these already prosper alongside that of Pettitt and Sims, which again does no more harm to the music halls than the music halls do to the waxworks or even the ratpit, although this last is

10. A disreputable music hall or tavern that provided entertainment.
11. Acts or specialty numbers in music halls or variety shows.
12. It was customary in eighteenth- and nineteenth-century English theaters for playgoers entering after act III of the main play to pay half price.

dropping into the limbo of discarded brutalities by the same progressive movement that has led the intellectual playgoer to discard Sardou and take to Ibsen. It has often been said that political parties progress serpentwise, the tail being today where the head was formerly, yet never overtaking the head. The same figure may be applied to grades of playgoers, with the reminder that this sort of serpent grows at the head and drops off joints of his tail as he glides along. Therefore it is not only inevitable that new theatres should be built for the new first class of playgoers, but that the best of the existing theatres should be gradually converted to their use, even at the cost of ousting, in spite of much angry protest, the old patrons who are being left behind by the movement.

The resistance of the old playgoers to the new plays will be supported by the elder managers, the elder actors, and the elder critics. One manager pities Ibsen for his ignorance of effective playwriting, and declares that he can see exactly what ought to have been done to make a real play of Hedda Gabler. His case is parallel to that of Mr Henry Irving, who saw exactly what ought to have been done to make a real play of Goethe's Faust, and got Mr Wills to do it. A third manager, repelled and disgusted by Ibsen, condemns Hedda as totally deficient in elevating moral sentiment. One of the plays which he prefers is Sardou's La Tosca! Clearly these three representative gentlemen, all eminent both as actors and managers, will hold by the conventional drama until the commercial success of Ibsen forces them to recognize that in the course of nature they are falling behind the taste of the day. Mr Thorne, at the Vaudeville Theatre, was the first leading manager who ventured to put a play of Ibsen's into his evening bill; and he did not do so until Miss Elizabeth Robins and Miss Marion Lea had given ten experimental performances at his theatre at their own risk.[13] Mr Charrington and Miss Janet Achurch, who, long before that, staked their capital and reputation on A Doll's House, had to take a theatre and go into management themselves for the purpose. The production of Rosmersholm was not a managerial enterprise in the ordinary sense at all: it was an experiment made by Miss Farr, who played Rebecca: an experiment, too, which was considerably hampered by the refusal of the London managers to allow members of their companies to take part in the performance. In short, the senior division would have nothing to say for themselves in the matter of the one really progressive theatrical movement of their time, but for the fact that Mr W. H. Vernon's effort to obtain a hearing for Pillars of Society in 1880 was the occasion of the first appearance of the name of Ibsen on an English playbill.[14]

13. *Hedda Gabler* in 1891.
14. Although Ibsen's name appeared on the playbill, the play's did not. *Pillars of Society* was retitled *Quicksands*. Vernon played Bernick.

But it had long been obvious that the want of a playhouse at which the aims of the management should be unconditionally artistic was not likely to be supplied either at our purely commercial theatres or at those governed by actor-managers reigning absolutely over all the other actors, a power which a young man abuses to provide opportunities for himself, and which an older man uses in an oldfashioned way. Mr William Archer, in an article in The Fortnightly Review, invited private munificence to endow a National Theatre;[15] and some time later a young Dutchman, Mr J. T. Grein, an enthusiast in theatrical art, came forward with a somewhat similar scheme.[16] Private munificence remained irresponsive: fortunately, one must think, since it was a feature of both plans that the management of the endowed theatre should be handed over to committees of managers and actors of established reputation: in other words, to the very people whose deficiencies have created the whole difficulty. Mr Grein, however, being prepared to take any practicable scheme in hand himself, soon saw the realities of the situation well enough to understand that to wait for the floating of a fashionable Utopian enterprise, with the Prince of Wales as President and a capital of at least £20,000, would be to wait forever. He accordingly hired a cheap public hall in Tottenham Court Road, and, though his resources fell far short of those with which an ambitious young professional man ventures upon giving a dance, made a bold start by announcing a performance of Ghosts to inaugurate The Independent Theatre on the lines of the Théâtre Libre of Paris. The result was that he received sufficient support both in money and gratuitous professional aid to enable him to give the performance at the Royalty Theatre; and throughout the following week he shared with Ibsen the distinction of being abusively discussed to an extent that must have amply convinced him that his efforts had not passed unheeded. Possibly he may have counted on being handled generously for the sake of his previous services in obtaining some consideration for the contemporary English drama on the continent, even to the extent of bringing about the translation and production in foreign theatres of some of the most popular of our recent plays; but if he had any such hope it was not fulfilled; for he received no quarter whatever. And at present it is clear that unless those who appreciate the service he has rendered to theatrical art in England support him as energetically as his opponents attack him, it will be impossible for him to maintain the performances of the Independent Theatre at the pitch of efficiency and frequency which will be needed if it is to have any wide effect on the taste and seriousness of the playgoing public. One of the most formidable and exasperating obstacles in his way is the detest-

15. "A Plea for an Endowed Theatre," 1 May 1889.
16. "A British 'Theatre [sic] Libre,'" Weekly Comedy, 30 November 1889.

able censorship exercised by the official licencer of plays, a public nuisance of which it seems impossible to rid ourselves under existing Parliamentary conditions. The licencer has the London theatres at his mercy through his power to revoke their licences; and he is empowered to exact a fee for reading each play submited to him, so that his income depends on his allowing no play to be produced without going through that ordeal. As these powers are granted to him in order that he may forbid the performance of plays which would have an injurious effect on public morals, the unfortunate gentleman is bound in honor to try to do his best to keep the stage in the right path: which he of course can set about in no other way than by making it a reflection of his individual views, which are necessarily dictated by his temperament and by the political and pecuniary interests of his class. This he does not dare to do: self-mistrust and the fear of public opinion paralyze him whenever either the strong hand or the open mind claims its golden opportunity; and the net result is that indecency and vulgarity are rampant on the London stage, from which flows the dramatic stream that irrigates the whole country; whilst Shelley's Cenci tragedy and Ibsen's Ghosts are forbidden, and have in fact only been performed once "in private": that is, before audiences of invited nonpaying guests. It is now so well understood that only plays of the commonest idealist type can be sure of a licence in London, that the novel and not the drama is the form adopted as a matter of course by thoughtful masters of fiction. The merits of the case ought to be too obvious to need restating: it is plain that every argument that supports a censorship of the stage supports with tenfold force a censorship of the press, which is admittedly an abomination. What is wanted is the entire abolition of the censorship and the establishment of Free Art in the sense in which we speak of Free Trade. There is not the slightest ground for protecting theatres against the competition of music halls, or for denying to Mr Grein as a theatrical entrepreneur the freedom he would enjoy as a member of a publishing firm. In the absence of a censorship a manager can be prosecuted for an offence against public morals, just as a publisher can. At present, though managers may not touch Shelley or Ghosts, they find no difficulty in obtaining official sanction, practically amounting to indemnity, for indecencies from which our uncensured novels are perfectly free. The truth is that the real support of the censorship comes from those Puritans who regard Art as a department of original sin. To them the theatre is an unmixed evil, and every restriction on it a gain to the cause of righteousness. Against them stand those who regard Art in all its forms as a department of religion. The Holy War between the two sides has played a considerable part in the history of England, and is just now being prosecuted with renewed vigor by the Puritans. If their opponents do not display equal energy, it is quite possible that we shall presently have a reformed censorship ten times more odious than the existing one, the very absurdity of which causes it to be exercised with a halfheartedness that prevents the licencer from doing his worst as well as his best. The wise policy for the friends of Art just now is to use the Puritan agitation in order to bring the matter to an issue, and then to make a vigorous effort to secure that the upshot shall be the total abolition of the censorship.

As it is with the actors and managers, so it is with the critics: the supporters of Ibsen are the younger men. In the main, however, the Press follows the managers instead of leading them. The average newspaper dramatic critic is not a Lessing, a Lamb, or a Lewes:[17] there was a time when he was not necessarily even an accustomed playgoer, but simply a member of the reporting or literary staff told off for theatre duty without any question as to his acquaintance with dramatic literature. At present, though the special nature of his function is so far beginning to be recognized that appointments of the kind usually fall now into the hands of inveterate frequenters of the theatre, yet he is still little more than the man who supplies accounts of what takes place in the playhouses just as his colleague supplies accounts of what takes place at the police court: an important difference, however, being that the editor, who generally cares little about Art and knows less, will himself occasionally criticize, or ask one of his best writers to criticize, a remarkable police case, whereas he never dreams of theatrical art as a subject upon which there could be any editorial policy. Sir Edwin Arnold's editorial attack on Ibsen[18] was due to the accidental circumstance that he, like Richelieu,[19] writes verses between whiles. In fact, the dramatic critic of a newspaper, in ordinary circumstances, is at his best a good descriptive reporter, and at his worst a mere theatrical newsman. As such he is a person of importance among actors and managers, and of no importance whatever elsewhere. Naturally he frequents the circles in which alone he is made much of; and by the time he has seen so many performances that he has formed some critical standards in spite of himself, he has also enrolled among his personal acquaintances every actor and manager of a few years' standing, and become engaged in all the private likes and dislikes, the quarrels and friendships, in a word, in all the partialities which personal relations involve, at which point the value of his verdicts may be imagined. Add to this that if he has the misfortune to be attached to a paper to which

17. Gotthold Ephraim Lessing (1729–81), German dramatist and drama critic (*Hamburg Dramaturgy*, 1767–69); Charles Lamb (1755–1834), essayist, dramatist, and author of many works about the drama; George Henry Lewes (1817–78), English dramatist and critic of drama and theater (*On Actors and the Art of Acting*, 1875).

18. *Daily Telegraph*, 14 March 1891.

19. Armand Jean du Plessis, Cardinal Duc de Richelieu (1585–1642), powerful French statesman.

theatrical advertisements are an object, or of which the editor and proprietors (or their wives) do not hesitate to incur obligations to managers by asking for complimentary admissions, he may often have to choose between making himself agreeable and forfeiting his post. So that he is not always to be relied on even as a newsman where the plain truth would give offence to any individual.

Behind all the suppressive forces with which the critic has to contend comes the law of libel. Every adverse criticism of a public performer is a libel; and any agreement among the critics to boycott artists who appeal to the law is a conspiracy. Of course the boycott does take place to a certain extent; for if an artist, manager, or agent shews any disposition to retort to what is called a "slating" by a lawyer's letter, the critic, who cannot for his own sake expose his employers to the expenses of an action or the anxiety attending the threat of one, will be tempted to shun the danger by simply never again refering to the litigiously disposed person. But although this at first sight seems to sufficiently guarantee the freedom of criticism (for most public persons would suffer more from being ignored by the papers than from being attacked in them, however abusively) its operation is really restricted on the one side to the comparatively few and powerful critics who are attached to important papers at a fixed salary, and on the other to those *entrepreneurs* and artists about whom the public is not imperatively curious. Most critics get paid for their notices at so much per column or per line, so that their incomes depend on the quantity they write. Under these conditions they fine themselves every time they ignore a performance. Again, a dramatist or a manager may attain such a position that his enterprises form an indispensable part of the news of the day. He can then safely intimidate a hostile critic by a threat of legal proceedings, knowing that the paper can afford neither to brave nor ignore him. The late Charles Reade,[20] for example, was a most dangerous man to criticize adversely; but the very writers against whom he took actions found it impossible to boycott him; and what Reade did out of a natural overflow of indignant pugnacity, some of our most powerful *entrepreneurs* occasionally threaten to do now after a deliberate calculation of the advantages of their position. If legal proceedings are actually taken, and the case is not, as usual, compromised behind the scenes, the uncertainty of the law receives its most extravagant illustration from a couple of lawyers arguing a question of fine art before a jury of men of business. Even if the critic were a capable speaker and pleader, which he is not in the least likely to be, he would be debarred from conducting his own case by the fact that his comparatively wealthy employer and not himself would be the defendant in the case. In short, the law is against

20. (1814–84), playwright and novelist.

straightforward criticism at the very points where it is most needed; and though it is true that an ingenious and witty writer can make any artist or performance acutely ridiculous in the eyes of ingenious and witty people without laying himself open to an action, and indeed with every appearance of good-humored indulgence, such applications of wit and ingenuity do criticism no good; whilst in any case they offer no remedy to the plain critic writing for plain readers.

All this does not mean that the entire Press is hopelessly corrupt in its criticism of Art. But it certainly does mean that the odds against the independence of the Press critic are so heavy that no man can maintain it completely without a force of character and a personal authority which are rare in any profession, and which in most of them can command higher pecuniary terms and prospects than any which journalism can offer. The final degrees of thoroughness have no market value on the Press; for, other things being equal, a journal with a critic who is goodhumored and compliant will have no fewer readers than one with a critic who is inflexible where the interests of Art and the public are concerned. I do not exaggerate or go beyond the warrant of my own experience when I say that unless a critic is prepared not only to do much more work than the public will pay him for, but to risk his livelihood every time he strikes a serious blow at the powerful interests vested in artistic abuses of all kinds (conditions which in the long run tire out the strongest man), he must submit to compromises which detract very considerably from the trustworthiness of his criticism. Even the critic who is himself in a position to brave these risks must find a sympathetic and courageous editor-proprietor who will stand by him without reference to the commercial advantage—or disadvantage—of his incessant warfare. As all the economic conditions of our society tend to throw our journals more and more into the hands of successful moneymakers, the exceeding scarcity of this lucky combination of resolute, capable, and incorruptible critic, sympathetic editor, and disinterested and courageous proprietor, can hardly be appreciated by those who only know the world of journalism through its black and white veil.

On the whole, though excellent criticisms are written every week by men who, either as writers distinguished in other branches of literature and journalism, or as civil servants, are practically independent of this or that particular appointment as dramatic critic (not to mention the few whom strong vocation and force of character have rendered incorruptible) there remains a great mass of newspaper reports of theatrical events which is only called dramatic criticism by courtesy. Among the critics properly so called opinions are divided about Ibsen in the inevitable way into Philistine, idealist, and realist (more or less). Just at present the crossfiring between them is rather confusing. Without being necessarily an Ibsenist, a critic may see at a glance that abuse of the sort quoted on pages 161–62 is worthless; and he may for the credit of his cloth attack it on that ground. Thus we have Mr A. B. Walkley, of The Speaker, one of the most able and independent of our critics, provoking Mr Clement Scott beyond measure by alluding to the writers who had just been calling the admirers of Ibsen "muckferreting dogs," as "these gentry," with a goodhumored but very perceptible contempt for their literary attainments. Thereupon Mr Scott publishes a vindication of the literateness of that school, of which Mr Walkley makes unmerciful fun.[21] But Mr Walkley is by no means commited to Ibsenism by his appreciation of Ibsen's status as an artist, much less by his depreciation of the literary status of Ibsen's foes. On the other hand there is Mr Frederick Wedmore, a professed admirer of Balzac, conceiving such a violent antipathy to Ibsen that he almost echoes Sir Edwin Arnold, whose denunciations are at least as applicable to the author of Vautrin[22] as to the author of Ghosts. Mr George Moore, accustomed to fight on behalf of Zola against the men who are now attacking Ibsen, takes the field promptly against his old enemies in defence not of Ibsenism, but of Free Art.[23] Even Mr William Archer expressly guards himself against being taken as an Ibsenist doctrinaire. In the face of all this, it is little to the point that some of the critics who have attacked Ibsen have undoubtedly done so because—to put it bluntly—they are too illiterate and incompetent in the sphere of dramatic poetry to conceive or relish anything more substantial than the theatrical fare to which they are accustomed; or that others, intimidated by the outcry raised by Sir Edwin Arnold and the section of the public typified by Pastor Manders (not to mention Mr Pecksniff), against their own conviction join the chorus of disparagement from modesty, caution, compliance: in short, from want of the courage of their profession. There is no reason to suppose that if the whole body of critics had been endowed with a liberal education and an independent income, the number of Ibsenists among them would be much greater than at present, however the tone of their adverse criticism might have been improved. Ibsen, as a pioneer in stage progress no less than in morals, is bound to have the majority of his contemporaries against him, whether as actors, managers, or critics.

Finally, it is necessary to say, by way of warning, that many of the minor combatants on both sides have either not studied the plays at all, or else have been so puzzled that they have allowed themselves to be misled by the attacks of the idealists into reading extravagant immoralities between the lines, as, for instance, that Oswald in Ghosts is really the son of

21. *The Speaker*, 21 March and 11 April 1891; *Sunday Times*, 5 April 1891.
22. *La Dernière incarnation de Vautrin* (1847) by Honoré de Balzac (1790–1850).
23. George Augustus Moore (1852–1933), Anglo-Irish novelist and dramatist, in *The Hawk*, 17 June 1890, on the Théâtre Libre production of *Ghosts*.

Pastor Manders, or that Lövborg is the father of Hedda Tesman's child. It has even been asserted that horrible exhibitions of death and disease occur in almost every scene of Ibsen's plays, which, for tragedies, are exceptionally free from visible physical horrors. It is not too much to say that very few of the critics have yet got so far as to be able to narrate accurately the stories of the plays they have witnessed. No wonder, then, that they have not yet made up their minds on the more difficult point of Ibsen's philosophic drift: though I do not myself see how performances of his plays can be quite adequately judged without reference to it. One consequence of this is that those who are interested, fascinated, and refreshed by Ibsen's art misrepresent his meaning benevolently quite as often as those who are perplexed and disgusted misrepresent it maliciously; and it already looks as if Ibsen might attain undisputed supremacy as a modern playwright without necessarily converting a single critic to Ibsenism. Indeed it is not possible that his meaning should be fully recognized, much less assented to, until Society as we now know it loses its self-complacency through the growth of the conviction foretold by Richard Wagner when he declared that "Man will never be that which he can and should be until, by a conscious following of that inner natural necessity which is the only true necessity, he makes his life a mirror of nature, and frees himself from his thraldom to outer artificial counterfeits. Then will he first become a living man, who now is a mere wheel in the mechanism of this or that Religion, Nationality, or State."[24]

["THE LITTLE GEORGIA MAGNET"]
C/Un (*Bradford Observer*, 16 November 1891)

I was present on Saturday afternoon at a most curious display of what Theosophists would call psychic force at the Alhambra. This was a performance by a young American lady, *petite* and rather pretty, called Miss Abbott.[1] She was introduced by an American agent, who gave a serious account of the development of his protégé. According to the gentleman it was discovered at a very early age that she was endowed with a strange psychical force, which, however, had no connexion with muscular power,

24. *The Art Work of the Future* (1849).
    1. Annie May Abbott (Priscilla Rawlinson, 1868–1943), known as "the little Georgia Magnet."

and which enabled her practically to do whatever she pleased. If she decided to remain in a room the united force of the family could not move her from it. Some very extraordinary examples of her powers were given to the spectators at the Alhambra. She spread out her open hands and laid on them a billiard cue inclined at an angle of about 45 degrees. The cue appeared to rest lightly on her palms, but the united force of six gentlemen, who were chosen by a committee of which Mr Hollingshead was a member,[2] could not move the cue. In another experiment a number of strong and heavy men laid themselves face downwards on a set of chairs. Miss Abbott then placed one finger on the hand of one of the committee, and the chairs were immediately displaced and the whole company fell to the ground. As a third illustration a strong and heavy man attempted to lift her by her bare elbows, but was unable to move her. She then placed a handkerchief between his hand and her flesh, and he was able to lift her with the greatest ease. As far as one can see, the committee selected consisted of respectable and representative persons.

"SPECTATOR'S" BOOK[1]
C/Ps (*The Star*, 9 January 1892, Signed "C. di B." [Corno di Bassetto])

Before going more particularly into the merits of this book of Playhouse Impressions, I may as well betray a secret. A. B. Walkley is none other than our Mr Spectator. Now we are justly proud of our Mr Spectator. He is, without exception, the best dramatic critic in London; and it was The Star that discovered him. We challenge the entire Press to produce his equal. The only paper that does so is The Speaker, whose champion, however, proves on examination to be A.B.W. himself. Before he came, the critic was Mr William Archer, and "W.A." is there still, a man preeminently to be reckoned with in the literature of the theatre. But in the art of playhouse impressionism he is nowhere beside "Spectator." A careful examination of his work will shew that he is hampered with a conscience, and has moments of sentiment. He receives his impressions on certain moral conditions; and he has a soft side which may be reached at any moment by inculcating a compound of fairy tale fantasy and domestic pathos, which

2. John Hollingshead (1827–1904), English dramatist and manager.
1. *Playhouse Impressions*. By A. B. Walkley. (London: Fisher Unwin, 1892.) [G.B.S.]

goes straight to the sentimental part like a spoonful of Koch's[2] lymph to a bit of tuberculosis tissue, and at once sets up virulent indulgence and overration. No such frailty is to be found in our own impressionist. He has no scruples, no conscience: he gives himself with both hands to the actor and dramatist to work their spells upon; and would not spare his nearest and dearest if his confidence were abused by the least jar of his artistic sensibility. It must not be inferred that he is vindictive: not at all. Vengeance is a department of morality; and A.B.W. is absolutely unmoral: that is of the essence of his attitude. He says to the artist "Here I am, my friend, in a highly sensitive condition. Impress me; and I will describe my impressions. Do not ask who made me a judge and ruler over thee; for, believe me, I set up no such pretension. I am not a judge, because, like Necessity, I know no law. I am not a ruler, because I have no view as to what is good for you or me. I have no prepossessions except those of artistic temperament. I sit down in my stall and present my sensitised surface to you virginally blank as the *tabula rasa* of Locke's celebrated baby in the Essay on Human Understanding.[3] The raising of the curtain will be simply the removal of the cap from the camera. If you disgust me, as Sardou did with his torture scene in La Tosca, I shall describe my disgust. If you start a train of quaint and delicious fancies through my head, as the Pierrot family did in L'Enfant Prodigue,[4] I shall write them all down. With the effect of my descriptions on the sum taken at the payboxes I have nothing to do. The impressions you give me may revolt the paying public when I describe them; but that is your lookout, not mine. Now you know what you have to expect. Therefore, if you will excuse the shoppiness of a Shakespearean quotation, "Leave thy damnable faces, and begin."[5] That is "Spectator's" program; and it is by his power of carrying it out that he beats us all as a critic. Whilst we are laboriously measuring the difference between what the performance is and what it ought to be, and complaining because it is not the latter: whilst we are padding our notices with the story of the play, or moralizing, or immoralizing, or backing our side in every political or religious issue raised by the dramatist, A.B.W. simply develops his negative in an ink bath; etches it with charming ingenuity, humor, and grace; and presents you with a perfect black-and-white picture of what you are inquiring about. Do not suppose, though, that he does

2. Robert Koch (1843–1910), who in 1905 would win the Nobel Prize for Medicine.

3. In his *Essay Concerning Human Understanding* (1690), John Locke (1632–1704) denies the existence of innate ideas and believes that a child's mind is a *tabula rasa* (blank slate), with knowledge coming from experience and reflection on sensory and intellectual perceptions.

4. Shaw had reviewed *L'Enfant prodigue* (1883) by André Wormser (1851?-1926) and Michel Carré *fils* (1865–1945) in *The World*, 8 April 1891.

5. *Hamlet*, III.ii.

not argue. To refrain from that luxury would be inhuman; and A.B.W. is none of your university professors who imagine that a writer's first duty is to dehumanize himself in order that he may be impartial. Any fool can see that impartiality is the negation of criticism; and it is A.B.W.'s chief care to humanize himself to the highest point before exposing himself to playhouse impressions. In this condition the drama stimulates his whole system; and the consequent need of exercise for his wit leads him to intellectual fencing, at which he displays imperturbable politeness and address. His bout with a "scientific" critic of the school of Mr Molton, and his neat spiflication of Mr Henry Arthur Jones's attempt to try an old thrust of Burke's on the realist school,[6] should be carefully studied by amateurs; but experts will appreciate his skill more by seeing him stroll through the fencing saloon, goodnaturedly shewing the other combatants here and there how this attack could be done more neatly, or why that parry will not do. A.B.W.'s *sang froid*, however, is exasperating to combatants who have lost their tempers. For instance, when discussing the prejudice against actors, he observes with great sweetness:

> I am not defending the prejudice. I am merely trying to appreciate it. Why will not the actors do the same? Why will they not frankly accept the situation, and regard themselves—not without a certain pride—as a class apart?

The spectacle of A.B.W. "merely trying to appreciate it," so infuriated Mr Irving that he has hardly smiled since; and it is well known that his recent frenzied denuciation of certain mysterious "creatures of the swamp and mist" would never have been uttered had he not maddened himself by reading The Speaker. If Mr Irving were a true connoisseur in literature, he would have promptly sent A.B.W. a coop of chickens, 12 dozen of champagne, a family box in perpetuity at the Lyceum, and a honeyed profession of high delight and edification over his scholarly and interesting observations.

I confess that if I were an actor myself, I could bear any sort of disparagement of my calling, from evangelical denunciation upwards, more equanimously than the tolerance of "Spectator." For instance, here is Mr William Archer, who, as the bass in Judas Maccabeus puts it, is somewhat "fearful in praise." The actors cannot altogether relish his ruthless treatment of the whole affair as so much paint, wigs, limelight, and masquerade, or his open declaration that "our devotion to this poor, tawdry, claptrap art of the theatre" can only be explained and justified by the

---

6. Possibly Edmund Burke's (1729–97) statement "all the contortions of the sibyl without the inspiration."

few and far between occasions when some stroke of genius intensifies a moment of idle makebelieve into a moment of real and searching experience. This principle of resisting illusion to the utmost instead of meeting it halfway really amounts to a refusal to accept the situation. Exactly as criticism of novels is admittedly impossible except upon the understanding that the critic will not use the argument that the novelist is a professional liar; just so can no actor be expected to stand up to criticism that begins with Dr Johnson's *coup de Jarnac*[7] at Garrick, "Punch has no feelings." Accordingly, A.B.W. at once agrees to consider the *coup de Dr Johnson* as a blow beneath the belt. "The point, my good fellow," he says to the actor, "is the effect of your performance on my imagination, not that of your profession on your moral character." And he is right; for such considerations must utterly corrupt the artistic purity of impressionistic criticism. That is why I—and, I suggest, Archer—get hopelessly beaten in point of critical integrity by "Spectator." I claim, however, that we err by transcension, not by shortcoming; and I sympathize with Mr Irving's preference of even the *coup de Dr Johnson* to such a diabolical refinement of the mind-your-own-business principle as that reached in the concentration of all critical recognition on the *dramatis persona*, and the utter ignoring of the sympathy-craving human being behind it. If I were an actor I should much rather have a man call me Punch than imply that it was nothing to him whether I was Punch or not. And so "Spectator," the perfect critic, is called a creature of the swamp and mist; whilst we imperfect ones escape with a few after-dinner sarcasms, well up to the standard of work required on such convivial occasions, but necessarily too amateurish to disturb our good humor.

To say that "Spectator" passes for a brilliant critic in England is to pay him a doubtful compliment; for it cannot be denied that the national genius does not lie in that direction; and in the kingdom of the blind, the one-eyed is king.[8] Even I cut quite a figure here as a critic; yet, if I had space to print my notice of L'Enfant Prodigue in parallel columns with A.B.W.'s "Pierrotics," my greatest admirer would admit that I wrote like an auctioneer in comparison. It is in Paris that playhouse impressions are really well done; and if I were asked to name some of the masters of the French school, I should unhesitatingly include "Spectator" (an Englishman), and Theodore Child (an American)[9] as among the best. "Spectator" makes no secret of his study of the French critics, and evidently considers

7. An unexpected and decisive attack. Guy Chabot, Baron de Jarnac (1509–72) so defeated his enemy in 1568.

8. "In the country of the blind the one-eyed man is king" is a proverb that was later the basis of "The Country of the Blind" (1904) by H(erbert) G(eorge) Wells (1856–1946).

9. (1846–92), London journalist who was Paris correspondent for *The World*.

that he learnt his business, as far as it can be learnt, chiefly from Jules Lemaître, to whom he has a quaint habit of attributing every good thing he quotes, even though he may have introduced it a dozen pages earlier as the latest *mot* of Anatole France, or as a titbit from Montaigne, myself, or some other famous author.[10] Lemaître, in fact, is his Mrs Harris;[11] and I am convinced that if he ever does anything so trite as to quote "After life's fitful fever he sleeps well," or "There's a divinity that shapes our ends," he will add, "as Jules Lemaître says."[12] And this is our "Spec's" only weakness.

A SHELLEY CELEBRATION
C/Un (*The Daily Chronicle*, 16 July 1892)

Quite the oddest celebration that the Shelley Centenary is likely to have was that which took place on Thursday afternoon at the Bedford Park Club. It will be remembered that the Shelley Society lately formed a joint committee with the Independent Theatre Society for the commemoration of Shelley's birth in 1792 by a performance of The Cenci. That committee immediately found itself in conflict with her Majesty's Reader of Plays, who refused to license any performance of Shelley's tragedy. On a previous occasion his authority had been evaded by the expedient of a "private" performance, which came off at the Grand Theatre, Islington, before an enormous audience, all of whom, except certain illustrious guests like Browning, had obtained admission without payment at the doors by subscribing to the Shelley Society for the year then current. The censor, thus baffled, could only sit down and watch for the demoralizing effect of the forbidden performance on the public, which, however, was not one penny the worse for it. This year found the censor fairly on his mettle. The Independent Theatre had followed the example of the Shelley Society in producing Ibsen's Ghosts without a licence. When the committee applied again for the Islington Theatre, they found that a clause in the new lease

10. Anatole France, pseudonym of Jacques-Anatole-François Thibault (1844–1922), French novelist and journalist who won the Nobel Prize for Literature in 1921; Michel Eyquem de Montaigne (1533–92), French moralist and essayist.
    11. In Dickens's *Martin Chuzzlewit*, "the words" Mrs Gamp "spoke of Mrs Harris, lambs could not forgive . . . nor worms forget."
    12. The quotations are from *Macbeth*, III.ii and *Hamlet*, V.ii.

expressly barred unlicensed performances. When they tried the Royalty, where Ghosts had found a night's hospitality, they found that never again would the management risk the forfeiture of its licence by defying the Lord Chamberlain. Further attempts proved equally fruitless. Mr Beerbohm Tree did what he could to move the censorship, offering his theatre freely for the performance, but Mr E.F.S. Pigott,[1] lenient as he is to the most hazardous sallies in farcical comedy and burlesque, remained inexorable, and finally forced Mr Tree to forgo the distinction of commemorating Shelley at his house. Mr Charrington, at the Avenue Theatre, then threw himself into the breach, and offered to run any risk, and defy any authority on such an occasion; but the committee now felt that they had no right to expose any manager to the resentment of a despotic ruler, and contented themselves with inviting the nation to contemplate the spectacle of the London theatres closed against The Cenci, on the centenary of Shelley's birth, and opened on the one hand to Jane[2] and on the other to Die Walküre, which is vulnerable to the same technical "moral" objection as The Cenci. The nation, so far, has contemplated the spectacle with heroic equanimity, and the censor, up to four o'clock on Thursday afternoon, remained master of the situation. At that hour, however, he appears to have been circumvented by Miss Florence Farr. This young lady, it will be remembered, astonished London a couple of years ago by producing Rosmersholm, the most strangely tragic of Ibsen's prose plays, at the Vaudeville Theatre, and bringing off a couple of performances with considerable glory, and actually without pecuniary loss. Miss Farr thereby marked herelf out as the actress *par excellence* for Beatrice Cenci, and the part was offered to her when the original Beatrice, Miss Alma Murray, was prevented by circumstances from resuming her old rôle. When the censor proved one too many for the Shelley Society, Miss Farr seems to have resolved to prove one too many for the censor. At any rate, she has managed to perform the prison scenes from the fifth act of the tragedy at the Bedford Park Club in spite of his interdict. No doubt the circumstances were enough to nerve a less mettlesome person than Miss Farr to brave a good deal in the way of unfavorable conditions; but when the curtain rose and revealed a tiny little bonnet box of a dungeon, its chill gloom heavily discounted by a dazzling limelight, which made every thread in the canvas wall glitter fiercely, it was evident that Miss Farr's work was cut out for her. Fortunately, the audience maintained an honorable gravity, and she pulled the scenes through as resolutely as if she was on the Lyceum stage, the curtain falling amid a surprising volume of

1. Pigott (1824–95), later Lord Lathom, was Licenser of Stage Plays in the Lord Chamberlain's Office.
2. (1890) by Harry Nicholls (1852–1926) and William Lestocq (1851?–1920).

applause, considering the smallness and selectness of the audience. Miss Ella Dresser, as the boy Bernardo, spoke her lines very prettily; Miss Florence Hunter volunteered for the thankless part of Lucretia; and Messrs Orlando Barnett, Fisher White, and Lewin Mannering[3] stood up bravely to the limelight, which, to tell the truth, was much harder on their costumes and venerable make-up than on the white robe and striking beauty of Beatrice. Altogether the performance was a quaint but plucky assertion of the right of Free Commemoration, and one which would, perhaps, have seemed more hopeful to the poet than the Horsham proposal to establish a Shelley Library[4] which "shall absorb existing libraries and be governed in such a manner as to secure the support of all sections of the community." Whilst cordially wishing well to that project, one cannot help thinking that if the library is to be particularly Shelleyan the support of all sections of the community is likely to be rather further off than the license which Miss Farr has recognized the necessity of doing without. The audience at Bedford Park was necessarily a limited one, the Press being represented only by Mr William Archer, Mr Walkley, and Mr H. M. Paget; the Shelley Society by Dr Furnivall and Mr John Todhunter, the Universities by Mr York Powell,[5] and the stage by Mrs Theodore Wright, Miss Marion Lea, and Miss Frances Ivor.

BERNARD SHAW REPLIES TO THE CRITICS OF WIDOWERS' HOUSES
(Letter to the Editor, *The Star*, 19 December 1892)

The critics of my play Widowers' Houses have now had their say. Will you be so good as to let the author have a turn? I know that I have had a full meal of advertisement, and that to ask for more seems greedy and ungrateful; but I said at the outset that I would boom this business for all I was

3. Barnett (b. 1867); J. Fisher White (1865–1945); Doré Lewin Mannering (1879–1932).

4. A committee at Horsham, in Shelley's native county, Sussex, proposed to found a Shelley Library and Museum.

5. Henry Marriott Paget (1856–1936), who was Farr's brother-in-law; F. York Powell (1850–1904), a lecturer and tutor at Christ Church, would in 1894 become Regius Profesor of Modern History at Oxford.

worth; and if I omited a "reply to my critics" I should feel that I had not done my complete utmost.

I have read every criticism of the play I could get hold of; and I think it is now clear that "the new drama" has no malice to fear from the serious critics. A few of the humorists have, of course, shewn all the unscrupulousness of their speciality; but they have amused us; and for that be all their sins forgiven them. There has been a touch of temper, too: one gentleman's blood boiled to such an extent that he literally "saw red," and solemnly assured the public that I wore a coat of that revolutionary hue. But the influential critics have, it seems to me, been not merely fair, but generous in their attitude. The care with which every possible admission in my favor has been made, even in the notices of those who found the play intolerably disagreeable and the author intolerably undramatic, shews that the loss of critical balance produced by the first shock of Ibsen's Ghosts was only momentary, and that the most unconventional and obnoxious agitator-dramatist, even when he has gone out of his way to attack his critics, need not fear a Press vendetta. I have had fair play from my opponents, and considerably more than that from my partisans; and if this is how I fare, I do not see what anybody else need fear.

However, the fairness of criticism is one thing, its adequacy quite another. I do not hesitate to say that many of my critics have been completely beaten by the play simply because they are ignorant of society. Do not let me be misunderstood: I do not mean that they eat with their knives, drink the contents of their fingerbowls, or sit down to dinner in ulsters and green neckties. What I mean is that they do not know life well enough to recognize it in the glare of the footlights. They denounce Sartorius, my house-knacking widower, as a monstrous libel on the middle and upper class because he grinds his money remorselessly out of the poor. But they do not (and cannot) answer his argument as to the impossibility of his acting otherwise under our social system; nor do they notice the fact that though he is a bad landlord he is not in the least a bad man as men go. Even in his economic capacity I have made him a rather favorable specimen of his class. I might have made him a shareholder in a match factory where avoidable "phossy jaw" was not avoided, or in a tram company working its men seventeen and a half hours a day, or in a railway company with a terrible deathroll of mangled shunters, or in a whitelead factory, or a chemical works: in short, I might have piled on the agony beyond the endurance of my audience, and yet not made him one whit worse than thousands of personally amiable and respected men who have invested in the most lucrative way the savings they have earned or inherited. I will not ask those critics who are so indignant with my "distorted and myopic outlook on society" what they will do with the little money their profession may enable them to save. I will simply tell them what they m u s t do with it, and that is to follow the advice of their stockbroker as to the safest and most remunerative investment, reserving their moral scruples for the expenditure of the interest, and their sympathies for the treatment of the members of their own families. Even in spending the interest they will have no alternative but to get the best value they can for their money without regard to the conditions under which the articles they buy are produced. They will take a domestic pride in their comfortable houses full of furniture made by "slaughtered" (*i.e.* extra-sweated) cabinet makers, and go to church or to dinner in shirts sewn by women who can only bring their wages up to subsistence point by prostitution. What will they say to Sartorius then? What, indeed, can they say to him now?—these "guilty creatures sitting at a play"[1] who, instead of being struck to the soul and presently proclaiming their malefactions, are naïvely astonished and revolted at the spectacle of a man on the stage acting as we are all acting perforce every day. I can turn Sartorius from a house knacker into a dramatic critic quite easily without robbing the drama of its essential truth, and certainly without robbing the satire of its pungency. The notion that the people in Widowers' Houses are abnormally vicious or odious could only prevail in a community in which Sartorius is absolutely typical in his unconscious villainy. Like my critics, he lacks conviction of sin. Now, the didactic object of my play is to produce conviction of sin, to make the Pharisee who repudiates Sartorius as either a Harpagon[2] or a diseased dream of mine, and thanks God that such persons do not represent his class, recognize that Sartorius is his own photograph. It is vain for the virtuous dramatic critic to tell me that he does not own slum property: all I want to see is the label on his matchbox, or his last week's washing bill, in order to judge for myself whether he really ever gives a second thought to Sartorius's tenants, who make his matchboxes and wash his stockings so cheaply.

As to the highly connected young gentleman, naturally straightforward and easygoing, who bursts into genuine indignation at the sufferings of the poor, and, on being shewn that he cannot help them, becomes honestly cynical and throws off all responsibility whatever, that is nothing but the reality of the everyday process known as disillusion. His allowing the two business men to get his legs under their mahogany, and to persuade him to "stand in" with a speculation of which he understands nothing except that he is promised some money out of it, will surprise no one who knows the City and has seen the exploitation of aristocratic names by City promoters spread from needy guinea-pig colonels, and lords with courtesy titles, to eldest sons of the noblest families. If I had even represented

1. *Hamlet*, II.ii.
2. Title character of *The Miser* (1668) by Molière.

Harry Trench as letting himself in for eighteen months hard labor for no greater crime than that of being gambler enough to be the too willing dupe of a swindler, the incident would be perfectly true to life. As to the compensation speculation in the third act being a fraud which no gentleman would have countenanced, that opinion is too innocent to be discussed. I can only say that as the object of the scheme is to make a haul at the expense of the ratepayers collectively, it is much less cruel and treacherous in its incidence than the sort of speculation which made the late Mr Jay Gould universally respected during his lifetime. I shall be told next that the Prince of Wales is not a gentleman because he plays baccarat; that copper cornerers like M. Secretan, and cotton cornerers like Mr Steenstrand, are not admited into society; that Pearson's Weekly had no reputable subscribers; and that Panama is a dream of mine.[3]

There is a curious idea in the minds of some of my critics that I have given away my case by representing the poor man, Lickcheese, as behaving exactly as the rich man does when he gets the chance. These gentlemen believe that, according to me, what is wrong with society is that the rich, who are all wicked, oppress the poor, who are all virtuous. I will not waste the space of The Star by dealing with such a misconception further than to curtly but goodhumoredly inform those who entertain it that they are fools. I administer the remark, not as an insult, but as a tonic.

Most of the criticisms of my heroine, Blanche Sartorius, are summed up in the remark of the servant whom she throttles: "You ought to be ashamed of yourself, Miss Blanche, so you ought." I admit that she ought not to have vented her rage on the servant; but it must be remembered in extenuation that she had no sister. On another point in her conduct one critic makes an objection which, I confess, amazed me. Sartorius, as the son of a very poor woman, knows that the poor are human beings exactly like himself. But his daughter, brought up as a lady, conceives them as a different and inferior species. "I hate the poor" she says. "At least, I hate those dirty, drunken, disreputable people who live like pigs." The critic in question, whose bias towards myself is altogether friendly, cannot conceive that a young lady would avow such inhuman sentiments: hypocrisy,

3. Gould (1836–92) was an American railroad magnate and financial speculator whose activities in the gold market led to a panic in 1869, when the price of gold plummeted. Secretan (d. 1899) formed a French monopoly in 1888 to raise the price of copper; the following year, his speculations in copper resulted in collapsed prices and widespread panic. William Steenstrand (d. 1895) cornered the copper market in 1890; when the corner collapsed in September, he lost over £1 million, paying his stockholders 66¢ to the dollar. Pearson's Weekly published light literature for a popular market. In 1882, a French company headed by Ferdinand Marie de Lesseps (1805–94) began to dig a Panama Canal; French politicians stole a great deal of money from the company, which went bankrupt in 1889 after having excavated about 76 million cubic yards (58 million cubic meters) of earth.

he contends, would prevent her if her heart did not. I can only refer him, if he has really never heard such sentiments boasted of by ladies, to the comments of The Times and the St James's Gazette (to name no other papers written by gentlemen for gentlemen) on the unemployed, on the starving Irish peasants whose rents have since been reduced wholesale in the Irish land courts, or on the most heavily sweated classes of workers whose miserable plight has been exposed before the Housing of the Poor and Sweating Commissions, to prove that the thinkers and writers of Blanche Sartorius's party vie with each other in unconscious—nay, conscientious—brutality, callousness, and class prejudice when they speak of the proletariat. Hypocrisy with them takes the shape of dissembling sympathy with the working class when they really feel it, not of affecting it when they do not feel it. My friend and critic must remember the savage caricatures of William Morris, John Burns, Miss Helen Taylor,[4] Mrs Besant, &c., in which Punch once indulged, as well as the outrageous calumnies which were heaped on the late Mr Bradlaugh during his struggle to enter Parliament, and the remonstrance of The Saturday Review with the Government for not hanging myself, Mr Sidney Webb, and other London reformers in 1885–7, not to mention the cases of unsocial conduct by county gentlemen and magistrates that are exposed every week in the "Pillory" columns of Truth. Am I to be told that the young ladies who read these papers in our suburban villas are less narrow and better able to see across the frontiers of their own class than the writers whom they support? The fact is that Blanche's class prejudices, like those of the other characters in the play, are watered down instead of exaggerated. The whole truth is too monstrous to be told otherwise than by degrees.

Now comes the question, How far does all this touch the merits of the play as a work of art? Obviously not at all; but it has most decidedly touched the value of the opinions of my critics on that point. The evidence of the notices (I have sheaves of them before me) is irresistible. With hardly an exception the men who find my sociology wrong are also the men who find my dramatic workmanship bad; and vice versa. Even the criticism of the acting is biased in the same way. The effect on me, of course, is to reassure me completely as to my own competence as a playwright. The very success with which I have brought all the Philistines and sentimental idealists down on me proves the velocity and pene-

4. John Elliot Burns (1858–1943), a working-class man and social activist, led the successful Dock Strike of 1889 while he was a member of the London County Council. In 1892, as a member of the Labour Party, he entered Parliament. He and Helen Taylor (1831–1907), a social reformer and advocate of women's rights, were members of the Marxist Social Democratic Federation.

tration with which my realism got across the footlights. I am well accustomed to judge the execution I have done by the cries of the wounded.

On one point, however, I heartily thank my critics for their unanimous forbearance. Not one of them has betrayed the absurdities and impossibilities which abound in the political and commercial details of the play. They have even declared that here I am on my own ground, and that here consequently I rise, competent and entertaining, above criticism. Considering that I have made a resident in Surbiton eligible as a St Giles vestryman; that I have made the London County Council contemporary with the House of Lords Commission on the Housing of the Working Class; that I have represented an experienced man of business as paying seven percent on a first mortgage; that I have finished up with an unprecedented and farfetched mortgage transaction which will not stand criticism by any expert from the City: considering, in short, that I have recklessly sacrificed realism to dramatic effect in the machinery of the play, I feel, as may be well imagined, deeply moved by the compliments which have been paid me on my perfect knowledge of economics and business. Thanks, brothers, thanks.

In conclusion, let me say that whilst I shall not affect to attribute the difference between myself and most of my critics to anything else but the pretty plain fact that I know my subject much better than they do, I claim no much more for the play than that it has served its turn: better, perhaps, than a better play. My point of view is being reached by larger and larger masses of the people; and when it has become quite common, everybody will see a good many more faults in Widowers' Houses than have been yet discovered by anyone except yours truly.

UNCONSCIOUS VILLAINY AND WIDOWERS' HOUSES
X (Letter to the Editor, *The Speaker*, 31 December 1892)

I now, as an experienced critic, approach the question which is really the most interesting from the critical point of view. Is it possible to treat the artistic quality of a play altogether independently of its scientific quality? For example, is it possible for a critic to be perfectly appreciative and perfectly incredulous and half insensible at the same time? I do not believe it for a moment. No point in a drama can produce any effect at all unless the spectator perceives it and accepts it as a real point; and this primary condition being satisfied, the force of the effect will depend on the extent to which the point interests the spectator: that is, seems momentous to him. The spectacle of Hamlet fencing with an opponent whose foil is "unbated" and poisoned produces its effect because the audience knows the danger; but there are risks just as thrilling to those who know them, risks of cutting arteries in certain surgical operations, risks of losing large sums by a momentary loss of nerve in the money market, risks of destroying one's whole character by an apparently trifling step, perils of all sorts which may give the most terrible intensity to a scene in the eyes of those who have the requisite technical knowledge or experience of life to understand the full significance of what they are witnessing, but which would produce as little effect on others as the wheeling forward of a machine gun on a hostile tribe of savages unacquainted with "the resources of civilization." One can imagine the A.B.W. [Arthur Bingham Walkley] of the tribe saying, before the explosion, "This may be artillery—whatever artillery means—but it is not fighting," just as our own A.B.W., whom it is my glory to have floored and driven into mere evasion, says of my play "This may be the New Economics, which I do not profess to understand, but it is not drama." All I can say is that I find drama enough in it, and that the play has not fallen flat enough to countenance A.B.W.'s assumption that his anesthesia is my fault instead of his own. It has long been clear to me that nothing will ever be done for the theatre until the most able dramatists refuse to write down to the level of that imaginary monster, the British Public. We want a theatre for people who have lived, thought, and felt, and who have some real sense that women are human beings just like men, only worse brought up, and consequently worse behaved. In such a theatre the mere literary man who has read and written instead of living until he has come to feel fiction as experience and to resent experience as fiction, would be as much out of place as the ideal B.P. itself. Well, let him sit out his first mistaken visit quietly and not come again; for it is quite clear that it is only by holding the mirror up to literature that the dramatist pleases him, whereas it is only by holding it up to nature that good work is produced.[1] In such a theatre Widowers' Houses would rank as a trumpery farcical comedy; whereas, in the theatre of today, it is excitedly discussed as a daringly original sermon, political essay, satire, Drapier letter,[2] or what not, even

1. *Hamlet,* III.ii: "the purpose of playing [. . .] was and is to hold, as 'twere, the mirror up to nature [. . .]."
2. Jonathan Swift (1667–1745) published a series of satirical pamphlets, *The Drapier's Letters* (1724), supposedly by M. B. Drapier.

by those who will not accept it as a play on any terms. And all because my hero did not, when he heard that his income came from slum property, at once relinquish it (*i.e.* make it a present to Sartorius without benefiting the tenants) and go to the goldfields to dig out nuggets with his strong right arm so that he might return to wed his Blanche after a shipwreck (witnessed by her in a vision), just in time to rescue her from beggary, brought upon her by the discovery that Lickcheese was the rightful heir to the property of Sartorius, who had dispossessed and enslaved him by a series of forgeries unmasked by the faithful Cokane. (If this is not satisfactory I can reel off half a dozen alternative "dramatic" plots within ten minutes' thought, and yet I am told I have no dramatic capacity.) I wonder whether it was lack of capacity, or superabundance of it, that led me to forgo all this "drama" by making my hero do exactly what he would have done in real life: that is, apologize like a gentleman (in the favorable sense) for accusing another man of his own unconscious rascality, and admit his inability to change a world which would not take the trouble to change itself? A.B.W., panting for the renunciation, the goldfields, and the nuggets, protests that I struck "a blow in the air." That is precisely what I wanted to do, being tired of blows struck in the vacuum of stageland. And the way in which the blow, trifling as it was, has sent the whole critical squadron reeling, and for the moment knocked all the breath out of the body of the New Criticism itself, shews how absurdly artificial the atmosphere of the stalls had become. The critics who have kept their heads, counting hostile and favorable ones together, do not make five percent of the whole body.

THE AUTHOR TO THE DRAMATIC CRITICS
(Appendix 1 to *Widowers' Houses*, May 1893)

FELLOW CRITICS

It is one of my advantages that I can discuss criticism, not merely as an author, but as a critic. I have no illusions about critics being authors who have failed. I know, as one who has practised both crafts, that authorship is child's play compared to criticism; and I have, you may depend upon it, my full share of the professional instinct which regards the romancer as a mere adventurer in literature, and the critic as a highly skilled workman. Ask any novelist or dramatist whether he can write a better novel or play than I; and he will blithely say Yes. Ask him to take my place as critic for one week; and he will blench from the test. The truth is that the critic stands between popular authorship, for which he is not silly enough, and great authorship, for which he has not genius enough. It is certainly true that the status of popular author is much coveted by critics; but that is because the popular author is much better paid for much easier work. Thackeray, like many other eminent authors, coveted a government sinecure; but nobody therefore supposes that authors are merely unsuccessful sinecurists, or that a well paid post in the civil service would have been intellectually a promotion for Thackeray. He who publishes a critical essay well knows how few care to read such things; whereas some donkey of an author, with the imagination of a schoolboy, or some sentimental young lady perhaps, will turn out a story too absurd to be thinkable by an ordinarily competent critic, and yet have it bought by scores and hundreds of thousands of readers of fiction. It is the natural desire to wallow in the profits of romantic makebelieve instead of toiling for the scanty wages of "the intolerable fatigue of thought"[1] that drives the critic to envy the author.

You will now feel, fellow critics, that in turning dramatist I have not turned traitor. It is for the honor of our guild that I venture to suggest that even in the intellectual department the authors are getting ahead of us. I do not wish to rake up the case of Ibsen and his Ghosts again: I think it will be admited now that the most oldfashioned school for young ladies in the country would have made almost as good a job of that discussion as we did. It was not a question of our liking Ibsen or not liking him, agreeing with him or not agreeing with him. Whichever way our bias lay it was our business to analyze his position skilfully and pronounce on it coolly. Under no circumstances should we have forgotten ourselves so far as to scold at him and cry Fie! like a bevy of illiterate prudes. This, however, is what too many of us did; and now, since what is done cannot be undone, we had better put up a few posts to warn future critics off the dangerous places where we come to grief oftenest.

The first warning I propose is: Do not let us raise the cry of "Ibsen" whenever we find a modern idea in a play. See what it has led to in the following passages culled from criticisms—some of them friendly and able ones—of Widowers' Houses.

"As an ardent admirer of Ibsen's methods, he has not scrupled to follow the method of that writer to extremes." *Daily Telegraph.* "The lesson is trite in the case of creeds that the disciple not seldom distances the

---

1. "The insupportable fatigue of thought": William Cowper, *The Task* (1785), book 6.

master. Ibsen has justly been charged," &c., &c. *Athenæum.* "The London Ibsen [ironical].[2] One can see that all this is meant to be exceedingly Ibsenesque." *Sunday Sun.* "I really think it is time the Independent Theatre Society made an effort to secure a play that is not moulded on the lines laid down by the great and only Ibsen." *Pelican.* "Mr Shaw is a zealous Ibsenite." *Weekly Dispatch.* "A rather silly play by a rather clever man, which may be either worship or satire of Ibsenius the Great." *Saturday Review.* "Mr Shaw is the high priest, one may say, of Ibsenism." *Piccadilly.* "Like all the Ibsenians he ruins his argument," &c. *Modern Society.* "Mr Shaw is an Ibsenite and is consequently quite up to date." *Freeman's Journal.* "A promising young tigress of a daughter, who is drawn on the severest principles of Ibsenite heredity." *Western Mercury.*

Now the first two acts of Widowers' Houses were written in 1885, when I knew nothing about Ibsen; and I must add that the authors of the lines quoted above should have guessed this, because there is not one idea in the play that cannot be more easily referred to half a dozen English writers than to Ibsen; whilst of his peculiar retrospective method, by which his plays are made to turn upon events supposed to have happened before the rise of the curtain, there is not a trace in my work. The subjects which seem most strongly to suggest Ibsen to modern critics are (1) Heredity, (2) the Emancipation of Woman, (3) any adverse criticism whatever of our marriage laws and customs, and (4) any mixture of wickedness and goodness in the same character. It is therefore necessary to remind ourselves that modern English culture was saturated with the conception of heredity by Herbert Spencer, Darwin, Huxley, Tyndall, and Galton[3] before Ibsen's name was known here; that the Married Women's Property Act, the result of a long and strenuous crusade against what I may call the anti-Ibsenite ideal of marriage, was passed in England before A Doll's House was written; that the two most famous works on the subject of Women's Rights are Mary Wollstonecraft's Vindication and John Stuart Mill's [On the] Subjection of Women, dated respectively 1792 and 1869; and that those who may never have studied the complex characters in the fiction of Balzac, George Eliot, George Meredith,[4] and other well known modern writers, may at least be presumed to have read the history of King David in the Bible, and to have learnt from it that Nature does not keep heroism exclusively for one set of men and villainy exclusively for another, merely to enable us all to become dramatists and "paint character" with a bucket of whitewash and a jar of lampblack. These

2. Brackets are Shaw's.
3. Sir Francis Galton (1822–1911) wrote a pioneering treatise on eugenics (*Hereditary Genius*, 1869). Shaw refers to him in the preface (1924) to *Saint Joan* (1923).
4. (1828–1909), novelist, poet, and essayist.

things are the more important for a critic to observe, because matters have taken such a course in England for the last fifty years that the man who has neither the culture of the Bible nor that of the Evolutionist school is in ninetynine cases out of a hundred a man with no culture at all: a suspicion not to be lightly incurred by anyone whose calling it is to bring culture to bear on dramatic literature. Be warned therefore; for it is hard to see how a critic who has dipped into modern English literature even to the modest extent of reading one of Mr Grant Allen's novels, could write as if every idea in physics and morals that is not to be found in Chambers' Vestiges of Creation and Dr Watts' poems[5] must necessarily be a recent Norwegian importation.

The second warning is: Let us not try to encourage the hypocrisy of the theatre, already greater than that of the conventicle, by being more austere in our judgment of *dramatis personæ* than of real men and women. Imitate that excellent critic of mine (known to me only through his very agreeable notice of my play), the London correspondent of The Glasgow Herald, who says:

"The characters are depicted naturally, and not in the glorified form so common upon the conventional stage. . . . It was a treat for once to see a hero (like one of Thackeray's)[6] no better than one of his fellow men; to listen to the worldliness of the slum landlord and his clerk; and particularly to welcome a heroine who shews her temper to her betrothed, and still more to her father, and who, like other estimable womankind whom we frequently meet in real life, though rarely on the stage, is always ready to quarrel on a point of feminine dignity, but when 'cornered' is always anxious to forgive and to make friends again."

That is what I call a reasonable criticism. Now listen to some of the others:

"There can hardly be said to be a single estimable personage in the whole play." *Times.* "All his *dramatis personæ* are entirely selfish and despicable." *Daily Telegraph.* "Revolting picture of middleclass life. . . . Remorselessly the eccentric one [the author][7] laid bare his idealized essence of snobbishness compressed from all the worst specimens of his fellow-men, and bade us believe that he was painting from life. . . . The abominable Blanche appears in a worse light than ever; and the eccentricity ends with the smothering of what small spark of decency remained in the heart of the only person of the whole bunch who ever had any."

5. (Charles) Grant (Blairfindie) Allen (1848–99), Canadian-born writer of philosophy and fiction; Isaac Watts (1674–1748), a theologian who wrote over six hundred hymns.
6. William Makepeace Thackeray (1811–63), novelist, essayist, and caricaturist for *Punch.*
7. Shaw's brackets.

Morning Leader. "It is already impossible, we should hope, to find a set of people so peculiar and unsympathetic as those introduced in this play." *Morning Advertiser.* "In such a world what is to be done but to shew hands all round and caper to the tune of 'rogues all'?" *Globe.* "Mr Gilbert possesses an uncanny habit of turning up the seamy side of life's robe; but Mr Shaw's world has not rags enough to cover its nudity. He aims to shew with Zolaesque exactitude that middleclass life is foul and leprous. The play means that the middle class, even to its womanhood, is brutal at heart, or it means nothing." *Athenæum.* "A set of bloodsuckers. Everyone is ill conditioned, quarrelsome, fractious, apt to behave, at a moment's notice, like a badly brought-up child." *World.* "The mere word 'mortgage' suffices to turn hero into rascal. Mr Shaw will say that is his point: scratch a middleclass hero and you find a rascal." *Speaker.* "Revelation of a distorted and myopic outlook on society." *Sunday Sun.* "Very disagreeable heroine . . . all the other characters in the play—the poor parlormaid alone excepted—are as hateful as that heroine." *Era.* "Mr Shaw devotes all his energies to making his characters unsympathetic, sordid, soulless: ending even worse than they began." *Stage.* "Heartless young lady . . . cads of diverse temperaments." *Weekly Dispatch.* "He goes further than Ibsen, whose characters are a mixture of knaves and fools; whereas in Widowers' Houses they are all knaves." *Modern Society.* "Mr Shaw starts with a total disbelief in human nature." *Freeman's Journal.* "All the characters were villains except a pretty parlormaid." *Western Mercury.* "The moral seems to be the utter selfishness of human nature outside a progressive County Council." *Umpire.* "I could not help noticing that the only thoroughly decent character in the play was a sort of Mrs Harris in the shape of the parson, who was only allowed to be talked about, but who did not appear." Mr Ben Greet,[8] addressing the Church and Stage Guild.

I remember once hearing Mr Moody the Evangelist preach on the text "All have sinned and fallen short of the glory of God."[9] He declared strenuously that in morals a miss is as good as a mile, and that the most venial sin damns as effectually as the most atrocious crime. To have fallen short of the glory of God is enough, whether by an inch or a league does not matter. I must say that from any other point of view than Mr Moody's, the passages set forth above appear to me to be ludicrous exaggerations. Even

8. Later Sir (Philip Barling) Ben Greet (1857–1936), who in 1886 began to manage open-air productions of Shakespearean plays and would organize Shakespearean tours in the United Kingdom and the United States. In Dickens's *Martin Chuzzlewit* (1843–44), Mrs Harris, like the parson in Shaw's play, never appears (she is Mrs Gamp's imaginary friend).

9. Shaw's first publication was a letter in *Public Opinion*, 3 April 1875, on the American evangelists Dwight Lyman Moody (1837–1899) and Ira D. Sankey (1840–1908), who conducted a revival meeting in Dublin. The text is Romans, 3:23: "For all have sinned, and come short of the glory of God."

after making all allowance for the effect on the writers of the way in which, for the first time on the stage (as far as I know) they saw the citizen with his share in the guilt of our industrial system brought home to him, I still think that they might have paused to ask themselves in what respect Trench, Sartorius, Blanche, Cokane, and Lickcheese are any worse, I will not say than themselves, but than the characters in any of the comedies, ancient or modern, to which they have taken no exception on this score. I certainly had no intention of spoiling the moral of my play by making the characters at all singular; and I suggest that the following considerations will explain my apparent cynicism.

Formerly, a man was responsible only for his private conduct and for the maintenance of his own household. Today, as an inevitable consequence of Democracy, he is responsible for the state of the whole community which he helps to govern as a citizen and a voter. Now a man may discharge his private responsibility very well, and yet not even realize that his public responsibility exists. Just as Charles I was an excellent private gentleman and an intolerable king, so most men today are reasonably good friends and fathers, but execrable citizens. Sartorius is the ordinary man of business, voting for the candidate who promises to keep down the rates, and getting on the vestry solely to prevent the vestry from interfering with his property. And he does so in a hypocritical way only because that is the custom: not in the least because he is a Pecksniff. I have drawn him as a man of strong and masterful character, unscrupulous but not a lawbreaker, a kind and unselfish father, and much more reasonable and even magnanimous with Trench than the typical villa owner, who is a comparatively spiteful and huffy person. He is, in short, distinctly an exceptional and superior specimen of the middleclass man whose business it is to deal d i r e c t l y with the poor. His rascality—for from the social point of view he certainly is a callous rascal—does not lie in his refusing to spend money on his rookeries, since his plea that his tenants would burn his improvements is perfectly well founded. It lies altogether in his indifference to defects in our social system which produce a class of persons so poor that they are driven by constant physical privation to turn everything they can lay hands on into more fuel and more food. When we find a castaway at sea chewing his boots to appease his hunger, we do not stigmatize him as a creature too degraded to appreciate the right use of boots: we take him aboard and relieve his hunger, after which he wears his boots as appreciatively as a West End gentleman. But Sartorius is not ashamed to explain the disappearance of his banisters and cistern lids on the absurd ground that "these people do not know how to live in handsome houses." He has found out that there is no use in treating them goodnaturedly; and he has not enough social conscience to proceed to ask why there is no use, and to find out how, as a citizen and an elector, to remedy the abject poverty which makes a woman willing, for the sake of having a good warm, to burn the handrail that is put up to save her and her neighbors from falling downstairs. The point may not be obvious at once to a critic who has only to ring the bell for another scuttle of Wallsend[10] when his fire runs low, any more than it was obvious to Sartorius. Consequently, in every denunciation of Sartorius as a monster, we may see the hand of Sartorius himself.

I now come to a string of remonstrances partly brought on me by a passage in an interview published in the Star newspaper (November 29th, 1892), in which I declared that I wished to appeal to the audience "on the solid ground of political economy," and to have a blackboard on the stage with diagrams to illustrate my points, with much more chaff of the same kind. Here is the result:

"A kind of leading article of the slashing type." *Morning*. "An exposition in dialogue of the New Economics. . . . What has this farrago of newspaper leaders and Fabian essays to do with the play?" *Star*. "Undramatic attempt to cut up a Parliamentary Report into uneven stage lengths. . . . Published as one of the dialogues sometimes given in The Fortnightly Review it would be effective." *Echo*. "A discussion, with open doors, of the pros and cons of slum landlordism . . . a good sermon." *Black and White*. "A new form of didactic Socialistic demonstration, like the practicable laundries with the poor washerwomen at work which figured in a recent procession in Hyde Park." *Sunday Sun*. "It would be readable and might be useful as a Fabian pamphlet." *Weekly Dispatch*. "In no sense a drama, but a succession of dialogues in which the author sets forth his views concerning Socialist questions." *Lloyds*. "Not a play: a pamphlet." *Encore*. "The exposure of certain social sins connected with the letting of tenement houses afforded the sole *raison d'être* of Mr Shaw's feeble little play." *Observer*. "His propaganda: I beg pardon, his new play." *Penny Illustrated Paper*. "Merely a lecture." *Financial Observer*. "Mr Shaw wishes to utter a tirade against certain abuses; and he thinks the theatre a suitable pulpit for his utterances." *Colonies and India*. "The play is a pamphlet in dramatic form." *Western Mercury*. "The whole of the three acts is occupied with a dreary discussion of the ethics of slum property." *Birmingham Post*. "Three acts of dreary dissertation on the familiar text that 'rent is robbery.' " *Yorkshire Post*. "Mr Bernard Shaw is an amiable Fabian who believes that 'rent is robbery.' " *Yorkshire Evening Post*.

Now I think it must be evident at this rate to all who have read the play, that if I had written The Merchant of Venice it would have been denounced as a dissertation on the Jewish question, complicated by a crude

10. A type of coal, named for a city near Newcastle, in the coal-manufacturing area of northeast England.

exposition of the peculiar views of the Fabian Society on the law of contract. All I need say on the Fabian point is that any person who would like to see the difference between an essay on rent and Widowers' Houses can buy Fabian Essays, containing just such an essay by me, for ninepence. Fabian pamphlets, in which I have had a hand, can be obtained for a penny; and a comparison of them with this play will shew how little the critics quoted above know how merciful I have been to them. Let me say, however, that it is impossible for any fictionist, dramatic or other, to make true pictures of modern society without some knowledge of the economic anatomy of it. And since what the dramatist ought to know the critic ought to know, a course of Fabian literature would most unquestionably do incalculable good to both dramatists and critics, if they could be persuaded to go through it. For all that, I see that it would be useless to blame a critic today for not being an economist, or even an ordinarily competent politician and man of business. Nobody expects it from him; and he himself benightedly ridicules the idea. But what I do expect him to know is that "bluebook plays" hold the stage far better than conventionally idealist dramas. I need only mention the irrepressible Never Too Late to Mend[11] to prove that Widowers' Houses, far from being a play of so new a sort that its very title to the name of drama is questionable, is, on its bluebook side, a sample (whether good or bad is not here in question) of one of the most familiar, popular, and firmly established *genres* in English dramatic literature. It is a matter of experience that the dramatized or novelized bluebook or Fabian Essay (so to speak) has ten times as much chance of success as the mere romance, though it is also, of course, a much more difficult job for the writer. My warning therefore is against the folly of assuming that the reverse is the case, and that a play is handicapped by a basis of bluebook. A wary critic, if he wished to "slate" Widowers' Houses, would begin somewhat in this fashion: "Not even with all the advantages of his profound economic knowledge and his complete acquaintance with the wealth of dramatic material stored in our national bluebook literature was Mr Shaw able to produce a tolerable play." It is mere perversity to assume that the less a dramatist knows and cares about real life, the better his plays are likely to be.

There are a dozen other warnings that I could formulate for the sake of our younger and weaker brethren, who are being severely tested by the dramatic revival now beginning. But as I very much doubt whether they have read thus far into what must be to them a piece of heavy literature, I will indulge myself by laying down a just now rather weary pen, confident that the really able brothers of the craft will forgive my preaching, seeing that they best know how much the rest stand in need of a sermon. My

11. *It's Never Too Late to Mend* (1864) by Charles Reade.

sole object is to knock on the head a few empty formulas which take up the space in dramatic criticism which should be occupied by real ideas, and which have been trotted out in the last few years whenever a play has been produced with any pretension to represent modern life as it is really lived.

PLAYWRIGHT CUT PLAYWRIGHT.[1]
BERNARD SHAW ON GEORGE MOORE
C/X/Un (SDI, *The Star*, 27 June 1893)

"I want your opinion, Mr Shaw, of George Moore's Strike at Arlingford, from the Socialist point of view. It has just been published by Walter Scott, so your criticism will come in pat."

"What price has he published it at?" said the sage, with powerful interest.

"Five shillings."

"Hm! How many prefaces and appendices?"

"None."

The Man with a Red Beard was visibly revolted. "None!" he exclaimed. "Now just imagine wasting a book on a mere play. A man should never throw away an opportunity of talking about himself. It is wrong of Moore: very wrong; I must speak to him about it."

"He has indulged in a prefatory note of about five lines to say that in his own conception of the play the labor dispute is an externality to which he attaches little importance, and that what he applied himself to in the play was the development of a moral idea which he leaves the play itself to explain. Now, you are a bit of an expert in the labor question. Do you think Moore has made a mess of it or not?"

"No; because all the details which betray want of practical experience on his part could be corrected without essentially altering the play. And the economic point which brings about the tragedy is technically sound, new on the stage, probable, clearly intelligible, and of sufficient horse-power, so to speak, to drive the hero to destruction."

"What point is that?"

"The point that the moment you raise wages in any industry, a certain

1. "Diamonds cut diamonds"—John Ford (1586–after 1639?), *The Lover's Melancholy* (1629). Shaw might have got the phrase from *Polite Conversation* (1738) by Swift.

number of firms on the margin of the industry, who just scraped along by buying labor at the old starvation rate, have to put up the shutters and discharge their hands, leaving them, for the moment, penniless. No genuine labor leader lets that stop him. He knows that these marginal laborers are dragging all the rest down to their level, and that though they may have to look for fresh employment, the demand for labor cannot be reduced on the whole by a mere transfer of purchasing power from the capitalists to the workers through a rise in wages. But sometimes the temporary hardship is no joke to the sufferers, and a particularly hard case would undoubtedly be that of a mine only barely worth working at starvation level, but capable, at that level, of employing a large number of hands, and returning several thousands a year to the proprietors. You will remember that Moore makes the whole population of Arlingford dependent on a mine of this kind. When the strikers are almost beaten, their leader gets a big cheque for the strike fund. Then the lady who owns the pit shews him the books and convinces him that if he does not keep back the cheque and allow the strike to fail the mine will be closed and the strikers ruined. Moore has made his hero just the sort of weakling to turn traitor under these circumstances; and as he is in love with the lady into the bargain, there you have your drama with an unimpeachable economic motive."

"Would you not have done the same under the same circumstances, Mr Shaw?"

"Certainly not. However, it's an ingenious question, and does you credit as an interviewer. You want to find out whether I am disposed to quarrel with Moore over the Socialism in the play. That is what you are driving at, isnt it?"

The Star man blushed confessfully.

"I thought so. Well, the weak point of the play to me is the assumption throughout it all that Socialism is to a middleclass man exactly what keeping a turnpike was to old Mr Weller in Pickwick: the last resource of a soured and desperate wretch. John Reid, jilted by Lady Ann, takes to Socialism as being just a degree more suicidal than taking to drink. He is supposed to have renounced everything that makes life worth living in exchanging the position of a private secretary for that of a great labor leader. Now no man could possibly become a great labor leader with such ideas in his head. The position of labor leader is within the reach of every man, rich or poor, gentle or simple, Board-school pupil or University alumnus, who is strong enough to reach out his hand and take it. There are over eight million adult male working men in England to pick and choose labor leaders from. Out of the eight million less than a dozen persons have succeeded in raising themselves to the eminence claimed for John Reid: that is, the position of a Socialist leader of working class opinion, who is also a practical trade unionist and strike organizer of commanding reputation, national as well as local. If such men could be manufactured offhand out of minor poets and disappointed snobs crossed in love, we should have 12,000 field marshalls for every big strike, instead of less than 12: and if I said less than six, you would find it hard to contradict me. No; a labor leader may be far from an ideally virtuous republican; he may be an aristocrat, even an autocrat; he may laugh at the credulity and curse the folly of the mobs who cheer him; he may exhaust all the arts of the actor and the hypocrite in cajoling them, bullying them, stoking their enthusiasm up or down as may be necessary; he may be a bouncing liar and as great a blackguard as Napoleon; he may be utterly incapable of the attractively decent straightness and simplicity of private life that distinguishes such men as Burns and Mann;[2] but he must be an able man with all his will and his ambition enlisted on the labor side, and with a daimonic power of throwing himself into a labor conflict and fighting to win with all his might. Now the hero of The Strike at Arlingford is above all things a failure. That is the note of him from the beginning to end. And yet Moore asks me to believe for the sake of his play that this fellow is a great labor leader. Well, of course, I cannot; I know too much about it. It is as if I were asked to conceive Waterloo Bridge as a fabric of straw in order that it might collapse in the last act after bearing the traffic of London during the first and second. Mind: dont misunderstand me: I should not object at all if John Reid were represented as the sort of Socialist who, though fanatically enthusiastic, an eloquent speaker and a writer of gushing poems, has not a scrap of character underneath it all, and sooner or later disgraces himself in some transaction about a woman or a cheque or both. Such men turn up in every political and religious movement; and their eloquence may make them for a time very prominent in the eye of the public. But they never become real leaders; and though circumstances might make one of them the figurehead in a demonstration or strike he would not behave as John Reid does. He would not commit suicide under any circumstances; he would not hold back a cheque except for his own use; he would borrow money from Lady Ann as well as make love to her; and he would make himself scarce the moment the position became threatening. But Moore had no intention of painting a Socialist Tartuffe: he evidently means it to be taken that Reid, once outside Lady Ann's drawing room, is a John Burns; and the simple fact is that people who are John Burnses out of doors and John Reids in, dont exist in nature."

"Are there any other points—?"

2. Tom Mann (1856–1941), a member of both the S.D.F. and the Fabian Society, would the following year become secretary of the Independent Labour Party.

"No, I wont be drawn any further. You have me at an unfair advantage. It's unbecoming in the last degree for me, who am myself an Independent Theatre dramatist, to pick holes in the work of my only competitor so far except the author of Alan's Wife, whom I will abuse as much as you please for refusing to own up to his work.[3] But if I go on to point out Moore's artistic merits, I tranch on the province of your Mr Spectator. If your readers want to find out what The Strike is like, let them buy it."

TEN MINUTES WITH MR BERNARD SHAW
X/CPP, Vol. 1 (QI, *Today*, 28 April 1894)

"Do you assign an important part to the stagemanager?[1] Do you think that costumes, scenery, and general *mise-en-scène* have much to do nowadays with the success or failure of a play?"

"The stagemanager is as important a functionary as the conductor of an orchestra, and good ones are almost as rare. An adequate *mise-en-scène* is necessary to the complete effect of a theatrical representation, whether it is Box and Cox[2] or a grand opera. But if you ask what my choice would be between 'four boards and a passion'[3] and a sumptuous *mise-en-scène* without the passion, I am for the four boards. There is no rule that applies to all plays except the rule that no play should look shabby."

"Should a play simply aim at telling a story, or be used as a medium for embodying certain theories and ideas?"

"There is no such alternative presented to the playwright. You really cannot put the case exactly in that way. The greatest storytellers are the most inveterate moralists; and no man who is not an idiot can tell a story without shaping it in such a way as to move the sympathy of the audience by appealing to their moral ideas. Molière's plays are full of preaching;

---

3. At the time, neither Shaw nor J.T. Grein, who produced it for the Independent Theatre, knew the identity of the anonymous author of *Alan's Wife*, adapted from a Swedish story, "Befriad," by Elin Ameen. The play was a collaboration between Florence, later Lady Hugh Bell (1852–1930), and Elizabeth Robins, who acted the leading role.

1. Today we would use the term "director." In the English theater at this time, this person's duties traditionally included rehearsing and blocking actors—a condition that was undergoing drastic change partly through the efforts of such authors as Gilbert, Pinero, and Shaw, who assumed these functions.

2. (1847) by John Maddison Morton (1811–91).

3. Attributed to Lope de Vega Carpio (1562–1635).

whilst Joyce's Scientific Dialogues[4] are confined mostly to statements of objective fact. Joyce should be the ideal dramatist of the people who complain of moral didacticism in plays. For my part I prefer Molière, and so does the public."

"Are you an advocate of stage realism? Do the methods of the Théâtre Libre, for instance, appeal to you?"

"I am an advocate for stage illusion; stage realism is a contradiction in terms. I am only a realist in a Platonic sense. I am really a classicist, as far as my taste for other people's work goes. As to my own, I write what comes into my head, without reference to any theory of what is good or bad. I avoid what jars on me, either in sound or sense. I have never seen a performance of the Théâtre Libre. I should be satisfied with the Théâtre Français if I were allowed to make a clean sweep of the mass of superstitions which M. Antoine quite rightly protests against. Our own stage is in great need of reform, but it would take me too far to go into that. We require much greater force, vivacity, crispness, and alert intelligence in our actors. Our school is one of chronic sentimentality and solemn feebleness. A typical 'London leading man' is fit to be nothing else in the world than an undertaker's mute."

[ON CRITICISM]
C/X (statement in G. B. Burgin, "Some Literary Critics," *The Idler*, June 1894)

The difficulties that a critic gets into, as far as his relations with the persons criticized are concerned, arise mostly from the fact that the people criticized look upon criticisms as acts of justice to themselves, instead of as independent works of art. This, of course, is a ridiculous misunderstanding of the critic's position. When the public reads a column of criticism it wants to be entertained. It reads a criticism just as it reads a book, or watches an actor, or listens to a concert; and the critic must entertain it by his work exactly as an author or actor or any other artist does. Mere praise, which makes such delightful reading for the author, does not amuse the public at all; nor do purely judicial utterances, however finely balanced. The only judicial act that is popular for its own sake is blame: punishment, the Macaulay–on–Robert Montgomery sort of thing.[1] Con-

---

4. (1807) by Reverend Jeremiah Joyce (1763–1816).

1. In *The Edinburgh Review* (1830), Thomas Babington Macaulay (1880–59) mocked the idea that Robert Montgomery (1807–55), author of pious poems, was a serious poet.

sequently, if an author wants the advertisement of being made the subject of a long criticism, he must allow the critic to make him amusing or interesting in some way or other; and, however kindly, or even admiringly, that may be done, there is always something in the process that human nature—particularly literary and artistic human nature—shrinks from. Hence accusations of malice, complaints of injustice, coolnesses, quarrels, and so forth. And here let me give you a piece of practical advice. Never insult an author or artist by sparing his feelings. That is the one thing he will never forgive. If you are going to hit him, hit him straight in the face—exuberantly, as if you enjoyed it—and give him credit for being able to stand up to it.

CONCERNING STATE-AIDED AMUSEMENTS
C/X (*Sunday Times*, 9 December 1894)[1]

"Assuming it to be possible to establish a State-aided theatre, should you be sanguine of its good effect upon art?"

"That depends on the conditions of the time when it was established, and the form it took. But I certainly believe that art wants a freeing from commercial considerations. It is not possible for opera, for instance, to be self-maintaining in England. Sir Augustus Harris[2] is only enabled to carry on the Royal Italian Opera by a privately-subscribed subsidy. I think it could be carried on with much more regard to the interests of art if the subsidy were public instead of private. There is no theoretical reason why a Government which provides a National Gallery[3] should not also give us a State theatre. This would enable us to have what is most important: a frequent change of plays. Mr Irving, in his long management of the Lyceum, has given us comparatively few pieces: you had his stage cumbered for years with stuff like Mr Wills's vulgarization of Faust; and the Lyceum mutilation of Lear was an outrage to dramatic literature which could have been effectively prevented if it had occurred in a State-aided theatre. However, in comparing the National Gallery with the theatre, you must remember that a painter may steal a horse where an actor may not

1. Interview by, or revised by, Shaw.
2. (1852–96), theater manager who produced spectacular pantomimes at Drury Lane, then restored grand opera in England at Covent Garden.
3. The National Gallery, London, began its collection of art in 1824 but did not have a permanent home until 1838, when its new building in Trafalgar Square opened.

look over a hedge.[4] Salvini was not allowed to play even Samson[5] here, which most people of today do not regard as a very sacred subject; while the walls of our art galleries admit treatments of the most sacred topics from the Crucifixion downwards."

PREFACE TO THE THEATRICAL "WORLD" OF 1894
by William Archer (1895)

My qualification for introducing this annual record is, as I have vainly urged upon my friend the author, the worst qualification possible. For years past those readers of The World whose interest in art gave them an appetite for criticism, turned every Tuesday from a page on the drama by W.A. to a page on music by G.B.S. Last week the death of Edmund Yates[1] closed a chapter in the history of the paper; and G.B.S., having exhausted his message on the subject of contemporary music, took the occasion to write "Finis" at the end of his musical articles. But the old association was so characteristic, and is still so recent, that we have resolved to try whether the reader will not, just this once more, turn over the page and pass from G.B.S. to W.A., by mere force of habit, without noticing the glaring fact that the musical duties of G.B.S., by cutting him off almost entirely from the theatre, have left him, as aforesaid, quite the most unsuitable person to meddle in a book about the theatre and nothing else.

However, one can learn something about the theatre even at the opera: for instance, that there are certain permanent conditions which have nothing to do with pure art, but which deeply affect every artistic performance in London. No journalist, without intolerable injustice to artists and managers whose livelihood is at stake, can pass judgment without taking these conditions into account; and yet he may not mention them, because their restatement in every notice would be unbearable. The journalist is therefore forced to give his reader credit for knowing the difficulties under which plays are produced in this country, just as the writer of the leading article is forced to assume that his reader is acquainted with the British constitution and the practical exigencies of our system of party

4. "I will but look upon the hedge and follow you"—The Winter's Tale, IV.iv.
5. (1733) by Voltaire.
1. (1831–94), editor of The World.

government. And it is because the reader hardly ever does know these things that newspapers so often do more harm than good.

Obviously, Mr Archer, in reprinting his weeky articles exactly as they appeared, and thereby preserving all their vividness and actuality, preserves also this dependence of the journalist on the public for a considerate and well informed reading of his verdict. I need hardly add that he will not get it, because his readers, though interested in the art of the theatre, neither know nor care anything about the business of the theatre; and yet the art of the theatre is as dependent on its business as a poet's genius is on his bread and butter. Theatrical management in this country is one of the most desperate commercial forms of gambling. No one can foresee the fate of a play: the most experienced managers carefully select failure after failure for production; and the most featherheaded beginners blunder on successes. At the London West End theatres, where all modern English dramas are born, the minimum expense of running a play is about £400 a week, the maximum anything you please to spend on it. And all but the merest fraction of it may be, and very frequently is, entirely lost. On the other hand, success may mean a fortune of fifty thousand pounds accumulated within a single year. Very few forms of gambling are as hazardous as this. At roulette you can back red or black instead of yellow. On the turf you can take the low odds against the favorite instead of the high odds against the outsider. At both games you can stake as much or as little as you choose. But in the theatre you must play a desperate game for high stakes, or not play at all. And the risk falls altogether on the management. Everybody, from the author to the charwoman, must be paid before the management appropriates a farthing.

The scientific student of gambling will see at once that these are not the conditions which permanently attract the gambler. They are too extreme, too inelastic; besides, the game requires far too much knowledge. Consequently, the gambler pure and simple never meddles with the theatre: he has ready to his hand dozens of games that suit him better. And what is too risky for the gambler is out of the question for the man of business. Thus, from the purely economic point of view, the theatre is impossible. Neither as investment nor speculation, enterprise nor game, earnest nor jest, can it attract a single sovereign of capital. You must disturb a man's reason before he will even listen to a proposal to run a playhouse.

It will now be asked why, under these circumstances, have we a couple of dozen West End theatres open in London. Are they being run by people whose reason is disturbed? The answer is, emphatically, Yes. They are the result of the sweeping away of all reasonable economic prudence by the immense force of an artistic instinct which drives the actor to make opportunities at all hazards for the exercise of his art, and which makes the theatre irresistibly fascinating to many rich people who can afford to keep theatres just as they can afford to keep racehorses, yachts, or newspapers. The actor who is successful enough to obtain tolerably continuous employment as "leading man" in London at a salary of from twenty to forty pounds a week, can in a few years save enough to try the experiment of taking a theatre for a few months and producing a play on his own account. The same qualities which have enabled him to interest the public as an actor will help him, as actor-manager, to interest the rich theatre fanciers, and to persuade them to act as his "backers." If the enterprise thus started be watered now and then by the huge profits of a successful play, it will take a great deal to kill it. With the help of these profits and occasional subsidies, runs of ill luck are weathered with every appearance of brilliant prosperity, and are suspected only by experienced acting-managers, and by shrewd observers who have noticed the extreme skepticism of these gentlemen as to the reality of any apparently large success.

This system of actor-manager and backer is practically supreme in London. The drama is in the hands of Mr Irving, Mr Alexander, Mr Beerbohm Tree, Mr Lewis Waller, Mrs John Wood, Mr Hare, Mr Terry,[2] Mr Wyndham, Mr Penley, and Mr Toole. Nearly all the theatres other than theirs are either devoted, like the Adelphi and Drury Lane, to the routine of those comparatively childish forms of melodrama which have no more part in the development of the theatre as one of the higher forms of art than Madame Tussaud's or the Christy Minstrels,[3] or else they are opera houses.

We all know by this time that the effect of the actor-manager system is to impose on every dramatic author who wishes to have his work produced in first-rate style, the condition that there shall be a good part for the actor-manager in it. This is not in the least due to the vanity and jealousy of the actor-manager: it is due to his popularity. The strongest fascination at a theatre is the fascination of the actor or actress, not of the author. More people go to the Lyceum Theatre to see Mr Irving and Miss Ellen Terry than to see Shakespear's plays; at all events, it is certain that if Mr Irving were to present himself in as mutilated a condition as he presented King Lear, a shriek of horror would go up from all London. If Mr Irving were to produce a tragedy, or Mr Wyndham a comedy, in which they were cast for subordinate parts, the public would stay away; and the author would have reason to curse the self-denial of the actor-manager.

2. Waller (1860–1915), Edward O'Connor Terry (1844–1912).

3. Madame (Marie) Tussaud's is a wax museum in London. Edwin P. Christy (1815–62) established the minstrel show form in 1846; Christy's Minstrels, and its imitators, continued after his death.

Mr Hare's personally modest managerial policy is anything but encouraging to authors and critics who wish that all actor-managers were even as he. The absence of a strong personal interest on his part in the plays submited to him takes all the edge off his judgment as to their merits; and except when he is falling back on old favorites like Caste and Diplomacy, or holding on to A Pair of Spectacles,[4] which is as much a one-part actor-manager's play as Hamlet is, he is too often selecting all the failures of the modern drama, and leaving the successes to the actor-managers whose selective instincts are sharpened by good parts in them. We thus see that matters are made worse instead of mended by the elimination of personal motives from actor-management; whilst the economic conditions are so extremely unfavorable to anyone but an actor venturing upon the management of any but a purely routine theatre, that in order to bring up the list of real exceptions to the London rule of actor-management to three, we have to count Mr Daly and Mr Grein of the Independent Theatre along with Mr Comyns Carr.[5] Mr Grein, though his forlorn hopes have done good to the drama out of all apparent proportion to the show they have been able to make, tells us that he has lost more by his efforts than anybody but a fanatic would sacrifice; whilst Mr Daly, as the manager and proprietor of a London theatre (New York is his centre of operations), has had little success except in the Shakespearean revivals which have enabled him to exploit Miss Ada Rehan's unrivaled charm of poetic speech.

Taking actor-management, then, as inevitable for the moment, and dismissing as untenable the notion that the actor-manager can afford to be magnanimous any more than he can afford to be lazy, why is it that, on the whole, the effect of the system is to keep the theatre lagging far behind the drama? The answer is, that the theatre depends on a very large public, and the drama on a very small one. A great dramatic poet will produce plays for a bare livelihood, if he can get nothing more. Even if a London theatre would perform them on the same terms, the sum that will keep the poet for a year—or five years at a pinch—will not keep the theatre open for more than a week. Ibsen, the greatest living dramatic poet, produces a play in two years. If he could sell twenty thousand copies of it at five shillings apiece within the following two years, he would no doubt consider himself, for a poet, a most fortunate man in his commercial relations. But unless a London manager sees some probability of from

4. *Caste* (1867) by Robertson, *Diplomacy* (1878, English adaptation, by B. C. Stephenson and Clement Scott, of *Dora*, 1877) by Sardou, *A Pair of Spectacles* (1890) by Grundy.

5. Augustin Daly was American; Jacob Thomas Grein, Dutch. Joseph W. Comyns Carr (1842–1916), a popular dramatist, was English.

50,000 to 75,000 people paying him an average of five shillings apiece within three months, he will hardly be persuaded to venture. In this book the reader will find an acount of the production for the first time in England of Ibsen's Wild Duck, a masterpiece of modern tragicomedy, famous throughout Europe. It was by no means lacking in personal appeal to the actor-manager; for it contains two parts, one of which, old Ekdal, might have been written for Mr Hare, whilst the other, Hjalmar Ekdal, would have suited Mr Beerbohm Tree to perfection. What actually happened, however, was that no London manager could afford to touch it; and it was not until a few private persons scraped together a handful of subscriptions that two modest little representations were given by Mr Grein under great difficulties. Mr Tree had already, by the experiment of a few matinées of An Enemy of the People, ascertained that such first-rate work as Ibsen's is still far above the very low level represented by the average taste of the huge crowd of playgoers requisite to make a remunerative run for a play. The Wild Duck, therefore, had to give place to commoner work. This is how the theatre lags behind its own published literature. And the evil tends to perpetuate itself in two ways: first, by helping to prevent the formation of a habit of playgoing among the cultivated section of the London community; and second, by diverting the best of our literary talent from the theatre to ordinary fiction and journalism, in which it becomes technically useless for stage purposes.

The matter is further complicated by the conditions on which the public are invited to visit the theatre. These conditions, in my opinion, are sufficient by themselves to make most reasonable people regard a visit to the theatre rather as a troublesome and costly luxury to be indulged in three or four times a year under family pressure, than as the ordinary way of passing an unoccupied evening. The theatre managers will not recognize that they have to compete with the British fireside, the slippers, the easy chair, the circulating library, and the illustrated press. They persist in expecting a man and his wife to leave their homes after dinner, and, after worrying their way to the theatre by relays of train and cab or omnibus, pay seven-and-sixpence or half a guinea apiece for comfortable seats. In the United States, where prices are higher in other things, the same accommodation can be had for five and six shillings. The cheaper parts of the London theatre are below the standard of comfort now expected by third-class travelers on our northern railway lines. The result is, not that people refuse to go to the theatre at all, but that they go very seldom, and then only to some house of great repute, like Mr Irving's, or to see some play which has created the sort of mania indicated by the term "catching on." No doubt, when this mania sets in, the profits are, as we have seen, enormous. But when it does not—and this is the more frequent case—the acting-manager is at his wit's end to find people who will sit in his half-guinea stalls and seven-and-sixpenny balcony seats for nothing, in order to persuade the provincial playgoer, when his turn comes to see the piece "on tour" from an excellent seat costing only a few shillings, that he is witnessing a "great London success." In the long run this system will succumb to the action of competition, and to the growing discrepancy between the distribution of income in the country and the distribution of prices in the theatre; but the reader who wishes to intelligently understand the failures and successes recorded in this book, must take account of the fact that, with the exception of the shilling gallery, every seat in a West End London theatre is at present charged for at a rate which makes it impossible for theatrical enterprise to settle down from a feverish speculation into a steady industry.

Among other effects of this state of things is an extreme precariousness of employment for actors, who are compelled to demand unreasonably high salaries in order that they may earn in the course of the year discouragingly small incomes. As we have seen, the few who have sufficient adaptability and popularity to be constantly employed, save rapidly enough to become actor-managers and even to build theatres for themelves. The result is that it becomes more and more difficult to obtain a fine cast for a play. The "star system," which is supposed to have disappeared in London, is really rampant there as far as acting is concerned. Compare, for example, the Opera, where the actor-manager is unknown, with the Lyceum Theatre. Sir Augustus Harris can present an opera with a whole constellation of stars in it. One of the greatest operas in the world, sung by half a dozen of the greatest dramatic singers in the world, is a phenomenon which, as a musical critic, I have seen, and found fault with, at Covent Garden. Now try to imagine Mr Irving attempting to do for a masterpiece of Shakespear's what Sir Augustus Harris does for Lohengrin.[6] All the other stars are like Mr Irving: they have theatres of their own, and are competing with him as men of business, instead of cooperating with him as artists. The old receipt for an opera company, "Catalani[7] and a few dolls," is, leaving scenery and mounting out of the question, as applicable to a Shakespearean performance at the Lyceum today as it was to the provincial starring exploits of the late Barry Sullivan. One expects every month to hear that Mr Waring, Mr Fred Terry,[8] Mr Yorke Stephens, Mr Forbes-Robertson, Mr Brandon Thomas, and Mr Hawtrey are about to follow Mr Alexander

6. (1850) by Wagner.
7. Angelica Catalani (1779?-1849), Italian singer.
8. (1863–1933).

and Mr Waller into actor-management. We should then have sixteen actor-managers competing with one another in sixteen different theatres, in a metropolis hardly containing good actors enough to cast three good plays simultaneously, even with the sixteen actor-managers counted in. No doubt such an increased demand for actors and plays as six additional managers would set up might produce an increased and improved supply if the demand of the public for theatrical amusements kept pace with the ambition of actors to become actor-managers; but is there, under existing conditions as to growth of population and distribution of income, the slightest likelihood of such an upward bound of public demand without a marked reduction of prices?

There is yet another momentous prospect to be taken into consideration. We have at present nine actor-managers and only one actress-manager: Mrs John Wood. So far, our chief actresses have been content to depend on the position of "leading lady" to some actor-manager. This was sufficient for all ordinary ambitions ten years ago; but since then the progress of a revolution in public opinion on what is called the Woman Question has begun to agitate the stage. In the highest class of drama the century has produced, the works of Richard Wagner, we find the Elsa of Lohengrin, the most highly developed of the operatic *prima donnas* whose main function it was to be honored with the love of the hero, supplanted by a race of true heroines like Brynhild and Isolde,[9] women in no sense secondary to the men whose fate is bound up with their own, and indeed immeasurably superior in wisdom, courage, and every great quality of heart and mind, to the stage heroes of the middle Victorian period of Romance. The impulse felt in heroic music drama has now reached domestic prose comedy; and Esther Eccles and Diplomacy Dora[10] are succeeded by Nora Helmer, Rebecca West, Hedda Gabler, and Hilda Wangel. The change is so patent, that one of the plays criticized by Mr Archer in the pages which follow is called The New Woman.[11] Now it is not possible to put the new woman seriously on the stage in her relation to modern society, without stirring up, both on the stage and in the auditorium, the struggle to keep her in her old place. The play with which Ibsen conquered the world, A Doll's House, allots to the leading man the part of a most respectable bank manager, exactly the sort of person on whose quiet but irresistible moral superiority to women Tom Taylor insisted with the fullest public applause in his Still Waters Run Deep.[12] Yet

9. In Wagner's *Die Walküre* and *Tristan und Isolde*, respectively.
10. Esther Eccles is in Robertson's *Caste*. Shaw conflates Sardou's *Diplomacy* and the eponymous character of its English version.
11. (1894) by Grundy.
12. Taylor (1817–80), *Still Waters Run Deep* (1855).

the play ends with the most humiliating exposure of the vanity, folly, and amorous beglamorment of this complacent person in his attitude towards his wife, the exposure being made by the wife herself. His is not the sort of part that an actor-manager likes to play. Mr Wyndham has revived Still Waters Run Deep: he will not touch A Doll's House. The one part that no actor as yet plays willingly is the part of a hero whose heroism is neither admirable nor laughable. A villain if you like, a hunchback, a murderer, a kicked, cuffed, duped pantaloon by all means; but a hero *manqué*, never. Man clings to the old pose, the old cheap heroism; and the actor in particular, whose life aspiration it has been to embody that pose, feels with inexpressible misgiving, the earth crumbling beneath his feet as the enthusiasm his heroism once excited turns to pity and ridicule. But this misgiving is the very material on which the modern dramatist of the Ibsen school seizes for his tragicomedy. It is the material upon which I myself have seized in a play of my own criticized in this book, to which I can only allude here to gratify my friend the author, who has begged me to say something about Arms and the Man. I comply by confessing that the result was a misunderstanding so complete, that but for the pleasure given by the acting, and for the happy circumstance that there was suffi- cient fun in the purely comic aspect of the piece to enable it to filch a certain vogue as a novel sort of extravaganza, its failure would have been as evident to the public as it was to me when I bowed my acknowledg- ments before the curtain to a salvo of entirely mistaken congratulations on my imaginary success as a conventionally cynical and paradoxical castigator of "the seamy side of human nature." The whole difficulty was created by the fact that my Bulgarian hero [Sergius], quite as much as Helmer in A Doll's House, was a hero shewn from the modern woman's point of view. I complicated the psychology by making him catch glimpse after glimpse of his own aspect and conduct from this point of view himself, as all men are beginning to do more or less now, the result, of course, being the most horrible dubiety on his part as to whether he was really a brave and chivalrous gentleman, or a humbug and a moral cow- ard. His actions, equally of course, were hopelessly irreconcilable with either theory. Need I add that if the straightforward Helmer, a very honest and ordinary middleclass man misled by false ideals of womanhood, bewil- dered the public, and was finally set down as a selfish cad by all the Helmers in the audience, *a fortiori* my introspective Bulgarian never had a chance, and was dismissed, with but moderately spontaneous laughter, as a swaggering imposter of the species for which contemporary slang has invented the term "bounder"?

But what bearing have the peculiarities of Helmer and my misunder- stood Bulgarian on the question of the actress-manageress? Very clearly this, that it is just such peculiarities that make characteristically modern plays as repugnant to the actor as they are attractive to the actress, and that, consequently, the actress who is content to remain attached to an actor-manager as leading lady, forfeits all chance of creating any of the fascinating women's parts which come at intervals of two years from the Ibsen mint. Among the newest parts open to the leading lady, Paula Tanqueray[13] counts as "advanced," although she would be perfectly in her place in a novel by Thackeray or Trollope, to either of whom Nora Helmer would have been an inconceivable person. A glance at our theatres will shew that the higher artistic career is practically closed to the leading lady. Miss Ellen Terry's position at the Lyceum Theatre may appear an enviable one; but when I recall the parts to which she has been condemned by her task of "supporting" Mr Irving, I have to admit that Miss Janet Achurch, for instance, who made for herself the opportunity of "creating" Nora Helmer in England by placing herself in the position virtually of actress-manageress, is far more to be envied. Again, if we compare Miss Elizabeth Robins, the creator of Hedda Gabler and Hilda Wangel, with Miss Kate Rorke at the Garrick Theatre, or the records of Miss Florence Farr and Miss Marion Lea with that of Miss Mary Moore at the Criterion,[14] we cannot but see that the time is ripe for the advent of the actress-manageress, and that we are on the verge of something like a struggle between the sexes for the dominion of the London theatres, a struggle which, failing an honorable treaty, or the break-up of the actor-manager system by the competition of new forms of theatrical enterprise, must in the long run end disastrously for the side which is furthest behind the times. And that side is at present the men's side.

The reader will now be able to gratify his impatience, and pass on to Mr Archer's criticisms (if he has not done so long ago) with some idea of the allowances that must be made for circumstances in giving judgment on the curious pageant which passes before the dramatic critic as he sits in his stall night after night. He has had to praise or blame, advocate or oppose, always with a human and reasonable regard to what is possible under existing conditions. Most of his readers, preoccupied with pure ideals of the art of the theatre, know nothing of these conditions, and perhaps imagine that all that lies beyond their ken is the working of the traps and the shifting of the scenery. Perhaps these few hints of mine may help them to understand that the real secrets of the theatre are not those of the stage mechanism, but of the box office, the acting-manager's room, and the actor-manager's soul.

13. In Pinero's *The Second Mrs Tanquery* (1893).
14. Rorke (1866–1945), Moore (1861?-1931).

SLAVES OF THE RING[1]
(*Saturday Review*, 5 January 1895)

Of all wonderful scenes that the modern theatre knows, commend me to that in the first act of Wagner's Tristan, where Tristan and Isolde drink the death draught. There is nothing else for them to do; since Tristan, loving Isolde and being beloved by her, is nevertheless bringing her across the sea to be the bride of his friend King Mark. Believing themselves delivered by death from all bonds and duties and other terrestrial fates, they enter into an elysium of love in perfect happiness and freedom, and remain there until their brief eternity is cut short by the shouts of the sailors and the letting go of the anchor, and they find themselves still on earth, with all secrets told and barriers cast down between them, and King Mark waiting to receive his bride. The poison had been exchanged by a friendly hand for a love potion.

At what period Mr Sydney Grundy came under the spell of this situation, and resolved that he, too, would have a "new and original" turn at it, I do not know. It may be, since these dramatic imaginings are really the common heritage of the human imagination, and belong to no individual genius, however grandly he may have shaped them into a masterpiece of his art, that Mr Grundy may have found the situation in the air, and not at Bayreuth. Howbeit he conceived it somehow, and proceeded to make out of it the play entitled Slaves of the Ring, which differs from Wagner's Tristan in this very essential respect, that whereas Tristan is the greatest work of its kind of the century, Slaves of the Ring is not sufficiently typical or classical to deserve being cited even as the worst. It is not a work of art at all: it is a mere contrivance for filling a theatre bill, and not, I am bound to say, a very apt contrivance at that.

Here was the problem as it presented itself to Mr Grundy. Wanted, a married lady declaring her love for a man other than her husband under the impression that she and he are both dead, and consequently released from all moral obligations (this, observe, is the indispensable condition which appears to lie at the back of the popular conception of Paradise in all countries). The lady's conviction that she has passed the gates of death preserves her innocence as an English heroine. But what about the gen-

---

1. *Slaves of the Ring*. A new and original play in three acts. By Sydney Grundy. Garrick Theatre, 29 December 1894. [G.B.S.] Here and hereafter, such identification of Shaw's *Saturday Review* criticisms will be in footnotes, as they were in the *Saturday Review*; in Shaw's three-volume collection of these criticisms, *Our Theatres in the Nineties*, they are below the review's title. Although the reviews in this volume are from this collection, unless otherwise noted, the originals have also been consulted.

tleman? Wagner made the gentleman believe himself dead also, and so preserved his innocence. But the English stage gentleman is as frail as the English stage lady is pure: therefore Mr Grundy's Tristan, though perfectly alive and well aware of it, takes the deluded lady to his bosom. Hereupon Mr Grundy owes it to his character as a master of drama that Tristan's wife should overhear these proceedings; and he owes it to his reputation as a master of stage technique that she should announce her presence by turning up a lamp, which the other lady has previously had turned down for that express purpose (as every experienced playgoer in the house plainly foresees) on the somewhat emaciated pretext that she prefers to sit in the dark. But it is of course possible that this also is a reminiscence of Tristan and Isolde's love of night and death. At all events, Miss Rorke turns up the lamp with the expertness due to long practice; and then, the dramatic possibilities of the theme being exhausted, the parties get off the stage as best they can.

Here you have the whole play. Once this scene was invented, nothing remained for the author to do except to prepare for it in a first act, and to use up its backwash in a third. And concerning the first act, I can only say that my utter lack of any sort of relish for Mr Grundy's school of theatrical art must be my excuse if I fail, without some appearance of malice, adequately to convey my sense of the mathematic lifelessness and intricacy of his preliminaries. I am not alluding to the inevitable opening explanations on the subject of "the old Earl" and "the late Countess," which Mrs Boucicault industriously offers to Miss Kate Phillips, who replies with much *aplomb*, "I see your point."[2] Even if I could follow such explanations, I could not remember them. Often as I have sat them out, I have never listened to them, and I never will; though I am far from objecting to a device which gives me leisure to look at the scenery and dresses, and helps to attune the ear of the pit to the conversational pitch of the house. But I do expect the author to get through the task of introducing the persons of the drama to the audience in a lucid and easily memorable way, and not to leave me at the end of half an hour feeling like a boy on his first day at a new school, or a stranger at an At-Home in a new set. Mr Grundy somehow managed to plunge me into the densest confusion as to who was who, a confusion which almost touched aberration when I saw a double leading lady walk on to the stage, both of her in full wedding dress. Like the dying Mousquetaire in the Ingoldsby Legends,[3] when his friends tried to cure him of seeing a ghost by dressing up a nurse exactly like it, I exclaimed

2. Agnes Kelly Robertson (1833–1916), wife of the playwright-actor Dion (Dionysius Lardner) Boucicault (1822–90); Phillips (1856–1931).

3. *The Ingoldsby Legends* (1837) by Richard Harris Barham.

Mon Dieu! V'là deux!
By the Pope, t h e r e   a r e   t w o!

The spectacular effect alone of so much white silk was sufficiently unhing-ing. But when the two brides proceeded solemnly to marry oneanother with a wedding ring, I really did feel for a moment a horrible misgiving that I had at last broken through that "thin partition" which divides great wits from madness. It was only afterwards, when we came to the Tristan scene, for which all was mere preparation, that I realized how Mr Grundy's imagi-nation, excited solely by that one situation, and unhappily not fertilized by it sufficiently to bring its figures to life as created characters, was inert during this first act; so that in elaborating a tissue of artificialities to lead us to accept a situation which we would willingly have taken for granted without any explanations at all, he was unable to visualize the stage, even with two brides on it in full fig. Well was it for Mr Grundy that that act was under the wing of Mr Hare at the Garrick Theatre. Even as it was, there were moments when even the firmest faith that something must be com-ing presently shewed signs of breaking down.

The third act was better. There were no explanations, because, the murder being out, there was nothing more to explain. Unfortunately, though the plot was over, it was too late to begin the play. Further, the scene was in a conservatory, lit with so many lamps that Miss Rorke could not have made any particular difference by turning down one of them; so she jumped through a palm tree instead, and cried "Aha! I've caught you at last," just as the other lady, though now convalescent and in her right mind, was relapsing into her dream with Tristan. In spite of this and a few other claptraps,[4] there was a certain force at work in this act, a force which finally revealed itself as a burning conviction in Mr Grundy that our law and custom of making marriage indissoluble and irrevocable except by the disgrace of either party, is a cruel social evil. Under the stimulus of this, the only definite "view" anywhere discoverable in his works, he does manage to get some driving weight of indignant discon-tent into the end of the play, though even in the very heat of it he remains so captivated by worn-out French stage conventions that he makes one of his characters strike the supposed lover of his wife across the face with a white glove. Whereat it is really impossible to do anything but laugh and fish out one's hat to go. Being safely at home, well disposed to Mr Grundy, and desirous above all things to slip gently over the staring fact that the play might be a better one, let me note gratefully that there is no villain, no hero, a quadrille of lovers instead of a pair, and that Mr Grundy's imagination, stretched and tortured as it is on the Procrustean framework

4. Cheap tricks or devices to trap or catch applause.

of "the well-made play," yet bursts fitfully into activity—though not, alas! into rebellion—with angry vigor.

As to the acting, it is, on the whole, much worse than the play. Miss Kate Rorke, comely, ladylike, and self-possessed, turns her emotion on and off by her well established method with a businesslike promptitude that makes the operation as certain as the turning up and down of the lamp. I feel sure that Miss Rorke would regard what I call acting as mere hysteria; and indeed I should be loth to recommend it to her, as she is no doubt quite as popular, and perhaps a good deal happier, without it. Miss Calhoun,[5] equally experienced, also obliged with whatever was wanted at the right moment. Her outcries in the first act, and again in the last, were discordant and unconvincing; and she should have made the Tristan scene at least six times as effective. Mr Brandon Thomas, as a broken-hearted personage charged with the duty of accompanying the play by an explanatory lecture in the manner of Dumas *fils*,[6] was in a deplorable situation throughout. It happens that the plot devised by Mr Grundy to bring off his one scene has all the potentialities of a capital comedy plot. Mr Brandon Thomas divined this, and knew in his soul (as I read him) that if only he might be allowed the smallest twinkle of humor, he could make the play go like wildfire. Under these circumstances his enforced gravity had a baffled quality which was the more ludicrous because it looked as if he were killing the play, whereas the play was really killing him. Mr Gilbert Hare[7] had a more important part than he would have been cast for in any other theatre; but as he played it with great care and thoroughness to the very best of his ability, it would be churlish to grudge him his advantage. Mr Bourchier[8] had nothing to act, though, fundamentally, this observation is perhaps hardly more true of him than of the rest. Some comic relief gave an opportunity to Mr Hare and Miss Kate Phillips. Mr Hare, to be quite frank, had a very cheap job; but he got the last inch of effect out of it. He, also, was provided with a patent broken heart, though he happily kept it to himself until a moment before his final exit. Miss Phillips was hampered in the first two acts by that sort of comic part which is almost as much a nuisance as a relief; but she played a little scene with Mr Hare in the last act very cleverly, and was, it seemed to me, the only lady in the cast whose artistic sensitiveness had survived the case-hardening of professional routine. The stage-mounting and coloring

5. Eleanor Calhoun (1862–1957).

6. The plays of French writer Alexandre Dumas *fils* (1824–95) were usually considered realistic social dramas, chiefly problem plays or thesis plays, rather than well-made plays; yet their affinities are really to the latter and their treatment of social issues is superficial.

7. (1869–1951).

8. Arthur Bourchier, actor and dramatist (1863–1927).

were solidly and expensively Philistine, the dresses in the last act, and the style of domestic decorations in the first, epitomizing the whole history of plutocracy in England during the expiring century.

TWO NEW PLAYS[1]
(Saturday Review, 12 January 1895)

The truth about Mr James's play is no worse than that it is out of fashion. Any dramatically disposed young gentleman who, cultivating sentiment on a little alcohol, and gaining an insight to the mysteries of the eternal feminine by a couple of squalid intrigues, meanwhile keeps well aloof from art and philosophy, and thus preserves his innocence of the higher life of the senses and of the intellect, can patch up a play tomorrow which will pass as real drama with the gentlemen who deny that distinction to the works of Mr Henry James. No doubt, if the literary world were as completely dominated by the admirers of Mr Rider Haggard[2] as the dramatic world is by their first cousins, we should be told that Mr James cannot write a novel. That is not criticism: it is a mere begging of the question. There is no reason why life as we find it in Mr James's novels— life, that is, in which passion is subordinate to intellect and to fastidious artistic taste—should not be represented on the stage. If it is real to Mr James, it must be real to others; and why should not these others have their drama instead of being banished from the theatre (to the theatre's great loss) by the monotony and vulgarity of drama in which passion is everything, intellect nothing, and art only brought in by the incidental outrages upon it. As it happens, I am not myself in Mr James's camp: in all the life that has energy enough to be interesting to me, subjective volition, passion, will, make intellect the merest tool. But there is in the centre of that cyclone a certain calm spot where cultivated ladies and gentlemen live on independent incomes or by pleasant artistic occupa-

---

1. GUY DOMVILLE. A play in three acts. By Henry James [1843–1916]. St James's Theatre, 5 January 1895. AN IDEAL HUSBAND. A new and original play of modern life. By Oscar Wilde. Haymarket Theatre, 3 January 1895. [G.B.S.]
2. Later Sir Henry Rider Haggard (1856–1925), whose romantic novels include *King Solomon's Mines*, its sequel *Allan Quartermain*, and *She*. The first has been filmed three times, the second twice, and the third, considered the apotheosis of Victorian romance, at least nine times. In *Getting Married*, Shaw has St John Hotchkiss refer to Mrs George by the full appelation of Haggard's mythical ruler: "SHE WHO MUST BE OBEYED."

tions. It is there that Mr James's art touches life, selecting whatever is graceful, exquisite, or dignified in its serenity. It is not life as imagined by the pit or gallery, or even by the stalls: it is, let us say, the ideal of the balcony; but that is no reason why the pit and gallery should excommunicate it on the ground that it has no blood and entrails in it, and have its sentence formulated for it by the fiercely ambitious and wilful professional man in the stalls. The whole case against its adequacy really rests on its violation of the cardinal stage convention that love is the most irresistible of all the passions. Since most people go to the theatre to escape from reality, this convention is naturally dear to a world in which love, all powerful in the secret, unreal, daydreaming life of the imagination, is in the real active life the abject slave of every trifling habit, prejudice, and cowardice, easily stifled by shyness, class feeling, and pecuniary prudence, or diverted from what is theatrically assumed to be its hurricane course by such obstacles as a thick ankle, a cockney accent, or an unfashionable hat. In the face of this, is it good sense to accuse Mr Henry James of a want of grip of the realities of life because he gives us a hero who sacrifices his love to a strong and noble vocation for the Church? And yet when some unmannerly playgoer, untouched by either love or religion, chooses to send a derisive howl from the gallery at such a situation, we are to sorrowfully admit, if you please, that Mr James is no dramatist, on the general ground that "the drama's laws the drama's patrons give."[3] Pray, which of its patrons?—the cultivated majority who, like myself and all the ablest of my colleagues, applauded Mr James on Saturday, or the handful of rowdies who brawled at him? It is the business of the dramatic critic to educate these dunces, not to echo them.

Admiting, then, that Mr James's dramatic authorship is valid, and that his plays are *du théâtre* when the right people are in the theatre, what are the qualities and faults of Guy Domville? First among the qualities, a rare charm of speech. Line after line comes with such a delicate turn and fall that I unhesitatingly challenge any of our popular dramatists to write a scene in verse with half the beauty of Mr James's prose. I am not now speaking of the verbal fitness, which is a matter of careful workmanship merely. I am speaking of the delicate inflexions of feeling conveyed by the cadences of the line, inflexions and cadences which, after so long a course of the ordinary theatrical splashes and daubs of passion and emphasis, are as grateful to my ear as the music of Mozart's Entführung aus dem Serail would be after a year of Ernani[4] and Il Trovatore. Second, Guy Domville is a

3. Samuel Johnson, Prologue for the opening of the Drury Lane Theatre under David Garrick's management in 1747: "The drama's laws the drama's patrons give, / For we that live to please, must please to live."

4. *Abduction from the Seraglio* (1782); *Ernani* (1844) by Verdi.

story, and not a mere situation hung out on a gallows of a plot. And it is a story of fine sentiment and delicate manners, with an entirely worthy and touching ending. Third, it relies on performers, not for the brute force of their personalities and popularities, but for their finest accomplishments in grace of manner, delicacy of diction, and dignity of style. It is pleasant to be able to add that this reliance, rash as it undeniably is in these days, was not disappointed. Mr Alexander, having been treated little better than a tailor's dummy by Mr Wilde,[5] Mr Pinero, and Mr Henry Arthur Jones successively, found himself treated as an artist by Mr James, and repaid the compliment, not only, as his manager, by [his] charming XVIII century stage setting of the piece, but, as actor, by his fine execution of the principal part, which he touched with great skill and judgment. Miss Marion Terry, as Mrs Peveril, was altogether charming: every movement, every tone, harmonized perfectly with the dainty grace and feeling of her lines. In fact, had the second act been equal to the first and third, and the acting as fine throughout as in the scenes between Mr Alexander and Miss Terry (in which, by the way, they were well supported by Mr Waring), the result would have been less doubtful. It will be a deplorable misfortune if Guy Domville does not hold the stage long enough to justify Mr Alexander's enterprise in producing it.

Unfortunately, the second act dissolved the charm rather badly; and what was more, the actors felt it. The Falstaffian make-up of Mrs Saker, and the senseless drunken scene, which Mr Alexander played with the sobriety of desperation, made fuss instead of drama; and the dialogue, except for a brief and very pretty episode in which Miss Millard and Mr Esmond took part, fell off into mere rococo.[6] Little of this act can be remembered with pleasure except Miss Millard's "Forgive me a little," and a few cognate scraps of dialogue. It had better have been left out, and the wanderings of the prodigal taken for granted. And, to weight it still further, it contained a great deal of the gentleman who played Lord Devenish, and played him just as he might have played an elderly marquis in a comic opera, grimacing over a snuff box, and withering all sense and music out of Mr James's lines with a diction which I forbear to describe. He was very largely responsible for the irritation which subsequently vented itself on the author; and I am far from sure that I ought not to borrow a weapon from the Speaker of the House of Commons, and go to the extreme length of naming him.[7]

Guy Domville is preceded by a farce (called in the bill a comedy) by

5. George Alexander produced Oscar Wilde's *Lady Windermere's Fan* (1892), in which he played Lord Windermere.
6. Mrs Edward Saker (Marie O'Brien, 1847–1912); Evelyn Millard (1869–1941); Henry Vernon Esmond (1869–1922).
7. The actor was William Gerald Elliott (b. 1858).

Julian Field, entitled Too Happy by Half. It is deftly turned out from old and seasoned materials, and is capital fun for the audience and for Mr Esmond and Miss Millard. Miss Millard is not yet quite experienced enough to do very easy work quite well: she is the least bit crude occasionally.

Mr Oscar Wilde's new play at the Haymarket is a dangerous subject, because he has the property of making his critics dull. They laugh angrily at his epigrams, like a child who is coaxed into being amused in the very act of setting up a yell of rage and agony. They protest that the trick is obvious, and that such epigrams can be turned out by the score by anyone lightminded enough to condescend to such frivolity. As far as I can ascertain, I am the only person in London who cannot sit down and write an Oscar Wilde play at will. The fact is that his plays, though apparently lucrative, remain unique under these circumstances, says much for the self-denial of our scribes. In a certain sense Mr Wilde is to me our only thorough playwright. He plays with everything: with wit, with philosophy, with drama, with actors and audience, with the whole theatre. Such a feat scandalizes the Englishman, who can no more play with wit and philosophy than he can with a football or a cricket bat. He works at both, and has the consolation, if he cannot make people laugh, of being the best cricketer and footballer in the world. Now it is the mark of the artist that he will not work. Just as people with social ambitions will practise the meanest economies in order to live expensively; so the artist will starve his way through incredible toil and discouragement sooner than go and earn a week's honest wages. Mr Wilde, an arch-artist, is so colossally lazy that he trifles even with the work by which an artist escapes work. He distils the very quintessence, and gets as product plays which are so unapproachably playful that they are the delight of every playgoer with twopenn'orth of brains. The English critic, always protesting that the drama should not be didactic, and yet always complaining if the dramatist does not find sermons in stones[8] and good in everything, will be conscious of a subtle and pervading levity in An Ideal Husband. All the literary dignity of the play, all the imperturbable good sense and good manners with which Mr Wilde makes his wit pleasant to his comparatively stupid audience, cannot quite overcome the fact that Ireland is of all countries the most foreign to England, and that to the Irishman (and Mr Wilde is almost as acutely Irish an Irishman as the Iron Duke of Wellington) there is nothing in the world quite so exquisitely comic as an Englishman's seriousness. It becomes tragic, perhaps, when the Englishman acts on it; but that occurs too seldom to be taken into account, a fact which intensifies the humor of the situation, the total result being the Englishman utterly unconscious of his real self, Mr Wilde keenly obser-

8. The phrase is from As You Like It, II.i.

vant of it and playing on the self-unconsciousness with irresistible humor, and finally, of course, the Englishman annoyed with himself for being amused at his own expense, and for being unable to convict Mr Wilde of what seems an obvious misunderstanding of human nature. He is shocked, too, at the danger to the foundations of society when seriousness is publicly laughed at. And to complete the oddity of the situation, Mr Wilde, touching what he himself reverences, is absolutely the most sentimental dramatist of the day.

It is useless to describe a play which has no thesis: which is, in the purest integrity, a play and nothing else. The six worst epigrams are mere alms handed with a kind smile to the average suburban playgoer; the three best remain secrets between Mr Wilde and a few choice spirits. The modern note is struck in Sir Robert Chiltern's assertion of the individuality and courage of his wrongdoing as against the mechanical idealism of his stupidly good wife, and in his bitter criticism of a love that is only the reward of merit. It is from the philosophy on which this scene is based that the most pregnant epigrams in the play have been condensed. Indeed, this is the only philosophy that ever has produced epigrams. In contriving the stage expedients by which the action of the piece is kept going, Mr Wilde has been once or twice a little too careless of stage illusion: for example, why on earth should Mrs Chevely, hiding in Lord Goring's room, knock down a chair? That is my sole criticism.

The performance is very amusing. The audience laughs conscientiously: each person comes to the theatre prepared, like a special artist, with the background of a laugh ready sketched on his or her features. Some of the performers labor intensely at being epigrammatic. I am sure Miss Vane Featherston and Miss Forsyth[9] could play Lady Macbeth and Medea with less effort than Lady Basildon and Mrs Marchmont, who have nothing to do but sit on a sofa and be politely silly for ten minutes. There is no doubt that these glimpses of expensive receptions in Park Lane, with the servants announcing titles *ad libitum*, are enormously attractive to social outsiders (say ninetynine hundredths of us); but the stage reproduction is not convincing: everybody has an outrageous air of being at a party; of not being used to it; and, worst of all, of enjoying themselves immensely. Mr Charles Hawtrey [as Lord Goring] has the best of the fun among the principals. As everyone's guide, philosopher, and friend, he has moments in which he is, I think, intended to be deep, strong, and tender. These moments, to say the least, do not quite come off; but his lighter serious episodes are excellent, and his drollery conquers without effort. When Miss Neilson[10] sits still and lets her gifts of beauty and grace be eloquent for

9. Featherston (1864–1948); Helen Forsyth (d. 1901).
10. Ada Neilson (1846–1905).

her, she is highly satisfying; but I cannot say the same for the passages in which she has to take the stage herself and try to act. She becomes merely artificial and superficially imitative. Miss Fanny Brough makes Lady Markby, an eminently possible person, quite impossible; and Miss Maude Millett,[11] playing very well as Mabel Chiltern, nevertheless occasionally spoils a word by certain vowel sounds which are only permissible to actresses of the second rank. As an adventuress who, like the real and unlike the stage adventuress, is not in love with anyone, and is simply selfish, dishonest, and third-rate, Miss Florence West[12] is kinetoscopically realistic. The portrait is true to nature; but it has no artistic character: Miss West has not the art of being agreeably disagreable. Mr Brookfield, a great artist in small things, makes the valet in the third act one of the heroes of the performance. And Mr Waller is handsome and dignified as the ideal husband, a part easily within his means. His management could not have been more auspiciously inaugurated.

KING ARTHUR[1]
(Saturday Review, 19 January 1895)

Mr Irving is to be congratulated on the impulse which has led him to exclaim, on this occasion, "Let us get rid of that insufferably ignorant specialist, the dramatist, and try whether something fresh cannot be done by a man equipped with all the culture of the age." It was an inevitable step in the movement which is bringing the stage more and more into contact with life. When I was young, the banquets on the stage were made by the property man: his goblets and pasties, and epergnes laden with grapes, regaled guests who walked off and on through illusory wainscoting simulated by the precarious perspective of the wings. The scene-painter built the rooms; the costumier made the dresses; the armor was made apparently by dipping the legs of the knights in a solution of salt of spangles and precipitating the metal on their calves by some electro-process; the leader of the band made the music; and the author wrote the verse and invented the law, the morals, the religion, the art, the jurispru-

---

11. (1867–1920).
12. (Mrs Lewis Waller, 1862–1913).
    1. KING ARTHUR. A drama in a prologue and four acts. By J. Comyns Carr. Lyceum Theatre, 12 January 1895. [G.B.S.]

dence, and whatever else might be needed in the abstract department of the play. Since then we have seen great changes. Real walls, ceilings, and doors are made by real carpenters; real tailors and dressmakers clothe the performers; real armorers harness them; and real musicians write the music and have it performed with full orchestral honors at the Crystal Palace and the Philharmonic. All that remains is to get a real poet to write the verse, a real philosopher to do the morals, a real divine to put in the religion, a real lawyer to adjust the law, and a real painter to design the pictorial effects. This is too much to achieve at one blow; but Mr Irving made a brave step towards it when he resolved to get rid of the author and put in his place his dear old friend Comyns Carr as an encyclopedic gentleman well up to date in most of these matters. And Mr Comyns Carr, of course, was at once able to tell him that there was an immense mass of artistic and poetic tradition, accumulated by generations of poets and painters, lying at hand all ready for exploitation by any experienced dealer with ingenuity and literary faculty enough to focus it in a stage entertainment. Such a man would have to know, for instance, that educated people have ceased to believe that architecture means "ruins by moonlight" (style, ecclesiastical Gothic); that the once fashionable admiration of the Renascence and "the old masters" of the XVI and XVII centuries has been swept away by the growth of a genuine sense of the naïve dignity and charm of XIII century work, and a passionate affection for the exquisite beauty of XV century work, so that nowadays ten acres of Carracci, Giulio Romano, Guido, Domenichino, and Pietro di Cortona will not buy an inch of Botticelli, or Lippi, or John Bellini:[2] no, not even with a few yards of Raphael thrown in; and that the whole rhetorical school in English literature, from Shakespear to Byron, appears to us in our present mood only another side of the terrible *dégringolade* from Michael Angelo to Canova and Thorwaldsen, all of whose works would not now tempt us to part with a single fragment by Donatello, or even a pretty foundling baby by Della Robbia.[3] And yet this, which is the real art culture of England today, is only dimly known to our dramatic authors as a momentary bygone craze out of which a couple of successful pieces, Patience and The Colonel,[4] made some money in their day. Mr Comyns Carr knows better. He knows that Burne-Jones has made himself the greatest among English decorative painters by picking up the tradition of his art where Lippi left it, and

2. Annibale Carracci (1560–1609); Giulio Romano (Giulio Pippi de Giannuzzi, c. 1499–1546); Guido da Siena (fl. second half of the thirteenth century); Domenichino (Domenico Zampieri, 1581–1641); Pietro di Cortona (Pietro Berretini, 1596–1669); Alessandro Botticelli (1444–1510); Fra Filippo Lippi (1406–69); Giovanni Bellini (1428–1516).

3. Antonio Canova (1757–1822); Bertel Thorwaldsen (or Thorvaldsen, 1770–1844); Donatello (1386–1466); Luca della Robbia (1399–1474).

4. (1821) by Scribe and Germain Delavigne (1790–1868).

utterly ignoring "their Raphaels, Correggios, and stuff."[5] He knows that William Morris has made himself the greatest living master of the English language, both in prose and verse, by picking up the tradition of the literary art where Chaucer left it, and that Morris and Burne-Jones, close friends and cooperators in many a masterpiece, form the highest aristocracy of English art today. And he knows exactly how far their culture has spread and penetrated, and how much simply noble beauty of Romanesque architecture, what touching loveliness and delicate splendor of XV century Italian dresses and armor, what blue from the hills round Florence and what sunset gloom deepening into splendid black shadow from the horizons of Giorgione[6] will be recognized with delight on the stage if they be well counterfeited there; also what stories we long to have as the subject of these deeply desired pictures. Foremost among such stories stands that of King Arthur, Lancelot, and Guinevere; and what Mr Comyns Carr has done is to contrive a play in which we have our heart's wish, and see these figures come to life, and move through halls and colonnades that might have been raised by the master builders of San Zeno or San Ambrogio, out into the eternal beauty of the woodland spring acting their legend just as we know it, in just such vestures and against just such backgrounds of blue hill and fiery sunset. No mere dramatic author could have wrought this miracle. Mr Comyns Carr has done it with ease, by simply knowing whom to send for. His long business experience as a man of arts and letters, and the contact with artists and poets which it has involved, have equipped him completely for the work. In Mr Irving's theatre, with Burne-Jones to design for him, Harker and Hawes Craven to paint for him, and Malory[7] and Tennyson and many another on his bookshelves, he has put out his hand cleverly on a readymade success, and tasted the joy of victory without the terror of battle.

But how am I to praise this deed when my own art, the art of literature, is left shabby and ashamed amid the triumph of the arts of the painter and the actor? I sometimes wonder where Mr Irving will go to when he dies: whether he will dare to claim, as a master artist, to walk where he may any day meet Shakespear whom he has mutilated, Goethe whom he has travestied, and the nameless creator of the hero-king out of whose mouth

5. Sir Edward Burne-Jones (1833–98), English painter of the Royal Academy, was a leader of the Pre-Raphaelite movment. Corregio (Antonio Allegri, 1494–1534) was an Italian painter. The quotation is from Oliver Goldsmith, *Retaliation* (1774).

6. Giorgione (Giorgio Barbarelli, 1477–1510).

7. Joseph Cunningham Harker (1855–1957), painter who would design scenery and costumes for Shaw's plays; Hawes Craven (1837–1910), chief scenic artist at the Lyceum; Sir Thomas Malory (d. 1471), author of *Le Morte D'Arthur*.

he has uttered jobbing verses. For in poetry Mr Comyns Carr is frankly a jobber and nothing else. There is one scene in the play in which Mr Irving rises to the height of his art, and impersonates, with the noblest feeling, and the most sensitive refinement of execution, the King Arthur of all our imaginations in the moment when he learns that his wife loves his friend instead of himself. And all the time, whilst the voice, the gesture, the emotion expressed are those of the hero-king, the talk is the talk of an angry and jealous costermonger, exalted by the abject submission of the other parties to a transport of magnanimity in refraining from reviling his wife and punching her lover's head. I do not suppose that Mr Irving said to Mr Comyns Carr in so many words "Write what trash you like: I'll play the real King Arthur over the head of your stuff"; but that was what it came to. And the end of it was that Mr Comyns Carr was too much for Mr Irving. When King Arthur, having broken down in an attempt to hit Lancelot with his sword, left Guinevere groveling on the floor with her head within an inch of his toes, and stood plainly conveying to the numerous bystanders that this was the proper position for a female who had forgotten herself so far as to prefer another man to him, one's gorge rose at the Tappertitian[8] vulgarity and infamy of the thing; and it was a relief when the scene ended with a fine old Richard III effect of Arthur leading his mail-clad knights off to battle. That vision of a fine figure of a woman, torn with sobs and remorse, stretched at the feet of a nobly superior and deeply wronged lord of creation, is no doubt still as popular with the men whose sentimental vanity it flatters as it was in the days of the Idylls of the King.[9] But since then we have been learning that a woman is something more than a piece of sweetstuff to fatten a man's emotions; and our amateur King Arthurs are beginning to realize, with shocked surprise, that the more generous the race grows, the stronger becomes its disposition to bring them to their senses with a stinging dose of wholesome ridicule. Mr Comyns Carr miscalculated the spirit of the age on this point; and the result was that he dragged Mr Irving down from the height of the loftiest passage in his acting to the abyss of the lowest depth of the dialogue.

Whilst not sparing my protest against this unpardonable scene, I can hardly blame Mr Comyns Carr for the touch of human frailty which made him reserve to himself the honor of providing the "book of the words" for Burne-Jones's picture-opera. No doubt, since Mr Carr is no more a poet than I am, the consistent course would have been to call in

8. Tappertit is a character in Dickens's *Barnaby Rudge* (1841).
9. Poem by Tennyson, about King Arthur and the knights of the Round Table, based on Malory's *Morte D'Arthur*.

Mr William Morris to provide the verse. Perhaps, if Mr Irving, in his black harness, with his visor down and Excalibur ready to hand and well in view, were to present himself at the Kelmscott Press fortified with a propitiatory appeal from the great painter, the poet might, without absolutely swearing, listen to a proposal that he should condescend to touch up those little rhymed acrostics in which Merlin utters his prophecies, leaving the blank verse padding to Mr Comyns Carr. For the blank verse is at all events accurately metrical, a fact which distinguishes the author sharply from most modern dramatists. The ideas are secondhand, and are dovetailed into a coherent structure instead of developing into one-another by any life of their own; but they are sometimes very well chosen; and Mr Carr is often guided to his choice of them by the strength and sincerity of their effect on his own feelings. At such moments, if he does not create, he reflects so well, and sometimes reflects such fine rays too, that one gladly admits that there are men whose originality might have been worse than his receptivity. There are excellent moments in the love scenes: indeed, Lancelot's confession of his love to Guinevere all but earns for the author the poet's privilege of having his chain tested by its strongest link.

The only great bit of acting in the piece is that passage of Mr Irving's to which I have already alluded: a masterly fulfilment of the promise of one or two quiet but eloquent touches in his scene with Guinevere in the second act. Popularly speaking, Mr Forbes-Robertson as Lancelot is the hero of the piece. He has a beautiful costume, mostly of plate armor of Burne-Jonesian design; and he wears it beautifully, like a XV century St George, the spiritual, interesting face completing a rarely attractive living picture. He was more than applauded on his entrance: he was positively adored. His voice is an organ with only one stop on it: to the musician it suggests a clarionet in A, played only in the chalumeau register; but then the chalumeau, sympathetically sounded, has a richly melancholy and noble effect. The one tune he had to play throughout suited it perfectly: its subdued passion, both in love and devotion, affected the house deeply; and the crowning moment of the drama for most of those present was his clasping of Guinevere's waist as he knelt at her feet when she intoxicated him by answering his confession with her own. As to Miss Ellen Terry, it was the old story, a born actress of real women's parts condemned to figure as a mere artist's model in costume plays which, from the woman's point of view, are foolish flatteries written by gentlemen for gentlemen. It is pathetic to see Miss Terry snatching at some fleeting touch of nature in her part, and playing it not only to perfection, but often with a parting caress that brings it beyond that for an instant as she relinquishes it, very loth, and passes on to the next length of arid sham-feminine twaddle in blank verse, which she pumps out in little rhythmic strokes in a desperate and all too obvious effort to make music of it. I should prove myself void of the true critic's passion if I could pass with polite commonplaces over what seems to me a heartless waste of an exquisite talent. What a theatre for a woman of genius to be attached to! Obsolete tomfooleries like Robert Macaire, schoolgirl charades like Nance Oldfield,[10] blank verse by Wills, Comyns Carr, and Calmour,[11] with intervals of hashed Shakespear; and all the time a stream of splendid women's parts pouring from the Ibsen volcano and minor craters, and being snapped up by the rising generation. Strange, under these circumstances, that it is Mr Irving and not Miss Terry who feels the want of a municipal theatre. He has certainly done his best to make everyone else feel it.

The rest of the acting is the merest stock company routine, there being only three real parts in the play. Sir Arthur Sullivan (who, in the playbill, drops his knighthood whilst Burne-Jones parades his baronetcy) sweetens the sentiment of the scenes here and there by penn'orths of orchestral sugarstick, for which the dramatic critics, in their soft-eared innocence, praise him above Wagner. The overture and the vocal pieces are pretty specimens of his best late work. Some awkwardness in the construction of the play towards the end has led the stagemanager into a couple of absurdities. For instance, when the body of Elaine is done with, it should be taken off the stage and not put in the corner like a portmanteau at a railway station. I do not know what is supposed to happen in the last act: whether Guinevere is alive or a ghost when she comes in at Arthur's death (I understood she was being burnt behind the scenes), or what becomes of Lancelot and Mordred, or who on earth the two gentlemen are who come in successively to interview the dying Arthur, or why the funeral barge should leave Mr Irving lying on the stage and bear off to bliss an imposter with a strikingly different nose. In fact I understand nothing that happened after the sudden blossoming out of Arthur into Lohengrin, Guinevere into Elsa, Mordred into Telramund, and Morgan le Fay into Ortruda[12] in the combat scene, in which, by the way, Mr Comyns Carr kills the wrong man, probably from having read Wagner carelessly. But I certainly think something might be done to relieve the shock of the whole court suddenly bolting and leaving the mortally wounded king floundering on the floor without a soul to look after him. These trifles are mere specks of dust on a splendid picture; but they could easily be brushed off.

10. Title character of a one-act comedy (1883) by Charles Reade.
11. Alfred Cecil Calmour (d. 1912).
12. The second in each pair of names is a character in *Lohengrin*.

THE INDEPENDENT THEATRE[1]
(*Saturday Review*, 26 January 1895)

Now that the fashionable productions at the Lyceum, the Haymarket, and the St James's have been attended to, the Independent Theatre claims a modest word for two plays, one which it would have produced had the Queen's reader of plays permited, and another which it actually has produced. The Independent Theatre is an excellent institution, simply because it is independent. Its disparagers ask what it is independent of, knowing well that no question is so difficult to answer as that to which the answer is obvious. It is, of course, independent of commercial success. It can take a masterpiece of European dramatic literature, which, because it is a masterpiece, is above the level of commercial practicability fixed by the average taste of a hundred thousand playgoing Londoners, and produce it for at least a night or two. What is more, it has done it. If Mr Grein had not taken the dramatic critics of London and put them in a row before Ghosts and The Wild Duck, with a certain small but inquisitive and influential body of enthusiasts behind them, we should be far less advanced today than we are. The real history of the drama for the last ten years is not the history of the prosperous enterprises of Mr Hare, Mr Irving, and the established West End theatres, but of the forlorn hopes led by Mr Vernon, Mr Charrington, Mr Grein, Messrs Henley and Stevenson,[2] Miss Achurch, Miss Robins and Miss Lea, Miss Farr, and the rest of the Impossibilists.[3] Their commercial defeat has been slaughterous: each scaling party has gained the rampart only to be hurled back into the moat with empty pockets, amid plentiful jeering from the baser sort, with their opportunities of a share in the ordinary lucrative routine of their profession considerably diminished, and their acquaintances, after the manner of acquaintances, rather ashamed of them. For my part, I take off my hat to them. Besides, that is the way things get done in England; so, as a

---

1. THYRZA FLEMING. In four acts. By Dorothy Leighton. The Independent Theatre (Terry's), 4 January 1895. THE FIRST STEP. A Dramatic Moment. By William Heinemann [1863–1920]. London: John Lane, 1895. [G.B.S.]

2. William Ernest Henley (1849–1903) and Robert Louis Stevenson (1850–94) had collaborated on several plays, one of which, *Beau Austin* (1884), Shaw mentions later in this review, and another of which, *Robert Macaire* (based on *L'Aubèrge des Adrets*, which Charles Selby had already turned into a popular melodrama), was published (1892) but unproduced; Shaw comments on the latter in his review of 8 June 1895.

3. Term used by political radicals of the period to indicate people with impractical political views. Here, of course, Shaw ironically indicates people with supposedly impractical theatrical ideas.

prudent man, I always make friends with able desperadoes, knowing that they will seize the citadel when the present garrison retires.

The special danger of the Independent Theatre is its liability to its subscribers for the production of half a dozen new plays every season. No author whose play strikes, or is aimed at, the commercially successful pitch will give it to Mr Grein. Until, for one reason or another, the author has come to the conclusion that his play is either too good or too bad or too new for the regular theatres, his manuscript does not come Mr Grein's way. Now Nature is lavish of plays that are too bad for the ordinary theatre, and niggard of plays that are too good: much more niggard than Mr Grein dare be of new plays if he wishes to give his subscribers enough performances to make them feel that they are having some sort of value for their subscriptions. It lies, therefore, in the very nature of the case that the majority of the performances of the Independent Theatre, taken by themselves, will not justify its existence; and the late reconstitution of the enterprise as The Independent Theatre, Limited, in no way modifies this rather hard condition. We must make up our minds to accept one really remarkable play a year as a sufficient excuse for half a dozen indifferent ones, including perhaps an occasional dismal failure. And I think our London managers, if they were wise, would help and cherish the Independent Theatre as a sort of laboratory in which they can have experiments tried on the public from time to time without the cost and responsibility incurred by, for example, Mr Beerbohm Tree in the experiments he made at the Haymarket with Beau Austin and An Enemy of the People.

Thyrza Fleming, with which Mr Grein has inaugurated the *régime* under which he divides the responsibilities of managing director with Miss Dorothy Leighton, is a courageous attempt at a counterblast to The Heavenly Twins,[4] sometimes sinking to the level of a mere skit, as in the schoolgirlish caricature of Ideala as Theophilia, and sometimes rising into tolerable drama, or swerving into mere abstract discussion. The contest between Miss Leighton's talent and Sarah Grand's genius is an unequal one; and the play evades the challenged issue in a sufficiently ridiculous way. Sarah Grand's heroine married a gentleman with "a past"; discovered it on her wedding day; and promptly went home, treating him exactly as he would have been conventionally expected to treat her under like circumstances. To this Miss Leighton says, in effect: "Let me shew you what a frightful mistake it is for a woman to take such a step." She accordingly creates a heroine who leaves her husband on their wedding day, and presently returns repentant to confess that she was wrong, the proof being that her husband is really a blameless gentleman with no past

---

4. A popular novel (1893) by the feminist Frances E. McFall, written under the pseudonym Sarah Grand (1854–1943); Shaw refers to it in his preface to *Getting Married*.

at all. It is exactly as if Shakespear had written Othello as a confutation of the Tue-la of Dumas *fils*.[5] Leaving this aspect of the play out of the question, one may say that it shews a promising turn on Miss Leighton's part for the theatre. Its main fault is that at the height of her argument she has not written the play at all, but simply stated its intellectual basis in the style proper to the Royal Institution.[6] If she will translate these passages into the idiomatic, vernacular language by which feeling, which is for her the true material of drama, leaps into expression; and if she will allow her characters, when they are no longer wanted, to simply walk off the stage without making farfetched excuses, her play will do very well. Even as it is, it would have carried off its shortcomings if the title part had been better presented. Miss Esther Palliser,[7] who a year ago was a slender and attractive young lady making a place for herself in the front rank of the oratorio singers, has taken as little heed to her physical training as any German *prima donna*; and her performance can only be described as a fairly intelligent reading aloud of the part by rote. It was just a degree better than having it read from the book by the prompter. As to the blameless Colonel, the incorrigibly goodnatured Mr Bernard Gould, talented, handsome, and proof (thanks to a rare soundness of head and heart) against all the crazy illusions of stageland, lent his engaging personality for the part, and shewed us what it was like with his usual cleverness. The considerateness and adroitness with which he steered Miss Palliser among the smaller shipping was delightful; but between them the scenes on which Miss Leighton's play chiefly depended for its success left the imagination inexpressibly untouched. Mr Gould's only real chance, in fact, was in the scenes with Miss Winifred Fraser,[8] whose charm in sympathetic and rather fragile parts is becoming sufficiently well known to render it unnecessary to compliment her on the victim of the Heavenly Twins. Mr Bonney[9] was rather interesting; and Miss [A.] Beaugarde, as Jones the maid, managed, perhaps through inexperience,

---

5. Shaw makes a similar comparison in a book review in the *Pall Mall Gazette*, 11 September 1886. In an essay, *L'Homme-Femme: réponse à M. Henri D'Ideville* (1872), Dumas *fils* says that since an adulterous wife is not truly a woman, is not part of God's conception, and is purely animal, then "Kill her." This essay was so popular, or notorious, that it underwent numerous editions that year and prompted an anonymous satire with an extremely long title, beginning *Tue-la! ou elle te tuera! ou l'homme-femme! ou la femme-homme! ou ni homme ni femme* . . . (1872).

6. In 1799, Benjamin Thompson founded The Royal Institution of Great Britain (in London), which sponsors lectures for the promotion and extension of science and other useful knowledge.

7. (b. 1872).

8. Fraser (Mrs George R Foss, b. 1868/72).

9. William E. Bonney (1860?-1916).

to put the real female domestic servant on the stage for the first time within my experience.

So much for the play which has been produced. The other, frustrated by that insane institution for the taxation of authors, the Censorship of the Lord Chamberlain, is Mr William Heinemann's First Step. In this instance Mr Pigott has been the instrument of the irony of fate, the flavor of which can be fully relished only in view of the following facts, not hitherto publicly collated. A few years ago certain matters in Central America required the presence of a plenipotentiary from the Colonial Office. This mission was entrusted to Mr Sydney Olivier,[10] a gentleman who, having an esoteric reputation as a sort of lucid George Meredith, is at present, no doubt, awaiting discovery by Mr Le Gallienne[11] in the dignified security of Downing Street. Last year Mr Olivier wrote a play entitled A Freedom in Fetters, embodying his observations of human nature as developed in the British colonist by a tropical climate. The Censor, after one horrified glimpse into this strange region, refused to allow the play to be performed. The spectacle of a subordinate court official appointed by patronage, arbitrarily suppressing an upper division civil servant appointed by strenuous competitive examination, and one moreover of Mr Olivier's standing and personal character, was an exceptionally piquant addition to the scandals of the Censorship; and Mr Olivier sought the usual remedy: publication. But the first publisher approached sided with the Censor, and refused to publish the play on moral grounds. That publisher was Mr William Heinemann, who thereupon proceeded to write a play himself, and was immediately suppressed by Mr Pigott, to the accompaniment, one fancies, of a hollow laugh from the Colonial Office. Mr Heinemann, with admirable consistency, refused to publish his own play, and sent it on to Mr John Lane of the Bodley Head, who has duly issued five hundred copies of it to clear Mr Heinemann from the imputation of having written something worse than the intentional and gross indecencies which Mr Pigott has licensed from time to time, as I, an old musical critic, well know from my experience of comic opera books. Of course there is nothing of that sort in Mr Heinemann's work any more than there was in Mr Olivier's; only the hero and heroine are living together without being legally married, which is against Mr Pigott's rule of thumb for determining whether a play is "moral" or not.

In Mr Heinemann's play, the grounds on which it is assumed that this unconventional arrangement is beneficial to the hero are so inadequately conveyed that if the pair were married, the play would gain rather than

10. He had served as Acting Colonial Secretary in British Hondouras, 1890–91.
11. Richard Le Gallienne (1866–1947), poet and novelist, was book reviewer for *The Star*.

lose in verisimilitude, though, no doubt, the heroine would tumble out of her place in Mr Heinemann's imagination as a woman with certain noble qualities which have led her to sacrifice her reputation for the sake of helping a man of genius. In such an error of the feminine imagination, and in its fearfully real consequences, there is material for a tragedy. And there is always drama to be got out of a man who is on with the new love before he is off with the old, particularly when, as Mr Heinemann begins by suggesting, the man has character and temperament enough to be interesting. But all this slips through Mr Heinemann's fingers on the introduction of good-for-nothings in the second act. In drawing these Mr Heinemann discovered that he could do that sort of sketching rather well; and immediately he abandoned his attempt at the higher manner, and turned his hero and heroine into a pair of loose-lived Bohemians of the commonest clay. Consequently, after having taken the trouble to conceive the man as a great dramatic poet, and the woman as having sufficient generosity and force of character to make a compact with him involving a heavy sacrifice on her part, we are put off with a drunken squabble which might have been better carried on by the most dissolute couple picked from the gallery of a third-rate music hall. This is worse than Rossini's lazy way of beginning with a Te Deum and finishing with a galop;[12] for he at least gave us the Te Deum, whereas Mr Heinemann only gives us the exordium, and then tails off at once into his galop. I would not stand such trifling from an author, much less from my natural enemy, a publisher. The opening of the First Step is an abandoned and derelict fragment; and I invite Mr Heinemann to turn to again like a man and rescue it.

POOR SHAKESPEAR![1]
(*Saturday Review*, 2 February 1895)

What a pity it is that the people who love the sound of Shakespear so seldom go on the stage! The ear is the sure clue to him: only a musician can understand the play of feeling which is the real rarity in his early plays. In a deaf nation these plays would have died long ago. The moral attitude in them is conventional and secondhand: the borrowed ideas,

12. Gioacchino Antonio Rossini (1792–1868).
1. ALL'S WELL THAT ENDS WELL. Performance by the Irving Dramatic Club at St George's Hall, 22 and 24 January 1895. [G.B.S.]

however finely expressed, have not the overpowering human interest of those original criticisms of life which supply the rhetorical element in his later works. Even the individualization, which produces that old-established British speciality, the Shakespearean "delineation of character," owes all its magic to the turn of the line, which lets you into the secret of its utterer's mood and temperament, not by its commonplace meaning, but by some subtle exaltation, or stultification, or slyness, or delicacy, or hesitancy, or whatnot in the sound of it. In short, it is the score and not the libretto that keeps the work alive and fresh; and this is why only musical critics should be allowed to meddle with Shakespear: especially early Shakespear. Unhappily, though the nation still retains its ears, the players and playgoers of this generation are for the most part deaf as adders. Their appreciation of Shakespear is sheer hypocrisy, the proof being that where an early play of his is revived, they take the utmost pains to suppress as much of it as possible, and disguise the rest past recognition, relying for success on extraordinary scenic attractions; on very popular performers, including, if possible, a famously beautiful actress in the leading part; and, above all, on Shakespear's reputation and the consequent submission of the British public to be mercilessly bored by each of his plays once in their lives, for the sake of being able to say they have seen it. And not a soul has the hardihood to yawn in the face of the imposture. The manager is praised; the bard is praised; the beautiful actress is praised; and the free list comes early and comes often,[2] not without a distinct sense of confering a handsome compliment on the acting manager. And it certainly is hard to face such a disappointment without being paid for it. For the more enchanting the play is at home by the fireside in winter, or out on the heather of a summer evening—the more the manager, in his efforts to realize this enchantment by reckless expenditure on incidental music, colored lights, dances, dresses, and elaborate rearrangements and dislocations of the play—the more, in fact, he departs from the old platform with its curtains and its placards inscribed "A street in Mantua," and so forth, the more hopelessly and vulgarly does he miss the mark. Such crown jewels of dramatic poetry as Twelfth Night and A Midsummer Night's Dream fade into shabby colored glass in his purse; and sincere people who do not know what the matter is, begin to babble insufferably about plays that are meant for the study and not for the stage.

Yet once in a blue moon or so there wanders on to the stage some happy fair whose eyes are lodestars and whose tongue's sweet air's more tunable

2. An allusion to "Vote early and vote often," which according to William Porcher Miles (1822–99), in a speech in the United States House of Representatives, 31 March 1858, was advice openly given at election time in northern American cities.

than lark to shepherd's ear.[3] And the moment she strikes up the true Shakespearean music, and feels her way to her part altogether by her sense of that music, the play returns to life and all the magic is there. She may make nonsense of the verses by wrong conjunctions and misplaced commas, which shew that she has never worked out the logical construction of a single sentence in her part; but if her heart is in the song, the protesting commentator-critic may save his breath to cool his porridge: the soul of the play is there, no matter where the sense of it may be. We have all heard Miss Rehan perform this miracle with Twelfth Night, and turn it, in spite of the impossible Mr Daly, from a hopelessly ineffective actress show into something like the exquisite poem its author left it. All I can remember of the last performance I witnessed of A Midsummer Night's Dream is that Miss Kate Rorke got on the stage somehow and began to make some music with Helena's lines, with the result that Shakespear, who had up to that moment lain without sense or motion, immediately began to stir uneasily and shew signs of quickening, which lasted until the others took up the word and struck him dead.

Powerful among the enemies of Shakespear are the commentator and the elocutionist: the commentator because, not knowing Shakespear's language, he sharpens his reasoning faculty to examine propositions advanced by an eminent lecturer from the Midlands, instead of sensitizing his artistic faculty to receive the impression of moods and inflexions of feeling conveyed by word-music; the elocutionist because he is a born fool, in which capacity, observing with pain that poets have a weakness for imparting to their dramatic dialogue a quality which he describes and deplores as "sing-song," he devotes his life to the art of breaking up verse in such a way as to make it sound like insanely pompous prose. The effect of this on Shakespear's earlier verse, which is full of the naïve delight of pure oscillation, to be enjoyed as an Italian enjoys a barcarolle, or a child a swing, or a baby a rocking cradle, is destructively stupid. In the later plays, where the barcarolle measure has evolved into much more varied and complex rhythms, it does not matter so much, since the work is no longer simple enough for a fool to pick to pieces. But in every play from Love's Labor's Lost to Henry V, the elocutionist meddles simply as a murderer, and ought to be dealt with as such without benefit of clergy. To our young people studying for the stage I say, with all solemnity, learn how to pronounce the English alphabet clearly and beautifully from some person who is at once an artist and a phonetic expert. And then leave blank verse patiently alone until you have experienced emotion deep enough to crave for poetic expression, at which point verse will seem an

---

3. *A Midsummer Night's Dream*, I,i: "O happy fair! / Your eyes are lodestars, and your tongue's sweet air / More tunable than lark to shepherd's ear."

absolutely natural and real form of speech to you. Meanwhile, if any pedant, with an uncultivated heart and a theoretic ear, proposes to teach you to recite, send instantly for the police.

Among Shakespear's earlier plays, All's Well That Ends Well stands out artistically by the sovereign charm of the young Helena and the old Countess of Rousillon, and intellectually by the experiment, repeated nearly three hundred years later in A Doll's House, of making the hero a perfectly ordinary young man, whose unimaginative prejudices and self-ish conventionality make him cut a very fine mean figure in the atmosphere created by the nobler nature of his wife. That is what gives a certain plausibility to the otherwise doubtful tradition that Shakespear did not succeed in getting his play produced (founded on the absence of any record of a performance of it during his lifetime). It certainly explains why Phelps, the only modern actor-manager tempted by it, was attracted by the part of Parolles, a capital study of the adventurous yarn-spinning society-struck coward, who also crops up again in modern fiction as the hero of Charles Lever's underrated novel, A Day's Ride: A Life's Romance.[4] When I saw All's Well announced for performance by the Irving Dramatic Club, I was highly interested, especially as the performers were free, for once, to play Shakespear for Shakespear's sake. Alas! at this amateur performance, at which there need have been none of the miserable commercialization compulsory at the regular theatres, I suffered all the vulgarity and absurdity of that commercialism without its efficiency. We all know the stock objection of the Brixton Family Shakespear[5] to All's Well: that the heroine is a lady doctor, and that no lady of any delicacy could possibly adopt a profession which involves the possibility of her having to attend cases such as that of the king in this play, who suffers from a fistula. How any sensible and humane person can have ever read this sort of thing without a deep sense of its insult to every charitable woman's humanity and every sick man's suffering is, fortunately, getting harder to understand nowadays than it once was. Nevertheless, All's Well was minced with strict deference to it for the members of the Irving Dramatic Club. The rule for expurgation was to omit everything that the most pestiferously prurient person could find improper. For example,

4. (1863) by Lever (1806–72). Shaw pays tribute to this work in the preface to *Major Barbara*.

5. Thomas Bowdler (1754–1825), clergyman and editor, is famous for his expurgated editions called *The Family Shakespeare*, "in which nothing is added to the original text, but those words and expressions are omitted which cannot with propriety be read aloud in a family," first published in 1807. Thomas Perronet Thompson (1783–1869) coined the derogatory word "bowdlerization." As Brixton (which is in the Borough of Lambeth) was in 1895 a lower middle-class London suburb, a "Brixton Family Shakespear" would be a lower middle-class family's copy of one of Bowdler's Shakespearean editions.

when the noncommissioned officer, with quite becoming earnestness and force, says to the disgraced Parolles: "If you could find out a country where but women were that had received so much shame, you might begin an impudent nation," the speech was suppressed as if it were on all fours with the obsolete Elizabethan badinage which is and should be cut out as a matter of course. And to save Helena from anything so shocking as a reference to her virginity, she was robbed of that rapturous outburst beginning

> There shall your master have a thousand loves—
> A mother and a mistress and a friend, &c.

But perhaps this was sacrificed in deference to the opinion of the editor of those pretty and handy little books called the Temple Shakespear,[6] who compares the passage to "the nonsense of some foolish conceited player": a criticism which only a commentator could hope to live down.

The play was, of course, pulled to pieces in order that some bad scenery, totally unconnected with Florence or Rousillon, might destroy all the illusion which the simple stage directions in the book create, and which they would equally have created had they been printed on a placard and hung up on a curtain. The passage of the Florentine army beneath the walls of the city was managed in the manner of the end of the first act of Robertson's Ours,[7] the widow and the girls looking out of their sitting-room window, whilst a few of the band gave a precarious selection from the orchestral parts of Berlioz's version of the Rackóczy March.[8] The dresses were the usual fancy ball odds and ends, Helena especially distinguishing herself by playing the first scene partly in the costume of Hamlet and partly in that of a waitress in an Aerated Bread shop,[9] set off by a monstrous auburn wig which could by no stretch of imagination be taken for her own hair. Briefly, the whole play was vivisected, and the fragments mutilated, for the sake of accessories which were in every particular silly and ridiculous. If they were meant to heighten the illusion, they were worse than failures, since they rendered illusion almost impossible. If they were intended as illustrations of place and period, they were ignorant

6. A pocket edition of Shakespeare's plays, one play per volume, published by J. M. Dent & Sons, who gave the edition that name. The editor of the *All's Well That Ends Well* volume, who wrote an introduction to the play, was Israel Gollancz (1864–1930).

7. (1866).

8. (1846) by Hector Berlioz (1803–69).

9. Aerated Bread Shops were inexpensive vegetarian restaurants in London. Their name indicates their speciality. In act III of *John Bull's Other Island* (1904), Larry Doyle says that when he first went to London he was enchanted by the accent of a waitress in an Aerated Bread shop.

impostures. I have seen poetic plays performed without costumes before a pair of curtains by ladies and gentlemen in evening dress with twenty times the effect: nay, I will pledge my reputation that if the members of the Irving Dramatic Club will take their books in their hands, sit in a Christy Minstrel semicircle, and read the play decently as it was written, the result will be a vast improvement on this St George's Hall travesty.

Perhaps it would not be altogether kind to leave these misguided but no doubt well intentioned ladies and gentlemen without a word of appreciation from their own point of view. Only, there is not much to be said for them even from that point of view. Few living actresses could throw themselves into the sustained transport of exquisite tenderness and impulsive courage which makes poetry the natural speech of Helena. The cool young woman, with a superior understanding, excellent manners, and a habit of reciting Shakespear, presented before us by Miss Olive Kennett, could not conceivably have been even Helena's thirtysecond cousin. Miss Lena Heinekey, with the most beautiful old woman's part ever written in her hands, discovered none of its wonderfully pleasant good sense, humanity, and originality: she grieved stagily all through in the manner of the Duchess of York in Cibber's Richard III. Mr Lewin Mannering did not for any instant make it possible to believe that Parolles was a real person to him. They all insisted on calling him *parole*, instead of Parolles, in three syllables, with the *s* sounded at the end, as Shakespear intended: consequently, when he came to the couplet which cannot be negotiated on any other terms:

Rust, sword; cool, blushes; and, Parolles, thrive;
Theres place and means for every man alive,

he made a desperate effort to get even with it by saying:

Rust, rapier; cool, blushes; and, p a r o l e, thrive,

and seemed quite disconcerted when he found that it would not do. Lafeu is hardly a part that can be acted: it comes right if the right man is available: if not, no acting can conceal the makeshift. Mr Herbert Everitt was not the right man; but he made the best of it. The clown was evidently willing to relish his own humor if only he could have seen it; but there are few actors who would not have gone that far. Bertram (Mr Patrick Munro), if not the most intelligent of Bertrams, played the love scene with Diana with some passion. The rest of the parts, not being character studies, are tolerably straightforward and easy of execution; and they were creditably played, the king (Mr Ernest Meads) carrying off the honors, and Diana (Mrs Herbert Morris) acquiting herself with com-

parative distinction. But I should not like to see another such performance of All's Well or any other play that is equally rooted in my deeper
affections.

WHY NOT SIR HENRY IRVING?
(*Saturday Review*, 9 February 1895)

In an oldfashioned play revived the other day by Mr Terry, a kitchen
discussion of literature leads to the question "Who wrote Shakespear?"[1]
Let me put a cognate question. Who writes Mr Irving's lectures? Of
course, I must not altogether exclude the hypothesis that he writes them
himself; but I had rather flatter him by assuming that he contents
himself with jotting down a scenario, and orders some literary retainer to
write the dialogue, enjoining him especially to put in plenty of art and
learning, and not to forget some good declamatory passages, in the
manner of the late Mr Wills, for elocutionary display. At all events, this is
what is suggested by the report of his recent discourse at the Royal
Institution. Dr Johnson—"Punch, sir, has no feelings"—Homer—
"poetry, music, sculpture, painting"—Hamlet—Shakespear—"the poor
player of Wittenberg"—Hogarth—Edmund Kean—Raphael and Michael
Angelo—Praxiteles and Phidias—the Colosseum and the Parthenon—
"Roscius a name that lives in history":[2] who could not deliver the lecture
verbatim from these notes as easily as Mr Percy Fitzgerald could write a
book from them?[3] And would we stand it from anybody but Henry
Irving? Some years ago Mr William Archer lectured on the drama at the
Royal Institution. What would the directors have said to Mr Archer had
he put them off with stuff which any sufficiently oldfashioned auctioneer
could improvize at a sale of theatrical prints? No: let us deal faithfully
with Mr Irving in this matter, and not treat him like a spoiled child. The

---

1. In Townley's *High Life Below Stairs*, which Edward Terry revived at his theater
beginning 14 January 1895, Kitty exclaims, "Shikspur! Shikspur! Who wrote it!" "Why, Ben
Jonson," replies Sir Harry's Servant, whereupon the Duke's Servant contradicts him: "O, I
remember, it was Kolly Kibber!"

2. William Hogarth (1697–1764), British painter and engraver; Praxiteles and Phidias
(fourth century B.C.), Greek sculptors; Quintus Roscius (d. 62 B.C.), Roman comic actor, the
most famous of his day.

3. Percy Hetherington Fitzgerald (1834–1925) was a prolific editor and author of numerous books, including *The Kembles* and *Henry Irving*.

other evening, after King Arthur, he wished us all a happy new year. He wished it heartily, respectfully, and so on; and then, with a friendly impulse to get on more intimate terms with us, he asked whether he might wish it to us "affectionately." Naturally, the house immediately shook hands with him, so to speak: I among the rest. Consequently, I hold myself privileged now to drop all insincere ceremony, and tell Mr Irving bluntly what every competent person thinks of his lecture. Their opinion may not seem consistent with their applause; but Mr Irving must remember that we now applaud him, not critically, but affectionately, and that we allow him to play like a child at being a learned lecturer, just as we indulge him, every evening at the Lyceum, with a broadsword combat the solemn absurdity of which quite baffles my powers of description. If we treat his orations as lectures, do we not also treat Mr Gladstone's tree-felling exploits as acts of statesmanship? No one can say that we are not indulgent to our favorites.

Mr Irving, however, began his lecture seriously and well, by putting forward "a formal claim to have acting classified o f f i c i a l l y among the fine arts." We all know what official recognition of a fine art means; but for the benefit of the millions of persons who never know anything, and therefore are not included in such general expressions as "we all," Mr Irving explicitly said "Official recognition of anything worthy is a good, or at least a useful thing. It is a part, and an important part, of the economy of the State: if it is not, of what use are titles and distinctions, names, badges, offices, in fact all the titular and sumptuary ways of distinction?" Here the "formal claim" is put as precisely as Mr Irving himself feels he can deco-rously put it. I, who am not an actor, and am therefore not hampered by any personal interest in the claim, can put it much more definitely. What Mr Irving means us to answer is this question: "The artist who composed the music for King Arthur is Sir Arthur Sullivan; the artist who composed the poem which made King Arthur known to this generation died Lord Tennyson; the artist who designed the suit of armor worn by King Arthur is Sir Edward Burne-Jones; why should the artist who plays King Arthur be only Mister Henry Irving?" That is clearly Mr Irving's meaning, since his art lacks no other sort of recognition or advancement[4] than this.

Here let me plead against any envious and base-minded view of this claim. Mr Irving is entitled to an entirely honorable construction: we owe him an unhesitating assumption that his jealousy is for the dignity of his art and not of himself, and that it would never have been advanced if the friend of Sir Joshua Reynolds[5] had been Sir David Garrick, and if every

4. *Hamlet*, III.ii: "I lack advancement."
5. (1723–92), English painter and president of the Royal Academy of Arts from its founding in 1768, to provide exhibitions of art and schools of art training.

successive P.R.A.[6] had had for his officially recognized peer the leading actor of his day. The theatre at present only boasts one title, that of Sir Augustus Harris, who was knighted, not on the excellent ground of his public services as opera impresario, but through the perfectly irrelevant accident of his having been sheriff when the Emperor of Germany visited the City. Who can deny that the actor is regarded as less worthy of official honors than the musician, the painter, or the poet? We have Sir Arthur Sullivan, Sir A. C. Mackenzie, and Sir Charles Hallé (a purely "executive" artist);[7] and we have Sir Edward Burne-Jones, Sir John Millais, and Sir Frederick Leighton.[8] No one questions the social position of these gentlemen; and an expression of any doubt as to whether it was right to go to a concert or to the Royal Academy Exhibition would be considered an unheard-of eccentricity. But numbers of respectable English people still regard a visit to the theatre as a sin; and numbers more, including most of those who have become accustomed to meeting even rank and file actors and actresses in society where thirty years ago they would as soon have expected to meet an acrobat, would receive a proposal from an actor for the hand of their daughter with a sense of *mésalliance* which they would certainly not have if the suitor were a lawyer, a doctor, a clergyman, or a painter. Such people, being intellectually and socially mere sheep, are very much influenced by titles: indeed, that influence is the *raison d'être* of titles; and there can be no doubt that if the next list of birthday honors[9] were to include the names of Sir Henry Irving, Sir John Hare, and Sir Charles Wyndham, the boycott would lose half its force and all its credit at one stroke. On this account it is tenable, not only that Mr Irving might with perfect propriety and dignity accept an official honor which we should expect a great poet, for instance, to refuse just as a great commoner is expected to refuse a peerage, but that he is quite right, on behalf of his profession, to claim it as his due before it is offered. His lecture is such a claim; and in advancing it, he has done worthily and courageously: worthily, because a title can add nothing to his personal eminence, and courageously, because many unworthy persons will wound him by seeing nothing in the act but a vain man grasping at a handle for his name.

But since this was Mr Irving's meaning, why was he too shy to say so in plain words, with the i's dotted and the t's crossed? Why observe that "the

6. President of the Royal Academy (of Arts).

7. Sir Alexander Campbell Mackenzie (1847–1935) was a composer; Sir Charles Hallé (1819–95) founded the Hallé Orchestra in Manchester in 1857 and conducted its concerts.

8. Millais (1829–96) was a painter; Leighton (1830–96), a painter and sculptor.

9. At the celebration of the Queen's (or King's) official birthday, she or he, on a Birthday Honours List, may bestow recognition in the form of a title.

philologists define the word Art, as we have it, as coming through the Latin from the Greek. In this language the root word means &c., &c., &c." In the Royal Institution an actor should not meddle with philology, for precisely the same reason as a philologist should not meddle with acting. And even when an actor exercises his right as an artist to talk about art, he should be careful to speak from his knowledge and not from his imagination, lest he unknowingly fall into the style of a Cabinet Minister proposing the health of the President of the Royal Academy, and be received by irreverent Slade scholars[10] with the thumb to the nose. For example:

"What is there in the works of genius, howsoever they may be represented, which touches the heart with emotion? We feel it as we gaze on the beauty which Canova wrought in marble, which Raphael and Velasquez and Vandyke and Reynolds and Gainsborough depicted on canvas,[11] which Michael Angelo piled up to the dome of St Peter's or as we listen to the tender strains of Mozart, the sad witchery of Mendelssohn, or the tempestuous force of Wagner."

I have no doubt Mr Irving, reading this over, and not for the life of him being able to see what I have to complain of in it, will think me nothing short of a wizard when I tell him that I have discovered from it that he does not know Arnolfo from Brunelleschi in architecture, nor Carpaccio from Guido in painting, nor Rossini from Rubinstein in music.[12] One does not illustrate Michael Angelo's genius from the dome of St Peter's, which was another man's affair, nor do you lump Canova with Velasquez or Raphael with Gainsborough, any more than you lump Blondin and the late Mr Spurgeon[13] with Henry Irving. As to the "sad witchery" put forward as Mendelssohn's general characteristic, I can only wish Mr Irving better luck next time. Never did man make a worse shot in the dark. And yet Mr Irving has a fine ear; for he hears the music of Mozart, Mendelssohn, and Wagner, as aforesaid, "in Nature's choral forces: that mighty gamut of creation which rises from the tiniest whisper of whirring wings in the insect world, through the sighing of the night wind, the crackle of swaying corn, the roar of falling water, and the mighty voice of

10. Holders of scholarships or professorships in Fine Art, endowed by Felix Slade (1790–1868) at Oxford, Cambridge, and London Universities.

11. Velázquez (1599–1660); Sir Anthony Vandyke (or Van Dyck, 1599–1641); Thomas Gainsborough (1727–88).

12. Arnolfo di Cambio (d. 1302); Filippo Brunelleschi (1377–1446); Vittore Carpaccio (c. 1460–1526); Anton Rubinstein (1829–94).

13. Blondin (pseudonym of Jean-François Gravelet, 1824–97), a Frenchman, crossed Niagara Falls on a tightrope in 1859; Charles H. Spurgeon (1834–92) was an English Baptist preacher.

the sounding sea, up to the hiss of the lightning flash and the crash of the thunderbolt."

This quotation, by the way, also proves that Mr Irving does not know fine literature from a penny-a-liner's fustian: though that, alas! we have known ever since we heard him, as Mephistopheles, threatening to do all manner of horrible things to Faust in a passage not at all unlike the above.

Here I can imagine some goodnatured reader asking me why I go on like this at our favorite actor: whether I deliberately wish to be disagreeable. My answer is, yes. I do deliberately want to make it impossible for Mr Irving, or any other member of his profession, ever hereafter to get on the Royal Institution or any other platform, and, with stores of firsthand experience to draw on for a sincere and authoritative, and consequently enormously interesting and valuable lecture on his art, to put us off with two columns of stereo concerning which I can tell Mr Irving, with the utmost exactitude, and without fear of contradiction, that if he wrote it himself he wasted his time, and that if—as I prefer to believe—he got it written for him, he need not have paid the writer a farthing more than one-and-sixpence an hour, at which rate I will undertake to procure him, in the reading room of the British Museum and at the shortest notice, as much literary matter to match his sample as he wants. And of all the critics who paid Mr Irving flowery little compliments on his exhibition next day, there is not one who does not know this as well as I know it. Someday, no doubt, I, too, shall succumb to Mr Irving's charm and prestige. But for the present I prefer to say what I think. I can well understand that it is natural for an actor to resort to his art on the platform, and to a c t the lecturer from a written part rather than venture, without experience, to be the lecturer. But surely, if Mr Irving could so happily come before the curtain at the Lyceum, and wish an audience of friends that affectionate happy new year, he could equally come before a still more select circle of friends in Albemarle Street, and, having told them frankly what he knew about his own art, plead that whether it be ranked as a creative art, like Sir Frederick Leighton's (or like Liszt's[14] playing of Beethoven's sonatas, according to a memorable and luminous criticism of Wagner's), or an executive art like Sir Charles Hallé's, it is no less worthy than theirs of a recognition which, though it could make no personal difference to him, would make all the difference in the world to the status of his profession. Of course, that would not be acting; but then acting is the one thing that is intolerable in a lecture. Even on the stage it is a habit that only the finest actors get rid of completely.

14. Franz Liszt (1811–86), composer.

A PURIFIED PLAY[1]
(*Saturday Review*, 16 February 1895)

After all, things begin to march a little at the theatre. Here is Mr Comyns Carr accepting and producing a play by an untried author who is apparently a literate person, conversant with politics and society, capable of intellectual interests, and even of recognizing a certain degree of delicacy of manner and feeling as an enhancement of human intercourse. If "Mr Ward" were a celebrated novelist like Mr Henry James, or a noted wit like Mr Oscar Wilde, one could understand a manager consenting to overlook his education in consideration of his reputation; but as nobody ever heard of the author of A Leader of Men until his play was announced, it is difficult to avoid the conclusion that Mr Comyns Carr is so far an innovator that he does not regard even an unknown author as being any the worse for a little cultivation, or even a good deal of it. The significance of this can only be appreciated by those who know the theatrical world well enough to understand how strongly it is still dominated by the tradition that crudity, vulgarity, and profligacy, no further disguised than "evening dress" can disguise any wastrel, are the natural characteristics of playhouse entertainments. The force of this insane faith in blackguardism is apparent enough in the huge sums lavished by managers and syndicates on stage shows with nothing to redeem their obvious silliness but a promise of as much lewdness as the audience will stand, even with all public sense of responsibility relieved by that sanction which the Lord Chamberlain never seems to withhold from anything that is openly and intentionally vile. Where it is less apparent, but far more mischievous, is in the timidity of the managers who are struggling against it, and who are, of course, heavily handicapped by the determination of the same official to thrust the drama back into the gutter whenever an attempt is made to deal seriously with social questions on the stage.

I have not dragged this public grievance of the censorship in here merely to ventilate it out of season as well as in season. It is true that no question of censorship arises on the play Mr Ward has written. But it arises very pointedly indeed on the much better play he did not write, but evidently would have written but for the certainty of seeing it strangled at its birth by Mr Pigott. Mr Ward, like all dramatic authors, has had to choose between infanticide and abortion; and he has chosen abortion.

1. A LEADER OF MEN. A new and original comedy. By Charles E. D. Ward [a pseudonym]. Comedy Theatre, 9 February 1895. [G.B.S.]

What he meant to put on the stage was that most dramatic page of our political history in which Mr Gladstone, the late Charles Stewart Parnell, and the lady who was then Mrs O'Shea were the principal figures.[2] Lord Killarney, Mr Llewellyn, M. P., and Mrs Dundas are as clearly stage names for these three as Morton Stone, M. P., is a stage name for Mr Timothy Healy.[3] We all know their story as it was played out on the larger stage which Mr Pigott, doubtless to his own great scandal, is not empowered to purify: how the issue of a bitter political conflict became suddenly bound up with that of an intensely exciting and tragic personal struggle between the two political leaders, in which it was at once apparent that the fiercer, younger, more terrible, least popular of the combatants, trapped between the compulsive force of his affections on the one side, and, on the other, of the stubborn resistance of that unnatural deficiency in our law which makes a mistaken marriage indissoluble except at the cost of social disgrace to the woman and political ruin to the man, was going down, and his cause with it, beneath a well timed blow from his opponent, driven home with the colossal weight of our public hypocrisy and the Nonconformist[4] Conscience. Probably there is not a playwright in the country who has not thought of giving artistic life and form to that drama, only to relinquish the project at the thought of Mr Pigott, and to pass on, possibly, to some farcical comedy theme sufficiently salacious to be sure of a licence.

Mr Ward, being a young hand, did not wholly submit to the despot. But neither did he defy him, being still sufficiently modest to content himself with an expurgated version of the tragedy. Accordingly, we have Mr Llewellyn, a "labor leader" rejoicing in the novelty of a following in the House of Commons, on the eve of forcing a crucial division—presumably concerning the unemployed—on the Prime Minister, a grand old man called Lord Killarney. Both leaders, in an amative and parental way respectively, flirt with a Mrs Dundas, who has positively declined to live with an exceedingly objectionable husband. Llewellyn declares his love; and Mrs Dundas, ladylike, bids him begone. This he is maladroit enough to do, whereupon it becomes necessary for the lady to explain that what she

2. Captain William Henry O'Shea (1840–1905), a member of the Irish Parliamentary Party in England's Parliament, cited Parnell (1846–91), who had been living with O'Shea's wife Katharine (c. 1845–1921) and who was that Party's leader, as co-respondent in a divorce action. In 1890, the court ruled in O'Shea's favor. As a result of the scandal, Parnell, who had persuaded Prime Minister Gladstone (known as the "Grand Old Man") to introduce the First Home Rule Bill for Ireland, which in 1885 was defeated by 341 votes to 311, was deposed, lost his power, and died in 1891.

3. Timothy Michael Healy (1855–1931), an Irish M. P. who would become the first Governor-General of the Irish Free State, opposed Parnell's leadership.

4. Not a member of the Church of England.

really meant was that she returns his love. People thereupon begin to talk; and Mr Timothy Healy, *alias* Morton Stone, M. P., rebels, and is bullied by his leader in the most trenchant Committee Room 15 style.[5] Lord Killarney, also disquieted by the talking, goes to the lady and suggests that she shall go back to her husband in order to place herself above suspicion. She instantly overwhelms him with a tirade in which she recites the horrors of her marriage one by one, fitting each instance with the biting anticlimax "therefore I must go back to him." She then goes to Llewellyn's house, and is about, by taking up her quarters there, to save the Government, ruin the labor leader, and bring down Mr Pigott's blue pencil on the whole play, when another lady, also enamored of the labor leader, persuades her to think better of it. This ending, however moral, being most discouragingly unhappy, as purely moral endings usually are, Mr Dundas considerately expires behind the scenes, and thereby enables the play to comply not only with Mr Pigott's ethical code, but also with the public demand that virtue shall cost nothing.

It is a public duty to point out here that the process of adapting the play to Mr Pigott has consisted in taking a real episode which made a profound moral impression on the nation, and ruthlessly demoralizing it. Suppose Mr Ward had been permitted to dramatize the famous case with the utmost exactitude! Suppose he had introduced his hero in the second act as Mr Fox, and in the third as Mr Preston; suppose he had made him descend from the window of Mrs Dundas's house by a fire escape at the sound of Mr Dundas's latchkey, and immediately reappear at the front door in the character of a casual visitor delighted to see his old friend back again, still he could have gone no further than he actually has gone: that is, represented a married woman as deliberately transfering her declared affection from her husband to another man. The difference in point of adultery would have been a mere technical difference of no moral significance whatever. But there would have been the very serious difference that in the real story the adultery brought tragic consequences which may yet nerve us to bring our marriage law into harmony with those of most other highly civilized communities, whereas in the perversion made for Mr Pigott the consequences are that the lady and her lover live happily ever after, the husband being slaughtered by Providence like a Chicago pig for their convenience. Such are the results of handing over the drama to be purified by a respectable householder at a guinea an act or two guineas for three.

5. An oak-paneled room in an upper floor of the House of Commons, overlooking the Thames, Committee Room 15 was the scene of arguments among members and factions of the Irish Parliamentary Party. Its debates there in December 1890 were decisive factors in Parnell's downfall.

Allowing for the shackles in which the author had to work, the play is by no means an unwelcome one, though how far its simpliciity and refinement of feeling and its chivalrous idealism of sentiment are qualities of the author's youth, and how far of his genius, remains to be seen. The character drawing has hardly any individualization. The young women, a little etherealized, are feminine enough, and very sympathetically and tenderly handled; but then they are all the same young woman with different names. It is much the same with the men: one fails to catch any idiosyncracy. Even the attempt, made for the sake of comic relief, to make one of them a bounder and another an idiot, came off very faintly, though it was, one must admit, powerfully reinforced by the artists entrusted with the two parts in question. The flashes of wit in the play, brilliant enough in themselves, made no effect, because they did not illuminate either the character of the utterers or any irony in the dramatic situation. And the persons of the drama belong rather to the world of imagination than of reality. Even the feeling, which is the author's most effective quality so far, is imaginative feeling, and never has quite the conviction that experience alone brings; but it is fine and intellectual as well as abundant. Every act was saved by some stroke of it: indeed the play was triumphantly rescued, act by act, rather than carried safely and surely through; yet the total result was a very considerable success for a young author making his first attempt with a difficult and ambitious theme.

The acting, as far as the gentlemen in the cast were concerned, several times touched the point of making me think it the very worst I had ever seen. I will not venture to criticize Mr Fred Terry; for, frankly, I did not understand his proceedings. It did not seem to me that any person, labor leader or other, would have spoken the author's words as Mr Terry spoke them, or accompanied them with the gestures he used. Nor did his tones and gestures strike me as having that beauty and grace which one looks for as the differentia between a skilled actor and an ordinary gentleman who has not specialized himself in these directions. I do not for a moment accuse Mr Fred Terry of being a bad actor. The position he occupies is, I presume, hardly to be won without considerable competence. Neither is mine. And yet I could see neither appropriateness in the design, nor skill and elegance in the execution of his impersonation of Robert Llewellyn. If the fault is with me, I can only express my regret. Mr H. B. Irving was not good as Louis Farquhar: he was gratuitously tragic, and introduced the heroics of facial expression into drawing room comedy in a way that he will not dream of five years hence; but he is industriously and successfully learning to act; and that is for him at present the whole duty of man. If Mr Dennis's Lord Killarney was not a very remarkable performance, that was perhaps as much the author's fault as the actor's. Something was supposed to be wrong with Mr Carne's acting as the Archdeacon.[6] The defect was really in his wig, which was a powdered servant's wig, and gave him an irresisitible air of being his own coachman.

Fortunately for Mr Ward, the women's parts, on which the play chiefly depends, were in capable hands. Miss Marion Terry and Miss Alma Murray not only know the technical routine of their business—which is really saying a good deal nowadays—but their execution has a cultivated artistic character throughout; and each has an original and completely formed style. The two styles—Miss Murray's carefully guarded, and a little reticent and fastidious; Miss Terry's delicately frank and sympathetic— contrast very happily, making the scene between the two women in the last act a very pretty piece of work indeed. Unfortunately the public, accustomed to tolerate any sort of bumptious bungling, provided a big effect is pulled off now and then by some actor or actress for whom it has a purely personal admiration, did not shew half as much appreciation of this scene as of Miss Terry's big curtain points, which, to be sure, were admirably done, but which would have been just as loudly applauded had they been crudely thrown at our heads by the youngest and rawest of our leading ladies. When, in this third act, Miss Murray and Miss Terry left the stage, and the men came on, it was as if we had suddenly passed from a first-rate theatre to a country house infested with amateurs. Miss May Harvey,[7] with a pretty but rather colorless part, was too strong for it: her opportunities evidently lie in tragicomic parts of a much more forcible kind. Still, that is more her grievance than the author's: one does not complain of receiving overweight.

AN OLD NEW PLAY AND A NEW OLD ONE[1]
(*Saturday Review*, 23 February 1895)

It is somewhat surprising to find Mr Oscar Wilde, who does not usually model himself on Mr Henry Arthur Jones, giving his play a five-chambered

---

6. Henry Brodribb Irving (1870–1919), Henry Irving's son; Will Dennis (1859–1914); Joseph Carne.

7. (d. 1930).

1. THE IMPORTANCE OF BEING EARNEST. A trivial comedy for serious people. By Oscar Wilde. St James's Theatre, 14 February 1895. ? A play in ? acts. By ?. Opéra Comique, 16 February 1895. THE SECOND MRS TANQUERAY. A play in four acts. By Arthur W. Pinero. London: W. Heinemann. 1895. [G.B.S.]

title like The Case of Rebellious Susan.[2] So I suggest with some confidence that The Importance of Being Earnest dates from a period long anterior to Susan. However it may have been retouched immediately before its production, it must certainly have been written before Lady Windermere's Fan. I do not suppose it to be Mr Wilde's first play: he is too susceptible to fine art to have begun otherwise than with a strenuous imitation of a great dramatic poem, Greek or Shakespearean; but it was perhaps the first which he designed for practical commercial use at the West End theatres. The evidence of this is abundant. The play has a plot: a gross anachronism; there is a scene between the two girls in the second act quite in the literary style of Mr Gilbert, and almost inhuman enough to have been conceived by him; the humor is adulterated by stock mechanical fun to an extent that absolutely scandalizes one in a play with such an author's name to it; and the punning title and several of the more farcical passages recall the epoch of the late H. J. Byron. The whole has been varnished, and here and there veneered, by the author of A Woman of No Importance;[3] but the general effect is that of a farcical comedy dating from the seventies, unplayed during that period because it was too clever and too decent, and brought up to date as far as possible by Mr Wilde in his now completely formed style. Such is the impression left by the play on me. But I find other critics, equally entitled to respect, declaring that The Importance of Being Earnest is a strained effort of Mr Wilde's at ultra-modernity and that it could never have been written but for the opening up of entirely new paths in drama last year by Arms and the Man. At which I confess to a chuckle.

I cannot say that I greatly cared for The Importance of Being Earnest. It amused me, of course; but unless comedy touches me as well as amuses me, it leaves me with a sense of having wasted my evening. I go to the theatre to be moved to laughter, not to be tickled or bustled into it; and that is why, though I laugh as much as anybody at a farcical comedy, I am out of spirits before the end of the second act, and out of temper before the end of the third, my miserable mechanical laughter intensifying these symptoms at every outburst. If the public ever becomes intelligent enough to know when it is really enjoying itself and when it is not, there will be an end of farcical comedy. Now in The Importance of Being Earnest there is plenty of this rib-tickling: for instance, the lies, the deceptions, the cross purposes, the sham mourning, the christening of two grown-up men, the muffin eating, and so forth. These could only have been raised from the farcical plane by making them occur to characters who had, like Don Quixote, convinced us of their reality and obtained

2. (1894) by Henry Arthur Jones.
3. (1893) by Wilde.

some hold on our sympathy. But that unfortunate moment of Gilbertism breaks our belief in the humanity of the play. Thus we are thrown back on the force and daintiness of its wit, brought home by an exquisitely grave, natural, and unconscious execution on the part of the actors. Alas! the latter is not forthcoming. Mr Kinsey Peile as a manservant, and Miss Irene Vanbrugh as Gwendolen Fairfax,[4] alone escaped from a devastating consciousness of Mr Wilde's reputation, which more or less preoccupied all the rest, except perhaps Miss Millard [as Cecily Cardew], with whom all comedy is a preoccupation, since she is essentially a sentimental actress. In such passages as the Gilbertian quarrel with Gwendolen, her charm rebuked the scene instead of enhancing it. The older ladies were, if they will excuse my saying so, quite maddening. The violence of their affectation, the insufferable low comedy soars and swoops of the voice, the rigid shivers of elbow, shoulder, and neck, which are supposed on the stage to characterize the behavior of ladies after the age of forty, played havoc with the piece. In Miss Rose Leclerq [as Lady Bracknell] a good deal of this sort of thing is only the mannerism of a genuine if somewhat impossible style; but Miss Leclerq was absent through indisposition on the night of my visit; so that I had not her style to console me. Mr Aynesworth's easygoing Our Boys[5] style of play suited his part rather happily; and Mr Alexander's graver and more refined manner [as John Worthing] made the right contrast with it. But Mr Alexander, after playing with very nearly if not quite perfect conviction in the first two acts, suddenly lost confidence in the third, and began to spur up for a rattling finish. From the moment that began, the play was done with. The speech in which Worthing forgives his supposed mother, and the business of searching the army lists, which should have been conducted with subdued earnestness, was bustled through to the destruction of all verisimilitude and consequently all interest. That is the worst of having anyone who is not an inveterate and hardened comedian in a leading comedy part. His faith, patience, and relish begin to give out after a time; and he finally commits the unpardonable sin against the author of giving the signal that the play is over ten minutes before the fall of the curtain, instead of speaking the last line as if the whole evening were still before the audience. Mr Alexander does not throw himself genuinely into the comedy: he condescends to amuse himself with it; and in the end he finds that he cannot condescend enough. On the whole I must decline to accept The Importance or Being Earnest as a day less than ten years old; and I am altogether unable to perceive any uncommon excellence in its presentation.

4. Frederick Kinsey Peile (1862–1934); (later Dame Irene) Vanbrugh (1872–1949).
5. E. Allan Aynesworth (1865–1959) played Algernon Moncrief. In 1875, Our Boys by H. J. Byron ran for a then-record 1,362 performances; it was frequently revived thereafter.

I am in a somewhat foolish position concerning a play at the Opéra Comique, whither I was bidden this day week. For some reason I was not supplied with a program; so that I never learnt the name of the play.[6] I believe I recognized some of the members of the company—generally a very difficult thing to do in a country where, with a few talented exceptions, every actor is just like every other actor—but they have now faded from my memory. At the end of the second act the play had advanced about as far as an ordinary dramatist would have brought it five minutes after the first rising of the curtain; or, say, as far as Ibsen would have brought it ten years before that event. Taking advantage of the second interval to stroll out into the Strand for a little exercise, I unfortunately forgot all about my business, and actually reached home before it occurred to me that I had not seen the end of the play. Under these circumstances it would ill become me to dogmatize on the merits of the work or its performance. I can only offer the management my apologies.

I am indebted to Mr Heinemann for a copy of The Second Mrs Tanqueray, which he has just published in a five-shilling volume, with an excellent photographic portrait of the author by Mr Hollyer.[7] Those who did not see the play at the St James's Theatre can now examine the literary basis of the work that so immoderately fascinated playgoing London in 1893. But they must not expect the play to be as imposing in the library as it was on the stage. Its merit there was relative to the culture of the playgoing public. Paula Tanqueray is an astonishingly well drawn figure as stage figures go nowadays, even allowing for the fact that there is no cheaper subject for the character draughtsman than the ill-tempered sensual woman seen from the point of view of the conventional man. But off the stage her distinction vanishes. The novels of Anthony Trollope, Charles Lever, Bulwer Lytton, Charles Reade, and many other novelists, whom nobody praised thirty years ago in the terms in which Mr Pinero is praised now, are full of feats of character drawing in no way inferior—to say the least—to Mr Pinero's. The theatre was not ready for that class of work then: it is now; and accordingly Mr Pinero, who is in literature a humble and somewhat belated follower of the novelists of the middle of the XIX century, and who has never written a line from which it could be guessed that he is a contemporary of Ibsen, Tolstoy,[8] Meredith, or Sarah Grand, finds himself at the dawn of the XX hailed as a man of new ideas, of daring originality, of supreme literary distinction, and even—which is perhaps oddest—of consummate stagecraft. Stagecraft, after all, is very narrowly limited by the physical conditions of stage representation; but

---

6. *An M. P.'s Wife*. A play in four acts. Anon. (adapted from T. Terrell's novel *A Woman of Heart*).

7. Frederick Hollyer (1837–1933), pioneer of natural photographic portraits,

8. Count Leo (Lev) Nikolayevich Tolstoy (1828–1910), Russian novelist and dramatist.

when one turns over the pages of The Second Mrs Tanqueray, and notes the naïve machinery of the exposition of the first act, in which two whole actors are wasted on sham parts, and the hero, at his own dinner party, is compelled to get up and go ignominiously into the next room "to write some letters" when something has to be said behind his back; when one follows Cayley Drummle, the confidant to whom both Paula and her husband explain themselves for the benefit of the audience; when one counts the number of doors which Mr Pinero needs to get his characters on and off the stage, and how they have finally to be supplemented by the inevitable "French windows" (two of them); and when the activity of the postman is taken into consideration, it is impossible to avoid the conclusion that what most of our critics mean by mastery of stagecraft is recklessness in the substitution of dead machinery and lay figures for vital action and real characters. I do not deny that an author may be driven by his own limitations to ingenuities which Shakespear had no occasion to cultivate, just as a painter without hands or feet learns to surpass Michael Angelo in the art of drawing with the brush held in the mouth; but I regard such ingenuity as an extremity to be deplored, not as an art to be admired. In the Second Mrs Tanqueray I find little except a scaffold for the situation of a stepdaughter and stepmother finding themselves in the positions respectively of affianced wife and discarded mistress to the same man. Obviously, the only necessary conditions of this situation are that the persons concerned shall be respectable enough to be shocked by it, and that the stepmother shall be an improper person. Mr Pinero has not got above this minimum. He is, of course, sufficiently skilled in fiction to give Ellean, Mrs Cortelyon, Ardale, Tanqueray, and Cayley Drummle a passable air of being human beings. He has even touched up Cayley into a Thackerayan *flâneur* in order to secure toleration of his intrusiveness. But who will pretend that any of these figures are more than the barest accessories to the main situation? To compare them with the characters in Robertson's Caste would be almost as ridiculous as to compare Caste to A Doll's House. The two vulgar characters produce the requisite jar—a pitilessly disagreeable jar—and that is all. Still, all the seven seem good as far as they go; and that very little way may suggest that Mr Pinero might have done good creative work if he had carried them further. Unfortunately for this surmise, he has carried Paula further; and with what result? The moment the point is reached at which the comparatively common gift of "an eye for character" has to be supplemented by the higher dramatic gift of sympathy with character, of the power of seeing the world from the point of view of others instead of merely describing or judging from one's own point of view in terms of the conventional systems of morals, Mr Pinero breaks down. I remember that when I saw the play acted I sat up very attentively when Tanqueray said to Paula "I know what you were at Ellean's age. You hadnt a thought that wasnt a wholesome one; you hadnt an impulse that didnt tend towards good; you never harbored a notion you couldnt have gossiped about to a parcel of children. And this was a very few years back, &c., &c." On the reply to that fatuous but not unnatural speech depended the whole question of Mr Pinero's rank as a dramatist. One can imagine how, in a play by a master hand, Paula's reply would have opened Tanqueray's foolish eyes to the fact that a woman of that sort is already the same at three as she is at thirtythree, and that however she may have found by experience that her nature is in conflict with the ideals of differently constituted people, she remains perfectly valid to herself, and despises herself, if she sincerely does so at all, for the hypocrisy that the world forces on her instead of for being what she is. What reply does Mr Pinero put into her mouth? Here it is, with the stage directions: "A few—years ago! (*She walks slowly towards the door, then suddenly drops upon the ottoman in a paroxysm of weeping.*) O God! A few years ago!" That is to say, she makes her reply from the Tanqueray–Ellean–Pinero point of view, and thus betrays the fact that she is a work of prejudiced observation instead of comprehension, and that the other characters only owe their faint humanity to the fact that they are projections of Mr Pinero's own personal amiabilities and beliefs and conventions. Mr Pinero, then, is no interpreter of character, but simply an adroit describer of people as the ordinary man sees and judges them. Add to this a clear head, a love of the stage, and a fair talent for fiction, all highly cultivated by hard and honorable work as a writer of effective stage plays for the modern commercial theatre; and you have him on his real level. On that level he is entitled to all the praise The Second Mrs Tanqueray has won him; and I very heartily regret that the glamor which Mrs Patrick Campbell[9] cast round the play has forced me to examine pretensions which Mr Pinero himself never put forward rather than to acknowledge the merits with which his work is so concisely packed.

THE LATE CENSOR
(*Saturday Review*, 2 March 1895)

Mr E. F. Smyth Pigott, for twenty years examiner of stage plays to the Lord Chamberlain's department, has joined the majority. It is a great pity

9. Mrs Patrick Campbell (Beatrice Stella Tanner, 1865–1940) would in 1914 play Eliza Doolittle in the first English production of Shaw's *Pygmalion* (1912), directed by Shaw.

that the Censorship cannot be abolished before the appointment of a successor to Mr Pigott creates a fresh vested interest in one of the most mischievous of our institutions.

The justification of the Censorship is to be found in the assumption, repeatedly and explicitly advanced by the late holder of the office, that, if the stage were freed, managers would immediately produce licentious plays; actresses would leave off clothing themselves decently; and the public would sit nightly wallowing in the obscenity which the Censor now sternly withholds from them. This assumption evidently involves the further one, that the Examiner of Plays is so much better than his neighbors, as to be untainted by their assumed love of filth. This is where the theory of the Censorship breaks down in practice. The Lord Chamberlain's reader is not selected by examination either in literature or morals. His emoluments, estimated at about £800 a year, will fetch nothing more in the market than well connected mediocrity. Therefore it is necessary to give him absolute power, so that there may be no appeal from his blunders. If he vetoes serious plays and licenses nasty ones, which is exactly what the late Mr Pigott did, there is no remedy. He is the Tsar of the theatres, able to do things that no prime minister dare do. And he has the great advantage that in ninetyeight out of every hundred plays submitted to him (this is an official estimate), no question of morals is raised. He has nothing to do but read the play, pocket his two guineas, license the performance, and leave the manager and the author under the impression that he is a very agreeable, unobjectionable person, whose licence is cheap at the price since it relieves everyone of responsibility and makes things pleasant all round. It is not until the two per cent of plays in which received opinions and hardened prejudices are called in question, and offered for testing under the searching rays of the footlights—in other words, the plays on which the whole growth and continued vitality of the theatre depend—that the Censor has his opportunity of shewing how much better he is than the public by saying "You should listen to these plays, however much they may shock you. I have read them, and can certify that they will interest really cultivated people and help to set everybody thinking." But as the Censor never is any better than the average public, he does exactly the reverse of this. He shares its ignorant intolerance and its petulance under criticism, and uses his official authority to forbid the performance of the exceptional plays. The late Mr Pigott is declared on all hands to have been the best reader of plays we have ever had; and yet he was a walking compendium of vulgar insular prejudice, who, after wallowing all his life in the cheapest theatrical sentiment (he was a confirmed playgoer), had at last brought himself to a pitch of incompetence which, outside the circle of those unfortunate persons who have had to try and reason with him personally, can only be measured by reading his evidence before the Commission of 1892,[1] and the various letters of his which are just now finding their way into print. He had French immorality on the brain; he had American indecency on the brain; he had the womanly woman on the brain; he had the Divorce Court on the brain; he had "not before a mixed audience" on the brain; his official career in relation to the higher drama was one long folly and panic, in which the only thing definitely discernible in a welter of intellectual confusion was his conception of the English people rushing towards an abyss of national degeneration in morals and manners, and only held back on the edge of the precipice by the grasp of his strong hand.

In the Daily Telegraph of Monday last there was an obituary notice of Mr Pigott from the sympathetic pen of Mr Clement Scott, who is far too kindhearted to tell the truth on so sad an occasion, and who, I am afraid, will characterize my remarks, in his very ownest style, as "a cowardly attack on a dead man." Mr Scott tells us of Mr Pigott's "difficult and delicate duties," of his "admirable discretion," his "determination to persist in the path that seemed right to him," his conscientiousness, zeal, efficiency, tact, and so on. I do not question Mr Pigott's personal character: I have no doubt he was as excellent a man for all private purposes as Charles I.[2] But when Mr Scott's benevolence to Mr Pigott leads him to discredit my protests against the Censorship as "allegations that are as coarse as they are untrue," I must open Mr Scott's eyes a little. Not that I deny the coarseness. To accuse anyone of encouraging lewd farce at the expense of fine drama is to bring a coarse charge against him; but Mr Scott will admit that the policeman must not be put out of court because he has a coarse charge to prefer. The question is, Is the charge true? Mr Scott says no. I produce my evidence, and leave the public to judge.

Not very many seasons ago, in the exercise of my duties as a musical critic, I went to an opera at a certain West End theatre. (Mr Scott, not having enjoyed the advantage of a training as musical critic, misses these things.) There were two heroines, one a princess. The hero had to marry the princess, though he loved the other heroine. In the second act, the stage represented an antechamber in the palace of the bride's father on the night of the wedding. The door of the nuptial chamber appeared on the stage. It was guarded by an elderly duenna. The reluctant bridegroom arrived on his way to join his bride. The duenna presented him with the golden key of the chamber. Suddenly it occurred to him that if he were to

---

1. In 1892, a Select Committee of the House of Commons, before which Pigott testified on 23 May, investigated the system of stage censorship and reported that it worked satisfactorily.

2. King Charles I was beheaded in 1649.

criminally assault this lady, who was renowned at court for her austerity, her screams would rouse the court, and he would be consigned by the outraged monarch to a dungeon, thereby escaping his conjugal obligations. On proceeding to carry out this stratagem, he was taken aback by finding the old lady, far from raising an alarm, receive his advances with the utmost ardor. In desperation he threw her to the ground, and was about to escape when she, making no effort to rise, said, with archly affectionate reproach, "Dont you see where youve left me, duckie?" On this he fled; and presently a young man and a young woman entered and flirted until they were interrupted by the king. He, overhearing a kiss, supposed it to proceed from the bridal chamber of his daughter. He immediately went to the door; listened at the keyhole; and, hearing another kiss, remarked with an ecstatic shiver that it made him feel young again.[3] If that scene had not been presented to the public under the authority of the Lord Chamberlain it would be impossible for me to describe it in these columns. The sole justification for the Censorship is that, without its restraining hand, the scene would have been worse than it was. Pray how much worse could it have been?

Take another instance, this time of a well known farcical comedy which Mr Scott must have witnessed. I spare the details: suffice it to say that the piece contained three or four "laughs" which could not possibly have been explained or described at a dinner party, which is, if I mistake not, Mr Scott's test of propriety. I did not see the piece until, finding myself at Northampton on the eve of a political meeting in which I had to take part, I went into the theatre, and found this comedy "on tour" there.[4] Now Northampton is not like London: it is not large enough to support one theatre where improper jests are permitted, and another guaranteed safe for clergymen and their daughters. What was the result? The Censorship of public opinion—of that Monsieur Tout le Monde who is admited to be wiser than everyone except the Lord Chamberlain—acted spontaneously. The questionable points were either omited or slurred over in such a way that nobody could possibly catch their intention. Everything that Mr Pigott might have done, and did not do, to make the play decent was done without compulsion by the management in order to avoid offending that section of the public which does not relish smoking-room facetiousness.

These two typical cases, which, as Mr Scott knows better than anyone

3. *Incognita*, music by Lecocq, Herbert Bunning (1863–1937), and James Hamilton Clarke (1840–1912); libretto by F.C. Burnand; lyrics by Harry Greenbank (1866–90). Shaw reviewed it in *The World*, 12 October 1892. In his 1902 preface to *Mrs Warren's Profession*, he again summarizes this plot, which he says is of a play, not an opera. As the work is a play with music, either designation is reasonable.

4. *Jane* by Nicholls and Lestocq, on 5 September 1891.

else, I can easily multiply if he puts me to it, will, I hope, convince him that my statement that the Censorship does not withhold its approval from blackguardism on the stage is much better considered than his counterstatement that I have simply said the thing that is not. But if he demands equally direct proof of my statement that the Censorship suppresses fine work, he has me at a disadvantage; for I naturally cannot produce the plays that the Censorship has prevented from existing. And yet this is the very statement I chiefly desire to establish; for I do not in the least object to the licensing of plays which disgust me, if there are people who are entertained by them: what I object to is the suppression, because they disgust other people, of plays that entertain me. All I can do is to offer to produce a staggering list of authors who have not written for the stage since the evil day when Walpole established the Censorship to prevent Fielding from exposing the corruption of Parliament on the stage.[5] Fielding never wrote another play; and from his time to that of Dickens, who was once very fond of the stage, a comparison of our literature with our drama shews a relative poverty and inferiority on the part of the latter not to be paralleled in any of the countries where the Censor only interferes on political grounds. May I ask Mr Scott whether he thinks that Mr Grant Allen's The Woman Who Did would have been licensed by Mr Pigott if it had been a play, or whether The Heavenly Twins could have been written under the thumb of a Censor? Or, to come to actual plays, would Ibsen's Ghosts have been licensed had Mr Grein risked subjecting himself to a £50 penalty by making the attempt? Is Tolstoy's Dominion of Darkness[6] likely to be produced here as it has been elsewhere? Would Die Walküre be licensed as a spoken play? Would Shakespear, or the great Greek dramatists, have stood a chance with Mr Pigott? Mr Scott may reply that Mr Pigott actually did license Ibsen's plays. Fortunately, I am in a position to give both Mr Pigott's opinion of Ibsen's plays and his reason for licensing them. Here are his own words, uttered on one of the most responsible occasions of his official career:

"I have studied Ibsen's plays pretty carefully; and all the characters in Ibsen's plays appear to me morally deranged. All the heroines are dissatisfied spinsters who look on marriage as a monopoly, or dissatisfied married

5. Henry Fielding's political satires, Pasquin (1736) and The Historical Register for the Year 1736 (1737), attacked such targets as Sir Robert Walpole (1676–1745), who restricted the freedom of the London theaters by means of the Licensing Act of 1737, which limited them to two, Covent Garden and Drury Lane, and which brought dramatic performances under the authority and censorship of the Lord Chamberlain. After 1737, Fielding wrote three plays, none of them political satires, and he turned to the novel. Theatrical censorship in England lasted until 1968.

6. (1888), also translated as The Power of Darkness.

women in a chronic state of rebellion against not only the conditions which nature has imposed on their sex, but against all the duties and obligations of mothers and wives. As for the men, they are all rascals or imbeciles."

Not unnaturally, Mr Woodall[7] asked Mr Pigott on this why he did not think the plays sufficiently injurious to public morals to be suppressed. Mr Pigott replied that they were too absurd to do any harm. Thus the one great writer who has escaped what Mr Scott has called "the kindly blue pencil," was let pass, not because he was a great writer, but because Mr Pigott was so stupendously incompetent as to think him beneath contempt. I have suggested that Shakespear would have been vetoed by him; but he has anticipated that misgiving in the following remarkable utterance: "Shakespear himself was a member, I believe, at one time, of the Lord Chamberlain's company; but that did not prevent his plays being written." Imagine Mr Pigott, who refused to license The Cenci, confronted with the relationship between the king and queen in Hamlet, or with the closet scene in that play.

Let me add a few more touches to the sketch of Mr Pigott's mind. First, as to his notion of morality in an audience, of vice and virtue, of fine sentiment:

"The further east you go, the more moral your audience is. You may get a gallery full of roughs in which every other boy is a pickpocket, and yet their collective sympathy is in favor of self-sacrifice; collectively they have a horror of vice and a love of virtue. A boy might pick your pocket as you left the theatre, but have his reserve of fine sentiment in his heart."

This is immoral balderdash, nothing more and nothing less; and yet poor Mr Pigott believed it as firmly as he believed that Browning and George Meredith and James Russell Lowell,[8] in attending the Shelley Society's unlicensed performance of The Cenci, were indulging a vicious taste for immoral exhibitions.

Mr Pigott's highly praised tact, both as a critic and a controversialist, may be judged from the following *obiter dicta*:

"Managers' backers are in most cases men who do not care to keep a theatre—I will not say for the elevation of dramatic art, or for the public edification—but for purposes which can be openly avowed."

"Absolute free trade in theatre and theatrical representation may be left to the advocacy of disciples of Jack Cade, whose political economy is a sort

7. William Woodall (1832–1901), M.P., a parliamentary leader in the woman's suffrage movement, who was a member of the Commission of 1892.
8. (1819–91), American poet and essayist.

of Benthamism[9] burlesqued. These purveyors of theatrical scandals are equally in favor of absolute free trade in disorderly houses and houses of ill fame."

I must say I wish Mr Scott had not trifled so outrageously as he has with this great public question. It is a frightful thing to see the greatest thinkers, poets, and authors of modern Europe—men like Ibsen, Wagner, Tolstoy, and the leaders of our own literature—delivered helpless into the vulgar hands of such a noodle as this amiable old gentleman—this despised and incapable old official—most notoriously was. And just such a man as he was his successor is likely to be too, because a capable man means a known man; and a known man means one whose faults have become as public as his qualities. The appointment of Mr Archer, for instance, would awaken Mr Scott to the infamy of the Censorship as effectually as the appointment of Mr Scott himself would fortify Mr Archer's case against the institution. Yet the Lord Chamberlain cannot possibly find a better man than either one or other of these gentlemen. He will therefore have to appoint a nobody whose qualifications, being unknown, can be imagined by foolish people to be infinite. Is this, then, the time for Mr Scott to announce that "the dramatic world is well content with the control now vested in the Lord Chamberlain and his staff"? Who constitute the dramatic world? I take the first handful of names that comes to hand. Do Messrs Oscar Wilde, Sydney Grundy, Robert Buchanan, Henry Arthur Jones belong to it? Do Mr Hermann Vezin, Mr Lewis Waller, Mr Charles Charrington, Miss Alma Murray, Mrs Theodore Wright, Miss Janet Achurch, Miss Elizabeth Robins belong to it? Does Mr Scott himself belong to it? and, if so, do I?—does Mr Archer?—does Mr Walkley?—do the numerous critics who never refer to the Censorship except in terms of impatient contempt at such an anomaly? Would one of the managers who pay the Lord Chamberlain compliments now that they are in his power, waste a word on him if they were out of it? No: the dramatic world, Mr Scott may depend on it, wants the same freedom that exists in America and—oddly enough—in Ireland. Not, mind, a stage controlled by the County Council or any such seventyseven times worse evil than the present, but a stage free as the Press is free and as speech is free. When Mr Scott has dropped his tear over the lost friend whom he has forced me to handle so roughly, I shall thank him to come back to his own side and fight for that freedom. Abominations like the Censorship have quite enough flatterers without him.

9. Jeremy Bentham (1748–1832), English political philosopher and economist, led the Utilitarians, whose principle was that the foundation of morals and legislation was "the greatest happiness of the greatest number."

MR ARTHUR ROBERTS AS A GENTLEMAN
(*Saturday Review*, 9 March 1895)[1]

It is impossible to sit out an entertainment like Gentleman Joe without reflecting on the enormous part played in the theatre by hypnotic suggestion. At what point I fall a victim to it myself I, of course, do not know. No "professor" in the world can persuade me that a glass of paraffin oil is a bumper of Imperial Tokay. But as I look back on my earliest impressions of certain performances which completely dominated my imagination, I have to admit that my view of them was very far from being a sane and objective one. And now that it is my business as a critic to gain such a sane and objective view over the whole field of art, I sometimes find myself at the theatre in a state of distressingly complete sanity among neighbors who are in the wildest ecstasies at nothing. This was my predicament at Gentleman Joe. A variety of causes have produced a powerful hypnotic suggestion that Mr Arthur Roberts is a buffoon of almost superhuman powers, and that the musical farces "written around him," as the technical phrase goes, are immensely exhilarating, racy, up to date, and necessary to complete the experience of every dashing young undergraduate in the joy of life. The spell is undeniably successful, though nothing but the fear of seeming to pose as a superior person prevents me from adding that the weakness of its subjects has a great deal to do with its apparently irresistible strength. At any rate, it did not operate on me. When Mr Roberts, on the sands at Margate, turned to a gentleman who was about to annihilate a sand castle, and told him not to sit down on the Christmas pudding, I sat patiently enduring whilst all around me roared with merriment. And again, when, wishing to convey to the audience that one of the persons on the stage was beside himself, he tapped his forehead and said "Balmy on the crumpet," I, having long ago exhausted such delight as lurks in that fantastic expression, heaved a sigh amid general laughter. I do not deny that these sallies are funny in comparison with absolute vacuity; but surely, since private life supplies rather more than enough of them free of charge, one need not go to the trouble and expense of a visit to the theatre to procure them. Then there were certain humors which probably made a majority of the audience uneasy, and

---

1. GENTLEMAN JOE. A New Musical Farce. Words and Lyrics by Basil Hood [1864–1917]. Music by Walter Slaughter [1860–1908]. Prince of Wales' Theatre, 2 March 1895. [G.B.S.] Roberts (1852–1933), a popular performer, appeared in musical farces, light operas, music halls, and pantomime.

were not witty enough to excuse the company for condescending to them. For example, Mr Roberts, as Gentleman Joe, the hansom cabby, comes to see his sweetheart. He says to the butler "Where's Emma?" The butler replies "Emma is getting ready to see you, and is taking off her things." Mr Roberts receives this in such a way as to shew that the line may be construed to mean that the young lady is undressing herself completely; and the house, pleased at its own cleverness in finding this out, and at Mr Roberts's artfulness in suggesting it, laughs at the schoolboy indecency for fully half a minute. Again, Mr Roberts is conversing with Miss Kitty Loftus,[2] the sweetheart aforesaid, who has a piece of frilling in her hand. He asks her what it is. "That" she tells him "is frilling for me to wear." "Where?" he asks; and as "where" and "wear" make a sort of pun, there is a faint laugh from the quicker wits present. "In my hat" is Miss Loftus's answer. Whereupon Mr Roberts, by appropriate pantomime, makes it appear that he had supposed the frilling to belong to her undergarments; and there is again a huge guffaw. Now this sort of thing is to me mere silly misbehavior, and I want to have it banished from the stage. The question is, how is it to be done? The Censorship, even if there were no larger grounds for condemning it, is worse than useless here; for in the two instances given above, the first arose on a line which no Censor could possibly object to without exposing himself to the charge of having an intolerably prurient imagination; whilst the second enjoys the licence of the Lord Chamberlain, although the incident of the frilling is dragged in by the ears, for the express purpose of Mr Roberts's ribaldry, with an obviousness which even the most angelically innocent Censor could not possibly miss if he did his duty with any sort of intelligent vigilance. The Censorship of the public is of no use either, because part of any audience is sure to laugh: even the part who are annoyed cannot all help laughing; and the others will put up with an offensive passage or two for the sake of the rest of the entertainment sooner than make a fuss about an unpleasant matter. As for the critics, they must either complain of Mr Roberts's coarseness in general terms, thereby leaving the extent of the evil to the imagination, or else they must do what I have been compelled to do: that is, describe the objectionable passages with an exactitude which jars disagreeably on my readers and myself. There is, fortunately, another power to appeal to: the self-respect of the artist. Although the qualities found in Mr Roberts's performances by the hypnotized young gentlemen in the stalls of the Prince of Wales' Theatre are nine tenths imaginary, nonetheless must an actor possess a great deal of merit to outstrip all his competitors in the struggle to be rated as the most entertaining performer

2. (1867–1927).

of his class in London. Granted that the Arthur Roberts of the popular imagination has no objective existence; that dozens of artists at the music halls and in the provincial pantomimes can sing a comic song as well as he; that London is familiar with better dancers and pantomimists; and that his popularity is widest among people whose admiration is not worth having, still he has intense comic force, an eye for characteristic London street and shop types hardly inferior to Mr Phil May's,[3] much shrewdness and tact, and great skill and experience. Some day, when his younger admirers outgrow their taste for him, and the coming generations find him as oldfashioned as Mr Toole, he will take to acting, and probably earn a distinguished place as a low comedian. Mr Roberts, in short, has plenty of dignity as an artist if he will only stand on it. He dare not carry indecorum far enough to satisfy the people who like it, though he can and does go quite far enough to disgust the people who do not like it. When he says to Miss Jenoure[4] "May I take you on one side for a moment?" in such a way as to make the speech an insult, he simply throws away his own respectability and that of his art for nothing, since nobody can possibly be so feebleminded as to see any wit in the perception of such a point or any cleverness in the execution of it. I strongly recommend Mr Roberts to drop it; and I suggest to the author, Mr Basil Hood, who must be aware of the turn given to his lines, and to the management, who are equally responsible with the author and performer, that they should immediately signify to Mr Roberts that they would prefer not to have the three points I have mentioned made in future.

At the same time, I am of opinion that these entertainments would be far more enjoyable if they were not so depressingly moral. Let them be courageously written from the point of view of the devil's advocate; and then there will be conviction in them, interest in them, and wit in them. For example, I have not the slightest objection to Yvette Guilbert singing Les Vierges.[5] In that song you hear virtue attacked with bitter irony by a poet who does not believe in it and: I must not say by an artist who does not believe in it either, but at all events by one who has the power of throwing herelf with mordant intensity into the poet's attitude for the moment. Let us by all means have whole plays written like Les Vierges, in which the votaries of pleasure can religiously put forward their creed against the idealists and the Puritans. There would be life in that: pur-

3. Philip William (Phil) May (1864–1903) was a humorist, draftsman, and cartoonist, preeminent for comic delineations of street life and Bohemian life of the Victorian period.

4. Aida Jenoure (fl. 1887–1929).

5. (c. 1868–1944), French singer immortalized by the drawings of Henri de Toulouse-Lautrec (1864–1901), singing "The Virgins."

pose, honesty, reality, and the decency which arises spontaneously beside them. But a timidly conventional play like Gentleman Joe, with its abject little naughtinesses furtively slipped in under cover of the tamest propriety, and with a pitiful whoop at the end about a debauched clergyman riding in a cab with a lady, of whom Mr Roberts sings

> Perhaps she was his aunt,
> Or another Mrs Chant,[6]

all this is about as lively as the performances of the children who make faces at their teachers in Sunday school. The nearest approach to a witty line in Gentleman Joe is Mrs Ralli-Carr's reply to the question "Why dont you divorce your husband?" "I cant prove the cruelty"; but this faint attempt to say something scandalous with piquant indirectness was too subtle for the audience.

As usual in such entertainments, there is a tedious preliminary "exposition" of the relations between the characters. Nobody listens to it. Mr Roberts is a hansom cabman who is mistaken most impossibly for a lord. He has his moments of clever mimicry, as well as one good passage of acting, where he becomes respectful to the lady whom he has mistaken for a servant. The quaint line "Excuse me keeping my hat off" is the only one in the piece which shews the artist under the buffoon and caricaturist. A touch of cheap "John Anderson my jo"[7] sentiment in the duet with Miss Kitty Loftus in the last act was a huge relief after all the dead galvanized vivacity that preceded it. Miss Sadie Jerome, a dashing American lady, made a huge effect by launching her name "Potts" in one enormous consonantal convulsion at the end of her song. Miss Kate Cutler sang nicely; and Mr Philp, a rather throaty tenorino, just at the age at which throaty tenorinos are agreeable, delivered himself acceptably of a ballad.[8] Miss Jenoure, as Mrs Ralli-Carr, had a part in which she saw no harm. Possibly the author found her innocuousness disappointing. I did not.

The music, by Mr Walter Slaughter, does not contain a single novel or even passably fresh point either in melody, harmony, or orchestration. The song in the "old English" style, sung by Miss Cutler, was almost the only passage which Mr Slaughter seemed to have composed with any feeling or enjoyment.

---

6. Cockney euphemism for water closet. The joke may be a triple entendre, referring also to the social reformer Laura Ormiston Chant (1848–1923).

7. Ballad (1787–96) by Robert Burns (1759–96).

8. Jerome (1876–1950); Cutler (1870–1955); William Philp.

MR PINERO'S NEW PLAY
(*Saturday Review*, 16 March 1895)[1]

Mr Pinero's new play is an attempt to reproduce that peculiar stage effect of intellectual drama, of social problem, of subtle psychological study of character, in short, of a great play, with which he was so successful in The Profligate[2] and The Second Mrs Tanqueray. In the two earlier plays, it will be remembered, he was careful to support this stage effect with a substantial basis of ordinary dramatic material, consisting of a well worked-up and well worn situation which would have secured the success of a conventional Adelphi piece. In this way he conquered the public by the exquisite flattery of giving them plays that they really liked, whilst persuading them that such appreciation was only possible from persons of great culture and intellectual acuteness. The vogue of The Second Mrs Tanqueray was due to the fact that the commonplace playgoer, as he admired Mrs Patrick Campbell, and was moved for the twentieth time by the conventional wicked woman with a past, consumed with remorse at the recollection of her innocent girlhood, and unable to look her pure stepdaughter (from a convent) in the face, believed that he was one of the select few for whom "the literary drama" exists, and thus combined the delights of an evening at a play which would not have puzzled Madame Céleste[3] with a sense of being immensely in the modern movement. Mr Pinero, in effect, invented a new sort of play by taking the ordinary article and giving it an air of novel, profound, and original thought. This he was able to do because he was an inveterate "character actor" (a technical term denoting a clever stage performer who cannot act, and therefore makes an elaborate study of the disguises and stage tricks by which acting can be grotesquely simulated) as well as a competent dramatist on customary lines. His performance as a thinker and social philosopher is simply character acting in the domain of authorship, and can impose only on those who are taken in by character acting on the stage. It is only the make-up of an actor who does not understand his part, but who knows—because he shares—the popular notion of its externals. As such, it can never be the governing factor in his success, which must always depend

1. THE NOTORIOUS MRS EBBSMITH. An original play in four acts. By A. W. Pinero. Garrick Theatre, 13 March 1895. [G.B.S.]
    2. (1889).
    3. Céline Céleste (1814–82), a French dancer and an actress in melodrama, was popular in England and America.

on the commonplace but real substratum of ordinary drama in his works. Thus his power to provide Mrs Tanqueray with equally popular successors depends on his freedom from the illusion he has himself created as to his real strength lying in his acuteness as a critic of life. Given a good play, the stage effect of philosophy will pass with those who are no better philosophers than he; but when the play is bad, the air of philosophy can only add to its insufferableness. In the case of The Notorious Mrs Ebbsmith, the play is bad. But one of its defects: to wit, the unreality of the chief female character, who is fully as artificial as Mrs Tanqueray herself, has the lucky effect of setting Mrs Patrick Campbell free to do as she pleases in it, the result being an irresistible projection of that lady's personal genius, a projection which sweeps the play aside and imperiously becomes the play itself. Mrs Patrick Campbell, in fact, pulls her author through by playing him clean off the stage. She creates all sorts of illusions, and gives one all sorts of searching sensations. It is impossible not to feel that those haunting eyes are brooding on a momentous past, and the parted lips anticipating a thrilling imminent future, whilst some enigmatic present must no less surely be working underneath all that subtle play of limb and stealthy intensity of tone. Clearly there must be a great tragedy somewhere in the immediate neighborhood; and most of my colleagues will no doubt tell us that this imaginary masterpiece is Mr Pinero's Notorious Mrs Ebbsmith. But Mr Pinero has hardly anything to do with it. When the curtain comes down, you are compelled to admit that, after all, nothing has come of it except your conviction that Mrs Patrick Campbell is a wonderful woman. Let us put her out of the question for a moment and take a look at Mrs Ebbsmith.

To begin with, she is what has been called "a platform woman." She is the daughter of a secularist agitator: say a minor Bradlaugh. After eight years of married life, during which she was for one year her husband's sultana, and for the other seven his housekeeper, she has emerged into widowhood and an active career as an agitator, speaking from the platforms formerly occupied by her father. Although educated, well conducted, beautiful, and a sufficiently powerful speaker to produce a great effect in Trafalgar Square, she loses her voice from starvation, and has to fall back on nursing: a piece of fiction which shews that Mr Pinero has not the faintest idea of what such a woman's career is in reality. He may take my word for it that a lady with such qualifications woud be very much better off than a nurse; and that the plinth of the Nelson column, the "pitch" in the park, and the little meeting halls in poor parishes, all of which he speaks of with such an exquisitely suburban sense of their being the dark places of the earth, enter nowadays very largely into the political education of almost all publicly active men and women; so that the Duke of St Olpherts, when he went to that iron building in St Luke's, and saw "Mad Agnes" on the platform, might much more probably have found there a future Cabinet Minister, a lady of his own ducal family, or even a dramatic critic. However, the mistakes into which Mr Pinero has been led by his want of practical acquaintance with the business of political agitation are of no great dramatic moment. We may forgive a modern British dramatist for supposing that Mrs Besant, for example, was an outcast on the brink of starvation in the days when she graduated on the platform, although we should certainly not tolerate such nonsense from any intellectually responsible person. But Mr Pinero has made a deeper mistake. He has fallen into the common error of supposing that the woman who speaks in public and takes an interest in wider concerns than those of her own household is a special variety of the human species; that she "Trafalgar Squares" aristocratic visitors in her drawing room; and that there is something dramatic in her discovery that she has the common passions of humanity.

Mrs Ebbsmith, in the course of her nursing, finds a patient who falls in love with her. He is married to a shrew; and he proposes to spend the rest of his life with his nurse, preaching the horrors of marriage. Off the stage it is not customary for a man and woman to assume that they cannot cooperate in bringing about social reform without living together as man and wife: on the stage, this is considered inevitable. Mrs Ebbsmith rebels against the stage so far as to propose that they shall prove their disinterestedness by making the partnership a friendly business one only. She then finds out that he does not really care a rap about her ideas, and that his attachment to her is simply sexual. Here we start with a dramatic theme capable of interesting development. Mr Pinero, unable to develop it, lets it slip through his fingers after one feeble clutch at it, and proceeds to degrade his drama below the ordinary level by making the woman declare that her discovery of the nature of the man's feelings puts within her reach "the only one hour in a woman's life," in pursuance of which detestable view she puts on an indecent dress and utterly abandons herself to him. A clergyman appears at this crisis, and offers her a Bible. She promptly pitches it into the stove; and a thrill of horror runs through the audience as they see, in imagination, the whole Christian Church tottering before their eyes. Suddenly, with a wild scream, she plunges her hand into the glowing stove and pulls out the Bible again. The Church is saved; and the curtain descends amid thunders of applause. In that applause I hope I need not say I did not join. A less sensible and less courageous stage effect I have never witnessed. If Mr Pinero had created for us a woman whose childhood had been made miserable by the gloomy terrorism which vulgar, fanatical parents extract from the Bible, then he might fitly have given some of the public a very wholesome lesson by making the woman thrust the Bible into the stove and leave it there. Many of the most devoted clergymen of the Church of England would, I can assure him, have publicly thanked him for such a lesson. But to introduce a woman as to whom we are carefully assured that she was educated as a secularist, and whose one misfortune—her unhappy marriage—can hardly by any stretch of casuistry be laid to the charge of St Paul's teaching; to make this woman senselessly say that all her misfortunes are due to the Bible; to make her throw it into the stove, and then injure herelf horribly in pulling it out again: this, I submit, is a piece of claptrap so gross that it absolves me from all obligation to treat Mr Pinero's art as anything higher than the barest art of theatrical sensation. As in The Profligate, as in The Second Mrs Tanqueray, he has had no idea beyond that of doing something daring and bringing down the house by running away from the consequences.

I must confess that I have no criticism for all this stuff. Mr Pinero is quite right to try his hand at the higher drama; only he will never succeed on his present method of trusting to his imagination, which seems to me to have been fed originally on the novels and American humor of forty years ago, and of late to have been entirely starved. I strongly recommend him to air his ideas a little in Hyde Park or "the Iron Hall, St Luke's," before he writes his next play. I shall be happy to take the chair for him.

I should, by the way, like to know the truth about the great stage effect at the end of the second act, where Mrs Patrick Campbell enters with her plain and very becoming dress changed for a horrifying confexion apparently made of Japanese bronze wallpaper with a bold pattern of stamped gold. Lest the maker should take an action against me and obtain ruinous damages, I hasten to say that the garment was well made, the skirt and train perfectly hung, and the bodice, or rather waistband, fitting flawlessly. But, as I know nothing of the fashion in evening dresses, it was cut rather lower in the pectoral region than I expected; and it was, to my taste, appallingly ugly. So I fully believed that the effect intended was a terrible rebuke to the man's complaint that Mrs Ebbsmith's previous dress was only fit for "a dowdy demagogue." Conceive my feelings when everyone on the stage went into ecstasies of admiration. Can Mr Pinero have shared that admiration? As the hero of a recent play observes, "That is the question that torments me."[4]

A great deal of the performance is extremely tedious. The first twenty minutes, with its intolerable, unnecessary, and unintelligible explanations about the relationships of the characters, should be ruthlessly cut

4. Sergius in Shaw's Arms and the Man.

out. Half the stage business is only Mr Pinero's old "character actor" nonsense; and much of the other half might be executed during the dialogue, and not between the sentences. The company need to be reminded that the Garrick is a theatre in which very distinct utterance is desirable. The worrying from time to time about the stove should be dropped, as it does not in the least fulfil its purpose of making the Bible incident—which is badly stagemanaged—seem more natural when it comes.

Mr Hare, in the stalest of parts, gives us a perfect piece of acting, not only executed with extraordinary fineness, but conceived so as to produce a strong illusion that there is a real character there, whereas there is really nothing but that hackneyed simulacrum of a cynical and epigrammatic old libertine who has helped to carry on so many plots. Mr Forbes-Robertson lent himself to the hero, and so enabled him to become interesting on credit. Miss Jeffreys,[5] miraculously ill fitted with her part, was pleasant for the first five minutes, during which she was suggesting a perfectly different sort of person to that which she afterwards vainly pretended to become. The other characters were the merest stock figures, convincing us that Mr Pinero either never meets anybody now, or else that he has lost the power of observation. Many passages in the play, of course, have all the qualities which have gained Mr Pinero his position as a dramatist; but I shall not dwell on them, as, to tell the truth, I disliked the play so much that nothing would induce me to say anything good of it. And here let me warn the reader to carefully discount my opinion in view of the fact that I write plays myself, and that my school is in violent reaction against that of Mr Pinero. But my criticism has not, I hope, any other fault than the inevitable one of extreme unfairness.

I must change the subject here to say that Mr Clement Scott has been kind enough to let me know that he did not write the obituary notice which I ascribed to him throughout my recent utterance on the subject of the Censorship in these columns. Not that Mr Scott has changed his views on that subject. The continuity of his policy was strictly maintained by the actual writer of the article; so that the argument between us on that point remains, I am sorry to say, where it was. But as I have incidentally made it appear that Mr Scott wrote an anonymous obituary notice of his late friend, and made it the occasion for a defence of him against certain strictures of mine, I am bound not only to comply with Mr Scott's request to make it known that he did not write the article, but to express my sense of the very considerate terms in which he has pointed out my mistake, and to beg him to excuse it.

5. Ellis Jeffreys (1868–1943), sometimes listed as Ellice Jeffries.

THE CENSORSHIP OF PLAYS.
A TALK WITH MR BERNARD SHAW
C/QI (*Pall Mall Gazette*, 21 March 1895)

An omnibus journey to the vicinity of Fitzroy Square was rewarded by my finding Mr Bernard Shaw at home, writes our representative. Mounting two pair of stairs, I waited for him in a pleasant sitting room, where were many photographs and some charming old blue china in an antique cabinet. I had time to take note of Shirley and Jane Eyre,[1] standing cheek by jowl in a small bookcase with a play of Mr Wilde's. After some deprecatory observations upon himself as an authority in such matters, Mr Shaw said:

"I claim to have been the person who pointed out that the man selected as Examiner of Plays must inevitably be a Nobody."

"Why a Nobody?" I asked.

"Because the appointment of Somebody would have aroused a storm of indignation. If a man's a Somebody, his qualities are public property, and that means it is known that he is unfit to be the despot of the British drama. Now, Nobody's qualifications are unknown, and therefore people can imagine what they like."

"And the Examiner of Plays is of necessity a despot?"

"Necessarily. There's no appeal from his decision. I was once asked at the Playgoers' Club[2] if I could suggest a constitutional means of getting rid of him. I pointed out that the only means was to abolish the monarchy. A member of the club thereupon protested against my seditious language, and the subject dropped."

"What is your position, then, with regard to the Censorship? Do you object only to its present form, or do you want to have it abolished altogether?"

"I want" said Mr Shaw "to have it abolished altogether, root and branch; exterminated, annihilated. But, mind, if we are to have a censorship, I want Mr Redford[3] and the Lord Chamberlain. If we are to have a second Chamber I want the House of Lords. I want a notoriously arbitrary irresponsible veto, not a pseudo-democratic one."

"Then you are opposed to the suggestion of your friend, Mr Archer, that the London County Council should exercise the censorship?"

1. (1849 and 1847) by Charlotte Brontë (1816–55).
2. The Playgoers' Club, founded 1884, was an organization of theater devotées which invited actors and critics to be guest speakers.
3. George Alexander Redford (1846–1916) replaced E.F.S. Pigott as examiner of plays for the Lord Chamberlain.

"I am" replied Mr Bernard Shaw "most vehemently opposed to it, and I will tell you why. It would be found impossible in practice for a citizen of London to use his veto in such a fashion as to bear on the question of the censorship. For instance, probably the majority of the electors of Poplar do not agree with Mr McDougall's views on music halls any more than I do; but, if I were a Poplar elector, I should vote for Mr McDougall because his public services in other departments—such, for example, as the administration of our asylums—make it impossible to dispense with him on the single point of his Puritanism."[4]

"Then the democratic check, upon which Mr William Archer depends for his argument, is, in your view, a delusion?"

"Quite a delusion."

"You would have an authority elected for the purpose, a Theatre Board, just as we have a School Board?"

"That" returned Mr Shaw "would be the logical expedient, but it is obviously impossible; and even if it were possible, I should object to it."

"On what ground, Mr Shaw?"

"Well, I should answer, fundamentally on Mr Buchanan's ground, that the artist must be supreme in this matter."

"Do you mean to say that you would make him absolutely irresponsible?"

"No, I only claim the same freedom, as a playwright, that I already enjoy as an author. If I produce a pernicious play, let me be prosecuted for it, but dont let me be gagged by a Nobody."

"Or stifled by busybodies?"

"No busybody alive" replied Mr Shaw, with energy and emphasis, "can stifle a dramatist, that is to say, merely as a busybody. He must be an official, using the brute force of the State to curtail my liberty, on the assumption that I would make a bad use of it."

"But may he not be a better judge, Mr Shaw, of the use you are making of it than you yourself?"

"I see no reason to suppose so. If, however, a person of such extraordinary qualifications can be found, I submit that not only the censorship of the drama, but the government of the whole nation, and, if possible, of the entire universe, should be at once placed in his hands."

"In short," said I, "the real Censor is a Nobody, the ideal Censor is a God?"

"Precisely."

And beyond that Mr Shaw would not say one word on the censorship of plays.

---

4. John (later Sir John) McDougall (1844–1917) was a member of the London County Council. Among the committees on which he sat were Asylums and Theatres (including Music Halls). Honored for his work in behalf of the insane, he was also associated with the campaign for the purification of London Music Halls.

THE INDEPENDENT THEATRE REPENTS[1]
(*Saturday Review*, 23 March 1895)

The Independent Theatre is becoming wretchedly respectable. Nobody now clamors for the prosecution of Mr Grein under Lord Campbell's Act, or denounces myself and the other frequenters of the performances as neurotic, cretinous degenerates. This is not as it should be. In my barbarous youth, when one of the pleasures of theatregoing was the fierce struggle at the pit-door,[2] I learnt a lesson which I have never forgotten: namely, that the secret of getting in was to wedge myself into the worst of the crush. When ribs and breastbone were on the verge of collapse, and the stout lady in front, after passionately calling on her escort to take her out of it if he considered himself a man, had resigned herself to death, my hopes of a place in the front row ran high. If the pressure slackened I knew I was being extruded into the side eddies where the feeble and halfhearted were throwing away their chance of a good seat for such paltry indulgences as freedom to breathe and a fully expanded skeleton. The progressive man goes through life on the same principle, instinctively making for the focus of struggle and resisting the tendency to edge him out into the place of ease. When the Independent Theatre was started, its supporters all made for it, I presume—certainly I did— because it was being heavily squeezed. There was one crowded moment when, after the first performance of Ghosts, the atmosphere of London was black with vituperation, with threats, with clamor for suppression and extinction, with everything that makes life worth living in modern society. I have myself stood before the Independent footlights in obedience to my vocation (literally) as dramatic author, drinking in the rapture of such a hooting from the outraged conventional first-nighter as even Mr Henry James might have envied. But now that glory has departed to the regular theatres. My poor little audacity of a heroine who lost her temper and shook her housemaid has been eclipsed by heroines who throw the Bible into the fire. Mr Grein, no longer a revolutionist, is modestly bidding

1. A MAN'S LOVE, a Play in three acts, from the Dutch of J[an] C[ornelius] de Vos [(b. 1855), adapted (1890) by J. T. Grein and C. W. Jarvis]; and SALVÊ, a Dramatic Fragment in one act, by Mrs Oscar Beringer [Aimée Deniell, 1856–1936]. The Independent Theatre (Opéra Comique), 15 March 1895. [G.B.S.]

2. The door that leads to the rear of the ground floor of the auditorium, which was originally (and was so in Dublin during Shaw's youth) below the ground level. By the time Shaw wrote this, the old rows of pit seats near the orchestra in London theaters had been replaced by higher-priced stall seats and the term pit designated the more distant back rows.

for the position left vacant by the death of German Reed,[3] and will shortly be consecrated by public opinion as the manager of the one theatre in London that is not a real wicked Pinerotic theatre, and is, consequently, the only theatre in London that it is not wrong for good people to go to. His latest playbill is conclusive on this point. It begins with A Man's Love, from the Dutch of J. C. de Vos, and ends with Salvê, by Mrs Oscar Beringer. The first would be contemptuously rejected by Mr Hare as a sniveling, pietistic insult to the spirit of the age; and the second might without the least incongruity be played as a curtainraiser before Green Bushes or The Wreck Ashore.[4]

The defence to this grave disparagement will probably be that, in A Man's Love, the hero makes advances to his undeceased wife's sister, and that Salvê ends unhappily. I cannot allow the excuse. Any man, on the stage or off it, may make love to his sister-in-law without rousing the faintest sense of unexpectedness in the spectator. And when, as in Mr de Vos's play, the young lady tells him he ought to be ashamed of himself, and leaves the house without making her sister miserable by telling her why, the situation becomes positively triter than if he had not made love to her at all. There is only one Independent Theatre drama to be got out of such a theme; and that is the drama of the discovery by the man that he has married the wrong sister, and that the most earnest desire on the part of all concerned to do their duty does not avail against that solid fact. Such a drama occurred in the life of one of the greatest English writers of the XIX century,[5] one who was never accused by his worst enemies of being a loose liver. But Mr de Vos has not written that drama, or even pretended to write it. As to the unhappy ending of Salvê, unhappy endings are not a new development in the theatre, but a reversion to an older stage phase. I take it that the recently defunct happy ending, which is merely a means of sending the audience away in good humor, was brought in by the disappearance of the farce. Formerly you had The Gamester to begin with;[6] and then, when Beverley had expired yelling from the effects of swallowing some powerful mineral irritant, there was a screaming farce to finish with. When it suddenly occurred to the managers that for twentyfive years or so no experienced playgoer had ever been known to wait for the farce, it was dropped; and nothing was left in the bill except

---

3. Alfred German Reed (1847–95)—son of Mr. (Thomas, 1817–88) and Mrs. German Reed (née Priscilla Horton [1818–95], an American actress in mid-Victorian England), who had founded the German Reed entertainments, which parodied different styles of singing—continued in the old-fashioned but still popular tradition of his parents.

4. (1845) and (1830), melodramas by Buckstone.

5. Charles Dickens.

6. (1705) by Susannah Centlivre (1667–1723).

the play of the evening and a curtainraiser to keep the gallery amused whilst waiting for the plutocracy to finish their dinners and get down to their reserved seats. Still the idea of sending away the audience in a cheerful temper survived, and led to the incorporation of that function of the farce into the end of the play. Hence the happy ending. But in course of time this produced the same effect as the farce. The people got up and made for the doors the moment they saw it coming; and managers were reduced to the abject expedient of publishing in the program a request to the audience not to rise until the fall of the curtain. When even this appeal *ad misericordiam* failed, there was nothing for it but to abolish the happy ending, and venture on the wild innovation of ringing down the curtain the moment the play was really over. This brought back the old tragic ending of the farce days, which was of course immediately hailed, as the custom is whenever some particularly ghastly antiquity is trotted out, as the newest feature of the new drama.

So much then for the novelty of Mrs Beringer's idea of ending her little play by making the mother slay her long-lost cheeyild, and go mad then and there like Lucia di Lammermoor. Indeed, if Mrs Theodore Wright had struck up Spargi d'amaro pianto, with flute obbligato and variations, my old Italian operatic training would have saved me from the least feeling of surprise, though the younger generation would certainly have thought us both mad. The variations would have been quite in keeping with the bags of gold poured out on the table, and with the spectacle of a mother taking up the breadknife and transfixing her healthy young son full in the public view. Is it possible that Mrs Beringer has not yet realized that these mock butcheries belong to the babyhood of the drama? She may depend on it there is a solid reason for Hedda Gabler shooting herself behind the scenes instead of stabbing herself before them. In that, Ibsen shakes hands with the Greek dramatic poets just as clearly as Mrs Beringer, with her gory breadknife, shakes hands with the most infantile melodramatists of the Donizettian epoch. Salvê is not at all a bad piece of work of its naïve kind: indeed, except for a few unactable little bits here and there, it would merit high praise at the Pavilion or Marylebone the-atres;[7] but what, in the name of all thats Independent, has it to do with the aims of Mr Grein's society? To find any sort of justification for the performance I must turn to the acting: for let me say that I should consider Mr Grein quite in order in giving a performance of Robertson's Caste, followed by Box and Cox, if he could handle them so as to suggest fresh developments in stage art. Unfortunately, the management made an incomprehensible mistake in casting A Man's Love. It had at its dis-posal Miss Winifred Fraser and Miss Mary Keegan; and the two women's

7. The Marylebone Theatre, formerly the Pavilion Theatre, played melodramas.

parts in the play were well suited to their strongly contrasted personalities. Accordingly, it put Miss Keegan into the part which suited Miss Fraser, and Miss Fraser into the part which suited Miss Keegan. The two ladies did what they could under the circumstances; but their predicament was hopeless from the outset. The resultant awkwardness made the worst of the very clumsy devices by which the action of the play is maintained: impossible soliloquies, incidents off the stage described by people on it as they stare at them through the wings, and the like: all, by the way, reasons why the Independent Theatre should not have produced the work unless these crudities were atoned for by boldness or novelty in some other direction.

The two ladies being practically out of the question, the burden of the play fell upon Mr Herbert Flemming,[8] whose work presented a striking contrast to the sort of thing we are accustomed to from our popular "leading men." We all know the faultlessly dressed, funereally wooden, carefully phrased walking negation who is so careful not to do anything that could help or hinder our imaginations in mending him into a hero. His great secret is to keep quiet, look serious, and, above all, not act. To this day you see Mr Lewis Waller and Mr George Alexander struggling, even in the freedom of management, with the habits of the days when they were expected to supply this particular style of article, and to live under the unwritten law: "Be a nonentity, or you will get cast for villains," a fate which has actually overtaken Mr Waring because his efforts to suppress himself stopped short of absolute inanity. Only for certain attractive individual peculiarities which have enabled Mr Forbes-Robertson to place himself above this law occasionally as a personal privilege, our stage heroes would be as little distinguishable from oneanother as bricks in a wall. Under these circumstances, I was quite staggered to find Mr Flemming, though neither a comic actor nor a "character actor," acting—positively acting—in a sentimental leading part. He was all initiative, life, expression, with the unhesitating certainty of execution which stamps an actor as perfectly safe for every effect within his range. This amounted to a combination of the proficiency and positive power (as distinguished from negative discretion) of the old stock actor, with the spontaneity, sensitiveness, and touch with the cultivated nonprofessional world which the latest developments of the drama demand. Mr Flemming first made his mark here by his performances in certain Ibsen parts, and by his playing of the hero in Voss's Alexandra,[9] Stuttgart's pet tragedy. Yet when he appeared recently in such an absurd melodrama as Robbery Under Arms, he was as equal to the occasion as the veteran Mr Clarence

8. (1856–1908).
9. (1885) by Richard Voss (1851–1918).

Holt;[10] and his return without effort to the new style in A Man's Love is interesting as a sign that the new drama is at last beginning to bring in its harvest of technically efficient actors, instead of being, as it was at first, thrown into hands which were, with one or two brilliant exceptions, comparatively unskilled. The occasion was not a favorable one for Mr Flemming: quite the contrary. He was not on his mettle; he was in the unmistakable attitude of an experienced actor towards a play which he knows to be beyond saving; the extent to which he fell back on his mere stage habits shewed that he had refused to waste much time in useless study of a dramatically worthless character, and was simply using his professional skill to get through his part without damage to his reputation; and he was sometimes taken out of the character by his very free recourse to that frankly feminine style of play which is up to a certain point the secret, and beyond it the mere stage trick, of modern acting, and which is enormously effective in a man who, like Mr Flemming, is virile enough to be feminine without risk of effeminacy. Nonetheless this half-studied performance in a third-rate play at a depressing matinée (I was not present at the first performance) was striking enough to demand, at the present moment, all the attention I have given to it.

Mrs Theodore Wright, as the mother in Salvê, had no difficulty in touching and harrowing the audience to the necessary degree. Her acting, also, has the imaginative quality which the reviving drama requires. She made a mistake or two over Mrs Beringer's unactable bits, trying to worry some acting into them instead of letting them quietly slip by; but that was a fault on the right side; and one felt sorry for her sake when the breadknife reduced the little play to absurdity, and half spoiled the admirable effect of her playing in the scenes just before and after her journey of intercession. Happily, the audience did not mind the breadknife at all, and made her an ovation.

I must somewhat tardily acknowledge an invitation to witness a performance at the Royalty Theatre by a Miss Hope Booth,[11] a young lady who cannot sing, act, dance, or speak, but whose appearance suggests that she might profitably spend three or four years in learning these arts, which are useful on the stage. I watched her performance critically for ten minutes, and then went on to the Comedy Theatre, where I found Mr Grundy's Sowing the Wind[12] resuming its career. Miss Millard freshened the piece wonderfully: she did not, like Miss Emery, rise from a somewhat stolid average level to a forcible climax at one or two fixed points; but she

10. (1894) by Alfred Dampier (b. 1842) and Garnet Walch (1843–1913); Holt (1826–1903).
11. (1872–1933).
12. (1893).

was finer, swifter, and more responsive in feeling and utterance, and very like the ideal *ingénue* of the period indicated. Miss Millard is clearly a young lady with a future: a Mary Anderson[13] without that lady's solitary fault of being no actress. Mr Brandon Thomas repeated his old success by playing with genuine feeling as the father, and was forgiven accordingly for his Grundeian lecture on the sex question, "Sex against sex, &c.": the greatest nonsense possible. Mr Grundy can no more be cured of his tendency to hold forth in this fashion than of his habit of writing a play round a "situation," instead of developing a situation into a play; but in Sowing the Wind, the human interest of the old gentleman's heart and the young lady's good character, which is not the usual stage shoddy but a very real and worthy ladylikeness, keeps the piece alive. As to the rest of the acting, Miss Phillips plays excellently and refrains from caricature, in which all the rest indulge remorselessly. The only member of the original cast who shewed signs of staleness was Mr Sydney Brough,[14] who was possibly not in the vein on that particular evening.

L'ŒUVRE[1]
(*Saturday Review*, 30 March 1895)

M. Lugné-Poe[2] and his dramatic company called L'Œuvre came to us with the reputation of having made Ibsen cry by their performance of one of his works. There was not much in that: I have seen performances by English players which would have driven him to suicide. But the first act of Rosmersholm had hardly begun on Monday night when I recognized, with something like excitement, the true atmosphere of this most enthraling of all Ibsen's works rising like an enchanted mist for the first time on an English stage. There were drawbacks, of course. The shabbiness of the scenery did not trouble me; but the library of Pastor Rosmer got on my nerves a little. What on earth did he want, for instance, with

---

13. A beautiful American-born actress (1859–1940), popular in both America and England, but with limited talent, who retired from the theater after her marriage in 1889.
    14. (1868–1911).
    1. THÉÂTRE DE L'ŒUVRE DE PARIS. Performances at the Opéra Comique, London, of Ibsen's Rosmersholm and Master Builder, and of [Maurice] Maeterlinck's [1862–1949] L'Intruse [*The Intruder*, 1891] and Pelléas and Mélisande [1893], 25–30 March 1895. [G.B.S.]
    2. Aurélien-Marie Lugné-Poe (1869–1940).

Sell's World's Press?[3] That he should have provided himself with a volume of my own dramatic works I thought right and natural enough, though when he took that particular volume down and opened it, I began to speculate rather uneasily on the chances of his presently becoming so absorbed as to forget all about his part.[4] I was surprised, too, when it appeared that the Conservative paper which attacked the Pastor for his conversion to Radicalism was none other than our own Globe;[5] and the thrill which passed through the house when Rebecca West contemptuously tore it across and flung it down, far exceeded that which Mrs Ebbsmith sends nightly through the Garrick audiences. Then I was heavily taken aback by Mortensgard. He, in his determination to be modern and original, had entrusted the making-up of his face to an Ultra-Impressionist painter who had recklessly abused his opportunity. Kroll, too, had a frankly incredible wig, and a costume of which every detail was a mistake. We know Kroll perfectly well in this country: he is one of the many instances of that essential and consequently universal knowledge of mankind which enables Ibsen to make his pictures of social and political life in outlandish little Norwegian parishes instantly recognizable in London and Chicago (where Mr Beerbohm Tree, by the way, has just made a remarkable sensation with An Enemy of the People). For saying this I may be asked whether I am aware that many of our critical authorities have pointed out how absurdly irrelevant the petty parochial squabblings which stand for public life in Ibsen's prose comedies are to the complex greatness of public affairs in our huge cities. I reply that I am. And if further pressed to declare straightforwardly whether I mean to disparage these authorities, I reply, pointedly, that I do. I affirm that such criticisms are written by men who know as much of political life as I know of navigation. Any person who has helped to "nurse" an English constituency, local or parliamentary, and organized the election from the inside, or served for a year on a vestry, or attempted to set on foot a movement for broadening the religious and social views of an English village, will not only vouch for it that The League of Youth, An Enemy of the People, and Rosmersholm are as true to English as they can possibly be to Norwegian society, but will probably offer to supply from his own acquaintances originals for all the public characters in these plays.

3. *Sell's Dictionary of the World's Press and Advertiser's Reference* was a directory of daily, weekly, quarterly, half-yearly, and annual newspapers, magazines, and periodicals published in London and provincial cities in Great Britain, the colonies, and foreign countries.

4. This sentence was not an addition or revision in *Our Theatres in the Nineties* but appears in the original *Saturday Review* article. When Shaw wrote it, only one volume of one dramatic work by him had been published (1893): the first of his five plays thus far, *Widowers' Houses*.

5. An evening penny daily Conservative newspaper.

I took exception, then, to Kroll, because I know Kroll by sight perfectly well (was he not for a long time chairman of the London School Board?); and I am certain he would die sooner than pay a visit to the rector in a coat and trousers which would make a superannuated coffee-stall keeper feel apologetic, and with his haircutting and shampooing considerably more than three months overdue.

I take a further exception which goes a good deal deeper than this. Mlle Marthe Mellot, the clever actress who appeared as Rebecca West, Pelléas, and Kaia, played Rebecca in the manner of Sarah Bernhardt, the least appropriate of all manners for the part. Rebecca's passion is not the cold passion of the North—that essentially human passion which embodies itself in objective purposes and interests, and in attachments which again embody themselves in objective purposes and interests on behalf of others—that fruitful, contained, governed, instinctively utilized passion which makes nations and individuals great, as distinguished from the explosive, hysterical, wasteful passion which makes nothing but a scene. Now in the third and fourth acts of Rosmersholm, Mlle Mellot, who had played excellently in the first and second, suddenly let the part slip through her fingers by turning to the wrong sort of passion. Take, for example, the situation in the third act. Rosmer, who has hitherto believed that his wife was mad when she commited suicide, is now convinced (by Mortensgard) that she did it because he transferred his affection to Rebecca West. Rebecca, seeing that Rosmer will be utterly broken by his own conscience if he is left to believe that he is almost a murderer, confesses that it was she who drove the unfortunate wife to suicide by telling her certain lies. The deliberate character of this self-sacrifice is carefully marked by Ibsen both in Rebecca's cold rebuke to Kroll's attempt to improve the occasion by a gaol chaplain's homily, and in the scene with Madame Helseth in which she calmly arranges for her departure after the men have left her in horror. It was here that Mlle Mellot yielded to the temptation to have a tearing finish in the Bernhardt style. The confession became the mere hysterical incontinence of a guilty and worthless woman; the scene with Madame Helseth had to be spiced with gasps and sobs and clutches; and the curtain fell on applause that belonged not to Rosmersholm, but to Froufrou.[6] Rebecca West, therefore, still remains to be created in England. Her vicissitudes have already been curious enough to the student of acting. Miss Farr, the first to attempt the part here, played it as the New Woman, fascinated by Rebecca's unscrupulousness, asking amazed interviewers why such a useless Old Woman as Mrs Rosmer should not have been cleared out of Rosmer's way into the

---

6. (1869) by Henri Meilhac (1831–97) and Ludovic Halévy (1834–1908). Beginning 1888, Sarah Bernhardt played the role of Gilberte.

millrace, and generally combining an admirable clearness as to the logic of the situation with an exasperating insensibility to the gravity, or even the reality, of the issues. The result was that the point which Mlle Mellot has just missed was hit by Miss Farr, who, in spite of failures in whole sections of the play through want of faith in Rebecca's final phase of development, and in various details through the awkwardness of a somewhat amateurish attempt to find a new stage method for a new style of play, yet succeeded on the whole in leaving an impression of at least one side of Rebecca—and that the side which was then strangest—which has not been obliterated by any subsequent performance. A second attempt was made by Miss Elizabeth Robins; and from this a great deal was expected, Miss Robins having been remarkably successful in The Master Builder as Hilda Wangel, who is clearly the earlier Rebecca West of the "free fearless will." But that devastating stage pathos which is Miss Robbins's most formidable professional speciality, and which made her so heartrending in Alan's Wife, and so touching as Agnes in Brand, suddenly rose in Rosmersholm and submerged Rebecca in an ocean of grief. So that opportunity, too, was lost; and we still wait the perfect Rebecca, leaving Miss Farr with the honors of having at least done most to make us curious about her.

The performance of Maeterlinck's Pelléas and Mélisande, in which Mlle Mellot, who was altogether charming as Pelléas, brought down the house in the Rapunzel scene, settled the artistic superiority of M. Lugné-Poe's company to the Comédie Française. When I recall the last evening I spent at that institution, looking at its laboriously drilled upper-housemaid queens and flunkey heroes, and listening to the insensate, inhuman delivery by which every half Alexandrine is made to sound exactly like a street cry: when I compare this depressing experience with last Tuesday evening at the Théâtre de l'Œuvre, I can hardly believe that the same city has produced the two. In the Comédie Française there is nothing but costly and highly organized routine, deliberately used, like the ceremonial of a court, to make second rate human material presentable. In the Théâtre de l'Œuvre there is not merely the ordinary theatrical intention, but a vigilant artistic conscience in the diction, the stage action, and the stage picture, producing a true poetic atmosphere, and triumphing easily over shabby appointments and ridiculous incidents. Of course, this is so much the worse for the Théâtre de l'Œuvre from the point of view of the critics who represent the Philistinism against which all genuinely artistic enterprises are crusades. It is a stinging criticism on our theatre that ten years of constant playgoing in London seem to reduce all but the strongest men to a condition in which any attempt to secure in stage work the higher qualities of artistic execution—qualities which have been familiar for thousands of years to all art students—appears an aberration absurd enough to justify the reputable newspapers in publishing as criticism stuff which is mere streetboy guying. I am not here quarreling with dispraise of the Théâtre de l'Œuvre and M. Maeterlinck. I set the highest value on a strong Opposition both in art and politics; and if Herr Max Nordau were made critic of the Standard (for instance) I should rejoice exceedingly.[7] But when I find players speaking with such skill and delicacy that they can deliver M. Maeterlinck's fragile word-music throughout five acts without one harsh or strained note, and with remarkable subtlety and conviction of expression; and when I see these artists, simply because their wigs are not up to Mr Clarkson's English standard,[8] and the curtain accidentally goes up at the wrong time, denounced as "amateurs" by gentlemen who go into obedient raptures when M. Mounet-Sully[9] plasters his cheeks with white and his lips with vermillion, and positively howls his lines at them for a whole evening with a meaningless and discordant violence which would secure his dismissal from M. Lugné-Poe's company at the end of the first act, then: Well, what then? Shall I violate the sacredness of professional etiquet, and confess to a foreigner that the distinction some of our critics make between the amateur and the expert is really a distinction between a rich enterprise and a poor one, and has nothing in the world to do with the distinction made by the trained senses of the critic who recognizes art directly through his eyes and ears, and not by its business associations? Never! Besides, it would not be fair; no man, be he ever so accomplished a critic, can effectively look at or listen to plays that he really does not want to see or hear.

The interest taken in the performances culminated at that of The Master Builder on Wednesday. At first it seemed as if M. Lugné-Poe's elaborate and completely realized study of a self-made man breaking up, was going to carry all before it, a hope raised to the highest by the delightful boldness and youthfulness of Mlle Suzanne Desprès in the earlier scenes of Hilda. Unfortunately, Madam Gay as Mrs Solness was quite impossible; Miss Florence St John as Lady Macbeth would have

7. In 1893, Max Nordau (1849–1923) had published an attack on modern artists (including Ibsen), *Entartung*, translated two years later as *Degeneration*. At the time of this review, Benjamin Tucker (1854–1939), anarchist editor of *Liberty* (New York), asked Shaw to write a critique of it. He did so as an open letter to Tucker which appeared under the title "A Degenerate's View of Nordau" in the 27 July 1895 issue. Subsequently Shaw revised it as *The Sanity of Art*.

8. William (Willie) Clarkson (1865–1934) was considered the best wigmaker in England.

9. Jean Mounet-Sully (1841–1916), famous for tragic roles.

been better suited.[10] And in the second act, where Solness, the domina-
tor and mesmerizer of Kaia, becomes himself dominated and mesmer-
ized by the impulsive, irresponsible, abounding youth and force of Hilda,
Mlle Després lost ground, and actually began to play Kaia: Kaia prettily
mutinous, perhaps, but still Kaia. The last act, with a subjugated Hilda,
and a Mrs Solness, who was visibly struggling with a natural propensity
to cheerful commonsense, all but failed; and it was perhaps just as well
that an offensive Frenchman in the pit circle, by attempting to guy Mlle
Després, provoked a sympathetic demonstration from the decent members of the audience at the fall of the curtain. Probably he had been
reading the English papers.

Comparing the performance with those which we have achieved in
England, it must be admitted that neither Mr Waring nor Mr Waller were
in a position to play Solness as M. Lugné-Poe played him. They would
never have got another engagement in genteel comedy if they had worn
those vulgar trousers, painted that red eruption on their faces, and given
life to that portrait which, in every stroke, from its domineering energy,
talent, and covetousness, to its halfwitted egotism and crazy philandering
sentiment, is so amazingly true to life. Mr Waring and Mr Waller failed
because they were under the spell of Ibsen's fame as a dramatic magician, and grasped at his poetic treatment of the man instead of at the man
himself. M. Lugné-Poe succeeded because he recognized Solness as a
person he had met a dozen times in ordinary life, and just reddened his
nose and played him without preoccupation.

With Hilda it was a different matter. Except for the first five minutes, in
which she was so bright and girlish, Mlle Després could not touch Miss
Robins as Hilda Wangel. Whether Miss Robins would know Hilda if she
met her in the street, any more than Mr Waring would know Solness, I
doubt; but Miss Robins w a s Hilda; and it is an essential part of Hilda
that she does not realize her own humanity, much less that of the poor
wretch whom she destroys, or the woman whom she widows both before
and after his actual bodily death. This merciless insensibility, which gives
such appalling force to youth, and which, when combined with vivid
imagination, high brain power, and personal fascination, makes the
young person in search of the "frightfully thrilling" more dangerous than
a lion in the path, was presented by Miss Robins with such reality that
she made The Master Builder seem almost a one-part play. It was a great
achievement, the danger of which was realized here for the first time
perhaps, on Wednesday last, when Mlle Després failed to hold the house
at the critical moment. Had there been the most trifling bereavement in

10. Suzanne Després (Mme. Lugné-Poe, 1875–1951); Suzanne Gay. St John (1854–
1912) was a light opera singer.

the part to call forth the tear-deluge which swamped Rebecca and Mrs Lessingham,[11] Heaven only knows what would have happened to Miss Robins's Hilda. Happily the part is grief proof; and a Hilda who can even approach Miss Robins has not yet been seen in London.

Many thanks to the Independent Theatre for its share in bringing about the visit of the Théâtre de l'Œuvre to this country. Mr Grein could have rendered no better service to English art.

THE LIVING PICTURES
(*Saturday Review*, 6 April 1895)

I have been to the Living Pictures at the Palace Theatre. The moment Lady Henry Somerset[1] called public attention to the fact that they were obnoxious to the National Vigilance Association,[2] I resolved to try whether they would offend me. But this, like many other good resolutions of mine, remained unfulfiled until I was reminded of it by the address recently delivered by Mr William Alexander Coote,[3] the secretary of the Association, to the Church and Stage Guild, as reported verbatim in that excellent little paper the Church Reformer. In this address, Mr Coote said that he considered the Living Pictures "the ideal form of indecency." I at first supposed this to mean an ideally desirable form of indecency; but later on I found Mr Coote denouncing the pictures as "shameful productions, deserving the condemnation of all right-thinking people." That cured my procrastination, and incidentally brought five shillings into the till of the Palace Theatre. For I hurried off to see the Living Pictures at once, not because I wanted to wallow in indecency—no man in his senses would go to a public theatre with that object even in the most abandoned condition of public taste, privacy being a necessary condition of thoroughgoing indecency—but because, as a critic, I at once perceived that Mr Coote had placed before the public an issue of considerable

11. Elizabeth Robins played the title role in *Mrs Lessingham* (1894) by George Fleming (Constance Fletcher, b. 1858).

   1. Isabel, Lady Henry, Somerset (1851–1921) devoted herself to the promotion of temperance (she would become president of the Woman's Christian Temperance Union in 1898) and other moral causes.

   2. The National Vigilance Association was founded in 1885 to root out vice in both men and women.

   3. (1842–1919).

moment: namely, whether Mr Coote's opinion is worth anything or not. For Mr Coote is a person of real importance, active, useful, convinced, thoroughly respectable, able to point to achievements which we must all admit honorable to him, and backed by an Association strong enough to enable him to bring his convictions to bear effectively on our licensing authorities. But all this is quite compatible with Mr Coote being in artistic matters a most intensely stupid man, and on sexual questions something of a monomaniac.

I sat out the entire list of sixteen Living Pictures. Half a dozen represented naiads, mountain sprites, peris, and Lady Godiva, all practically undraped, and all, except perhaps Lady Godiva, who was posed after a well known picture by Van Lerius (who should have read Landor's imaginary conversation between Lady Godiva and her husband), very pretty.[4] I need hardly say that the ladies who impersonated the figures in these pictures were not actually braving our climate without any protection. It was only too obvious to a practised art critic's eye that what was presented as flesh was really spun silk. But the illusion produced on the ordinary music hall frequenter was that of the undraped human figure, exquisitely clean, graceful, and, in striking contrast to many of the completely draped and elaborately dressed ladies who were looking at them, perfectly modest. Many of the younger and poorer girls in the audience must have gone away with a greater respect for their own persons, a greater regard for the virtues of the bath, and a quickened sense of the repulsiveness of that personal slovenliness and gluttony which are the real indecencies of popular life, in addition to the valuable recreation of an escape for a moment into the enchanted land to which naiads and peris belong. In short, the living pictures are not only works of art: they are excellent practical sermons; and I urge every father of a family who cannot afford to send his daughters the round of the picture galleries in the Haymarket and Bond Street, to take them all (with their brothers) to the Palace Theatre.

This is how they struck me. Now let Mr Coote explain how they struck him.

"What cant to talk about 'Art' in connection with these living picture exhibitions! They are so obviously 'living.' Human nature is so very much in evidence. The nude as represented by the true artist on canvas never has the slightest tendency to demoralize. The artist's soul so consciously pervades the work that the beauty of form and pose hides that which would mar or vulgarize the picture. The subject is spiritualized, and becomes an inspiration for good and lovely thoughts. It is very different

4. Joseph Henri François Van Lerius (1823–76) drew *Lady Godiva* (1870); Walter Savage Landor (1765–1864) wrote a series of *Imaginary Conversations*, including *Leofric and Godiva* (1829).

with the 'living picture.' There is no art in it. Paradoxical as it may seem, there is no life in the living picture: it is even posed as a lifeless mass. There is a marked difference between the canvas or marble and the living picture, much to the disadvantage of the latter."

In discussing the above utterance, I do not want to take an unfair advantage of the fact that in writing about art I am a trained expert, and Mr Coote a novice. Mr Coote's object in undertaking a task so far beyond my powers as an explanation of the operation of the artist's soul is clearly to persuade us that he sees a distinction between an art that is false and an art that is true, and that it is his passionate devotion to the former that makes him so wroth with the latter. Let us see.

First, Mr Coote tells us that there is no art in the Palace picture. Well, I can quite believe that Mr Coote conceives that the posing and lighting of the figures so as to throw the figure into the required light and shadow is pure accident. Let me therefore make a suggestion. Let Mr Morton, the manager of the Palace, request Mr Dando,[5] the arranger of the pictures, to stand aside and entrust his functions for one night (on which a stall may be reserved for me at any price the management chooses to exact) to Mr William Alexander Coote. Let the entire resources of the establishment be placed absolutely under his direction; and let us then see whether he can take advantage of there being "no art in it" to produce a single tableau that will not be ludicrously and outrageously deficient in the artistic qualities without which Mr Dando's compositions would be hooted off the stage.

Now as to Mr Coote's assertion that the artist's soul spiritualizes his subject, and finds in it an inspiration for good and lovely thoughts. I can assure Mr Coote that he never made a greater mistake in his life. There are artists, and very able artists too, whose souls exactly resemble those of some members of the National Vigilance Association in debauching every subject, and finding in it an inspiration for obscene and unlovely thoughts. If Mr Coote, in the course of his next holiday, will travel from Padua to Mantua, and compare Giotto's[6] pictorial decoration of the arena chapel with Giulio Romano's decoration of the Palazzo Té, he will learn that the artist's soul can commune with the satyrs as well as with the saints. He need go no further than our own National Gallery to see the work of great artists who, like Paul Veronese, or Rubens,[7] materialize all their subjects and appeal to our love of physical splendor and vitality, exhibited under the same roof with those of the pre-Raphaelites (the real ones), whose works of art were also works of devotion. What is more, he will find the same artist

5. Charles Morton (1819–1904); Walter Pfeffer Dando (1852–1944).
6. (1266–1337).
7. Paolo Veronese (1528–88); Peter Paul Rubens (1577–1640).

expressing his devotional mood in one picture and his voluptuous mood in another; and if he will go as far as Venice—and the journey will be well worth his while—he can see there, in Titian's[8] Virgin of the Assumption, a union of the flesh and the spirit so triumphantly beautiful, that he will return abashed to the Church and Stage Guild, and apologize to them very humbly for having mixed up his account of his Vigilance stewardship with a sham lecture on a subject of which he does not know enough to be even conscious of his own ignorance.

Let me now help Mr Coote out of his difficulty. He admits by implication that works of art are above the law, and should be tolerated at all hazards. He then attempts to shew that the works he objects to are not "true art," and that therefore his hostility to them does not imply any hostility to Phidias and Raphael and the Royal Academy and so on. No person who really understands Art would make any such admission. A work of art is no more above the law than anything else. An old bridge may be a beautiful work of medieval art; but if it obstructs navigation, causes the river to silt up, or becomes insufficient for the traffic, it must come down. A palace may be a gem of the builder's art; but if its site is imperatively required for a better lighted and drained modern building, however ugly, or for a new thoroughfare, down it must come too. And if the living pictures, or M. Jules Garnier's illustrations to Rabelais, can be proved to be doing more harm than good, then Mr Coote is quite right to demand their suppression, works of art or no works of art.[9] Mr Coote is quite entitled to carry out all his aims, to forbid the circulation of cheap unexpurgated Shakespears; to make it a punishable offence for an artist to paint from a nude model; and to send the manager of the Palace Theatre to prison, if he can convince us that it is for the public interest that these things should be done. No plea as to the sacredness of art could in that case be admitted for a moment. If Mr Coote feels modest about claiming so much, let him consult the gentleman whom he describes as "that strange, peculiar, yet splendid man, Mr Stead." Mr Stead will, I think, as a matter of commonsense, at once assure him that I am right.

Having now got rid of the Art question, and pulled Mr Coote out of that morass on to solid ground, I am almost tempted to begin by exhorting him to go to his Bible, and ponder the saying "He which is filthy, let him be filthy still."[10] But no man in these islands ever believes that the Bible means what it says: he is always convinced that it says what he means;

8. Titian (Tiziano Vecelli, 1477–1576).

9. The National Vigilance Society seized a new edition of *Gargantua* (1534) and *Pantagruel* (1532) by François Rabelais (1494–1553), illustrated by Jules Arsène Garnier (1847–89).

10. Revelation, 22:11.

and I have no reason to hope that Mr Coote may be an exception to the rule. What, then, does Mr Coote found himself on? Apparently on this position, which I state in his own words: "Nothing in the management of our public entertainments can justify the exhibition of nude and semi-nude women as a means of amusement for a mixed audience." But why not, if the audience thinks the woman prettier and no less decent in that state than when fully draped, and she agrees with them; or if nudity or seminudity is appropriate to the character she is impersonating; or if she is performing athletic feats which skirts would hinder? Here is an instance which fulfils all three conditions. When Sir Augustus Harris first introduced at Covent Garden the Walpurgis ballet, which is one of the features of Gounod's Faust as performed at the Paris Grand Opéra, the dancer who impersonated Phryne dispensed with skirts altogether, and danced to the one exquisite tune that the ballet contains, in a costume which produced the illusion of nudity (I presume Mr Coote knows that it is only an illusion). She wore certain decorative ribbons, but no dress. She looked very graceful and quite modest; nobody in that huge theatre, which was crowded from floor to ceiling, objected in the least; it did not occur to us for a moment to complain of the absence of the ballet skirts and petticoats which make a woman look like an ostrich or a teetotum.

I will not pretend to misunderstand Mr Coote's objection to this. There are in the world a certain number of persons who, owing to morbid irritability in certain directions, are greatly incommoded by circumstances which are indifferent, or even agreeable, to the normal man. For instance, London is rather an ill-smelling place; and people with exceptionally acute noses suffer agonies on stagnant days when ordinary people notice nothing. Carlyle,[11] even in the comparative quietude of Chelsea, had to take special measures to keep the noises of the streets from his irritable ears; people with tender eyes have to resort to blue spectacles; humane people are made miserable by the treatment of our beasts of burden; and we find people oppressed by a special susceptibility to the dread inspired by hydrophobia, cholera, the Jesuits, the possibility of being damned, and many other contingencies which only occur to normal persons when they are out of health. On the other hand, we find people who are deficient in certain faculties: blind people, deaf people, colorblind people, people with no musical faculty, callous people, unsocial people, and so on. And we also find people in whom a deficiency in one respect is associated with an excess of sensitiveness in others. Now, it is quite impossible to legislate and administer with a view to the comfort of these abnormal people, even though there may, in so large a population as ours, be enough of any one variety of them to form an association and make a

11. Thomas Carlyle (1795–1881).

vigorous agitation. For instance, the Church will not modify the rite of communion because certain deplorable cases are on record in which the taste of the sacramental wine has brought on a ruinous attack of drink craze in the communicant. We do not suppress public meetings and abolish the right of free speech because people who are peculiarly suscep- tible to political excitement and the stimulus of platform oratory are led to behave foolishly and misuse their votes on such occasions. We do not prohibit "revivalist" prayer meetings because of the mischievously hysteri- cal condition into which weak people are thrown by them, a condition which the ignorant preacher glories in producing. We shall not stop the performances of The Notorious Mrs Ebbsmith because it has produced a case of suicide. In short, we shall not lead the life of invalids for the sake of a handful of unfortunate people to whom such a life is the only safe one.

The application of all this to Mr Coote's position is obvious. We have among us a certain number of people who are morbidly sensitive to sexual impressions, and quite insensible to artistic ones. We have certain sects in which such a condition is artificially induced as a matter of religious duty. Children have their affections repressed, and their susceptibility to emo- tional excitement nursed on sin, wrath, terror, and vengeance, whilst they are forbidden to go to the theatre or to amuse themselves with stories or "profane" pictures. Naturally, when such people grow up, life becomes to them a prolonged temptation of St Anthony. You try to please them by a picture which appeals to their delight in graceful form and bright warm color, to their share in the romance which peoples the woods and streams with sylphs and water maidens, to the innocent and highly recreative love of personal beauty, which is one of the great advantages of having a sex at all.[12] To your horror and discomposure, you are met with a shriek of "Nude woman: nude woman: police!" The one thing that the normal spectator overlooks in the picture is the one thing that St Anthony sees in it. Let me again put his protest in Mr Coote's own words: "Nothing can justify the exhibition of nude and seminude women as a means of amuse- ment for a mixed audience. They are shameful productions, and deserve the condemnation of all right-thinking people. The manager deserves, and should have, the immediate attention of the County Council." You remonstrate, perhaps, from the point of view of the artist. Mr Coote at once pleads: "They are so very obviously l i v i n g. Human nature is so very much in evidence." And there you have the whole of Mr Coote's pessimistic, misanthropic philosophy in two sentences. Human nature and the human body are to him nasty things. Sex is a scourge. Woman is

12. Among the many painters who drew this subject was Hieronymus Bosch (1450– 1516), c. 1500–1505.

a walking temptation which should be covered up as much as possible. Well, let us be charitable to Mr Coote's infirmity, and ask him, as kindly as may be, what good covering women up will do. Carmencita is covered up;[13] our skirt dancers are all petticoats; each of our serpentine dancers carries drapery enough to make skirts for a whole dozen schoolgirls. And yet they appeal far more to the sex instinct and far less to the artistic instinct than the Naiads and Phryne. There is only one solution of the difficulty; and that is for Mr Coote and those that sympathize with him to keep away from the Palace Theatre. Of course that will not protect them altogether. Every lownecked dress, every gust of wind that catches a skirt and reveals an ankle, perhaps every child in whom "human nature is in evidence" to the extent of a pair of sturdy little legs, may be a torment to the victims of this most pitiable of all obsessions. A quarrel with human nature admits of no fundamental remedy except the knife; and I should be sorry to see the members of the Vigilance Association cutting their own throats; they are useful and even necessary in keeping order among the people who suffer from morbid attractions instead of morbid repulsions. For it must not be forgotten that Mr Coote's error does not lie in his claim that the community shall suppress indecent exhibitions, but in his attempt to make nudity or seminudity the criterion of indecency. Perhaps I should qualify this statement of his position by limiting nudity to the female sex; for I notice that the seminudity which is quite a common spectacle in the case of male athletes is not complained of, though if there were anything in the Vigilance Association's view of such exhibitions as demoralizing, our women ought by this time to be much more demoralized than our men.

MR WILLIAM ARCHER'S CRITICISMS[1]
(Saturday Review, 13 April 15)

It is well that the critic should be criticized occasionally, not only by wrathful protests made in the heat of the moment while his notices are

13. Possibly a reference to a painting of the Spanish dancer La Carmencita (1892) by the American John Singer Sargent (1856–1925). Unlike the painting of Carmencita (c. 1878) by William Merritt Chase (1849–1916), also American, Sargent's has her bare shoulders covered with a shawl.
1. THE THEATRICAL "WORLD" OF 1894. By William Archer. With an introduction by G. Bernard Shaw, and a synopsis of the playbills of the year by Henry George Hibbert. London: Walter Scott. 1895. [G.B.S.]

still hot from the brain, but by a cool annual review of his whole year's worth. This involves republication in volume form of the critic's yearly output, which can only pretend to such honor in virtue of being more interesting than the day-before-yesterday's newspaper. Unhappily, most of our theatre criticism is born stale: it is hardly sufferable as news even on the day of its birth; and its republication would almost justify the immediate abolition of the freedom of the press. This is due solely to the fact that newspapers do not want good criticism and will not pay for it. Criticisms are like boots: the lowpriced ones are scamped, mechanical, and without individuality; the highpriced ones are sound, highly finished, and made by hand to the measure of their subject. Yet newspaper proprietors and editors who would not dream of walking down Bond Street in a pair of four-and-sixpenny boots, will buy criticism which would disgrace the humblest sort of oldfashioned police court reporter. I have known them to do the work themselves for the sake of getting into the theatre for nothing, or even let their wives do it on the same ground. In the provinces, dramatic criticism is incredibly bad. The great newspapers of Bradford, Manchester, Liverpool, and Birmingham are, of course, exceptions; but in the ordinary local paper the "criticism" is simply an advertisement which is not up to the level of literacy reached in the commonest kind of commercial correspondence. Sometimes there is a perceptible striving after perfection: for instance, instead of the stereotyped "Miss Smith was good as Juliet," you find "Miss Smith shewed talent as Juliet"; but this is rare. When there is a facetious sally, it signifies that the writer is a local wit who expects to be employed, as such, to write the topical allusions for the pantomime, and is consequently hopelessly enslaved by the manager. And the manager does not hesitate to use his power as a good advertisement customer to threaten and dictate freely if the notices are not of the most abjectly complimentary character. But nobody minds. If I were to suggest that an editor or proprietor who tolerates this sort of thing ought to be cut, expeled from his club, erased from the Institute of Journalists and treated generally like a runaway soldier, or a barrister who has sold his client, I should be poohpoohed for making an absurd fuss about nothing. Things are a little better in London; but even in London papers which ought to know better pay their critics meanly by the line, and make them feel that if they make themselves disagreeable to any person with the smallest influence (and the manager of a London theatre is always a person of some influence), they will probably be superseded by writers who may be depended on to give no trouble. I have repeatedly been urged by colleagues to call attention to some abuse which they themselves were not sufficiently strongly situated to mention; and I have twice had to resign very desirable positions on the critical staff of London papers of first-rate pretension: in one case because I was called upon as a recognized part of my duties to write corrupt puffs of the editor's personal friends, with full liberty, in return, to corruptly puff my own; and in the other, because my sense of style revolted against the interpolation in my articles of sentences written by the proprietor's wife to express her high opinion of artists, unknown to fame and me, who had won her heart by their hospitality.[2] I mention these matters because the public has hardly any suspicion of the extreme rarity of the able editor who is loyal to his profession and to his staff. Without such an editor even moderately honest criticism is impossible; and that is why the average critic is a man (or woman) who, not being allowed to say what he thinks, has long ago given up the habit of thinking as useless and dangerous. And the worst of it, from my particular point of view, is that dramatic criticism is one of the last departments of conduct on which even a tolerably scrupulous editor's conscience can be awaited. The same man who is particular and even fastidious about political and literary criticism often cannot be induced to regard criticism of the theatre as anything but pure news, and expects to have the fact that Mr Irving has produced a new play chronicled in exactly the same spirit as the fact that Her Majesty has taken a drive accompanied by the Princess Beatrice.

For quite a different set of limitations imposed on the critic by the economic conditions of modern theatrical enterprise, I must refer the reader to my excellent preface to Mr Archer's book. Mr Archer and I campaigned together for several years [in *The World*] under the editorship of the late Edmund Yates, who knew the value of genuine criticism, even musical criticism. We are intimate personal friends; and we roll each other's logs with a will. In my preface I imply that Mr Archer is the best of critics: in his epilogue he insists that there is nobody like G.B.S. If my judgment were not so exquisitely balanced that the slightest touch of personal bias upsets it, I should be a very poor critic: consequently my opinion as to Mr Archer's merits is flagrantly unjudicial. He has the reputation of being inflexible, impartial, rather cold but scrupulously just, and entirely incorruptible. I believe this impression is produced by his high cheekbones, the ascetic outline of his chin and jaw, and his habit of wearing a collar which gives his head the appearance of being wedged by the neck into a jampot. In reality he is half a dozen different men, most of them Scotch ancestors, especially a very grim Calvinist with an intense

2. In 1890, Shaw resigned as art critic of *Truth* because Horace Voules (1844–1909), its editor, wanted him to puff the work of Frederick Goodall (1822–1904), a Royal Academy artist whose work Shaw disliked. Henrietta Hodson (1841–1910), an actress married to Henry Labouchere (1831–1912), owner of *Truth*, may have been responsible for the efforts to puff Goodall. When Shaw's first review of a Royal Academy exhibition appeared in the *Observer* on 3 May 1891, unsigned, it was so cut, reedited, and filled with puffs by subeditor Clement Kinloch-Cooke (1854–1944) that Shaw resigned immediately.

belief in predestined damnation, who feels that it does the world good to be confronted with the hopelessness of its own doom. This particular Archer revels in La Tosca, in Alan's Wife, in Thérèse Raquin,[3] in Ghosts, and in Mrs Lessingham. To see some harmless and preferably rather lovable and interesting person annihilated with the most ferocious cruelty by the mere blind stroke of Fate positively edifies and exalts him. Then there is the sentimental Archer, a sniveling personage with whom I quarrel furiously, who gushes over Sweet Lavender,[4] weeps over Hedvig in The Wild Duck as "surely one of the loveliest characters in fiction," will blubber copiously (I prophesy) over Little Eyolf, and responds like an opening flower to the Amelia strain in his beloved Thackeray (an author I cannot abide).[5] These are the two extremes of Archer; and I rejoice that 1894 did not produce a play capable of fully bringing out the qualities of either of them. There are several intermediate Archers, all of them in evidence in this volume: Archer the humorist; Archer the dialectician (another Scotch Archer), gravely and patiently straightening out the argument of A Bunch of Violets[6] for Mr Grundy, as if the law of England for the next two centuries depended on the integrity of his logic; Archer the Cadi, sternly bastinadoing Mr Clement Scott for not seeing Ibsen's jokes; Archer the moralist, sermonizing me, in what I take to be the most shockingly bad criticism ever penned, for "dwelling on the seamy side of human nature to the exclusion of all else"; Archer the beglamored lover of literature and the theatre; and, finally, Archer the critic.

As I have said, I am no judge of Archer the critic, and can merely testify that he is honest, sober, careful, trustworthy, skilful, hardworking, and has been for many years in his present situation: all of which, though disgustingly prosaic, has more to do with the making of literary reputations than the public imagines. I shall confine myself here to the Archer whom I mentioned last but one, the Archer who describes himself as "born with an instinctive, unreasoning, unreasonable love for the theatre, the place of light and sound, of mystery and magic, where, at the stroke of the prompter's bell, a new world is revealed to the delighted sense." This is the Archer who has often told me that I have no love of art, no enjoyment of it, only a faculty for observing performances, and an interest in the intellectual tendency of plays. At first I thought this ridiculous; but there is always something in what he says; and I cannot deny that though I was for years a professional critic of books, for years more of pictures,

---

3. Zola's dramatization (1873) of his novel (1867), translated (1891) by Teixeira de Mattos, assisted by George Moore.
4. (1888) by Pinero.
5. A character in Vanity Fair (1847–48), whom Shaw considered insufferably cloying.
6. (1894).

and for yet more years of music, I go to no picture galleries now in London, I attend no concerts, and I read no current literature. Put an end to my professional business in the theatre, and I shall stop going there. Put an end to Archer's, and he will still, as he says, "find a melancholy fascination in the glare of the footlights." For him there is illusion in the theatre: for me there is none. I can make imaginary assumptions readily enough; but for me the play is not the thing, but its thought, its purpose, its feeling, and its execution. And as most modern plays have no thought, and are absurdly vulgar in purpose and feeling, I am mainly interested in their execution. But in these criticisms by Mr Archer (I must really remember my manners) there is little that is memorable about the execution; and that little has reference solely to its effect on the illusion. Even those pages in which, because they deal with such famous executants as Duse, Bernhardt, Rehan, and Calvé, the critic is compelled to take the execution as his main theme, he still makes the congruity of the artist's performance with the illusion of the story his criterion of excellence in the acting. In a very interesting comparison of Duse's Santuzza in Cavalleria Rusticana with Calvé's,[7] he declares that "the instinct of the world assigns a higher rank to pure mimetics than to even the highest so-called lyric acting." Now I confess that even to me the illusion created by Duse was so strong that the scene comes back to me almost as an event which I actually witnessed; whereas Calvé's performance was unmistakably an opera at Covent Garden. Looking at Duse, I pitied Santuzza as I have often pitied a real woman in the streets miserably trying, without a single charm to aid her, to beg back the affection of some cockney Turiddu. But who has ever seen in the streets anything like Calvé's Santuzza, with her passion, her beauty, her intensity, her singing borne aloft by an orchestra? To Mr Archer, this is the condemnation of Calvé's performance and the justification of Duse's. Every element, even though it be an element of artistic force, which interferes with the credibility of the scene, wounds him, and is so much to the bad. To him acting, like scenepainting, is merely a means to an end, that end being to enable him to make believe. To me the play is only the means, the end being the expression of feeling by the arts of the actor, the poet, the musician. Anything that makes the expression more vivid, whether it be versification, or an orchestra, or a deliberately artificial delivery of the lines is so much to the good for me, even though it may destroy all the verisimilitude of the scene. I do not for a moment set up this critical attitude of mine as standing to Mr Archer's

7. A French-born soprano, famous for her dramatic ability, Emma Calvé (1858–1942) performed Santuzza in the opera *Cavalleria Rusticana* (1890) by Pietro Mascagni (1863–1945). The great Italian actress Eleonora Duse (1859–1924) played Santuzza in the drama (1884) by Giovanni Verga (1840–1922), on which the opera is based.

in the relation of the right attitude to the wrong attitude. I only introduce it to make his own intelligible by contrast. Once his attitude is caught, and his sensitiveness to literature, which he calls "the divinest emanation of the human spirit" taken into account, his criticism becomes perfectly consistent, and its charm is seen to be a genuine imaginative quality which is quite independent of the adroit turn and fine intellectual texture of his sentences.

I had intended to devote this article almost entirely to my own preface; but I find myself with only space enough left to assure those gentlemen who are accusing me of advocating a *régime* of actress-manageresses, that I have advocated nothing at all. I have described the economic conditions of modern theatrical enterprise, with the results they have produced and seem likely to produce in the future. Among these last I enumerate the actress-manageress. I do not advocate her introduction, I simply announce her arrival. To state that she is "my remedy" for the state of things I have described is about as reasonable as to describe silence as Hamlet's remedy for death.

TWO BAD PLAYS[1]
(*Saturday Review*, 20 April 1895)

Last Saturday was made memorable to me by my first visit to the Adelphi Theatre. My frequent allusions to Adelphi melodrama were all founded on a knowledge so perfect that there was no need to verify it experimentally; and now that the experiment has been imposed on me in the course of my professional duty, it has confirmed my deductions to the minutest particular.

Should anyone rush to the conclusion hereupon that my attitude towards the Adelphi Theatre is that of a superior person, he will be quite right. It is precisely because I am able to visit all theatres as a superior person that I am entrusted with my present critical function. As a superior person, then, I hold Adelphi melodrama in high consideration. A really good Adelphi melodrama is of first-rate literary importance, because

---

1. THE GIRL I LEFT BEHIND ME [1893]. A Drama in four acts. By Franklin Fyles [1847–1911] and David Belasco [1853–1931]. Adelphi Theatre, 13 April 1895. DELIA HARDING. By Victorien Sardou. Adapted by J. Comyns Carr. Comedy Theatre, 17 April 1895. [G.B.S.]

it only needs elaboration to become a masterpiece. Molière's Festin de Pierre and Mozart's Don Juan are elaborations of Punch and Judy, just as Hamlet, Faust, and Peer Gynt are elaborations of popular stories. Unfortunately, a really good Adelphi melodrama is very hard to get. It should be a simple and sincere drama of acting and feeling, kept well within that vast tract of passion and motive which is common to the philosopher and the laborer, relieved by plenty of fun, and depending for variety of human character, not on the high comedy idiosyncrasies which individualize people in spite of the closest similarity of age, sex, and circumstances, but on broad contrasts between types of youth and age, sympathy and selfishnesss, the masculine and the feminine, the serious and the frivolous, the sublime and the ridiculous, and so on. The whole character of the piece must be allegorical, idealistic, full of generalizations and moral lessons; and it must represent conduct as producing swiftly and certainly on the individual the results which in actual life it only produces on the race in the course of many centuries. All of which, obviously, requires for its accomplishment rather greater heads and surer hands than we commonly find in the service of the playhouse.

The latest Adelphi melodrama, The Girl I Left Behind Me, is a very bad one. The only stroke in it that comes home is at the close of the second act, where the heroine sends her soldier lover, who has been accused of cowardice, off on a dangerous duty, and tells him that she loves him. The authors, I need hardly say, did not invent this situation, nor did they freshen it or add anything to it; but they at least brought it off without bungling it, and so saved the piece from the hostility of that sceptical spirit which is now growing among first-night audiences in a very marked degree. This is an inevitable reaction against the artificialities, insincerities, and impossibilities which form about three fourths of the stock in trade of those playwrights who seek safety and success in the assumption that it is impossible to underrate the taste and intelligence of the British public. But there is a profound error in this policy. It is true that the public consists largely of people who are incapable of fully appreciating the best sort of artistic work. It is even true that in every audience, especially on first nights, there is an appreciable number of persons whose condition is such that—to turn Tennyson's shallow claptrap into a terrible truth—they needs must hate the highest when they see it. But why should we credit these unhappy persons with that attribute of the highest character, the power of liking what pleases them, of believing in it, of standing by those who give it to them? For the most part they never enjoy anything; they are always craving for stimulants, whereas the essence of art is recreation; let their flatterer slip, as he always does sooner or later, and they are at his throat mercilessly before he can recover himself. But if you speak in their hearing as the great men speak (which is easy enough if you happen to be a great man), then you will find that their speciality is self-torture, and that they are always hankering, in spite of themselves, after their own boredom and bewilderment, driven, probably, by some sort of uneasy hope that Ibsen or Wagner or some other gigantic bore may exorcise the devils which rend them. The fact is, there is nothing the public despises so much as an attempt to please it. Torment is its natural element: it is only the saint who has any capacity for happiness. There is no greater mistake in theology than to suppose that it is necessary to lock people into hell or out of heaven. You might as well suppose that it is necessary to lock a professional tramp into a public house or out of a Monday popular concert, on the ground that the concert is the better and cheaper place of the two. The artist's rule must be Cromwell's: "Not what they want, but what is good for them." That rule, carried out in a kindly and sociable way, is the secret to success in the long run at the theatre as elsewhere.

My strong propensity for preaching is, I fear, leading me to deal with The Girl I Left Behind Me in rather too abstract a fashion. But it is only in its abstract bearing that the play provides interesting material to the critic. Instead of being natural and sincere, it is artificial and sanctimonious. The language, which should be vividly vernacular, is ineptly literary. Its fun runs too much on the underclothing of the ladies, which they tear up to make bandages for wounds, or offer, without detachment, to be used by gentlemen at a loss for towels after washing. The characters, instead of being consistent and typical, are patched and rickety, the author's grip constantly slipping from them. The villain and coward of the piece punches the hero's head with pluck and promptitude in the first act, lapses into abject poltroonery in the second, and in the third faces without concern a military emergency which drives all the rest into hysterical desperation. The hero, assaulted as aforesaid, ingloriously brings down the curtain with a stage villain's retort "You shall rrepent—thiss—bblow," and subsequently becomes the sport of circumstances, which turn out happily for him without much aid from himself. As to Kennion, the sympathetic general, I cannot believe that even in the army so incapable a man could rise to high command. It is, of course, usual on the stage for all army commanders to be superseded at critical moments by their daughters; but still there is no good reason why they should not have moments of efficiency when nothing but routine business is in hand. Private Jones, who is cordially received by his officer when he describes, with an air of conscious merit, how he has just run away on being actually fired at by the enemy, and who calmly quits his post as sentry (at a stockade which may be surprised at any moment) to sit down beside his sleeping lady love, and is supported in that proceeding by the general against a not unnatural remonstrance from his lieutenant: Private Jones is certainly consistent; but what he is consistent with is not himself—for as an individual human being he has no credible existence—but the trained incapacity of the Adelphi audience to understand true military valor. Instead of being, as he should be in a popular melodrama, a typically good soldier, he is a mere folly of the ignorant civil imagination. There is also a medical man, an army surgeon, who makes love to a girl of sixteen by way of comic relief. He relaxed the tension of the third act very happily by a slight but astonishingly effective alteration of a single syllable in the author's text. In the agony of the siege, when all hope was gone, he sat down with heroic calmness to write two documents: one a prescription which there was no apparent means of getting compounded, and the other a farewell—I did not quite catch to whom—probably to his mother. The last touching words of this communication were prefaced by the author with the sentence "I will add a postscript." The doctor, however, adroitly substituted "I will add a postcard," and sent the audience, just at the moment when their feelings could bear no further harrowing, into shrieks of refreshing laughter.

The third act, by the way, is an adaptation of the Relief of Lucknow,[2] which, as a dramatic situation, is so strong and familiar that it is hardly possible to spoil it, though the authors have done their best. The main difficulty is the foreknowledge of the hopelessly sophisticated audience that Mr Terriss will rush in at the last moment, sword in hand, and rescue everybody. The authors' business was to carry us on from incident to incident so convincingly and interestingly as to preoccupy us with the illusion of the situation sufficiently to put Mr Terriss out of our heads. Messrs Fyles and Belasco have not been equal to this. They have lamely staved off Mr Terriss for the necessary time by a flabbily commonplace treatment of the question of killing the women to save them from the Indians, and by bringing in the Indian chief's daughter to die in the stockade at the instant when the sound of her voice would have won quarter for the garrison. This is ill contrived, and only passes because the explanation is deferred until the last act, which is so transcendently imbecile that an absurdity more or less does not matter. As to the heroine, who had to kneel in the middle of the stage and rave her way through the burial service whilst her father, the general, hopped about, pulling horrible faces, and trying to make up his mind to shoot her, she was so completely out of the question from any rational human point of view, that I think the effort to impersonate her temporarily unhinged Miss

2. Dion Boucicault, *Jessie Brown, or The Relief of Lucknow* (1858).

Millward's[3] reason; for when the rescue came, and she had to wave the American flag instead of expressing her feelings naturally, she all but impaled the general on it in a frightful manner. Miss Millward and Mr Terriss and the rest of the company must bear with my irreverent way of describing the performance. I quite appreciate their skill, which is perhaps more indispensable for nonsense of this kind than for plays good enough to be comparatively "actor-proof"; but the better the skill, the more annoying it is to see it nine tenths wasted.

All the same, the evening was not a dull one. The play is not good drama, nor good melodrama; but it is tolerable pastime. I have spun out my criticism of it in order to leave as little room as possible for another play which was not tolerable even as pastime. When Mr Comyns Carr came before the curtain at the end of Sardou's Delia Harding at the Comedy Theatre on Wednesday, I found myself instinctively repeating the words of Sam Weller "You rayther want somebody to look after you, sir, ven your judgment goes out a wisitin'." Delia Harding is the worst play I ever saw. Taking it as a work bearing the same relation to the tastes of the upper middle class as the Adelphi drama to those of the lower middle class, I declare enthusiastically in favor of the Adelphi. Sardou's plan of playwriting is first to invent the action of his piece, and then to carefully keep it off the stage and have it announced merely by letters and telegrams. The people open the letters and read them, whether they are addressed to them or not; and then they talk either about what the letters announce as having occurred already or about what they intend to do tomorrow in consequence of receiving them. When the news is not brought by post, the characters are pressed into the service. Delia Harding, for instance, consists largely of the fashionable intelligence in Bellagio. As thus: "Stanley French arrived in Bellagio this morning," "Mr Harding will arrive in Bellagio tomorrow afternoon," "Miss Harding lives in that villa on the lake," "Sir Christopher Carstairs will remain here for another month at least," "This is my brother, Sir Arthur Studley," "Janet: we shall pack up and leave tomorrow morning," &c., &c., the person addressed invariably echoing with subdued horror "This morning!" "To-morrow afternoon!" "In t h a t villa!" and so on. The whole business was so stale, so obviously factitious, so barrenly inept, that at last the gallery broke out into open derision, almost as if they were listening to a particularly touching and delicate passage in a really good play. As for me, I felt ashamed and remorseful. The time has now come for pity rather than vengeance on the poor old "well-made play." Fifteen years ago I was almost alone in my contempt for these clumsy booby traps. Nowadays an actor cannot open a letter or toss off somebody else's glass of poison

---

3. Jessie Millward (1861–1932), William Terriss's leading lady and mistress.

without having to face a brutal outburst of jeering. At the Comedy on Thursday, some low fellow shouted out "Rats!" in the middle of the second act. Why was he not removed by the police? Such a step would be highly popular in the gallery: ninetynine out of every hundred people in it are incommoded by rowdyism, and are only too glad to be protected from neighbors who cannot express their disapproval or approval decently. At political meetings the public is not only allowed but expected to exercise a freedom of comment and interruption which no sane person would propose to tolerate in a theatre; but of late first nights have been disturbed by interruptions which would expose the interrupter to serious risk of a remarkably summary expulsion from a political meeting. Besides, public speakers are helped by interruptions: they deliberately provoke them for the sake of an effective retort. But the actor is helpless: he must not say a word that is not set down for him; and the nature of his work makes it terribly easy for any half drunk fool to cruelly disconcert and annoy him. Even the applause on first nights, the receptions and exit demonstrations, are silly enough: the rule ought to be silence whilst the curtain is up and as much noise as you please when it is down. But that is a matter of taste and custom rather than of police. Where the police ought to come in without mercy is in the case of offensive and disorderly remarks or exclamations shouted at the stage during the performance. One or two well chosen examples pursued to the police court would settle the matter for the next ten years.

The acting of Delia Harding calls for no special notice. Mr Mackintosh, who appeared as Stanley French, was warmly received.[4] His acting was not lacking in force; but his gesture and facial expression were grotesque and caricatured, though there was nothing in the part to give occasion for such extravagant handling.

SPANISH TRAGEDY AND ENGLISH FARCE[1]
(Saturday Review, 27 April 1895)

There is somewhere in Froissart a record of a hardy knight who discovered, as most men do in their middle age, that "to rob and pill is a good

4. William Mackintosh (1855–1929).
1. MARIANA [1892] and THE SON OF DON JUAN [1892]. By José Echegaray [1832–1916]. Translated from the Spanish by James Graham. Two volumes of the Cameo Series. London: [T.] Fisher Unwin. 1895. THE LADIES' IDOL. A new and original farcical comedy in three acts. By Arthur Law [1844–1913]. Vaudeville Theatre, 18 April 1895. [G.B.S.]

life."[2] When Mr Fisher Unwin sent me The Son of Don Juan I began at the end, as my custom is (otherwise I seldom reach the end at all), and found the following:

> LAZARUS (*speaking like a child, and with the face of an idiot*). Mother—the sun—the sun; give me the sun. For God's sake— for God's sake—for God's sake, mother, give me the sun.

To a person familiar with Ibsen's Ghosts, this was sufficient to establish a warm interest in an author who, like Froissart's knight, takes his goods so boldly where he finds them. I had never heard of José Echegaray before; but I soon learnt, from Mr Graham's sketch of his life, that he is a celebrated Spanish dramatist, and that it will be decorous for me in future to pretend to know all about him. To tell the truth, I wish I had some other authority than Mr Graham to consult; for though I have no excuse for questioning the entire trustworthiness of the little memoir he has prefixed to The Son of Don Juan, I can hardly bring myself to believe more than half of it. No doubt Echegaray is a greater physicist than Newton, and a greater mathematician than De Morgan and Professor Karl Pearson rolled into one.[3] Perhaps he really did walk out of a drawing room ignorant of a word of German, and presently return a master of that intractable tongue, and intimate with the secrets of Hegel[4] and all the other philosophers of the Fatherland. And why should there be any difficulty in believing in that discussion on fencing, which again made him leave the room, only to come back so consummate a swordsman that no professional in Madrid could as much as keep hold of his foil when confronted with him? And yet, somehow, I dont believe it. It is all the fault of that unfortunate musical criticism which I practised so long and assiduously. A musical critic gets supplied gratuitously with biographies of distinguished artists, compiled by musical agents or other experts in fiction, and circulated to the press and to persons with whom the artist desires to do business. These biographies seldom appear among the books of reference in first-rate libraries. They all contain at least two anecdotes, one to illustrate the miraculous powers of their hero's brain, and another to exhibit his courage and dexterity in personal combat. Mind, I do not say these anecdotes are untrue; I simply confess apologetically that I never find myself able to believe them. When I receive

---

2. *Chronicles of England, France, Spain, Portugal, Scotland, Brittany, Flanders, and other places adjoining* (1400) by Jean Froissart (1337–1410).

3. Sir Isaac Newton (1642–1727); Augustus De Morgan (1806–71); Karl Pearson (1857–1936).

4. Georg Wilhelm Friedrich Hegel (1770–1831).

from an agent or a bookseller a life of Sarasate, or Mr Edison,[5] or any other celebrated person, I try to believe as much of it as I can; and the breakdown of my faith must not be taken as a breakdown of the celebrated person's credit. Besides, after all, Mr Graham's memoir of Echegaray may not mean anything so very staggering. There is something momentous at first sight in the statement that "the first three years of the dramatist's life were passed in the capital of Spain"; but now I come to think of it, the first three years of my life (and more) were passed in the capital of Ireland, which was a much harder trial. Again, the attention he gave to "the infinitesimal calculus, theoretical and applied mechanics, hydrostatics, curve tracing, descriptive geometry and its applications, solid geometry, and so on into the dimmest heights of science," might have happened to many a university don. I remember once buying a book entitled How to Live on Sixpence a Day, a point on which at that time circumstances compelled me to be pressingly curious. I carried out its instructions faithfully for a whole afternoon; and if ever I have an official biography issued, I shall certainly have it stated therein, in illustration of my fortitude and self-denial, that I lived for some time on sixpence a day. On the whole, I am willing to take Mr Graham's word for it that Echegaray is, apart from his capacity as a dramatic poet, an exceptionally able man, who, after a distinguished university career, turned from the academic to the political life; attained Cabinet rank, with its Spanish inconveniences of proscription and flight at the next revolution; and in 1874, being then fortytwo years of age, and in exile in Paris, took to writing plays, and found himself famous in that line by the time his political difficulties had settled themselves.

As a dramatist, I find Echegaray extremely readable. Mr Graham has translated two of the most famous of his plays into a language of his own, consisting of words taken from the English dictionary, and placed, for the most part, in an intelligible grammatical relation to oneanother. I say for the most part; for here and there a sentence baffles me. For example: "The hall is approached by two or three saloons, whether in front of it, whether in converging lines, but in such a fashion that they are partly visible." This is a hard saying, which I humbly pass on to the stage-manager in the hope that he may be able to make more out of it than I can. Happily, the dialogue is pellucid as to its meaning, even where it is least vernacular. If Mrs Patrick Campbell, for instance, plays Mariana (and she might do worse: it would be a far wiser choice than Juliet), I shall, if she uses Mr Graham's translation, listen eagerly to the effect on

5. Pablo de Sarasate (1844–1908), Spanish violinist; Thomas Alva Edison (1847–1931), Scottish-born American whose inventions included the phonograph and the electric light.

the audience of such a speech as "The sickness of the journey has not left me. I suspect that I am going to have a very violent megrim." I fear it is useless to pretend to accept Mr Graham's work as a translation after this: it is clearly only a crib, though in some of the burning passages it rises to considerable force and eloquence. In such passages the full meaning can be gathered from the words alone; for most nations express themselves alike when they are red-hot; but in passages of comedy the word is often nothing, and the manner and idiom everything, in proof whereof I will undertake to recast any scene from, say, The School for Scandal, in such a manner that without the least alteration of its meaning it will become duller than an average sample of the evidence in a bluebook. Therefore, as I do not know a word of Spanish, I can only guess at the qualities which have eluded Mr Graham's crib.

Echegaray is apparently of the school of Schiller, Victor Hugo, and Verdi: picturesque, tragic to the death, shewing us the beautiful and the heroic struggling either with blind destiny or with an implacable idealism which makes vengeance and jealousy points of honor. Mariana is a lineal descendant of Ruy Blas or Don Carlos.[6] In The Son of Don Juan, the modern scientific culture comes in, and replaces the "villain" of the older school, the Sallustio or Ruy Gomez,[7] by destiny in the shape of hereditary disease. In spite of the line "Give me the sun, mother," for which Echegaray acknowledges his indebtedness to Ibsen, his treatment of the Ghosts theme is perfectly original: there is not in it a shadow of the peculiar moral attitude of Ibsen. Echegaray remorselessly fixes all the responsibility on Don Juan (Alving), who is as resolutely vicious as Shelley's Count Cenci. Ibsen, on the contrary, after representing Mrs Alving as having for years imputed her late husband's vices to his own wilful dissoluteness, brings home to her the conviction that it was really she herself and her fellow Puritans who, by stamping men and women of Alving's temperament into the gutter, and imposing shame and disease on them as their natural heritage, had made the ruin into which Alving fell. Accordingly, we have those terrible scenes in which she desperately tries to reverse towards the son the conduct that was fatal to the father, plying Oswald with champagne and conniving at his intrigue with his own half-sister. There is not the slightest trace of this inculpation of respectability and virtue in The Son of Don Juan. Indeed, had Echegaray adapted Ibsen's moral to the conditions of domestic life and public opinion in Spain, the process would have destroyed all that superficial re-

6. (1838) by Hugo and (1787) Schiller, respectively.
7. Sallustio is a character in Ruy Blas, Ruy Gomez in Verdi's Ernani and Hugo's Hernani, on which Ernani is based.

semblance to Ghosts which has led some critics hastily to describe Echegaray's plays as a wholesale plagiarism. The fact that the doctor who is only mentioned in Ghosts actually appears on the stage in The Son of Don Juan is a point, not of resemblance, but of difference; whilst the fact that Mrs Alving and Manders have no counterparts in the Spanish play, and that the dissipated father, who does not appear in Ghosts at all, is practically Echegaray's hero, will make it plain to anyone who has really comprehended Ghosts that the story has been taken on to new ground nationally, and back to old ground morally. Echegaray has also created a new set of characters. Paca, the woman of Tarifa; the poor little consumptive Carmen, betrothed to Lazarus (Oswald); Timoteo and Nemesio, the shattered old boon companions of Don Juan; Dolores, the wife of Don Juan, who is not even twentieth cousin to Mrs Alving: all these are original creations. Echegaray makes his puppets dance ruthlessly. He writes like a strong man to whom these people are all "poor devils" whom he pities and even pets, but does not respect. This again contrasts strongly with the Norwegian feeling. Ibsen never presents his play to you as a romance for your entertainment: he says, in effect, "Here is yourself and myself, our society, our civilization. The evil and good, the horror and the hope of it, are woven out of your life and mine." There is no more of that sort of conscience about Echegaray's plays than there is about Hernani, or, for the matter of that, The Babes in the Wood.[8] The woman who looks at Hedda Gabler or Mrs Alving may be looking at herself in a mirror; but the woman who looks at Mariana is looking at another woman, a perfectly distinct and somewhat stagey personality. Consequently the howl of rage and dread that follows each stroke of Ibsen's scalpel will not rise when one of our actresses pounces on Mariana: we shall only whimper a little because our childish curiosity is not indulged in the last scene to the extent of letting us see whether Daniel kills Pablo and then himself, or whether Pablo kills Daniel. This last scene, or epilogue, as it is called, is magnificently dramatic; so much so that if some adapter will change the name of the piece from Mariana to Daniel, and transfer all the lady's best speeches to the gentleman, some of our actor-managers will probably produce it as soon as they realize its existence: say in twenty years or so. Unless, indeed, the actress-manageress arrives in the meantime and snaps it up.

I can best convey a notion of the style and dramatic method of Echegaray by a couple of quotations. In both of the plays just translated, a narrative by the principal character makes an indelible impression on the imagination, and comes into action with great effect at the climax of the

8. (1860) by Tom Taylor.

tragedy. Both narratives are characteristically modern in their tragicomedy. Here is Mariana's:

"Listen. I was eight years old. It must have been two or three o'clock in the morning. I was sleeping in my crib; and I dreamt that I was giving a great many kisses to my doll, because it had called me 'mamma.' The doll soon began to kiss me in return, but so fiercely that it caused me pain; and the doll became very large; and it was my mother. She was holding me in her arms; and I—I was not sleeping now: it was no dream: I was awake. Behind my mother there was a man standing. It was Alvarado, who was saying 'Come.' My mother said 'No: not without her.' And he said 'Devil take it, then, w i t h her.' The rest was like another dream—a nightmare—anything that whirls you away and will not let you breathe. My mother dressed me as people dress lunatics or dolls, pulling me about, shaking me, nearly beating me. And Alvarado was all the time hurrying her with whispers of 'Quick, quick, make haste.' I have never gone through anything like it: trivial: ludicrous as it was, it was horrible. She could not get the little socks rightly on me; she could not manage to button my boots; my drawers were put on the wrong way, the petticoats left with the opening at the side, my dress half loose, though I kept saying 'It wants to be fastened: its should be fastened.' And all the time Alvarado was saying 'Quick, quick, make haste, make haste.' I was wound up in a cloak of my mother's; and a hat ribbon was tied round my head so that it nearly choked me. Then my mother snatched me up in her arms; and we got into a carriage and went very fast. Then I heard a kiss; and I thought 'My God, who was that for, who was that for: nobody has kissed me.' Ah, my own mother, my own mother!"

At the end of the play, Daniel, Mariana's lover, in persuading her to elope, picks up her cloak, and by trying to wrap her in it and carry her out to the carriage, reminds her of this passage in her childhood, and of Alvarado, whose son Daniel is. She calls in her husband, who kills her; and the two men disappear to fight it out to the death in the garden as the curtain falls.

Don Juan's narrative is an instance of the same dramatic device.

"It was a grand night—a grand supper. There were eight of us—each with a partner. Everybody was drunk—even the Guadalquiver. Aniceta went out on the balcony and began to cry out 'Stupid, insipid, waterish river: drink wine for once,' and threw a bottle of Manzanilla into it. Well, I was lying asleep along the floor, upon the carpet, close to a divan. And on the divan there had fallen, by one of the usual accidents, the Tarifena: Paca the Tarifena. She was asleep; and in her tossings to and fro her hair had become loose—a huge mass; and it fell over me in silky waves—a great quantity, enfolding me as in a splendid black mantle of perfumed lace. The dawn arrived: a delightful morning, the balcony open, the East with splendid curtains of mist and with little red clouds; the sky blue and stainless; a light more vivid kindling into flame the distant horizon. Slowly the crimson globe ascended. I opened my eyes wide; and I saw the sun, I saw it from between the interlaced tresses of the Tarifena. It inundated me with light; and I stretched forth my hand instinctively to grasp it. Something of a new kind of love—a new desire—agitated me; great brightness, much azure, very broad spheres, vague yet burning aspirations for something very beautiful. For a minute I understood that there is something higher than the pleasures of the senses: for a minute I felt myself another being. I wafted a kiss to the sun, and angrily pulled aside the girl's hair. One lock clung about my lips: it touched my palate and gave me nausea. I flung away the tress; I awoke the Tarifena; and vice dawned through the remains of the orgy, like the sun through the vapors of the night, its mists, and its fire-colored clouds."

I need only add that Don Juan is on the stage at the end of the play when the heir to his debauchery says "Give me the sun, mother." On the whole, though I am afraid some of our critics will be as nauseated as Don Juan was by that stray lock of the Tarifena's hair, I suspect the Spaniards will compel us to admit that they have produced a genius of a stamp that crosses frontiers, and that we shall yet see some of his work on our own stage.

Mr Arthur Law, the author of The Ladies' Idol, the latest Vaudeville piece, did not remind me of Echegaray in any way; but his piece is not bad fun for all that. Only, when I come upon as clever an actor as Mr Weedon Grossmith,[9] I like to see his powers well drawn out; and this social duty Mr Arthur Law has not, I regret to say, performed. The audience, convinced that Mr Grossmith is one of the funniest of men, laughs whenever he opens his mouth. He accordingly opens his mouth very often, and shuts it again, with hilarious results; but he has really very little more to do. Mr Beauchamp's Purley is a capital piece of acting; Mr Volpé, as Wix, is a credible and natural Brixton paterfamilias, and does not "character-act";[10] and Mr Little, though still rather too much the funny man and too little the artist, is amusing. Miss Beringer, Miss Palfrey, and Miss Homfrey acquit themselves competently in the women's parts.[11] It is true that The Ladies' Idol is not a very difficult piece to play; but after the exasperating bad acting one constantly sees at the theatres where high comedy and "drama" prevail, it is a relief to see even simple work creditably done.

9. (1852–1919).

10. John Beauchamp (1851?-1921); Frederick Volpé (1865–1932).

11. C.P. Little (d. 1914); Esmé Beringer (1875–1972); May Lever Palfrey (Mrs Weedon Grossmith, c. 1867–1929); Gladys Homfrey (1849?-1932).

THE PROBLEM PLAY: A SYMPOSIUM
ST (*The Humanitarian*, May 1895)

I do not know who has asked the question, Should social problems be freely dealt with in the drama?—some very thoughtless person evidently. Pray what social questions and what sort of drama? Suppose I say yes, then, vaccination being a social question, and the Wagnerian music drama being the one complete form of drama in the opinion of its admirers, it will follow that I am in favor of the production of a Jennerian tetralogy at Bayreuth.[1] If I say no, then, marriage being a social question, and also the theme of Ibsen's Doll's House, I shall be held to condemn that work as a violation of the canons of art. I therefore reply to the propounder that I am not prepared to waste my own time and that of the public in answering maladroit conundrums. What I am prepared to do is to say what I can with the object of bringing some sort of order into the intellectual confusion which has expressed itself in the conundrum.

Social questions are produced by the conflict of human institutions with human feeling. For instance, we have certain institutions regulating the lives of women. To the women whose feelings are entirely in harmony with these institutions there is no Woman Question. But during the present century, from the time of Mary Wollstonecraft onwards, women have been developing feelings, and consequently opinions, which clash with these institutions. The institutions assumed that it was natural to a woman to allow her husband to own her property and person, and to represent her in politics as a father represents his infant child. The moment that seemed no longer natural to some women, it became grievously oppressive to them. Immediately there was a Woman Question, which has produced Married Women's Property Acts, Divorce Acts, Woman's Sufrage in local elections, and the curious deadlock to which the Weldon and Jackson cases have led our courts in the matter of conjugal rights.[2] When we have achieved reforms enough to bring our institutions as far into harmony with the feelings of women as they now are with the feelings of men, there will no longer be a Woman Question. No conflict, no question.

Now the material of the dramatist is always some conflict of human feelings with circumstances; so that, since institutions are circumstances, every social question furnishes material for drama. But every

---

1. In 1796, the English physician Edward Jenner (1749–1823) introduced vaccination against smallpox. Wagner's music dramas were, and are, performed at Bayreuth.
2. See *The Quintessence of Ibsenism*, "The Womanly Woman," note 6.

drama does not involve a social question, because human feeling may be in conflict with circumstances which are not institutions, which raise no question at all, which are part of human destiny. To illustrate, take Mr Pinero's Second Mrs Tanqueray. The heroine's feelings are in conflict with the human institutions which condemn to ostracism both herself and the man who marries her. So far, the play deals with a social question. But in one very effective scene the conflict is between that flaw in the woman's nature which makes her dependent for affection wholly on the attraction of her beauty, and the stealthy advance of age and decay to take her beauty away from her. Here there is no social question: age, like love, death, accident, and personal character, lies outside all institutions; and this gives it a permanent and universal interest which makes the drama that deals with it independent of period and place. Abnormal greatness of character, abnormal baseness of character, love, and death: with these alone you can, if you are a sufficiently great dramatic poet, make a drama that will keep your language alive long after it has passed out of common use. Whereas a drama with a social question for the motive cannot outlive the solution of that question. It is true that we can in some cases imaginatively reconstruct an obsolete institution and sympathize with the tragedy it has produced: for instance, the very dramatic story of Abraham commanded to sacrifice his son, with the interposition of the angel to make a happy ending; or the condemnation of Antonio to lose a pound of flesh, and his rescue by Portia at the last moment, have not completely lost their effect nowadays—though it has been much modified—through the obsolescence of sacrificial rites, belief in miracles, and the conception that a debtor's person belongs to his creditors. It is enough that we still have paternal love, death, malice, moneylenders, and the tragedies of criminal law. But when a play depends entirely on a social question—when the struggle in it is between man and a purely legal institution—nothing can prolong its life beyond that of the institution. For example, Mr Grundy's Slaves of the Ring, in which the tragedy is produced solely by the conflict between the individual and the institution of indissoluble marriage, will not survive a rational law of divorce, and actually fails even now to grip an English audience because the solution has by this time become so very obvious. And that irrepressibly popular play It's Never Too Late to Mend will hardly survive our abominable criminal system. Thus we see that the drama which deals with the natural factors in human destiny, though not necessarily better than the drama which deals with the political factors, is likely to last longer.

It has been observed that the greatest dramatists shew a preference for the nonpolitical drama, the greatest dramas of all being almost elementarily natural. The minor dramatist leads the literary life, and dwells in the world of imagination instead of in the world of politics, business, law, and the platform agitations by which social questions are ventilated. He therefore remains, as a rule, astonishingly ignorant of real life. He may be clever, imaginative, sympathetic, humorous, and observant of such manners as he has any clue to; but he has hardly any wit or knowledge of the world. Compare his work with that of Sheridan, and you feel the deficiency at once. Indeed, you need not go so far as Sheridan: Mr Gilbert's Trial by Jury is unique among the works of living English playwrights, solely because it, too, is the work of a wit; and a man of the world. Incidentally, it answers the inquiry as to whether social questions make good theatrical material; for though it is pointless, and, in fact, unintelligible except as a satire on a social institution (the breach of promise suit), it is highly entertaining, and has made the fortune of the author and his musical collaborator.[3] The School for Scandal, the most popular of all modern comedies, is a dramatic sermon, just as Never Too Late to Mend, the most popular of modern melodramas, is a dramatic pamphlet: Charles Reade being another example of the distinction which the accomplished man of the world attains in the theatre as compared to the mere professional dramatist. In fact, it is so apparent that the best and most popular plays are dramatized sermons, pamphlets, satires, or bluebooks, that we find our popular authors, even when they have made a safe position for themselves by their success in purely imaginative drama, bidding for the laurels and the percentages of the sociological dramatist. Mr Henry Arthur Jones takes a position as the author of The Middleman and The Crusaders,[4] which The Silver King, enormously popular as it was, never could have gained him; and Mr Pinero, the author of The Second Mrs Tanqueray and The Notorious Mrs Ebbsmith, is a much more important person, and a much richer one, than the author of Sweet Lavender. Of course, the sociology in some of these dramas is as imaginary as the names and addresses of the characters; but the imitation sociology testifies to the attractiveness of the real article.

We may take it then that the ordinary dramatist only neglects social questions because he knows nothing about them, and that he loses in popularity, standing, and money by his ignorance. With the great dramatic poet it is otherwise. Shakespear and Goethe do not belong to the order which "takes no interest in politics." Such minds devour everything with a keen appetite: fiction, science, gossip, politics, technical processes, sport, everything. Shakespear is full of little lectures of the concrete English kind, from Cassio on temperance to Hamlet on suicide. Goethe, in his German way, is always discussing metaphysical points. To master

---

3. *Trial by Jury* (1875) concerns a lawsuit for breach of promise. Gilbert's musical collaborator is of course Sir Arthur Sullivan.

4. (1889) and (1891), respectively.

Wagner's music dramas is to learn a philosophy. It was so with all the great men until the present century. They swallowed all the discussions, all the social questions, all the topics, all the fads, all the enthusiasms, all the fashions of their day in their nonage; but their theme finally was not this social question or that social question, this reform or that reform, but humanity as a whole. To this day your great dramatic poet is never a socialist, nor an individualist, nor a positivist, nor a materialist, nor any other sort of "ist," though he comprehends all the "isms," and is generally quoted and claimed by all the sections as an adherent. Social questions are too sectional, too topical, too temporal to move a man to the mighty effort which is needed to produce great poetry. Prison reform may nerve Charles Reade to produce an effective and businesslike prose melodrama; but it could never produce Hamlet, Faust, or Peer Gynt.

It must, however, be borne in mind that the huge size of modern populations and the development of the press make every social question more momentous than it was formerly. Only a very small percentage of the population commits murder; but the population is so large that the frequency of executions is appalling. Cases which might have come under Goethe's notice in Weimar perhaps once in ten years come daily under the notice of modern newspapers, and are described by them as sensationally as possible. We are therefore witnessing a steady intensification in the hold of social questions on the larger poetic imagination. Les Misérables,[5] with its rivulet of story running through a continent of essays on all sorts of questions, from religion to main drainage, is a literary product peculiar to the XIX century: it shews how matters which were trifles to Eschylus become stupendously impressive when they are multiplied by a million in a modern civilized state. Zola's novels are the product of an imagination driven crazy by a colossal police intelligence, by modern hospitals and surgery, by modern war correspondence, and even by the railway system: for in one of his books the hero is Jack the Ripper and his sweetheart a locomotive engine.[6] What would Aristophanes[7] have said to a city with fifteen thousand lunatics in it? Might he not possibly have devoted a comedy to the object of procuring some amelioration in their treatment? At all events we find Ibsen, after producing, in Brand, Peer Gynt, and Emperor and Galilean, dramatic poems on the grandest scale, deliberately turning to comparatively prosaic topical plays on the most obviously transitory social questions, finding in their immense magnitude under modern conditions the stimulus which, a hundred years ago, or four thousand, he would only have received from the eternal strife of man

5. (1862) by Victor Hugo.
6. *The Human Beast* (1890).
7. (c. 445-c. 385 B.C.), Greek author of satiric comedies.

with his own spirit. A Doll's House will be as flat as ditchwater when A Midsummer Night's Dream will still be as fresh as paint; but it will have done more work in the world; and that is enough for the highest genius, which is always intensely utilitarian.

Let us now hark back for a moment to the remark I made on Mr Grundy's Sowing the Wind:[8] namely, that its urgency and consequently its dramatic interest are destroyed by the fact that the social question it presents is really a solved one. Its production after Les Surprises de Divorce (which Mr Grundy himself adapted for England)[9] was an anachronism. When we succeed in adjusting our social structure in such a way as to enable us to solve social questions as fast as they become really pressing, they will no longer force their way into the theatre. Had Ibsen, for instance, had any reason to believe that the abuses to which he called attention in his prose plays would have been adequately attended to without his interference, he would no doubt have gladly left them alone. The same exigency drove William Morris in England from his tapestries, his epics, and his masterpieces of printing, to try and bring his fellow-citizens to their senses by the summary process of shouting at them in the streets and in Trafalgar Square. John Ruskin's writing began with Modern Painters; Carlyle began with literary studies of German culture and the like: both were driven to become revolutionary pamphleteers. If people are rotting and starving in all directions, and nobody else has the heart or brains to make a disturbance about it, the great writers must. In short, what is forcing our poets to follow Shelley in becoming political and social agitators, and to turn the theatre into a platform for propaganda and an arena for discussion, is that whilst social questions are being thrown up for solution almost daily by the fierce rapidity with which industrial processes change and supersede oneanother through the rivalry of the competitors who take no account of ulterior social consequences, and by the change in public feeling produced by popular "education," cheap literature, facilitated traveling, and so forth, the political machinery by which alone our institutions can be kept abreast of these changes is so old-fashioned, and so hindered in its action by the ignorance, the apathy, the stupidity, and the class feuds of the electorate, that social questions never get solved until the pressure becomes so desperate that even governments recognize the necessity for moving. And to bring the pressure to this point, the poets must lend a hand to the few who are willing to do public work in the stages at which nothing but abuse is to be gained by it.

Clearly, however, when the unhappy mobs which we now call nations and populations settle down into ordered commonwealths, ordinary bread

8. An error for *Slaves of the Ring.*
9. As *Mamma.*

and butter questions will be solved without troubling the poets and philosophers. The Shelleys, the Morrises, the Ruskins and Carlyles of that
day will not need to spend their energies in trying to teach elementary
political economy to the other members of the commonwealth; nor will
the Ibsens be devising object lessons in spoiled womanhood, sickly con-
sciences, and corrupt town councils, instead of writing great and enduring dramatic poems.

I need not elaborate the matter further. The conclusions to be drawn are:

1. Every social question, arising as it must from a conflict between
human feeling and circumstances, affords material for drama.

2. The general preference of dramatists for subjects in which the conflict is between man and his apparently inevitable and eternal rather than
his political and temporal circumstances, is due in the vast majority of
cases to the dramatist's political ignorance (not to mention that of his
audience), and in a few to the comprehensiveness of his philosophy.

3. The hugeness and complexity of modern civilizations and the development of our consciousness of them by means of the press, have the
double effect of discrediting the comprehensive philosophies by revealing
more facts than the ablest man can generalize, and at the same time
intensifying the urgency of social reforms sufficiently to set even the
poetic faculty in action on their behalf.

4. The resultant tendency to drive social questions on to the stage, and
into ficton and poetry, will eventually be counteracted by improvements
in social organization, which will enable all prosaic social questions to be
dealt with satisfactorily long before they become grave enough to absorb
the energies which claim the devotion of the dramatist, the storyteller,
and the poet.

AT THE THEATRES[1]
(*Saturday Review*, 4 May 1895)

On the whole, I am inclined to congratulate Mr Godfrey on Mrs John
Wood, rather than Mrs John Wood on Mr Godfrey, in the matter of Vanity

1. VANITY FAIR. A Caricature. By G[eorge] W[illiam] Godfrey [1844–97]. Court Theatre,
27 April 1895. THE PASSPORT [1894]. By B. C. Stephenson and W[illiam] Yardley [1849?–
1900]. Terry's Theatre, 25 April 1895. A HUMAN SPORT. A Drama in one act. By Austin
Fryers [pseudonym of W. E. Cleary]. Globe Theatre, 1 May 1895. [G.B.S.]

Fair. Mrs John Wood is herself a character; and by providing her with some new dialogue Mr Godfrey has given himself an air of creation; but I doubt if the other parts can be said to bear him out on this point. When I saw the piece, on the third night, Mr Arthur Cecil[2] was still so unequal to the mere taskwork of remembering long strings of sentences which were about as characteristic and human as the instructions on the back of a telegram form, that he had to be spoonfed by the prompter all the evening. Mr Anson[3] as Bill Feltoe, the blackmailer, had a part which was certainly memorable in the sense that he could preserve the continuity of his ideas; but it did not go beyond that. The play, as a drama, is nothing. As an entertainment "written round" Mrs John Wood, it is a success. But it also pretends to be Vanity Fair, a picture of society. Mr Godfrey guards himself by calling it a caricature; but he nonetheless presents it as a morality, a satire, a sermon. And here he appeals to the love of the public for edification. Dickens's group of cronies at the Maypole inn,[4] with their cry of "Go on improvin' of us, Johnny," exactly typifies the playgoing public in England. When an English playgoer is not by temperament, if not by actual practice, nine tenths a chapelgoer, he is generally ten tenths a blackguard; and so, if you cannot produce a genuine drama, and conquer him legitimately in that way, you must either be licentious at the cost of your respectability, or else moral and idealistic. Mr Godfrey, running short for the moment of character and drama, of course chose the respectable alternative, and resorted to idealism. He moralizes on fine lady spectators at murder trials, on matrimonial scandals in high life, on Christianity conquering Africa with the Maxim gun, and on the prevarications of the Treasury Bench. As further evidence of the corruption of society, he instances the interest taken in it by eminent explorers, in Buffalo Bill, and in foreign violinists, the inference being, as I understand it, that to invite Mr Stanley to dine, or Herr Joachim to play a partita by Bach,[5] is a proceeding as fraught with degenerate heartlessness as to shew your "horror" of a crime by rushing down to the court to gloat over the trial, or to give a gentleman who pays your wife's bills the right to call you to account for being seen in her company. Mr Godfrey's explanation of all this depravity is simple. It is the work of the New Woman and of the Problem Play.

You are now in a position to appreciate the scene at the beginning of the

2. (1843–96).
3. George William Anson (1847–1920).
4. In *Barnaby Rudge*.
5. Buffalo Bill (pseudonym of William Frederick Cody, 1846–1917), former buffalo hunter and Indian fighter, now organizer and star of a Wild West show; Joseph Joachim (1831–1907), Hungarian violinist; Johann Sebastian Bach (1685–1750), German composer.

third act, where Mr Arthur Cecil, as the gently cynical Thackerayan observer of Vanity Fair, receives, with the assistance of the prompter, the wondering questions of Miss Nancy Noel as to whether the relations between young men and young women ever really were as they are represented in the novels of Sir Walter Scott. To which I regret to say Mr Cecil does not hesitate to reply in the affirmative, without mentioning that no change that has taken place in this century has been more obviously a change for the better than the change in the relations between men and women. "Goodnight, little girl " he adds with unction, after a brief reference to his guide, philosopher, and friend in the prompter's box, "Trust to the teachings of your own pure heart. God bless you!"

Mr Godfrey must excuse me; but that sort of social philosophy is not good enough for me. It does not matter, perhaps, because I am far from attributing to the claptap play the devastating social influence he apparently attaches to the problem play (which I am getting rather anxious to see, by the way). But I must at least declare my belief that Mr Godfrey will never succeed as a critic of society by merely jumbling together all the splenetic commonplaces that sound effective to him, and tacking on an Adelphi moral. In order to make a stage drawing room a microcosm of Vanity Fair, you may, I grant, mix your sets to any extent you please; but you need not therefore produce an impression that the sort of man who never reads a serious book or ventures above burlesque and farcical comedy at the theatre has been led into his habit of not paying his bills, and of winking at his wife's relations with useful acquaintances, by The Heavenly Twins and Ibsen's plays. I do not say that Mr Godfrey has produced such impressions intentionally: my quarrel with him is that he has begun to criticize life without first arranging his ideas. The result is, that it is impossible for the most credulous person to believe in Mrs Brabazon-Tegg's Grosvenor Square reception even to the extent of recognizing it as a caricature. It is not that the real thing is more respectable, or that the most extravagant bits (the scene with the sham millionaire, for instance) are the least lifelike: quite the contrary. But a drawing room is not like Margate sands for all that: however loose the selection of guests, there is enough logic in it to keep the music, bad though it may be, in one predominant key. It requires a very nice knowledge of what is reasonable to be safely outrageous in society of any grade; and this knowledge is as essential to the dramatist depicting society on the stage as to the diner-out who wishes to be allowed the privilege of unconventionality. In putting the drawing room on the stage, Mr Godfrey's master is obviously Mr Oscar Wilde. Now Mr Wilde has written scenes in which there is hardly a speech which could conceivably be uttered by one real person at a real At-Home; but the deflection from commonsense is so subtle that it is evidently produced as a tuner tunes a piano: that is, he first tunes a fifth perfectly, and then flattens it a shade. If he could not tune the perfect fifth he could not produce the practicable one. This condition is imposed on the sociological humorist also. For instance, Don Quixote's irresistibly laughable address to the galley slaves, like the rest of his nonsense, is so close to the verge of good sense that thickwitted people, and even some clever ones, take the Don for a man of exceptionally sound understanding. Nonetheless he is a hopeless lunatic, the sound understanding which he skirts so funnily being that of Cervantes. Mr Godfrey fails to produce the same effect because he tries to say the absurd thing without precisely knowing the sensible thing, with the result that, though he makes epigrams most industriously, he never tickles the audience except by strokes of pure fun, such as Mrs Brabazon-Tegg's "Dont disturb my maid: she's upstairs doing my hair." There are passages which are effective because they give voice to grievances or allude to abuses upon which the audience feels, or feels obliged to pretend to feel, highly indignant; but this is not art or drama: the effect would be the same if the point were made on a political platform: indeed, it would be better there. For example, in Mrs Brabazon-Tegg's dream of her trial for bigamy, she is made to complain of the practice of eminent counsel accepting retainers in more cases than they can possibly attend to. The complaint would be more effective at an ordinary public meeting, because the trial represented on the stage is precisely the sort of one from which no counsel would dream of absenting himself. Such effect, then, as Mrs Brabazon-Tegg's speech from the dock actually does produce is due, not to the author's knowledge of his subject, but to the extraordinary spontaneity and conviction with which Mrs John Wood delivers herself.

There is one point on which I am unable to say whether Mr Godfrey was satirical or sincere. When Mrs Brabazon-Tegg's conscience is awakened, she does what most rich people do under similar circumstances: that is to say, the most mischievous thing possible. She begins to scatter hundred pound cheques in conscience money to various charities. Whether Mr Godfrey approves of this proceeding I do not know; but he at any rate conquered my respect by remorselessly making his woman of fashion presently reduce all the cheques to five pounds and replunge into fashionable life not a whit the better for her hard experience. This seems to indicate that Mr Godfrey has that courage of his profession in which most of our dramatists are shamelessly wanting. For its sake he may very well be forgiven his random satire, and even—on condition that he undertakes not to do it again—the insufferable conversations of Mr Arthur Cecil and Miss Granville.[6]

The Passport, at Terry's, is an amusing piece, with thirteen parts, of

6. Charlotte Granville (b. 1863).

which no less than eight are very well acted. I was not surprised at this except in the case of Miss Gertrude Kingston,[7] who, when I last saw her, was a clever lady with a certain virtuosity in the art of dress, and made of metal hard enough to take a fine edge, but still not then a skilled actress, though the critics had instinctively recognized her as a person to whom it was best to be civil, perhaps because she so suggested that terrible person, the lady who has walked straight from her drawing room on to the stage. Most of that is gone now, except what was worth keeping in it. Miss Kingston's utterance and movements are acquiring a definite artistic character; and the circulation of feeling, which is more important to the stage artist than the circulation of the blood, seems to be establishing itself in spite of the refractory nature of the conducting medium; whilst her cleverness is still conspicuous, and her dresses make me feel more keenly than ever that I have left one corner of critical journalism unconquered: to wit, the fashion article. In short, Miss Kingston confronted me in The Passport as a rising actress, holding my interest from her entrance to her final exit, and indeed determining the success of the play, which, without her, might have broken down badly in the second and third acts, hampered as they are with the stuff about Bob, Algy, and Violet which is neither sensible, amusing, nor credible. The main thread of the story is presented by a very powerful combination of artists: Mr Yorke Stephens, Mr Maltby, Mr Giddens, Mr Mackay, Miss Gertrude Kingston, Miss Cicely Richards, and Miss Fanny Coleman.[8] Their parts are all funny; and some of them are individual and interesting, notably the exasperating but fascinating young widow with the impossible memory, and the perfectly normal respectable maid, an excellent character, played admirably by Miss Cicely Richards. Mr Yorke Stephens is a little underparted: after the first act, which he carries off with all the debonair grace and smartness of style which distinguish him, he takes the part a little too easily. Even a widower could not be so completely unembarrassed on his wedding day; and however obvious it may be that the misunderstandings created by the widow can be explained away, still, whilst they last, they need the assistance of a little alarm on the part of the bridegroom. As to the play, it is not a mere farcical imbroglio in which neither the figures who work the puzzle nor the places in which they work it have any real individuality: the scenes and circumstances, both in the frontier railway station and in the London house, are fully imagined and realized. The value

7. (1866–1937), actress-manager who played numerous Shavian roles and for whom Shaw wrote *Great Catherine*.
8. Alfred Maltby (1842?-1901); George Giddens (1845–1920); J. L. Mackay (b. 1867); Richards (1850?-1933); Coleman (1840–1919).

and, alas! the rarity of this is shewn by the comparative freshness and interest of the action, and the genial indulgence with which the audience accepts the complications of the last two acts, which are, it must be confessed, anything but ingenious, not to mention the silly episode of Algy, Violet, and Bob as aforesaid.

The one act piece, A Human Sport (in the evolutionary sense), by Mr Austin Fryers, produced at the Globe Theatre at a matinée in aid of the Actors' Benevolent Fund on Wednesday last, is hardly a drama at all: it is rather the exhibition of an incident which does not develop in any way. An ironmaster (I think it was an ironmaster) has some operation spoiled by a workman getting drunk at the critical moment. In order to prevent this occuring again, he resolves to take a step which, simple and obvious as it is, has not, as far as I am aware, ever been thought of before: namely, to take the man into partnership so as to increase his self-respect. With this view he invites him to tea. The drunkard recognizes in his master's wife and mother-in-law his own deserted daughter and wife. Finding that respectability will involve a reunion with his family, he pretends to get drunk again, and is promptly kicked out as incorrigible. This unconventional and rather amusing notion has been ruined by Mr Austin Fryers's inveterate sentimentality. The "human sport," instead of behaving sportively, plunges into the stalest maudlin pathos over his longlost daughter. If Mr Austin Fryers will cut out the daughter, and make the sport get really drunk in order to escape from respectability and his wife, the play will do very well. Or if he will write a temptation scene round the decanter of brandy, and make the wife rush in and struggle with her husband for the glass until the contest is decided in her favor by the sound of their daughter's voice singing a hymn in the next room, the whole ending with the partnership and domesic bliss, that will be equally satisfactory. But I implore Mr Austin Fryers not to mix his *genres*. Let us have the new ideas in the new style, or the old tricks in the old style; but the new ideas combined with the old tricks in no style at all cannot be borne. Mr James Welch,[9] as the sport, pulled the play through by a piece of acting impressive enough to keep the audience believing, up to the last moment, that something really interesting was imminent. If only for Mr Welch's sake, Mr Austin Fryers, who is by no means deficient in ability, should extirpate that daughter, and build the part into something worthy of the actor's rare talent.

9. (1865–1917), who had played Lickcheese in the first production of *Widowers' Houses*, Major Petkoff in that of *Arms and the Man*.